D1094739

© Scriptum Publishers

Photography: Thijs Tuurenhout
Aerial photography: Karel Tomeï
Text: Rinus Antonisse
Translation: Jonathan Ellis
Design: www.manifestarotterdam.nl
Lithography and printing: Balmedia bv

ISBN 978 90 5594 369 2

ZEELAND

Op de nachtelijke satellietfoto oogt Zeeland als een duistere vlek. Ingeklemd tussen de oplichtende woon- en werkgebieden van de Randstad, Antwerpen-Gent en, aan de andere kant van de Noordzee, zuidelijk Engeland met metropool Londen. Hier en daar duiden witte speldeprikjes op menselijke activiteiten in de Delta, maar de duisternis overheerst.

Overdag vallen vanuit de lucht de bijzondere kenmerken van Zeeland meteen op. Een archipel, een land van overkanten. De grillige lijnen van de eilanden. Omgeven door water. Overal aanwezig in de vorm van zeearmen, meren, kreken, kanalen en sloten. Het ruikt er zilt en zompig. De naam van Nederlands zuidwestelijke Delta klopt precies: zee en land.

Een provincie die door de rust en de ruimte uitnodigt tot onthaasten. De weidsheid van de deltawateren, met zwermen vogels en een enkele voorbij varende boot. Grote verstedelijkte gebieden, zoals in de volgepakte Randstad, ontbreken. Op twee plaatsen, in Vlissingen-Oost en bij het kanaal Gent-Terneuzen, bepaalt een industrieel havenlandschap de horizon.

De geschiedenis is overal nadrukkelijk aanwezig. Het verhaal van ontworsteld land, van een eeuwige strijd tegen de zee. Door inpolderingen is veel land gewonnen, maar de zee heeft ook veel vruchtbare polders terug genomen. Het is als met eb en vloed, die in een oerritme twee keer per 25

On a night satellite photograph, Zeeland looks like a dark blot. It seems hemmed in between the shining residential and industrial areas of the Randstand (that conglomeration of Amsterdam, Utrecht, Rotterdam, and The Hague), Antwerp-Ghent, and, on the other side of the North Sea, England with the metropolis of London. Here and there, pinpricks of light indicate some human activity in the Delta, but darkness has the upper hand.

During the day, the special characteristics of Zeeland are instantly noticeable from the air. An archipelago; a country of opposite shores. The capricious lines of the islands. Surrounded by water. It is omnipresent, in the shape of sea arms, lakes, brooks, canals, and streams. It smells brackish and boggy. The name given by the Dutch to their southwesterly province is perfectly chosen: zee en land – sea and land.

A province that, with its peace and space, encourages a less hurried lifestyle. The vast expanses of the delta waters, the swarms of birds, and the occasional sailing boat. Large conurbations, such as those in the overcrowded Randstand, are absent here. In two places, in Vlissingen-East and near to the Ghent-Terneuzen canal, the horizon is delineated by an industrial harbour landscape.

History is everywhere emphatically present. The story of land that in a century-long struggle has been wrestled from the grips of the sea. A lot of land has been reclaimed, but the sea has also taken back many fruitful polders. It is just like ebb and flood, the primordial rhythm of coming and going that repeats itself twice every

25 hours. Rising, turning, and receding tides.

Two thousand years ago, the landscape was totally different: a broad expanse of marshy fens behind low coastlines. Dissected by narrow waterways, that reached the sea through narrow openings in the dunes. The territory of a handful of farmers and shepherds. The Romans, who arrive around 175 AD, call it "a country drenched in water."

As the sea rose, so that dunes were breached in various places and the salt water created a network of tidal gullies that reached far into the higher sandy ground of Brabant and Flanders. The transport of sand and clay changed the marshy fens into a gravely landscape that is so characteristic of Zeeland.

For several centuries, the inhospitable area remains uninhabited; people only again settle there in the sixth century. They choose the higher places on the ridges of the creeks. But these are not safe from storm tides. Low mounds are thrown up, and on them are built farmhouses. As happened in delta areas throughout the world, trading settlements spring up on the edges of the area.

The inhabitants must be constantly on guard not only against the water, but also against attacks from the Norse Men. At the end of the ninth century they constructed protective ramparts. And these "burgs" (ramparts) are celebrated even today in names such as Domburg, Middelburg, Oost-Souburg, Oostburg, and Burgh. In Burgh in particular, the contours have been clearly preserved.

uur komen en gaan. Opkomend, kenterend en afgaand getij.

Tweeduizend jaar geleden ligt er een heel ander landschap: een uitgestrekt veenmoeras achter lage strandwallen. Doorsneden door smalle wateren, die via nauwe openingen in de duinen de zee bereiken. Domein van een handvol landbouwers en schaapherders. De Romeinen, die er omstreeks 175 na Christus binnentrekken, noemen het 'een land doordrenkt met water.'

Door het rijzen van de zee breekt de duinenrij op verschillende plaatsen door en het zoute water zorgt voor een stelsel van getijdengeulen, die doordringen tot aan de hogere zandgronden van Brabant en Vlaanderen. Door aanvoer van zand en klei verandert het veenmoeras in een schorrenlandschap, nog altijd zo karakteristiek voor Zeeland.

Enkele eeuwen blijft het onherbergzame gebied onbewoond; pas vanaf de zesde eeuw vestigen zich weer mensen. Ze zoeken de hoogste plaatsen van de kreekruggen op. Die zijn echter niet veilig bij stormvloeden. Er worden lage woonheuvels opgeworpen, met daarop boerderijen. Zoals wereldwijd in deltagebieden het geval is, ontstaan aan de rand handelsnederzettingen.

Naast de voortdurende strijd tegen het water, moeten de bewoners zich ook teweer stellen tegen invallen van de Noormannen. Eind negende eeuw bouwen ze ter bescherming ringwalburgen. Terug te vinden in namen als Domburg, Middelburg,

Oost-Souburg, Oostburg en Burgh. Vooral van die in Burgh zijn de contouren goed bewaard gebleven.

Na het jaar 1000 beginnen de mensen met aanleg van dijkjes en afdammen van kreken. Een grote stormvloed in 1134 is aanleiding voor een volledige bedijking van de bewoonde gebieden. Die komt – met schop, spade en mand als belangrijkste gereedschap – vrij snel tot stand. Het land kan beter worden ontwaterd, tot voordeel van land- en tuinbouw en veeteelt.

De bevolking neemt toe; de meeste oudere kerkdorpen zijn in de periode 1200-1300 ontstaan. Middelburg en Zierikzee ontwikkelen zich tot plaatsen met stedelijke allures. Er is meer ruimte voor wonen en werken nodig en de mensen, met de monniken uit Vlaamse kloosters voorop, gaan vanuit de verdediging ten aanval tegen de zee.

De lijnen van het huidige Zeeland krijgen meer en meer gestalte. Kerngebieden van grote polders op Walcheren, Zuid-Beveland en Schouwen. Met als kenmerken veel natuurlijke elementen. Hogere kreekruggen afgewisseld door lagere, zilte poelgronden. Rondom het oude land komen stap voor stap nieuwe polders. Het ontstaan ervan wordt door het dijkenpatroon weergegeven.

Een of meermalen per generatie teisteren overstromingen het lage deltaland. Soms moet land worden prijs gegeven. Het Verdronken Land van

After the year 1000, the people started constructing dykes and dams in the creeks. A great storm tide in 1134 led to the decision to build dykes around the inhabited areas. These are constructed relatively quickly – even though the principle tools are spade, shovel, and basket. The land can now be better irrigated, and this is an advantage both for agriculture and for raising livestock.

The population increases; the majority of the old church villages are founded between 1200 and 1300. Middelburg and Zierikzee develop into places with suburban allure. There is a growing need for space for work and housing, and the people, led by the monks of the Flemish monasteries, set off from their defences to attack the sea.

The contours of present-day Zeeland come increasingly into focus. Core areas of large polders at Walcheren, Zuid-Beveland, and Schouwen. With natural elements as an important characteristic. High creek ridges contrasted with lower, brackish wetlands. Step by step, new polders sprang up around the existing land. Their emergence is illustrated by the patterns of the dykes.

Once or more each generation, floods threaten the low delta area. Sometimes land has to be sacrificed. The Drowned Land of Saeftinge and of Reimerswaal, the Southland of Schouwen, Orisant Island near North Beveland, the islands of Koezand, Schoneveld, Waterdunen, and Wulpen in West Zeeuws-Flanders – they all live on forever under water.

An archaeological treasure trove lies under the delta: the drowned villages. The result of storm tides, but also of military inundations (especially during the Eighty Year War). Only names remind us of the villages of Emelisse, Stuivezand, Soelekerke, Tolsende. At many of the places where the land has again been reclaimed, you find potholes – called wells – and deep grooves.

The fight against both the sea and the Spaniards doesn't prevent Zeeland developing into one of the most important provinces in the republic of the Seven United Netherlands. This is because of its location, because of the presence of the sea that is not only an archenemy but also emerges as a friend. Trade, shipping, and fishing flourish, even though the Zeeland archipelago is threatened from all sides.

The fall of Antwerp in 1585 is the turning point. The fleeing Flemish and Branbanters pour into Zeeland and many remain. Their knowledge of crafts and sciences bring a new élan to social life. Zeeland, together with Holland, play first fiddle during the foundation of the United East Indian Company (and later too the West Indian).

Merchant shipping and privateering laid the foundations for many flourishing towns and villages. Middelburg develops into a proud merchant town, and in the second half of the 17th century has 30,000 inhabitants. Country estates spring up, a tangible expression of the wealth around. In the course of the following century, decline sets in. The arrival in 1795 of the French brings about much change. The once so proud region becomes run down.

Saeftinge en van Reimerswaal, het Zuidland van Schouwen, het eiland Orisant bij Noord-Beveland, de eilanden Koezand, Schoneveld, Waterdunen en Wulpen in West-Zeeuws-Vlaanderen – ze liggen voor altijd onder water.

Onder de Delta ligt een archeologische schat verborgen: de verdronken dorpen. Gevolg van stormvloeden, maar ook door militaire inundaties (met name tijdens de Tachtigjarige Oorlog). Alleen naamgeving herinnert nog aan dorpen als Emelisse, Stuivezand, Soelekerke, Tolsende. Op veel plaatsen waar het overstroomde land is her-wonnen, liggen kolkgaten (welen genaamd) en diepe geulen.

Het gevecht tegen de zee én tegen de Span-jaarden, weerhoudt Zeeland niet zich te ontwikke-len tot een van de belangrijkste gewesten in de republiek der Zeven Verenigde Nederlanden. Dat is te danken aan de ligging, aan de aanwezigheid van de zee, die behalve erfvijand ook vriend blijkt. Handel, scheepvaart en visserij floreren, ook al lijkt de Zeeuwse archipel aan alle zijden belaagd.

De val van Antwerpen in 1585 vormt een keer-punt. Vluchtende Vlamingen en Brabanders stro-men Zeeland binnen en velen blijven er. Hun ambachtelijke en wetenschappelijke kennis geven nieuw elan aan het maatschappelijk leven. Zeeland speelt met Holland eerste viool bij de oprichting van de Verenigde Oostindische Compagnie (en later de Westindische).

Koop- en kaapvaart leggen de basis voor

bloeiende steden en dorpen. Middelburg groeit uit tot een trotse koopmansstad, met in de tweede helft van de zeventiende eeuw 30.000 inwoners. Buitenplaatsen ontstaan als teken van rijkdom. In de loop van de volgende eeuw dient het verval zich aan. De komst van de Fransen in 1795 brengt vele veranderingen. Het eens zo fiere gewest verpaupert.

Veel wordt eind negentiende eeuw verwacht van de aanleg van een spoorlijn (1868), waarvoor onder meer Kreekrakdam en Sloedam worden aangelegd. Ook het Kanaal Terneuzen-Gent (1827), het Kanaal door Zuid-Beveland (1866) en het Kanaal door Walcheren (1873) ontstaan. De economische uitstraling valt tegen; Zeeland blijft een landbouwprovincie en ontwikkelt een schaal- en schelpdierencultuur.

Ondanks grote verwoestingen in Zeeuws-Vlaanderen en het onder water zetten van Walcheren (door geallieerde bombardementen op de zeeweringen), zorgt de Tweede Wereldoorlog niet voor een nieuw keerpunt. Dat komt wél in 1953, wanneer de zee onbarmhartig toeslaat. Ruim 136.000 hectare land overstroomt, 1835 mensen en honderdduizenden dieren laten het leven. De schade bedraagt 1,5 miljard gulden.

De watersnoodramp is een breuklijn in de tijd. 'Voor en na de ramp' wordt een ijkpunt. Uitvoering van het Deltaplan geeft Zeeland een ander gezicht. Op de Westerschelde na, worden de zee-

At the end of the 19th century, much was expected from the construction of a railroad link (1868); the Kreekrakdam and Sloedam were built for this. The Terneuzen-Ghent Canal (1827), the Canal from Zuid-Beveland (1866), and the Canal through Walcheren (1873) were also constructed. But the economic reality is disappointing; Zeeland remains an agricultural province and develops a seafood and shellfish culture.

Despite widespread devastation in Zeeland-Flanders and the flooding of Walcheren (through the allied bombardment of the sea defences), the Second World War is not a new turning point. That takes place in 1953, when the sea strikes mercilessly. More than 136,000 hectares are flooded, 1835 people and hundreds of thousands of animals lose their lives. The damage amounts to 1.5 billion guilders.

The "Watersnoodramp" (the Flood Disaster) forms a break in time; "before and after the disaster" becomes a measuring point. The execution of the Delta Plan gives Zeeland a new face. With the exception of the Wester-schelde, the sea channels are all shut off by enormous dams. In the Oosterschelde, the tidal movements are retained thanks to the construction of a flood barrier that was the subject of aggressive protests. The islands were forged together.

And the final act was the construction of the 6.6 kilometre Westerschelde Tunnel between Ellewoutsdijk and Terneuzen (2003). This puts an end to sailing between the two shores. The trusted water transport returns as a summer network of tourist ferries. Zeeland quickly develops into a recreational bastion. Holiday parks and camping areas are the new villages; yacht harbours replace agricultural wharfs.

The enclosure of the Delta also offers opportunities for industrialisation. Chemical factories are built near deep-water channels. In 1973, a fiercely debated nuclear power station comes online near Borssele. Farming is modernised and mechanised. The way the land is put to use means that many historic elements disappear from the countryside. Greenhouse nurseries grow in number. The polder landscape becomes flatter and covered in glass.

As the new millennium dawns, so the tide turns again in Zeeland. It is still a very green province with space, water, and peace and quiet. With all the special characteristics of the delta waterways: the dynamics of the tide, fresh and salt water, marshes, dykes, polders, creeks, and wells. A green-blue oasis, surrounded by overfull living and working areas. It is under pressure.

Politicians think that Zeeland — which still has less than 380,000 inhabitants — must grow. They are putting everything on economic development. More harbour and industrial-related activities in Vlissingen-East and the Channel zone of Zeeland-Flanders. New "economic pillars" for agriculture. The advent of aquaculture. Expansion of recreational facilities, both on the coast and inland

"Welcome to Zeeland!" chant the politicians. To the many thousands of tourists who especially want to enjoy the sea, sun, and sand. And to new inhabitants, who will have to contribute to keeping the province habitable; who will make sure that it has modern facilities in the areas of

gaten afgesloten met grote dammen. In de Oosterschelde blijft getijwerking behouden door aanleg van een, via actie zwaar bevochten, stormvloedkering. De eilanden worden aaneen gesmeed.

Met als sluitstuk de aanleg van de 6,6 kilometer lange Westerscheldetunnel tussen Ellewoutsdijk en Terneuzen (2003). Aan het varen tussen overkanten komt een eind. Het veer keert weer als zomers netwerk van toeristische pontjes. Zeeland ontwikkelt zich in snel tempo tot een recreatief bolwerk. Vakantieparken en kampeerterreinen als nieuwe dorpen, jachthavens in plaats van landbouwhavens.

De ontsluiting van de Delta biedt ook kansen voor industrialisatie. Chemische fabrieken vestigen zich aan diep vaarwater. Vanaf 1973 is bij Borssele een omstreden kernenergiecentrale in bedrijf. De landbouw mechaniseert en moderniseert. Door landinrichting verdwijnen veel historische elementen uit het landschap. Glastuinbouw rukt op. Het polderland vervlakt en verglast.

Bij het betreden van een nieuw millenium kentert het getij in Zeeland andermaal. Nóg is het een provincie met veel ruimte, groen, water en rust. Met de bijzondere karakteristieken van de deltawateren: de dynamiek van het getij, zout en zoet water, schorren, dijken, polders, kreken en welen. Een groen-blauwe oase, omringd door volle woon- en werkgebieden. Die staat onder druk.

Bestuurders vinden dat Zeeland – nog geen 380.000 inwoners – moet groeien. Ze zetten in op economische ontwikkeling. Meer haven- en indus-triegebonden activiteiten in Vlissingen-Oost en Kanaalzone Zeeuws-Vlaanderen. Nieuwe 'econo-mische dragers' voor de landbouw. Komst van aquacultures. Uitbreiding van recreatieve voorzie-ningen, zowel aan de kust als in het achterland.

'Welkom in Zeeland', roepen de bestuurders. Tot de vele duizenden toeristen, die vooral willen genieten van zon, zee en strand. En tot nieuwe inwoners, die ertoe moeten bijdragen dat de pro-vincie leefbaar blijft en kan beschikken over eigen-tijdse voorzieningen op gebied van onderwijs, gezondheidszorg en cultuur. Het betekent woeke-ren met ruimte, rust en duisternis. Hoogbouw is één van de gevolgen.

Nu de deltawerken zijn afgerond, blijkt dat er aan de strakke en stoere dammen nadelen verbonden zijn. De abrupt van het getij afgesloten wateren vertonen ziekteverschijnselen, zoals blauw-algplagen. In de Oosterschelde vlakken de platen en slikken af en schuiven de geulen dicht. De natuur mist node de bijzondere overgangen van zout op zoet water. Sanering van de deltawateren is nodig.

Als compensatie voor de 'verstening' – door uitbreiding steden en dorpen, nieuwe recreatiepar-ken en bedrijfsvestigingen – wordt nieuwe natuur gemaakt. Hier en daar een postzegel groen, maar langs de zuidkust van Schouwen-Duiveland en Tholen zorgt het plan Tureluur voor grote plas-

education, healthcare, and culture. It means conjuring with space, peace, and darkness. High-rise construction is one of the consequences.

Now the delta works have been completed, it has emerged that there are disadvantages to the severe and rigid dams. The water that has been abruptly shut off from the tides is now showing signs of sickness, such as blue algae plagues. In the Oosterschelde, the shallows and mud flats are being eroded and the gullies becoming bloc-ked. Nature is reluctantly missing the special transition from salt water to fresh. It is vital that the delta waters be put in order.

As compensation for the increased building – the expansion of towns and villages, new recreation parks, and business accommodation – new nature is being created. Here and there a tiny patch of green, but along the south coast of Schouwen-Duiveland and Tholen, the Tureluur plan is creating expansive tracts of swampy marshland that is an Eldorado for birds. The Delta area is, after the Wadden Sea, the second largest bird area in the Netherlands.

Since the completion of the Delta plan, security against flooding seems to be guaranteed. The rising sea level, partly due to climate change and partly to the settling of the seabed, means that the barriers need constant adjustment. The people of Zeeland know better than anyone that it is a constant struggle between man and the elements.

There is a limit to the extent to which the dykes can be strengthened. Other solutions will be required. Back to the past: a first barrier and then, at a certain distant, a second. In this way, the encroaching water encounters two obstacles. The "non-land" between the two dykes can be used for nature and sea culture. Another option is to give the water more room.

For this, consideration is being given to a controlled return of polder land to the sea and to nature. For the people of Zeeland, this is a topsy-turvy world. No longer are they turning their backs on the sea. The tide is turning yet again. This new approach in the struggle against the sea is called "unpoldering." And so change is continuous. The only constant is the meeting of the elements: the game of wind, weather, and water.

Since the formation of the archipelago in the South-Westerly Delta in the fourth century AD, Zeeland has always been a place of opposite shores. Islands with their own character. And other peculiarities: the make-up of the population, dialect, local costumes, characteristic customs. Schouwen and Duiveland, Tholen and St. Philips Island, North and South Beveland, Walcheren, and the mainland of East and West Zeeland-Flanders.

For centuries, the islands – under their collective name of Zeeland – have known their own isolation and tempo. It is an area of opposite shores. For the people in Zeeland-Flanders that opposite shore is Middle Zeeland, for those in Beveland it is Zeeland-Flanders. And so on. Ferry services maintain the connections between those opposite shores.

The fatal flood of February 1953 prompted radical change. The Delta Plan – which closed the Canals to the

drasse gebieden, die voor de vogels een dorado zijn. Na de Waddenzee is de Delta tweede vogelge-bied van Nederland.

Veiligheid tegen overstromingen lijkt na uitvoe-ring van het deltaplan te zijn gegarandeerd. Stij-ging van de zeespiegel, mede door klimaatveran-dering, en het inklinken van de bodem noodzaken tot regelmatige aanpassing van de zeeweringen. Zeeuwen weten het als geen ander: het blijft een voortdurende worsteling van mens en elementen.

Het almaar versterken van de dijken houdt een keer op. Andere oplossingen zijn gewenst. Terug naar vroeger: eerste waterkeringen, met op enige afstand een tweede. Het opdringende water stuit zo tweemaal op barrières. Het 'onland' tussen de dijken is bruikbaar voor natuur en zeecultuur. Andere optie is het water meer ruimte geven.

Daarvoor is in beeld het gecontroleerd terug-geven van polderland aan de zee en de natuur. Een voor de Zeeuwen omgekeerde wereld. Niet meer met de rug naar de zee gekeerd. Het getij kentert weerom. De nieuwe benadering van de strijd tegen de zee is 'ontpolderen' gedoopt. Zo is er continu verandering. Blijvend is slechts de ont-moeting van elementen: het spel van wind, wolken en water.

21

inds het ontstaan van de archipel in de Zuidwestelijke Delta, 4e eeuw na Christus, is Zeeland een land van overkanten. Eilanden met een eigen gezicht. En andere eigenaardigheden: samenstelling bevolking, dialect, streekdracht, kenmerkende gebruiken. Schouwen en Duiveland, Tholen en Sint-Philipsland, Noord- en Zuid-Beveland, Walcheren en het vaste land van Oost- en West-Zeeuws-Vlaanderen.

Eeuwenlang kennen de eilanden, verenigd onder de noemer Zeeland, hun eigen beslotenheid en tempo. Het is een land van overkanten. Voor de mensen in Zeeuws-Vlaanderen is die overkant Midden-Zeeland, voor die van Beveland is dat Zeeuws-Vlaanderen. Enzovoorts. Veerdiensten onderhouden de verbindingen tussen de overkanten.

De fatale stormvloed van februari 1953 zet een ingrijpende verandering in. Door uitvoering van het Deltaplan – afsluiting van de zeegaten in het Zuidwesten, behalve de Westerschelde - worden de eilanden aaneen gesmeed. De overkanten verdwijnen dam voor dam. Als eerste komen Noord- en Zuid-Beveland en Walcheren tot elkaar door het Drie-Eilandenplan, daarna volgen de eilanden in het noorden en oosten.

Er rest na het Deltaplan nog één overkant: die tussen Midden-Zeeland en Zeeuws-Vlaanderen. Daaraan komt in 2003 een einde door de inge-bruikname van de Westerscheldetunnel tussen Ellewoutsdijk op Zuid-Beveland (foto) en

sea in the South West with the exception of the Wester-schelde – forged all these islands together. Opposite shores disappear with each new dam. First it is North and South Beveland and Walcheren that are joined together by the Three-Island Plan; then it is the turn of the islands in the north and east.

After the Delta Plan, there is only one opposite shore: the one between Middle Zeeland and Zeeland-Flanders. And that disappears in 2003 when the Westerschelde Tunnel between Ellewoutsdijk on South Beveland (photo) and Terneuzen is opened. A tunnel with a length of 6.6 kilometres under the bed of the Wester-schelde. At its deepest point, it is 60 metres below NAP (the Amsterdam Ordnance Datum). There are two tun-nel tubes each for two lanes of traffic.

Now that the tunnel is in operation, the Provincial Steamboat services in Zeeland have come to an end. The last ferry connection with enormous double-decker boats between Vlissingen-Breskens and Kruiningen-Perkpolder has been discontinued. A ferry for cyclists and pedestrians is still being operated between Vlissingen and Breskens by the fast catamarans Prince Willem-Alexander and Princess Maxima. The network of ferry services between the former islands remains intact in the summer — but now for tourists.

Terneuzen. Een onder de bodem van de Westerschelde geboorde tunnel van 6,6 kilometer lengte,
met het diepste punt op 60 meter onder Normaal
Amsterdams Peil. Er zijn twee tunnelbuizen met
elk twee rijstroken.

Door de ingebruikname van de tunnel verdwijnen de Provinciale Stoombootdiensten in Zeeland.
De laatste veerverbindingen met grote dubbeldeks
boten tussen Vlissingen-Breskens en Kruiningen-
Perkpolder worden opgeheven. Alleen tussen
Vlissingen en Breskens blijft een fiets-voetveer
varen, met de snelle catamarans Prins Willem-
Alexander en Prinses Máxima. Het dichte netwerk
van veerdiensten tussen de voormalige eilanden
blijft 's zomers nog wel intact: nu als toeristische
pontjes.

Aan de westkant van het Grevelingenmeer houdt
de zware Brouwersdam (foto) de Noordzee tegen.
Op zomerse dagen is het stampvol recreanten, ter-
wijl aan de Grevelingenzijde de watersport flo-
reert.

The mighty Brouwers Dam (photo) on the west of the
Grevelingen Lake keeps back the North Sea. In summer,
it is overrun with visitors, while water sports flourish on
the Grevelingen side of the dam.

Sinds 1930 wordt uit de zoetwaterbel onder de duinen bij Haamstede drinkwater opgepompt. Vooral door de sterke toename van het toerisme op Schouwen-Duiveland groeit het waterverbruik explosief. De zoetwaterbel teert in, het zoute zeewater dringt op. Als oplossing wordt zoet oppervlaktewater uit het Haringvliet naar infiltratievijvers in de duinen (foto) getransporteerd, ter aanvulling van de natuurlijke voorraad.

Since 1930, drinking water has been pumped up out of the fresh water bubble under the dunes near Haamstede. Water usage has increased dramatically, largely due to the rapid rise in tourism on Schouwen-Duiveland. The fresh water bubble is shrinking; salt water is encroaching. As a solution, fresh surface water is transported from Haringvliet (photo) to infiltration ponds; it supplements the natural reserves.

De vuurtoren in de duinen van Schouwen bij Haamstede (foto) siert het verdwenen bankbiljet van 250 gulden. De vuurtorenwachter hoeft niet meer dagelijks vele trappen op en af; het lichtsysteem is geautomatiseerd.

The lighthouse near Haamstede (photo) in the dunes of Schouwen used to be on the 250-guilder banknote before it was withdrawn. The lighthouse keeper no longer needs to climb endless stairs every day; the light system is fully automatic.

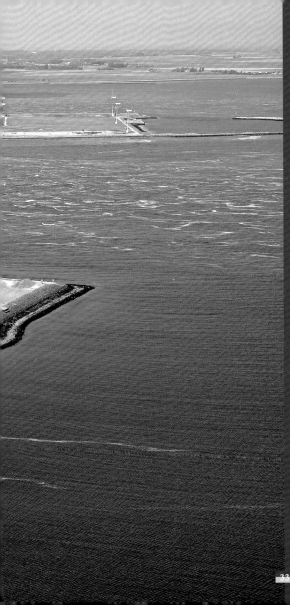

Om de unieke natuur en de visserij in de Oosterschelde te behouden, wordt deze zeearm niet met
een dichte dam afgesloten, maar met een bijzonder waterbouwkundig werk, waardoor het getij
grotendeels gehandhaafd blijft: de stormvloedkering. Op een speciale fundering in de Ooster-
scheldemonding komen 65 enorme betonnen pijlers te staan, met stalen schuiven ertussen. Die
worden bij stormvloed gesloten en houden zo de
Noordzee tegen.

De pijlers worden met behulp van het speciale
hefschip Ostrea in drie sluitgaten geplaatst, van
zuid naar noord: Roompot, Schaar van de
Roggenplaat en Hammen (foto). De stormvloedkering, gebouwd voor 200 jaar, wordt in oktober
1986 in gebruik genomen en werkt in de praktijk
prima. Het gebied rond de Oosterschelde is veel
beter beschermd tegen stormvloeden.

Voor de bouw van de stormvloedkering wordt in
het midden van de Oosterschelde het werkeiland
Neeltje Jans – een zandplaat – aangelegd. Nadat
het werk is voltooid biedt het onder meer ruimte
aan het recreatief themapark Waterland Neeltje
Jans, met als centraal gebouw het opvallende
Delta Plaza (foto). Eén pijler is als reserve een-
zaam in het bouwdok achtergebleven.

*The Oosterschelde is unique in its nature and its fishing
and this had to be preserved. And so this sea arm was not
shut off with a dam, but with a special hydraulic system*

allowing the tides largely to continue: the storm surge barrier. Special foundations were laid in the mouth of the Oosterschelde on which 65 enormous concrete pillars were erected, with steel sliding partitions between them. These are closed during the storm tide and thus keep out the North Sea.

The pillars were placed by the special lifting ship Ostrea in three enclosing gaps, from south to north: Roompot, Schaar van de Roggenplaat, and Hammen (photo). The Storm Surge Barrier, built to last for 200 years, was taken into use in October 1986 and works very successfully. The area around the Oosterschelde is now far better protected against storm floods.

When the Storm Surge Barrier was built, a special construction island – a sand flat – was built; it was called Neeltje Jans. When the work was completed, the island became the site for several attractions, including the theme park "Waterland Neeltje Jans," which has, as its central building, the remarkable Delta Plaza (photo). A solitary pillar has remained in the dock as reserve.

Brouwershaven (foto) is een van de Zeeuwse smal-steden. De positie als overscheephaven verdwijnt in 1872 door aanleg van de Nieuwe Waterweg. Graaf Floris V, graaf van Holland, is in 1286 stich-ter van Brouwershaven, dat door handel op Engeland en de Oostzee (uitvoer van haring, mee-krap, zout, invoer van wol en steenkool) tot bloei komt. Bewaard gebleven monumenten bewijzen dat. Opvallend is de grote Sint-Nicolaaskerk uit de 14e eeuw, een driebeukige hallekerk.

Brouwershaven (photo) is one of Zeeland's narrow towns. Its importance as transit harbour disappeared in 1872 with the opening of the Nieuwe Waterweg. Count Floris V, lord of Holland, was the founder of Brouwenshaven in 1286; it flourished thanks to the trade with England and the East Sea (export of herring, madder, salt, and the import of wool and coal). Some of the preserved monuments demonstrate all this. The large St. Nicolas Church from the 14th century is, with its three naves, a remarkable building.

In de vorm van de Zeeuwse dorpen zijn twee typen te onderscheiden: het voorstraatdorp (met de belangrijkste straat rechtuit tussen kerk en zeedijk) en het ringdorp. De ringdorpen zijn kenmerkend voor de oudste delen van de provincie: de vroeg bewoonde kerngebied, ofwel het oudland van Schouwen, Walcheren en Zuid-Beveland. In de jongere polders zijn de dorpen meer volgens rechte lijnen en hoeken aangelegd.

Het Schouwse Dreischor (foto) is een gaaf schoolvoorbeeld van een ringdorp, met de kerk in het midden en de woningen rondom. De plaats wordt al in 1206 vermeld. Het is altijd een landbouwdorp geweest, met als belangrijke gewassen meekrap en vlas. De oorspronkelijk aan Sint-Adriaan gewijde tweebeukige hallenkerk dateert grotendeels uit de 15e eeuw. Opmerkelijk aan de ring is het oude raadshuis ('t plaesen'uus) uit 1637, met bij de ingang de spreuk: Doet wel en vreest niemant.

There are two basic types of villages in Zeeland: the "main road" village (with a main street running directly between the church and the sea dyke) and the ring village. The ring villages are characteristic of the oldest parts of the province: the area that was first inhabited, the old land of Schouwen, Walcheren, and South Beveland. In the more recent polders, the villages are increasingly constructed with straight lines and right angles.

Dreischoor in Schouwen (photo) is a textbook example of a ring village, with the church in the centre and the houses around it. The place is mentioned as far back as 1206. It has always been an agricultural community, with flax and madder as its most important crops. The church with double naves dating, largely, from the 15th century was initially dedicated to St Adriaan. A remarkable feature of the ring is the old town hall ('t plaesen'uus) from 1637, with, above the entrance, the motto: "Do good and fear nobody."

De inwoners van de welvarende koopmansstad Zierikzee willen uiting geven aan hun rijkdom. Ze kiezen voor bouw van wat de grootste en hoogste toren (foto) van Nederland moet worden. De fundering, omvangrijker dan die van de Utrechtse Domtoren, wordt in 1454 gelegd. Pas in 1535 kunnen klokken worden geplaatst. Dan is het met de welvaart van Zierikzee ver gedaan en er is geen geld meer om de Sint-Lievens Monstertoren de gedachte hoogte te geven. Desondanks is het ontwerp van Rombout Keldermans een tot in wijde omtrek zichtbaar bouwwerk geworden, waarvan in 1972 een 15 jaar durende restauratie werd afgerond.

The inhabitants of the prosperous trading town of Zierikzee wanted to flaunt their wealth. They decided to build the largest and highest tower (photo) in the Netherlands. The foundation, larger than that for the Dom tower in Utrecht, was laid in 1454. The bells had to wait until 1535 before they could be hung. By then, the prosperity of Zierikzee had passed, and there was no money to give the St. Lievens Monster Tower its projected height. Nevertheless, this design of Rombout Keldermans is visible for many miles around. In 1972, a restoration that had lasted 15 years was completed.

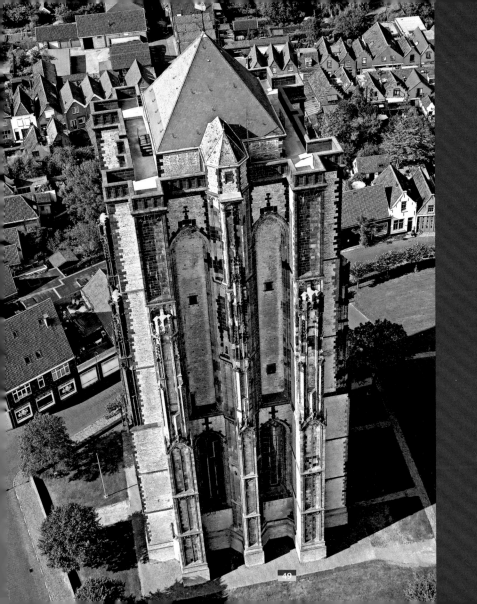

De Nieuwe Haven in Zierikzee, kort na 1600 aangelegd, is de thuisbasis van een aantal viskotters (foto), waarmee mossels in de Oosterschelde opgevist worden. De vroegere rijkdom van de stad is af te zien aan enkele oprijzende monumentale gebouwen.

The New Harbour in Zierikzee, that was built shortly after 1600, is the homeport to a number of cutters (photo) used for mussel fishing in the Oosterschelde. The former prosperity of the city is illustrated by a number of impressive buildings.

Er zijn weinig steden in Nederland waar het historisch erfgoed zo goed bewaard is, als in Zierikzee. Het stadje bezit evenveel monumenten als Delft, waaronder 14e eeuwse stadspoorten. Het belang en de welvaart van Zierikzee komen onder meer tot uiting in het stadhuis (foto) met twee Vlaamse topgevels (circa 1554). De kern van het gebouw bestaat uit de vleeshal met ranke toren.

There are few towns in the Netherlands where the historic heritage is so well preserved as in Zierikzee. The small town has as many monuments as Delft, including the 14th century city gates. The importance and the prosperity of Zierikzee is illustrated by the town hall (photo) crowned with two Flemish top gables (c. 1554). At the heart of the building is the meat hall with its slender towers.

Tussen Schouwen-Duiveland en Goeree-Overflakkee is in het kader van het Deltaplan in 1965
de Grevelingendam (foto) opgeworpen. Bij de
aanleg wordt gebruik gemaakt van een nieuwe
sluitmethode: een kabelbaan deponeert stortma-
terialen in het water. Langs de dam ontstaat een
druk gebruikt recreatiegebied.

The Grevelingen Dam (photo) was erected in 1965
between Schouwen-Duivenland and Goeree-Overflakkee
as part of the Delta plan. During construction, use was
made of a new enclosure method: a cable car was used to
drop debris into the water. A popular recreation area has
developed along the dam.

Aan de zuidkant van de Grevelingendam profiteert vissersdorp Bruinisse van de komst van het Grevelingenmeer. Dat uit zich in de aanleg van een grote jachthaven (foto).

To the south of the Grevelingen Dam, the fishing village of Bruinisse has profited from the creation of the Grevelingenmeer. The large yacht harbour (photo) is a clear demonstration of this.

Bij Bruinisse is het grote vakantiehuizencomplex
Aqua Delta gebouwd. In de nabijheid ligt
Grevelingenhout (foto). Het is een combinatie van
woongebied en golfbaan.

Near Bruinisse is a large holiday house complex, called
Aqua Delta. It is nearby to Grevelingenhout (photo), a
project that combines housing and a golf course.

Ten zuidoosten van Sint-Philipsland bevindt zich tussen Schelde-Rijnkanaal en Slaakdam (de verbinding tussen Tholen en Sint-Philipsland) het Rammegors (foto). Een nu nog zoet natuurgebied, gevormd door drooggevallen schorren en een voormalig zanddepot. Er zijn plannen om het gebied door toelaten van een lichte getijwerking weer te verzilten.

To the southeast of Sint Philipsland is the Rammegors (photo); it is situated between the Schelde-Rhine Canal and Slaak Dam (that connects Tholen and Sint Philipsland). The Rammegors is a freshwater area, formed by marshes that are now dry and a former sand depository. There are plans to make the area brackish by introducing limited tidal activity.

Het Thoolse dorp Sint-Annaland beschikt aan de Krabbenkreek, een zijtak van de Oosterschelde, over een jachthaven (foto). In de Krabbenkreek zelf is de wisselwerking van eb en vloed -- en daarmee het opslibproces – goed waarneembaar.

The village of Sint-Annaland on Tholen has a yacht marina (photo) on the Krabbenkreek, a tributary of the Oosterschelde. The ebb and flow of the tides — and with it the silting-up process — can be clearly observed in the Krabbenkreek.

78

Hoewel de dijken langs de Oosterschelde door de bouw van de stormvloedkering minder zwaar kunnen zijn dan die langs de open Westerschelde, moeten ze wel bestand zijn tegen zware stormen. Langs de Thoolse kust bij Stavenisse (foto) is te zien hoe in het verleden stukken dijk zijn weggeslagen; het gat is achterwaarts door een kaarsrechte dijk gedicht.

Although the dykes along the Oosterschelde – thanks to the construction of the Storm Surge Barrier – do not need to be as massive as those along the exposed Westerschelde, they still have to be able to repel heavy storms. Along the coast of Tholen near Stavenisse (photo), you can see how in the past sections of the dyke were destroyed; the hole has been plugged by a perfectly straight section of dyke.

In de omgeving van het huidige Sint-Maartensdijk
(foto) wonen al in het begin van onze jaartelling
mensen. Er zijn Germaanse en Romeinse aarde-
werkscherven gevonden die daarop duiden. Begin
13e eeuw ontstaat Haestinge, later Sint-
Maartensdijk genaamd. De laatgotische kerk
wordt in de 14e eeuw gebouwd.

*People have lived in the neighbourhood of the present St
Maartensdijk (photo) since the very earliest times.
Remains of German and Roman pottery found here prove
that. Haestinge – later renamed Sint-Maartensdijk –
dates back to the start of the 13th century. The late gothic
church was built in the 14th century.*

Scherpenisse (foto), gelegen in een van de oudste Thoolse polders (berucht om de vele dijkvallen), is een wat verloren dorpje uit begin 13e eeuw. De kerktoren heeft een houten opbouw. De watertoren uit 1923 is niet meer in gebruik.

Scherpenisse (photo), situated in one of the oldest Tholen polders (infamous for its many breached dykes), is a somewhat lost village from the beginning of the 13th century. The church towers have a wooden base. The water towers dating from 1923 are no longer in use.

Poortvliet op Tholen krijgt als enige plattelands-
district in Zeeland van de graaf het stadsrecht.
De gotische kruiskerk (foto) heeft een achtkantige
toren op een vierkante onderbouw uit circa 1350.

*Poortvliet on the island of Tholen is the only country
district in Zeeland that was granted city rights by the
Count. The gothic cruciform church (photo) has an eight-
sided tower built on a square base dating from around
1350.*

De stad Tholen (foto) – genaamd naar een tol op de Eendracht - ontwikkelt zich in de 15e eeuw tot een belangrijke plaats, met onder meer zoutwinning en meekrapteelt (wortels als grondstof voor rode verf). De welvaart verdwijnt na een grote brand in 1452, die bijna de hele stad in de as legt. Tholen blijft van belang, doordat het een van de stemhebbende steden in de Staten van Zeeland is (tot de Franse tijd, 1795). De gotische Grote of Onze Lieve Vrouwekerk, gesticht eind 13e eeuw, is een nooit voltooide kruisbasiliek.

The city of Tholen (photo) — named after the toll that had to be paid for using the river Eendracht — developed into a place of importance during the 15th century; it was a place where salt was won and where madder was grown (the roots of madder were used as a raw material for red dye). The prosperity disappears after a fire in 1452, that virtually razes the city to the ground. Tholen remains important, however, because it has a vote in the State of Zeeland (until the French period, 1795). The gothic Great or Our Lady's Church was founded in the 13th century; the cruciform basilisk was never completed.

89

De stad Tholen is als woongebied in trek bij Brabanders. Er komen gestaag nieuwe woonwijken (foto) bij. Ondanks deze Brabantse invasie, blijft de invloed van het reformatorische geloof aanzienlijk. Waar protestanten en katholieken kerken sluiten, bouwt de streng-gereformeerde geloofsgemeenschap juist nieuwe Godshuizen, wel met een eigentijdse uitstraling

The town of Tholen is an area that is particularly attractive to Brabanters. New housing areas are constantly being built (photo). Despite this invasion from Brabant, the influence of the reformed church is still considerable. Protestants and Catholics may be closing down their churches, but the strongly reformed communities are building new Houses of God, many with a contemporary look.

94

In het grensgebied van Zeeland en West-Brabant ontstaat in 1976 de 35 kilometer lange Schelde-Rijnverbinding (foto), als scheepvaartverbinding van Antwerpen naar Rotterdam en de Rijn. De verbinding loopt door de Kreekrakdam in de Hals van Zuid-Beveland, door de voormalige Eendracht langs Tholen en het Krammer-Volkerak. Er zijn twee sluiscomplexen: ten noorden van de Kreekrakdam en in de Philipsdam. De verbinding wordt in toenemende mate door duwvaart gebruikt.

In 1976, the 35-kilometre long Schelde-Rhine canal (photo), that provides a shipping lane from Antwerp to Rotterdam and the Rhine is opened in the area on the borders of Zeeland and West Brabant. The canal runs through the Kreekrak Dam in the Neck of South Beveland and through the former Eendracht, past Tholen and Krammer-Volkerak. There are two sets of locks: one to the north of the Kreekrak Dam, the other in the Philips Dam. The canal is increasingly used by pushing barges.

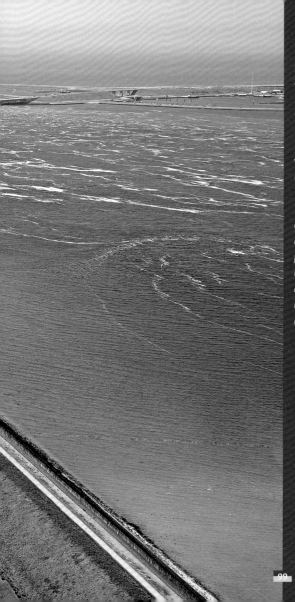

De noordkust van Noord-Beveland wordt door de eeuwen heen voortdurend belaagd door de zee. Er zijn vele dijkdoorbraken te noteren. Als bescherming bouwen de mensen achter de eerste zeewering een tweede waterkering. Tussenin ontstaan inlagen, die zich ontwikkelen tot waardevolle natuurgebieden en een pleisterplaats zijn voor vele vogels, zoals ter hoogte van de Anna Frisopolder (foto).

The north coast of North Beveland has, throughout the centuries, been under constant attack from the sea. The dykes have been breached on many occasions. For protection, people have now constructed a second dyke behind the first. The areas between the two have developed into valuable natural habitats and attract large numbers of birds as seen here near the Anna Friso Polder (photo).

Het grootste en diepste sluitgat in de Ooster-
scheldekering is de Roompot. Tussen de Noord-
Bevelandse wal en werkeiland Neeltje Jans staan
31 pijlers (foto).

The largest and deepest closing gap in the Oosterschelde
tidal barrier is the Roompot. There are 31 pillars (photo)
between the shore of North Beveland and the construction
island Neeltje Jans.

Ten behoeve van de deltawerken wordt op Noord-Beveland een werkhaven aangelegd. Later wordt deze Sophiahaven ingericht voor de watersport en komen er huizen aan de kant te staan. Vlakbij het recreatiecentrum Roompot (foto), een van de subtropische zwemparadijzen, die Zeeland rijk is.

For the works in the delta, a special harbour was constructed in North Beveland. Later, this harbour – the Sofia Harbour – was fitted out for recreational use and houses were built along the shore. Nearby is the recreational centre Roompot, that boasts one of the many sub-tropical swimming baths (photo) that are found throughout Zeeland.

Het is soms veel leuker dan varen. Bij hoogwater voor anker gaan op een zandplaat, die langzaam droog komt te liggen (foto). Een verschijnsel dat zich met name in de Oosterschelde voordoet.

It is sometimes more enjoyable than sailing: dropping anchor at high tide on a sand flat that slowly turns into dry land (photo). An occurrence that happens in particular in the Oosterschelde.

Nadat Noord-Beveland 60 jaar lang een drijvend eiland is geweest, wordt het opnieuw ingepolderd. Er ontstaan vrij grote polders, met grote akkers (foto), die van het eiland een vooraanstaand landbouwgebied maken. Door de malaise in de akkerbouw zijn veel veehouders, die elders met hun bedrijf weg moeten, naar Noord-Beveland gekomen: peeland wordt veeland.

After North Beveland had been a floating island for 60 years, it was once again turned into a polder. Fairly large polders are created, with large fields (photo), that transform the island into a leading farming area. As the problems hit agriculture, so many livestock breeders, who have to leave their farms elsewhere, come to North Beveland.

In de eerste helft van de 20e eeuw zijn er duizenden zeehonden in de Zeeuwse wateren. Door felle jacht en watervervuiling worden er begin jaren tachtig nog maar drie dieren geteld. Daarna groeit het aantal zeehonden weer licht, tot ongeveer 150 in 2004. De dieren zonnen, verharen en zogen hun jongen op de zandplaten in Ooster- en Westerschelde en Voordelta (foto). Ze liggen aan de rand van diepe geulen, waarin ze bij dreigende onraad meteen in kunnen wegzwemmen.

In the first half of the 20th century, there are thousands of seals in the Zeeland waters. But by the eighties, because of hunting and water pollution, there are only three animals left. The number of seals has since increased to around 150 in 2004. The animals sun, moult, and rear their young on the sand banks in the Ooster- and Westerschelde and at the mouth of the Delta (photo). They lie on the banks of deep gullies in which they can swim away at the first sign of danger.

Zeeland kan niet wachten op het gereedkomen van de deltawerken en wil eerder een vaste oeververbinding tussen Noord-Beveland en Schouwen-Duiveland. Dat wordt de vijf kilometer lange, rankgelijnde Zeelandbrug (foto), die in 1965 open gaat. Om de bouwkosten terug te verdienen wordt de eerste tijd tol geheven. De onderdelen voor de brug worden op een haventerrein bij Kats vervaardigd.

Zeeland does not want to wait for the completion of the Delta works and wants a permanent connection between North Beveland and Schouwen-Duiveland to be realised much sooner. That connection is the slender, five-kilometre long Zeeland Bridge (photo) that is opened in 1965. In order to recuperate the construction costs, toll is levied on all users of the bridge. The elements for the bridge are constructed on the harbour grounds in Kats.

Kats in de Oud-Noord-Bevelandpolder (foto) is een van de vele kleine Zeeuwse dorpen. Het eerste dorp duikt al in 1209 in de archieven op. Bij de Sint-Felixvloed in 1530 verdwijnt heel Noord-Beveland onder de golven. Eind 16e eeuw beginnen de herpolderingen en in 1598 wordt een nieuw Kats gesticht. Het is een Voorstraatdorp, met de belangrijkste straat loodrecht op de polderdijk. In Kats begint de Voorstraat bij de oude haven, om te eindigen bij de uit 1660 daterende witte kerk.

Kats in the Old North Beveland polder (photo) is one of many small Zeeland villages. The village is first mentioned in the records of 1209. In 1530, during the St. Felix Flood, the whole of North Beveland disappeared under the waves. The repoldering begins at the end of the 16th century, and in 1598 a new Kats is founded. The village is built along a single, main road that runs at a right angle from the polder dyke. In Kats, this single road starts at the harbour and ends at the white church that dates from 1660.

De Veerse Gatdam (foto) verbindt Walcheren met Noord-Beveland. Het is een toeristische trekpleister dankzij de aanwezigheid van breed Noordzeestand en het Veerse Meer.

The Gat Dam (photo) in Veere connects Walcheren and North Beveland. It is a tourist attraction thanks to the wide North Sea beach and the Veerse Meer.

In de binnenduinrand tussen Oostkapelle en Domburg wordt begin dertiende eeuw het kasteel Westhove gebouwd, dat onder meer dient als zomerverblijf voor de monniken uit de Abdij van Middelburg (foto). Door verbouwingen, brand en restauraties is van de oorspronkelijke middeleeuwse bebouwing weinig overgebleven. Naast het kasteel is een heemtuin aangelegd, waar de verschillende Zeeuwse landschapstypes worden getoond.

During the 13th century, the castle of Westhove was built on the inner edge of the dunes between Oostkapelle and Domburg; it was used among other things as the summer residence for the monks from the Abbey of Middelburg. Rebuilding, fire, and restoration means that little remains of the original building from the middle ages. A botanical garden, showcasing the diversity of landscapes in Zeeland, has been planted next to the castle.

Bij het kasteel Westhove tussen Oostkapelle en Domburg staat een historische oranjerie (foto). Die is ingericht tot biologisch museum en centrum voor natuur en landschap.

Near the castle of Westhove between Oostkapelle and Domburg is an historic orangery. This now houses a biological museum and a centre for nature and landscape.

De duinen langs de Walcherse kust zijn smal. Bij Westkapelle is al in de 16e eeuw de Westkappelse zeedijk aangelegd. Bij geallieerde bombardementen op de zeewering ontstaat in oktober 1944 een groot gat, waardoor landinwaarts grote kreken uitschuren. De reddingsbrigade beschikt er over een modern station (foto).

The dunes along the coast of Walcheren are narrow. A sea dyke was constructed near Westkapelle as early as the 16th century. In October 1944, during the allied bombing of the sea barrier, an enormous hole was blown in the dyke, and this resulted in large creeks being torn out of the island land inwards. The emergency services now have a modern station at their disposal (photo).

Westkapelle is een dorp met nog altijd een eigen karakter. Eigenlijk een zogenaamde smalstad (zonder vestingwerken): het krijgt in 1223 stadsrechten. De vuurtoren aan het begin van de Zuidstraat (foto) overheerst het dorpsbeeld. Het kustlicht is neergezet op een oorspronkelijke kerktoren.

Westkapelle is a village that still retains its own unique character. It is actually what is known as a "narrow town" (without fortification): it was awarded city rights in 1223. The lighthouse at the start of the Zuidstraat (photo) dominates the village. The coast light was installed in what had originally been a church tower.

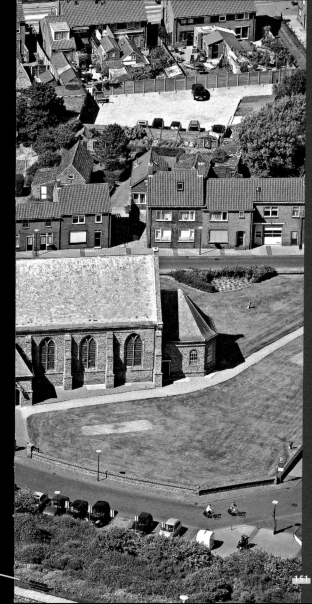

Door binnenwaartse verplaatsing van de duinen is Zoutelande steeds dichter aan zee komen te liggen. Toerisme is tegenwoordig de belangrijkste bestaansbron. De toren van de kerk (foto) bevat nog delen van laat 13e-eeuwse baksteengotiek.

As the dunes have been pushed ever farther inland, Zoutelande has come closer and closer to the sea. Tourism is now the most important source of income. The church tower (photo) still has sections featuring late 13th-century building-brick gothic.

Door aanleg van de Zandkreekdam en de Veersegatdam is in 1961 het Veerse Meer (foto) ontstaan. Het is ingericht als watersport- en oeverrecreatiegebied. In de zomer zijn de boten er nauwelijks te tellen. Van de diverse eilanden in het meer wordt druk gebruik gemaakt. Door aanleg van een ververskoker in de Zandkreekdam wordt het brakke water van het Veerse Meer doorgespoeld met zuiver, zout Oosterscheldewater.

The construction of the Zandkreek Dam and the Veersegat Dam in 1961 created the Veerse Meer (photo). It is now a water sport and recreation area. In the summer, it would be difficult to count the many boats. Much use is made of the many islands in the lake. A special system has been installed, which allows the brackish water to be flushed and refreshed with pure, salt water from the Oosterschelde.

Veere (foto) ontstaat in de 13e eeuw als nederzetting bij het veer op Campen (Noord-Beveland). De heren Van Borssele en Bourgondië brengen de stad veel welvaart. Haringvangst, kaapvaart en handel zijn belangrijk. Enkele eeuwen is het de exclusieve stapelplaats voor de Schotse handel. De rijkdom uit zich in monumentale huizen en gebouwen, waaronder het laatgotisch stadhuis van bouwmeester Keldermans (1517) en de Onze Lieve Vrouwekerk. Korenmolen de Koe is in 1909 op een bolwerkrest gebouwd.

Veere (photo) began in the 13th century as a settlement near the ferry (veer) on Campen (North Beveland). The Lords of Borssele and Burgundy bring the town much prosperity. Herring fishing, privateering, and trade are important. For several centuries, it is the exclusive warehousing spot for the Scottish trade. The wealth is apparent in the monumental houses and buildings, including the late gothic town hall by the master builder Keldermans (1517) and Onze Lieve Vrouwekerk (the Church of Our Lady). The corn mill "de Koe" (the cow) is erected in 1909 on a remnant of the fortifications.

De Onze Lieve Vrouwekerk (foto) in Veere – beter bekend als Grote Kerk – oogt fors. De toren is nooit afgebouwd; het geld ontbreekt. De bouw begint in 1332. De groei van de stad maakt diverse uitbreidingen noodzakelijk waarvoor onder anderen Antoon Keldermans en zijn zoon Rombout tekenen. Wegens geldgebrek wordt een deel als pakhuis verhuurd en de Fransen gebruiken de kerk als hospitaal en paardenstal. De brandweer vindt er onderdak en aannemers stallen er bouwmaterialen. Na restauratie vinden in de kerk culturele evenementen plaats.

The Onze Lieve Vrouwekerk (Church of Our Lady) (photo) — better known as the Great Church — appears massive. The tower was never completed; the money ran out. The building started in 1332. The growth of the city made several expansions necessary, and these were undertaken by several people, including Antoon Keldermans and his son Rombout. The lack of money resulted in a part of the church being rented out as warehouse, and the French made use of it as a hospital and stables. The fire brigade was stationed in it and building contractors stored their materials here. Following restoration, the church now houses cultural events.

Tot in de 19e eeuw wordt in heel Holland het ring-rijden beoefend. Noem het een vreedzame boeren-versie van het ridderlijke steekspel. Een ruiter moet op een ongezadeld paard in galop met een lans een ring van een draad afsteken. Dit oude gebruik heeft zich met name op Walcheren nog gehandhaafd, waar het zeer serieus als regionale sport wordt bedreven. De in 1950 opgerichte Zeeuwse Ringrijders Vereniging werkt jaarlijks een omvangrij-ke competitie af.

Het Huis van Oranje heeft speciale belangstel-ling voor het ringrijden. Dat blijkt onder meer uit het beschikbaar stellen van een koninklijke wisselbe-ker. Behalve door individuele rijders op paarden wordt het rienkrieën ook met rijtuigen beoefend: het sjeesjesrijden. Naast het wedstrijdelement is hieraan ook een dosis folklore verbonden. De deelnemers in authentieke sjezen gaan gekleed in oude streek-drachten. De man stuurt het rijtuig, de vrouw steekt de ring.

Provinciehoofdstad Middelburg is het bestuurlijk cen-trum van Zeeland. De stad is door de eeuwen heen altijd de belangrijkste van het gewest en dat uit zich onder meer in de monumentale gebouwen. Hoewel door het bombardement van de Duitsers in mei 1940 veel historische panden zijn verwoest, telt de stad nog ruim duizend monumenten, die herinneren aan een fier verleden. De grondslag wordt in het midden van de 9e eeuw gelegd door de aanleg van een ringwalburg, ter verdediging tegen binnenvallen-de Noormannen.

Pronkjuweel is het gotische stadhuis aan de Markt, gebouwd door de architectenfamilie Keldermans. Het wodt nu gebruikt door de in 2004 begonnen Roosevelt Academy, een mastersoplei-ding. Ook de na het bombardement ingrijpend gerestaureerde Abdij, met de 85 meter hoge toren die in de wandeling de Lange Jan wordt genoemd, maakt indruk. De eerste gebouwen van het complex zijn omstreeks 1150 verrezen. Lange tijd zijn de Norbertijner geestelijken de bewoners, nu is de Abdij zetel van het provinciaal bestuur.

Onderdeel van de Abdij zijn twee kerken: de Koorkerk (voor de kanunniken) en de Nieuwe Kerk (voor de parochianen). In de kerken bevinden zich de praalgraven van graaf Willem II en zijn broer Floris de Voogd en van de Zeeuwse admiraals Johan en Cornelis Evertsen (ontworpen door Rombout Verhulst). Beeldbepalend voor het silhouet van de stad is ook de koepelvormige Oostkerk, waaraan tussen 1644 en 1667 is gebouwd.

Middelburg krijgt in de tweede helft van de 12e eeuw stadsrechten en ontwikkelt zich tot een belangrijke handelsstad. Toppunt van de bloei ligt op het eind van de 17e eeuw; de stad huisvest dan meer dan 30.000 mensen. De kooplieden vervullen een belangrijke rol in de Verenigde Oustindische Compagnie (1602) en later de West-Indische Compagnie (1674). Deze WIC houdt zich, net als de in 1720 opgerichte Middelburgse Commercie-compagnie, onder meer bezig met de slavenhandel.

The sport of ring riding was practised throughout Holland until well into the 19th century. It could be considered apeaceful common-folks version of jousting between knights. A rider would ride bare back and try to skewer a ring suspended on a string with the tip of his lance. This old tradition has been preserved mainly in Walcheren, where it is seriously practised as a regional sport. Every year, the Zeeland Ring Riders Association holds an extensive competition.

The Royal House of Oranje is particularly interested in ring riding; they have instituted a royal challenge cup. Ring riding is not only practised by individuals on horseback, but also by couples in carriages: it is then called "sjeesjesrijden". It is more than just a competitive sport; there is also quite a bit of folklore attached to it. The participants drive authentic carriages (known as "sjezen") and dress in traditional regional costume. The man takes the reins; the woman tries to skewer the ring.

Middelburg is the provincial capital and administrative centre of Zeeland. Through the centuries, it has always been the most important city in the area and this is clearly show in its monumental buildings. Although the bombing by the Germans in May 1940 destroyed many historical buildings, the city still boasts more than a thousand monuments that are a reminder of a proud past. The origins of the city lay in the 9th century with the construction of a fortified mound to offer protection against invading Normans.

The jewel in the crown is the gothic city hall on the Markt (Market), built by the Keldermans, the celebrated family of architects. It has been used since 2004 as the headquarters of the Roosevelt Academy that offers training for Masters degrees. The Abbey, which was extensively restored after the bombing, is also impressive; its 85-metre tower is commonly called the Long John. The first buildings in this complex date back to around 1150. For a long time, the Norbertines were the spirituals inhabitants; the Abbey is now the seat of the provincial administration.

Two churches are part of the Abbey complex: the Koorkerk (the Choir Church – for the canons) and the Nieuwe Kerk (the New Church – for the parishioners). The churches contain the mausoleums of Count Willem II and his brother Floris the Guardian and of the admirals Johan and Cornelis Evertsen (designed by Rombout Verhulst). A distinguishing feature of the city's silhouette is the domed Oostkerk (East Church), that was built between 1644 and 1667.

Middelburg was granted city rights in the second half of the 12th century and developed into an important trading city. The height of its prosperity was at the end of the 17th century; the city then had more than 30,000 inhabitants. The tradesmen played an important role in the East Indies Company (1602) and later in the West Indies Company (1674). The WIC, in common with the Middelburg Commercial Company founded in 1720, was also involved in the slave trade.

TER EEUWIGE GEDACHTENIS
VAN DE
ONSTERFELIJKE ZIELEDEUGD
DE HOOGEDELEN
JOHAN EN CORNELIS EVERTSEN
LUITENANT-ADMIRALEN VAN ZEELAND
BEIDEN
STRIJDENDE VOOR HET VADERLAND
GESNEUVELD
IN DEN JARE MDCLXVI

DIT PRAALGRAF

De Gevangentoren in Vlissingen (foto), gelegen aan de rand van de boulevard is 40 jaar geleden gered van de sloop. Het is een restant van een eind 15e eeuw gebouwde stadspoort. Nu is er een restaurant in gevestigd.

The Prison Tower in Vlissingen (photo), situated just off the boulevard, was saved from demolition 40 years ago. It is the remains of the city gate that was built at the end of the 15th century. It is now in use as a restaurant.

Oud en nieuw bij elkaar aan de waterkant van Vlissingen: het in 1823 gebouwde arsenaal van de artillerie, met ernaast een uitkijktoren en eigentijdse woonflat. In het Arsenaal is thans een tentoonstelling over het onderwaterleven ingericht.

Old and new rub shoulders by the seashore in Vlissingen: the artillery arsenal, built in 1823, next to it a watchtower and a contemporary block of flats. In the Arsenal, there is an exhibition dealing with life under the water.

190

Goes, bijnaam Ganzestad, is streekcentrum voor de Bevelanden. De in 1651 aangelegde nieuwe haven (foto), is thans bestemd voor de pleziervaart. Langs de kade bevinden zich veel historische gebouwen, waaronder aan de Turfkade een woonhuis met een laatgotische trapgevel uit 1533.

Goes, nicknamed Ganzestad (Goose City), is the provincial centre of the collective Bevelands. The new harbour that was built in 1651, is now in use for recreational vessels. There are many historic buildings along the quay including on the Turfkade a house with a brick step gable dating from 1533.

Veel historie in het oude stadscentrum (foto) van Goes. Op de voorgrond het stadhuis aan de Grote Markt. Het oudste deel, met belfort, dateert uit de 14e eeuw. Daarachter de indrukwekkende Grote of Maria Magdalenakerk, die in 1423 is voltooid. In de kerk pronkt het Marcussenorgel uit 1643. Tegenover deze protestantse kerk staat de begin 20e eeuw gebouwde rooms-katholieke Maria Magdalenakerk.

There is much history in the old city centre (photo) of Goes. In the foreground is the town hall on the Grote Markt (the Main Market). The oldest part, with the belfry, dates from the 14th century. Behind this is the impressive Great or Maria Magdalena Church, that was completed in 1423. Inside the church, there is a magnificent Marcussen organ, dating from 1643. Opposite this protestant church is the Roman Catholic Maria Magdalena Church that was built in the early years of the 20th century.

203

Net buiten Goes verrijst in 1987 het Ooster-
scheldeziekenhuis (foto), dat twee oude
hospitalen, Bergzicht en Sint-Joanna, ver-
vangt. Het fungeert als streekziekenhuis voor
de Oosterscheldregio.

*In 1987, a new hospital — the Oosterschelde
Hospital (photo) — was opened just outside Goes;
it replaced two older hospitals — Bergzicht and St.
Joanna. It acts as the regional hospital for the
whole Oostschelde region.*

Omringd door akkers is aan het nieuwe Goese Meer een 18-holes golfbaan aangelegd (foto), die vanuit de lucht het patroon van een schorrengebied vertoont.

A new 18-hole golf course has been developed near the Goese Meer (Goes Lake). It is surrounded by fields and, from the air, shows all the characteristics of a mud flat landscape (photo).

Mensen willen graag aan het water wonen. In een polder ten noordoosten van Goes is daarin voorzien. Er is een geheel nieuwe woonwijk (foto) gebouwd. De huizen liggen op landtongen, omgeven door brede, speciaal gegraven waterpartijen.

People want to live near the water. This is now possible in the polder to the north east of Goes. A completely new housing estate (photo) has been built there. The houses are build on small heads of land, surrounded by specially dug water features.

Zuidwestelijk van het dorp Nisse ligt de Sluishoek
(foto), begrensd door de boomrijke Valdijk. Het is
een stukje lagere poelgrond, met hoofdzakelijk
weilanden. Bijzonder zijn de meidoornheggen, die
in het voorjaar voor een witte bloeipracht zorgen,
vandaar de naam heggengebied.

To the south west of the village of Nisse, on the
boundaries of the forested area of Valdijk, is the
Sluishoek (photo). It is a low-lying morass area, with
mainly meadows. Particularly unusual are the hawthorn
hedgerows that produce an abundance of white blooms in
the spring; people often call this the hedge area.

De kleine Nieuwe Kamerpolder (foto) van 31 hectare ontstaat al omstreeks 1400 en ligt midden tussen de dorpen Ellewoutsdijk en Ovezande. Het is een restant van de verzande geul de Kamer, die een zijtak vormt van de machtige stroomgeul Zwake.

The small Nieuwe Kamerpolder (the New Kamer Polder) (photo) covers some 31 hectares and was created around 1400 between the villages of Ellewoutsdijk and Overzande. It is the remnant of the Kamer channel which became silted up; it was a tributary of the Zwake, the major tidal channel.

Kapelle geldt als centrum van de Zeeuwse fruit-
teelt. De toren van de monumentale kerk (foto) in
het midden van het dorp, dateert uit de 14e eeuw
en valt op door vier hoektorentjes rond de spits.
Op de voorgrond het gemeentehuis van Kapelle.
Het dorp is in de 12e eeuw gesticht door de Heren
van Maalstede.

*Kapelle is the centre of Zeeland's fruit growing industry.
The tower of the monumental church (photo) in the
middle of the village dates from the 14th century; it is
unusual in having four corner turrets around the spire.
In the foreground is Kapelle's town hall. The village was
founded in the 12th century by the Gentlemen of
Maalstede.*

Het Kanaal door Zuid-Beveland, tussen Hansweert en Wemeldinge vormt een belangrijke schakel in de scheepvaartroute tussen Antwerpen-Gent en Rotterdam. Het kanaal is in 1866 open gesteld en enkele malen verbreed. Bij de jongste aanpassing zijn bij Hansweert nieuwe sluizen aangelegd (foto).

The Canal through South Beveland, that runs between Hansweert and Wemeldinge, is an important link in the shipping routes between Antwerp-Ghent and Rotterdam. The Canal was opened in 1866 and has since been widened on several occasions. In the latest redevelopment, new locks were installed near Hansweert (photo).

Yerseke geldt als hét centrum van de schelpdiercultuur: mossels, oesters en kreeften. Sinds het eind van de 19e eeuw worden de mossels gekweekt. De kweekpercelen bevinden zich in de Oosterschelde. Veel mosselzaad (piepjonge mosseltjes) wordt door de Zeeuwse vissers opgevist in de Waddenzee en uitgezet op de kweekpercelen. De Zeeuwse mossels vinden niet alleen in eigen land gretig aftrek, maar vooral ook in België.

Ook het kweken van oesters begint pas goed aan het eind van de 19e eeuw, in navolging van Franse cultures. De jonge oesters worden afgezet op oesterbanken, die voorzien zijn van speciaal materiaal (vroeger gekalkte dakpannen, nu lege mosselschelpen), waarop de jonge oesters zich kunnen hechten. Ze worden later uitgezaaid op kweekpercelen. Langs de Oosterschelde bij Yerseke bevinden zich nog oude oesterputten, waar de schelpdieren konden verwateren. Tijdens de strenge winter van 1962/63 krijgt de bedrijfstak een enorme dreun: ongeveer 90 procent van de oesters sterft. Veel kwekers stoppen en om de teelt weer op gang te brengen, worden, onder meer uit Brits Columbia, Japanse oesters ingevoerd. Die gedijen in de Oosterschelde zo goed, dat ze inmiddels een ware plaag vormen.

Yerseke is the undisputed centre of shellfish: mussels, oysters, and lobsters. Mussels have been cultivated here since the 19th century. The breeding beds are in the Oosterschelde. The fishermen of Zeeland fish up the mussel seed (tiny young mussels) in the Wad and release them in the breeding grounds. Zeeland mussels are not only eagerly sought after in the Netherlands, but also — and particularly — in Belgium.

Oyster cultivation also began at the end of the 19th century, inspired by the French cultivation. The young oysters are released on oyster beds that are made of a special material (they used to use chalked roof slates, now use is made of empty mussel shells), to which the young oysters can attach themselves. They are later sown out in breeding beds. Along the Oosterschelde near Yerseke, you can still find old oyster pits, in which the shellfish could be moved to fresh water. During the severe winter of 1962/62, the industry was severely damaged: about 90% of the oysters died. Many breeders ended their activities, and in order to revitalise the cultivation, Japanese oysters were imported, in particular from British Columbia. They flourish so well in the Oosterschelde, that they have since become something of a plague.

De komst van nieuwe sluizen bij Hansweert maakt de oude overbodig. Ze zijn gedempt (foto). Er wordt al vele jaren gezocht naar een passende functie voor het gebiedje langs het Kanaal door Zuid-Beveland.

The new locks at Hansweert made the old ones superfluous; they have been filled in (photo). For many years, people have tried to find a suitable use for the area along the Canal in South Beveland.

Voor het spoor- en wegverkeer zijn over het Kanaal door Zuid-Beveland bij het gehuchtje Vlake bruggen (foto) aangelegd. Dankzij de werkzaamheden voor de verbreding is ook de Vlaketunnel onder het kanaal gegraven, waardoor weg- en scheepvaartverkeer elkaar niet hinderen.

Bridges have been constructed over the canal near the hamlet of Vlake (photo) to carry road and rail traffic. Thanks to the activities around the widening of the canal, the Vlaketunnel was constructed under the canal so that road and water transport do not impede each other.

Aan het noordelijk eind van het Kanaal door Zuid-Beveland ligt Wemeldinge. De sluizen zijn daar vervallen, omdat het getij op het kanaal is toegelaten. De vrijkomende ruimte is benut voor jachthavens en woningbouw (foto).

Wemeldinge lies at the northern end of the Canal through South Beveland. The locks there are in bad repair, because the tide has now been let through into the canal. The area that has been won is now used for a yacht marina and housing (photo).

Aan de West-Zeeuws-Vlaamse kust probeert
Cadzand-Bad zich te ontwikkelen tot badplaats
van allure. Dus met veel vakantiehuizen en strand-
paviljoens (foto). De duinen ter plekke zijn nog
jong: ontstaan vanaf de 17e eeuw.

*Cadzand-Bad, on the coast of West Zeeland-Flanders, is
striving to establish itself as an exclusive resort. There is a
growing number of holiday homes and beach pavilions
(photo). The dunes here are fairly young; they developed
from the 17th century.*

In de 13e eeuw is Cadzand een apart eiland; er worden steeds stukjes land door inpolderingen – die behoren tot de oudste van West-Europa - aan toe gevoegd. In Cadzand (foto) en omgeving vestigen zich veel uit Frankrijk gevluchte Hugenoten. De Mariakerk uit het midden van de 13e eeuw is een voorbeeld van Schelde-gotiek. De toren is in 1677 afgebroken. Zwaar beschadigd in 1944, wordt de kerk bij de restauratie in 1954 voorzien van een klokketorentje.

In the 13th century, Cadzand was a separate island; gradually, more and more land was added to it through poldering; these were some of the oldest in Western Europe. Many Huguenots fleeing from France settled in Cadzand (photo). The Maria Church from the middle of the 13th century is an example of Schelde gothic. The tower was demolished in 1677. It was seriously damaged in 1944, and when it was restored in 1954, a bell tower was added.

241

Sluis (foto) is rond 1270 ontstaan als voorhaven van Brugge. De stad profiteert van de verzanding van het Zwin, waardoor de Vlaamse handelsstad moeilijker bereikbaar wordt. Vanwege de strategische ligging is de stad vaak strijdtoneel. Recent nog in de Tweede Wereldoorlog; bij de bevrijding op 1 november 1944 ligt Sluis grotendeels in puin. Ook het stadhuis met het enige echte belfort in Nederland (toren met vier uitgekraagde hoektorentjes) raakt zwaar beschadigd, maar wordt herbouwd. Sluis geniet bekendheid als winkelstad.

Sluis (photo) came into being in 1270 as an outport of Brugge. The city profited from the silting up of the Zwin, which made the Flemish trading town less accessible. The city was also the scene of conflict, given its strategic location. This was most recently the case in the Second World War; when it was liberated on November 1, 1940, it largely lay in ruins. The town hall that has the only true belfry in the Netherlands (a tower with four collarless corner towers) was also severely damaged, but has now been rebuilt. Sluis is famous as a shopping centre.

MOSSELEN

* Natuur met mosterdsaus
* in de witte wijnsaus

met brood en/of frites

Gegrild varkenshaasje met champignon
15,95

De Westerschelde is als toegangsweg tot de haven van Antwerpen niet afgesloten. De zeedijken zijn er wel fors versterkt en op zogenaamde Deltahoogte gebracht, waarbij het tracé soms een historische kronkel, zoals richting Baalhoek (foto) volgt.

The Westerschelde is the entrance to the harbour of Antwerp and has therefore not been closed. The sea dykes have been considerably strengthened and brought up to what is called Delta height. The dykes sometimes show an historic meandering, such as in the direction of Baalhoek (photo).

Behalve vissersplaats is Breskens ook een belangrijk watersportcentrum. Met diverse scheepswer-
ven en een grote haven voor zeegaande jachten
(foto). Aan de boorden van de Westerschelde zijn
enkele opvallende appartementencomplexen verrezen.

In addition to being a fishing community, Breskens is also
an important centre for water recreation. It has a variety
of ship wharves and a large harbour for sea-going yachts
(photo). A number of unusual apartment buildings have
risen on the banks of the Westerschelde.

Naast de veerhaven van Breskens, waar het fiets-
voetveer vanaf Vlissingen aanmeert, ligt op de
plaats van het voormalige fort Frederik Hendrik
een vakantiedorp (foto). De ontwerpers hebben
zich bij de vormgeving laten inspireren door het
verdedigingswerk, dat in 1810 door de Fransen ter
verdediging van de Scheldemonding als fort
Impérial is aangelegd.

*Next to the ferry terminal in Breskens, where the
pedestrian and bicycle ferry from Vlissingen comes in,
there is a holiday camp (photo) that has been built where
the former fort Frederik Hendrik used to stand. The
designers have allowed themselves to be completely
inspired by the fortifications that were built as a Fort
Impérial by the French in 1810 to protect the mouth of
the Schelde.*

Op talrijke plaatsen in Zeeuws-Vlaanderen slinge-
ren kreken zich door het landschap. Ze bezitten
belangrijke natuurwaarden, maar zijn ook nodig
voor de afwatering. Tussen Breskens en
Schoondijke ligt de Nieuwlandse kreek (foto).

*Creeks wind their way through many areas of the
Zeeland-Flanders landscape. They have a particular
natural value, but they are also essential for irrigation.
The Nieuwlandse creek (photo) is situated between
Breskens and Schoondijke.*

268

't Kerkje noemen de inwoners van Waterlandkerkje kortweg hun dorp (foto). Het heeft te maken met de oude heerlijkheid Waterland en de stichting van een hervormde kerk in 1669. Deze kerk is in 1708 door de Fransen in brand geschoten en in 1713 herbouwd.

The people living in Waterlandkerkje refer to their village simply as "'t Kerkje" (the Little Church) (photo). It is all revolves around the old domain of Westland and the founding of a reformed church in 1669. This church was set on fire by the French in 1708 and rebuilt in 1713.

Van IJzendijke is al begin 11e eeuw sprake; de plaats bloeit vooral dankzij de wolhandel. Door een reeks stormvloeden verdwijnt de stad in 1437. In 1587 ontstaat een nieuw IJzendijke (foto), aanvankelijk als verdedigingswerk dat door prins Maurits tot zeshoekige vesting wordt uitgebouwd. Tijdens de slag om West-Zeeuws-Vlaanderen in 1944 worden grote verwoestingen aangericht. Zo moet na de oorlog een nieuwe, derde, katholieke kerk worden gebouwd. De molen met Vlaamse kap uit 1841 staat op een bastionrest van de stadswallen.

IJzendijke was mentioned as long ago as the 11th century; the place owes its growth largely to the wool industry. The city disappears in 1437 as the result of a number of storm floods. In 1587, a new IJzendijke (photo) arises, initially as a fortification that Prince Maurits expanded into a six-sided fortress. Considerable damage was done to it in 1944 during the battle of West Zeeland-Flanders. As a result, a new catholic church — the third — was built after the war. The windmill with Flemish turret dating from 1841 is built on the remains of a bastion in the city walls.

Op vele plaatsen in Zeeland zijn vakantiedorpen verrezen. Vaak in combinatie met waterpartijen, zoals westelijk van Hoofdplaat (foto).

Holiday villages have sprung up in many places throughout Zeeland. Often combined with water features, such as those to the west of Hoofdplaat (photo).

Biervliet (foto) geniet enige bekendheid als woonplaats van Willem Beukel(s), die omstreeks 1400 het haringkaken uitvindt. De hervormde kerk uit 1660 is het oudste gebouw van Biervliet en bevat drie opvallende gebrandschilderde ramen. Korenmolen de Harmonie is in 1843 oorspronkelijk gebouwd als oliemolen.

Biervliet (photo) enjoys a certain fame as home of Willem Beukel(s) who, around 1400, discovered the process of gutting and preserving herring. The reformed church from 1660 is the oldest building in Biervliet and has three stained glass windows. The corn mill "de Harmonie" was originally built in 1843 as an oil mill.

Terneuzen is de grootste gemeente van Zeeland. De gelijknamige kern breidt gestaag uit, onder meer met een wijk tegen het gehucht Othene aan (foto). De appartementen vlak achter de speciaal daarvoor verbrede zeedijk bieden zicht op de Westerschelde.

Terneuzen is the largest county council in Zeeland. The city itself is expanding rapidly; there is a new district near the hamlet of Othene (photo). The apartments built immediately behind the specially widened sea dyke offer panoramas over the Westerschelde.

De provincie wil hoogbouw in het vlakke polderland zoveel mogelijk beperken. Naast de boulevards in Vlissingen is de Scheldedijk bij Terneuzen
een van de locaties waar torenflats (foto) het
beeld mogen bepalen.

*The province wants to restrict as far as possible high-rise
buildings in the flat polder landscape. The Scheldedijk
near Terneuzen is, together with the boulevards of
Vlissingen, one of the locations where high-rise flats
(photo) are allowed to dominate the skyline.*

Als centrumgemeente voor Zeeuws-Vlaanderen beschikt Terneuzen over een groot Scheldetheater (links op de foto). De voormalige veerhaven van de lijn Terneuzen-Hoedekenskerke is nu in gebruik als jachthaven.

As it is the centre for Zeeland-Flanders, Terneuzen boasts the large Schelde Theatre (left on the photo). The former ferry terminal for the Terneuzen-Hoedekenskerke route is now in use as a yacht marina.

Door de historie bepaald is Oost-Zeeuws-Vlaanderen een overwegend katholieke streek. Zo ook het dorpje Ossenisse (foto). Vlaamse abdijen, zoals Ten Duinen, hebben er veel grond in bezit. De aan Willibrordus gewijde kerk stamt uit 1915 en is in 1961 grondig gerestaureerd.

History has determined that East Zeeland-Flanders is largely a catholic region. This is true of the hamlet of Ossenisse (photo). Flemish abbeys, such as Ten Duinen, own a lot of land. The church dedicated to Willibrordus dates from 1915 and was completely restored in 1961.

Toegang Westerschelde tunnel nabij Ellewoutsdijk.

Entrance Westerschelde Tunnel.

In de archieven is in 991 al sprake van Axla, ofwel Axel (foto). Zoutwinning en turfsteken zijn aanleiding voor het ontstaan. Oorlogen en watersnoden kenmerken de geschiedenis. De kreken zijn ervan over gebleven. De watertoren uit 1937 doet niet meer als zodanig dienst. Er worden nu exposities in gehouden.

Records mention Axla or Axel (photo) as far back as 991. Production of salt and peat were the reasons for its existence. Its history is characterised by wars and floods. The creeks are reminders of this. The water tower dating from 1937 is no longer in use for its original purpose; exhibitions are now held there.

In de stad Hulst overheerst de basiliek gewijd aan Sint-Willibrord (foto). Rond 1200 is er de eerste kerk gebouwd, waarvan slechts enkele fragmenten bewaard zijn gebleven. De huidige vorm ontstond tijdens herbouw na een brand in 1468. Er hebben beroemde bouwmeesters aan gewerkt, onder wie leden van de familie Keldermans. De kerk is in 1935 tot basiliek verheven.

The city of Hulst is overshadowed by the basilisk dedicated to St Willibrord (photo). The first church was built here around 1200; only a few fragments of that church remain. The current form arose during the rebuilding that followed a fire in 1468. Many famous builders have worked on the building, including members of the Keldermans family. The church was promoted to a basilisk in 1935.

De Keldermanspoort in Hulst (foto) is in 1506 gebouwd als dubbele land- en waterpoort, met als bijnamen oude of dobbele poort. Bij het beleg van de stad in 1596 vindt een grondige vernieling plaats. De restanten zijn in ere hersteld.

The Keldermanspoort (Keldermans Gate) in Hulst was built in 1506 as a gate for both land and water; it was given the nickname of Old or Double Gate. When the town was sacked in 1596, the gate was totally destroyed. The remains were restored to their former glory.

In de Tachtigjarige Oorlog speelt Hulst een belangrijke rol in de strijd tussen de Staatse troepen van de Oranjes en de Spanjaarden. Er worden stadswallen en andere versterkingen aangelegd, met kenmerkende vormen (foto). Een deel van de vestigingwerken is gerestaureerd. De stadsmolen op het puntige bolwerk is in 1792 gebouwd.

In the Eighty Years War, Hulst played an important role in the battle between the State troops of the House of Orange and the Spanish. City walls and other defences were built, often with characteristic shapes (photo). A part of the fortifications has been restored. The city mill on the pointed rampart was built in 1792.

De Oost-Zeeuws-Vlaamse buurtschap Luntershoek
(foto) ligt zeer schilderachtig aan de rand van het
natuurgebied Groot Eiland, waar de Belgische
eigenaren overigens geen bezoekers toelaten.

*The East Zeeland-Flanders community Luntershoek
(photo) enjoys a picturesque setting on the edge of the
nature area Groot Eiland, to which, incidentally, the
Belgian owners do not allow any visitors.*

In het Verdronken Land van Saeftinghe, op de grens van Zeeuws-Vlaanderen en België, ligt een oerlandschap. Zo hebben grote delen van Zeeland er vóór de inpolderingen uit gezien. Een groot schorrengebied – een buitendijkse vlakte, dooraderd met een grillig patroon van kreken en geulen (foto). Het getij bepaalt er het ritme. Soms openbaart zich bij eb een slikkige geul, die bij opkomende vloed in rap tempo verandert in een watervlakte. Het woeste en ontoegankelijke gebied is het grootste brakwaterschor van Europa, met het grootste getijverschil in Nederland.

Waar nu eb en vloed heersen, hebben vruchtbare polders gelegen, welvarende dorpen en een imposant kasteel. Aanvankelijk trekken in Saeftinghe schaapherders rond. In de late Middeleeuwen ontstaan er twaalf polders. Het gebied overleeft in de 15e eeuw vele stormvloeden. De 16e eeuw wordt een tijd vol nieuwe rampspoed. De Sint-Felixvloed in 1530 houdt flink huis en tijdens de Allerheiligenvloed in 1570 breken de dijken opnieuw. Tijdens de Tachtigjarige Oorlog worden sluizen open gezet en dijken doorstoken. Saeftinghe vergaat.

In de 18e en 19e eeuw worden grote delen van het gebied opnieuw op zee gewonnen. De laatste inpoldering vindt in 1907 plaats: de Hertogin Hedwigepolder, nu in beeld als polder die andermaal terug gegeven moet worden aan het water, om de rivier weer meer ruimte te bieden. Saeftinghe is uitgegroeid tot natuurgebied met vele bijzondere planten en dieren. 's Winters verblijven er tienduizenden grauwe ganzen en eenden als smient en pijlstaart.

The Verdronken Land van Saeftinghe (the Drowned Land of Saeftinghe), on the border between Zeeland-Flanders and Belgium, displays a rudimentary, unspoiled landscape. This is how large tracts of Zeeland looked before the polders were engineered. An enormous salt marsh area – flats outside the dykes, with a filigree pattern made by creeks and gullies (photo). The tide sets the rhythm. Sometimes, at ebb, a slimy gully may appear that, as the tide rises, rapidly turns into an expanse of water. This wild and inaccessible area is the largest salt marsh in Europe, and has the greatest tidal difference in the Netherlands.

Where now ebb and flood rule, there were once fruitful polders, prosperous villages, and an imposing castle. Initially, shepherds moved around Saeftinghe. In the late middle ages, 12 polders were created. In the 15th century, the area survived many storm floods. But the 16th century became a time of natural catastrophes. In 1530, the St Felix flood causes extensive damage and in 1570, during the All Saints' Flood, the dykes are breached again. During the Eighty Years' War, the locks were opened and the dykes destroyed. Saeftinghe disappears.

In the 18th and 19th centuries, large parts of the area were once again wrested from the sea. The most recent polder was created in 1907: the Hertogin Hedwig (Countess Hedwig) Polder, that has now been nominated to be returned to the sea to create more room for the river. Saeftinghe has developed into a nature area with many unique plants and animals. In the winter, it becomes the home to tens of thousands of grey geese and ducks such as widgeon and pin-tail.

Bijnaam voor grensdorp Nieuw-Namen (foto) is de Kauter. Het heet aanvankelijk Hulsterloo, waar zich volgens de overlevering een deel van het dierenepos Van de Vos Reinaerde afspeelt. Sinds 1858, bij de oprichting van een eigen parochie, is het Nieuw-Namen. De Sint Josephkerk is in 1860 ingezegend.

The nickname of Nieuw-Namen (photo) – a village straddling the border – is the Kauter. It was originally known as Hulsterloo, where, according to tradition, a part of the animal fable of Reinaerde the Fox took place. Since 1858, with the founding of a separate parish, it became Nieuw-Namen. The St Joseph's Church was consecrated in 1860.

311

Auf einem nächtlichen Satellitenfoto sieht Zeeland aus wie ein dunkler Fleck, umschlossen von den hell erleuchteten Wohn- und Gewerbegebieten der Randstad, dem Gebiet um Antwerpen und Gent und – auf der anderen Seite der Nordsee – dem Süden Englands mit der Metropole London. Hier en da deuten weiße Stecknadelköpfe auf menschliche Tätigkeiten im Delta, aber die Dunkelheit herrscht vor.

Tagsüber kann man die Charakteristiken Zeelands aus der Luft sofort erkennen. Es ist ein Archipel, ein Land von einander gegenüberliegenden Seiten, von Inseln mit eigenwilligen Konturen, vom Wasser umgeben. Wasser ist in der Form von Meeresarmen, Seen, Prielen, Kanälen und Gräben allgegenwärtig. Zeeland riecht nach Salz und Sumpf. Das südwestlichste Delta der Niederlande trägt seinen Namen zu Recht: See und Land.

Die Provinz lädt mit ihrer Ruhe und ihrer Landschaft, der Weite der Deltagewässer, den Vogelschwärmen und ab und zu einem passierenden Schiff, dazu ein, die Seele baumeln zu lassen. Große urbanisierte Regionen, wie die dichtbevölkerte Randstad, gibt es nicht. Nur an zwei Stellen, in Vlissingen-Ost und am Kanal Gent-Terneuzen, dominiert eine industrielle Hafenlandschaft den Horizont.

Zeelands Geschichte ist allgegenwärtig. Es ist die Geschichte des ewigen Kampfes gegen die See, der das Land abgerungen wurde. Durch Eindeichung wurde viel Land gewonnen, die See aber hat sich auch viele fruchtbare Polder zurückerobert. Es ist die Geschichte der Gezeiten, die in ihrem uralten Rhythmus vom Fallen, Verweilen und Steigen des Wassers zweimal in 25 Stunden kommen und gehen.

Vor zweitausend Jahren sah es hier völlig anders aus. Hinter niedrigen Strandwällen erstreckten sich ausgedehnte Moorsümpfe, durchkreuzt von schmalen Gewässern, die sich durch enge Öffnungen ins Meer zwängten, bewohnt von einer Handvoll Bauern und Schafhirten. Die Römer, die etwa 175 nach Christus einmarschierten, nannten es "ein vom Wasser durchtränktes Land."

Der Meeresspiegel steigt und die Dünenreihe wird an einigen Stellen durchbrochen, das Salzwasser gräbt ein Netz von Gezeitenrinnen, die bis auf die höher gelegenen Sandböden von Brabant und Flandern reichen. Sand und Lehm werden abgelagert, die Moorsümpfe verwandeln sich in die für Zeeland noch immer so charakteristische Grodenlandschaft.

Das unwirtliche Gebiet bleibt einige Jahrhunderte lang unbewohnt, erst ab dem 6. Jahrhundert lassen sich wieder Menschen nieder. Sie suchen sich die höchstgelegenen Stellen der Platen aus. Aber auch diese bieten bei einer Sturmflut keine Sicherheit. Niedrige Wohnhügel werden aufgeworfen, auf denen Bauernhöfe entstehen. In ihrer Nähe entstehen Handelsniederlassungen, wie es überall auf der Welt in Deltagebieten der Fall ist.

Die Bewohner des Deltas mussten nicht nur unaufhörlich gegen das Wasser kämpfen, sondern sich auch gegen die Einfälle der Normannen wehren. Gegen Ende des 9. Jahrhunderts bauten sie Ringwallburgen zu ihrem Schutz. In dieser Zeit entstehen Ortsnamen wie Domburg, Middelburg, Oost-Souburg, Oostburg en Burgh. In Burgh sind die Konturen der Ringwallburg noch gut zu erkennen.

Nach der Jahrtausendwende beginnt man mit dem Bau von kleineren Deichen und dem Eindämmen von Prielen. Nach der großen Sturmflut im Jahre 1134 schließlich werden die bewohnten Gebiete vollständig eingedeicht. Mit Schaufel, Spaten und Korb als wichtigstem Handwerkzeug entstehen die Deiche in relativ kurzer Zeit. Jetzt kann das Land besser entwässert werden, was vor allem dem Ackerbau und der Viehzucht zugute kommt.

Die Bevölkerungsanzahl steigt; zwischen 1200 und 1300 entstehen die meisten älteren Kirchspiele. Middelburg und Zierikzee entwickeln sich zu Orten mit städtischem Charakter. Um den Bedarf an Wohnraum und Arbeitsstätten zu decken, gehen die Menschen, an vorderster Front die Mönche der flämischen Klöster, von der Verteidigung gegen die See zum Angriff über.

Die Konturen des heutigen Zeeland beginnen sich abzuzeichnen. Es sind die Kerngebiete der großen Polder auf Walcheren, Zuid-Beveland und Schouwen, die durch zahlreiche natürliche Elemente gekennzeichnet werden. Höher gelegene Platen wechseln sich ab mit niedriger gelegenen, salzigen Sumpfniederungen. Um das „alte" Land herum entstehen Schritt für Schritt neue Polder, deren Entstehen man anhand des Verlaufs der Deiche nachvollziehen kann.

Jede Generation im niedrig gelegenen Delta wird ein oder mehre Male vom Hochwasser heimgesucht. Manchmal gehen ganze Landstriche verloren. Das Verdronken Land van Saeftinge und von Reimerswaal, das Zuidland von Schouwen, die Insel Orisant bei Noord-Beveland, die Inseln Koezand, Schoneveld, Waterdunen und Wulpen in West-Zeeuws-Vlaanderen – sie liegen für immer unter Wasser.

Unter dem Delta verbirgt sich ein archäologischer Schatz: versunkene Dörfer. Sie verschwanden durch Sturmfluten, aber auch durch bewusst herbeigeführte Überflutungen während militärischer Auseinandersetzungen (vor allem während des Achtzigjährigen Krieges). An Dörfer wie Emelisse, Stuivezand, Soelekerke oder Tolsende erinnern nur noch ihre Namen. Wo man überschwemmtes Land zurückgewinnen konnte, finden sich oft Kolke und tiefe Rinnen.

Trotz des Kampfes gegen die See und gegen die Spanier gelingt es Zeeland, sich zu einer der wichtigsten Provinzen in der Republik der Sieben Vereinigten Niederlande zu entwickeln. Diese Entwicklung verdankt es seiner strategisch wichtigen Lage, denn die See ist nicht nur Erzfeind sondern auch Verbündete. Handel, Schifffahrt und Fischerei erleben eine Blütezeit, obwohl der Zeeuwse Archipel scheinbar von allen Seiten belagert wird.

Der Fall von Antwerpen 1585 stellt einen Wendepunkt dar. Menschen aus Flandern und Brabant flüchten nach Zeeland und viele von ihnen lassen sich auf Dauer nieder. Ihre handwerklichen und wissenschaftlichen Kenntnisse verhelfen dem öffentlichen Leben zu neuer Blüte. Zeeland ist zusammen mit Holland der wichtigste Partner bei der Gründung der Vereinigten Ostindischen (und später auch der Westindischen) Compagnie.

Die Kauf- und Kapschifffahrt bildet das Fundament für aufblühende Städte und Dörfer. Middelburg entwickelt sich zu einer stolzen Kaufmannsstadt, die in der zweiten Hälfte des 17. Jahrhunderts 30.000 Einwohner zählt. Als sichtbares Zeichen des Reichtums baut man sich Landhäuser. Im Laufe des 18. Jahrhunderts jedoch setzt der Verfall ein. Die Ankunft der Franzosen 1795 bringt viele Veränderungen mit sich mit. Die einst so stolze Provinz verarmt.

Ende des 19. Jahrhunderts (1868) kommt neue Hoffnung auf, als eine Eisenbahnstrecke gebaut wird, für die u.a. der Kreekrakdamm und der Sloedamm gebaut werden. Es folgen weitere Bauwerke: der Kanal Terneuzen-Gent (1827), der Kanal durch Zuid-Beveland (1866) und der Kanal durch Walcheren (1873). Die erwartete wirtschaftliche Blüte aber bleibt aus. In der Provinz Zeeland entwickelt sich vor allem die Landwirtschaft und die Krusten- und Schalentierzucht.

Trotz großer Verwüstungen in Zeeuws-Vlaanderen und der Überflutung von Walcheren (als die Alliierten die Seedeiche bombardieren) gibt es nach dem Zweiten Weltkrieg keine neue Wende. Die kommt erst im Jahre 1953, in dem die See unbarmherzig zuschlägt. Rund 136.000 Hektar Land stehen damals unter Wasser, 1835 Menschen und Hunderttausende von Tieren verlieren ihr Leben. Der Schaden beträgt 1,5 Milliarden Gulden.

Die Hochwasserkatastrophe führt zu einer neuen Zeitrechnung. „Vor bzw. nach der Katastrophe" wird zum neuen Bezugspunkt. Die Umsetzung des Deltaplans verändert das Aussehen von Zeeland auf immer. Mit Ausnahme der Westerschelde werden die Meeresmündungen mit großen Dämmen abgeschlossen. In der Oosterschelde erzwingen Bürgerinitiativen mit unermüdlichem Einsatz die Beibehaltung der Gezeiten durch Bau eines Sturmflutwehrs. Die Inseln von Zeeland sind nun miteinander verbunden.

Das Schlussstück ist der Bau des 6,6 km lange Westerscheldetunnels zwischen Ellewoutsdijk und Terneuzen (2003). Der Fährverkehr von der einen zur anderen Seite wird eingestellt, im Sommer jedoch gibt es ein Netzwerk kleinerer Fähren für Urlauber und Tagesausflügler. Zeeland entwickelt sich schnell zu einer touristischen Hochburg. Bungalowdörfer und Campingplätze sind die neuen Dörfer, statt der Häfen für den Umschlag landwirtschaftlicher Produkte werden Jachthäfen gebaut.

Die Erschließung des Deltas bietet auch Chancen für eine Industrialisierung. Am tiefen Fahrwasser siedeln sich chemische Fabriken an und 1973 wird bei Borssele ein umstrittenes Kernkraftwerk in Betrieb genommen. Die Landwirtschaft wird mechanisiert und modernisiert; durch die Flurbereinigung verschwinden viele historische Elemente aus der Landschaft. Die Gewächshauskultur breitet sich aus, die Polderlandschaft ist eintönig und verglast.

Zu Anfang des neuen Millenniums ändern sich die Zeiten in Zeeland noch einmal. Noch ist Zeeland eine Provinz mit viel Platz, Grün, Wasser und Ruhe und mit den besonderen Charakteristiken von Deltagewässern: der Dynamik der Gezeiten, Salz- und Süßwasser, Graden, Deichen, Poldern, Rinnen und Kolken. Eine grün-blaue Oase, umringt von überfüllten Wohn- und Gewerbegebieten. Die Oase ist bedroht.

Politiker setzen auf Wachstum für Zeeland mit seinen nicht einmal 380.000 Einwohnern. Sie eifern für wirtschaftliche Entwicklung, mit mehr hafen- und industriegebundenen Aktivitäten in Vlissingen-Ost und der Kanalzone Zeeuws-Vlaanderen. Sie sprechen von neuen „wirtschaftlichen Säulen" für die Landwirtschaft, z.B. der Aquakultur und wollen das touristische Angebot an der Küste und im Hinterland ausbauen.

„Willkommen in Zeeland", rufen die Politiker den Tausenden von Touristen zu, die vor allen Sonne, See und Strand suchen und den neuen Einwohnern, die dazu beitragen sollen, dass die Provinz lebendig bleibt und sich moderne Einrichtungen auf dem Gebiet von Bildung, Gesundheit und Kultur leisten kann. Das bedeutet wuchern mit Raum, Ruhe und Dunkelheit. Hochbau ist nur eine der Folgen dieser Entwicklung.

Nun, nachdem die Deltawerke fertig gestellt sind, zeigt sich, dass die kerzengeraden, mächtigen Dämme nicht nur Vorteile mit sich mitbringen. In den abrupt von den Gezeiten abgeschlossenen Gewässern entwickeln sich Krankheiten, wie z.B. Blaualgenbefall. In der Oosterschelde verflachen Sandbänke und Schlick und schieben die Fahrrinnen zu. Die Natur rächt sich für das Fehlen der Übergänge vom Salz- zum Süßwasser. Die Deltagewässer werden zum Sanierungsfall.

Als Ersatz für die „Versteinerung" – durch die Ausdehnung von Städten und Dörfern, den Bau neuer Feriendörfer und Gewerbegebiete – entsteht neue Natur in der Form einiger Grünflächen von Briefmarkengröße. An der Südküste von Schouwen-Duiveland und Tholen jedoch entstehen durch den Plan „Tureluur" (Rotschenkel) große Seen- und Sumpfgebiete, die ein Eldorado für Vögel sind. Nach dem Wattenmeer ist das Delta das zweitgrößte Vogelgebiet der Niederlande.

Durch die Fertigstellung des Deltaplans scheint Hochwasser für alle Zeit unmöglich zu sein. Die Erhöhung des Meeresspiegels jedoch, u.a. durch die Klimaveränderungen und das Absinken des Bodens, erfordert regelmäßige Anpassungen der Küstenbefestigungen. Die Menschen in Zeeland wissen besser als alle anderen, dass zwischen den Menschen und den Elementen niemals Friede herrscht.

Irgendwann können die Deiche nicht mehr erhöht und verbreitert werden; man muss andere Lösungen finden. So wie es früher war: Man baute eine erste Reihe von Wehren und in einigem Abstand dahinter eine zweite Reihe, so dass das herandrängende Wasser auf zwei Barrieren stößt. Das „Nichtland" zwischen den Deichen kann für Natur und Aquakultur genutzt werden. Eine andere Option ist es, dem Wasser mehr Platz einzuräumen.

Letzteres bedeutet kontrollierte Rückgabe von Polderland an die See und die Natur. Für die Einwohner von Zeeland ist das ein Paradox. Sie stehen nicht mehr mit dem Rücken zur See. Wieder ändern sich die Zeiten. Diesen neuen Ansatz im Kampf gegen die See nennt man „Entpoldern". Alles ändert sich fortwährend. Was bleibt, ist die Begegnung der Elemente: das Spiel von Wind, Wolken und Wasser.

Longitude D We

The Century Historical Series

EUROPEAN DIPLOMATIC HISTORY

1871-1932

BY

RAYMOND JAMES SONTAG

ASSOCIATE PROFESSOR OF HISTORY
PRINCETON UNIVERSITY

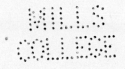
THE CENTURY CO.

NEW YORK   LONDON

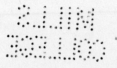

PRINTED IN U.S.A.

To my Mother

PREFACE

My purpose is to sketch briefly the diplomatic background of the existing relations between the great European powers. I have been brief, because I feel that the main lines of the story must be known before the details can be understood. I have told the story chronologically, because I believe that we must follow events as they unfold themselves if we are to understand why statesmen made the decisions they made. Where praise or blame seemed necessary, I have judged, not according to the standards of to-day, but by the standards which the statesmen themselves set; the reader must judge of the moral or practical worth of these standards.

Statesmen during the two generations we survey were trying to solve a riddle: how can desirable changes in the international *status quo* be effected, and undesirable changes prevented, without recourse to war? The attempts to solve this riddle have been made the central theme of the story, and have dictated the distribution of emphasis. I have, for instance, devoted more attention to the efforts of British and German statesmen to find some peaceful solution for the rivalry between their countries than to the events of July and August, 1914. In 1914 the search for a solution was abandoned as hopeless.

The riddle is to-day, as in 1871, unanswered. By seeing the ways in which statesmen have searched for an answer, the expedients they attempted, the success or failure of these expedients, we should be able more intelligently to grapple with this, one of the most pressing problems of our age.

Throughout I have profited from the advice and criticism of my wife and of my colleagues, students, and other friends. For this help I am very grateful. I owe an even

vii

greater debt to other workers in this field. Obviously a survey of so vast a field cannot be, even in large part, the fruit of exhaustive research. Where my knowledge is relatively complete I have not hesitated to differ from other students; in all other cases I have subordinated my views to those of students who have probed deeper. In a brief survey, detailed reference to the vast monographic literature would be out of place. I take, therefore, this opportunity to acknowledge my indebtedness.

R. J. SONTAG

PRINCETON, N. J.
November 22, 1932

CONTENTS

MAPS

CHAPTER I

BISMARCK'S LEAGUE OF PEACE, 1871–1881

EUROPEAN DIPLOMATIC HISTORY, 1871–1932

CHAPTER I

BISMARCK'S LEAGUE OF PEACE, 1871–1881

I. THE NEW MAP OF EUROPE

The Treaty of Frankfort, concluded in 1871 between the new French Republic and the new German Empire, closed one of the most confused and crowded quarter-centuries in European history. During these years every great European power fought with at least one of its neighbors. Political traditions which seemed part of the eternal order of things were demolished. For centuries France and Austria had struggled for Continental supremacy; Central Europe served as their battle-ground. The events of 1859 to 1871 wrote an abrupt finis to the story. Austria was unceremoniously ejected from Italy and Germany and was weakened by internal dissensions, which were intensified by the autonomy granted Hungary in 1867. France, shorn of Alsace-Lorraine, burdened with an indemnity and military occupation, fell suddenly from her place of leadership in Europe. Italy, on the other hand, attained unity for the first time since the days of ancient Rome, while Königgrätz and Sedan gave Continental hegemony to Prussian Germany. Would the new distribution of power endure? Would Germany, intoxicated by success, develop Napoleonic ambitions? Or would the old order return, tradition prove stronger than the chance victories and successes of a few years? These were some of the questions European statesmen asked themselves as they sought to find their bearings in a Europe from which most of the old landmarks had disappeared.

Few believed that the *status quo* established by the wars just passed would long remain unchallenged. Nearly all believed, and said when they spoke frankly, that war or the threat of war was the only means of effecting or preventing changes in the *status quo*. The French liked to speak of an "immanent justice" which would bring about the restitution of Alsace-Lorraine, but usually inherent justice was expected to operate through the traditional medium: some day there would be a Russo-German war; then France could demand the restitution of Alsace-Lorraine as the price of neutrality. Wars there had been; wars there would be. The map had been changed; new wars would bring new changes. War was "a legitimate and normal method of promoting national interests," wrote a prominent British liberal. He continued: "The truth is that in the world in which we were brought up, the crime was not to make war, but to make it unsuccessfully. . . . All the Governments of Europe, our own included, regarded war as a risk which had to be run, a legitimate gamble, as Churchill said of the Dardanelles Expedition, a 'continuation of policy' as the Germans defined it." The definition of war as a "continuation of policy" covers the ground precisely. National ambitions could be realized only to the extent that they were backed by national power— military, economic, intellectual, and moral. Lack of power meant lack of success, defeat, humiliation. In any crisis statesmen weighed their chances; if the issue was important and military victory probable, war was preferable to a diplomatic defeat. The task of the statesman was to see that his country was never confronted with the alternative of diplomatic defeat or military defeat. If a statesman blundered and found himself confronted with this alternative, he accepted diplomatic defeat unless he was desperate, as the Austrians were in 1914, or unless he had miscalculated the chances of military success, as did the Russians in their quarrel with Japan in 1904.

After 1871 three considerations modified the simplicity of the doctrine that war was the logical continuation of diplomatic policy. The first was a change in the character of war itself, resulting from the advance of science and industry. Most men continued to think of war in terms of earlier and comparatively harmless struggles, but responsible statesmen realized that a great war might well shake the foundations of European society. Moreover, with every passing year it became increasingly apparent that war between two states must almost inevitably spread until all Europe was involved. The alliance systems were largely the result of this realization. Every statesman tried to secure promises of assistance, or at least of neutrality, so he would know what to expect when the struggle began. Finally, popular government, conscription, and the rise of the press made vitally important the enthusiastic reception by public opinion of the decision for war. The increasingly hazardous nature of war, the realization that a localized duel was improbable, and the necessity for popular approval all made statesmen more eager for the peaceful solution of difficulties, more reluctant to risk war than formerly.

On the other hand, these same elements provoked an uneasy state of tension. If war was becoming more destructive, then adequate preparation became correspondingly more important. Armament bill was piled on armament bill, each increase provoking increases in neighboring countries. If wars could no longer be localized, then allies must be bound ever closer and must be supported unflinchingly; then too, the solidarity of rival alliance systems must be weakened, by threats, by cajolery, by lies. If public approbation of a war policy was essential, then the public mind must be prepared in advance to suspect and fear every possible antagonist so that, should a crisis suddenly arise, a slight stimulus would suffice to raise passions to the fighting point. As the hazards of the game rose, therefore, the play became more, rather than less, tense. In 1890 the aged German commander, Moltke, vividly described the prevailing mood:

"If the war which has hung over our heads, like the sword of Damocles, for more than ten years past, ever breaks out, its duration and end cannot be foreseen. The greatest powers of Europe, armed as they never have been armed before, will then stand face to face. No one can be shattered in one or two campaigns so completely as to confess itself beaten, and conclude peace on hard terms. It may be a Seven Years' War, it may be a Thirty Years' War—woe to him who first sets fire to Europe, and is the first to apply the torch to the magazine."

How could the fear of war be banished? How could preparation and counter-preparation be ended? By inculcating respect for the sanctity of treaties? By arbitration? By limitation of armaments? All three methods had advocates. But how could one decide by arbitration whether Russia or England should seize Persia; whether France or Germany should have Morocco; whether France or England should have the Sudan? Could arms be limited or treaties made inviolable without perpetuating a *status quo* which was intolerable to many nations? Here was the crux of the matter: until all the leading states were approximately content with the distribution of power, territory, wealth, and resources, efforts to change the *status quo* were inevitable. How could any nation compel change, compel the removal of irksome restrictions without recourse to the threat of armed action? No one could answer that question to the satisfaction of all contestants. So the race continued.

2. THE SEARCH FOR EQUILIBRIUM, 1871–1875

During the two decades following the Treaty of Frankfort, Germany was the stanchest bulwark of the *status quo,* and Germany to Europe meant Bismarck. At home, success silenced the storms of criticism which had broken over the earlier phases of his policy. After 1871 he still met with violent opposition on internal questions, but in foreign affairs his control was almost absolute. Both at home and abroad, the succession of lightning moves by which he had effected German unification and the ease with which he had duped or overcome all opponents gave him a reputation for superhuman sagacity. After 1871 his aloofness enhanced the romantic legend of his Olympian wisdom and power. Ten years of incessant strife had made him an old man before he was sixty, racked with pain, bitter, irascible.

To husband his strength he retired for long periods to his Baltic estates. There, mysterious and invisible, like Zeus on Ida, he studied the international scene. When he spoke, all men listened. His earth-shaking language could make nations tremble. When he was silent, statesmen sought eagerly to divine his will. Even to-day his gigantic form looms so large that it is difficult to realize that he was wrestling with forces which were largely beyond his control. His genius lay less in his capacity to dominate than in the rare intellectual honesty which made him recognize freely the logic of events and in the swift prescience which enabled him to adjust his course to currents his will could not change.

Bismarck's objective was simple: it was peace. At Versailles the German Empire had been proclaimed, but the proclamation did not make it a reality. All the jealousies, the loves, the hates accumulated over centuries between Bavarian, Prussian, Saxon, and the rest, must be sunk in the feeling of a common nationality; a common law must be devised; railroads and telegraphs must bind Germany together; a new economic system must be developed. All this took time, much time. Bismarck wanted no more territory; Germany, he said over and over, was a satiated state. But she must have leisure to digest her existing possessions. Internal problems set the end of Bismarck's foreign policy; all his acts were based on the imperative necessity of peace.

What elements menaced the peaceful existence of Germany? Geography and history, according to Bismarck. Germany lay in the center of Europe, between France, Austria, and Russia. A combination of these three would be fatal; Germany would be crushed in a vise. The union of two would be only slightly less dangerous; then Germany must become the slave of the third. Suppose Austria and France, remembering their defeats in 1866 and 1871, should ally. Then Russia would be in a position to compel German support of all Russian policies by threatening, in case of a refusal, to join France and Austria. Fear of a combination of Germany's neighbors was the nightmare which never ceased to haunt Bismarck.

How might the nightmare be prevented from becoming a reality? First of all, by keeping Germany strong. Force was to Bismarck the final argument in international affairs, and repeated army bills justified his boast that "he who attacks the German nation will find it armed to a man." The army was ready, but he preferred not to use it. Instead, he hoped to convince his neighbors of the desirability of friendly relations with Germany.

With Russia and Austria the task proved easy at first. Two bases existed for an understanding. All needed peace. The wars of 1859 and 1866 had exhausted Austria, while the creation of the Dual Monarchy in 1867 gave rise to serious constitutional problems which new wars would complicate. Russia, too, was preoccupied with internal problems. Every year the opposition to the autocracy became more violent, and the Tsar wished to concentrate his energies on the task of repressing the Nihilists. Fear of radicalism and devotion to conservative principles was common to all three emperors. Liberalism had triumphed in England, France, and Italy; socialism and anarchism were gaining adherents everywhere. A united front was needed to prevent the spread of revolutionary ideas eastward. In 1872 the three emperors met in Berlin, and agreed to work for peace and conservatism. In the following year the informal union attained written form in the "Dreikaiserbund," the League of the Three Emperors. By this agreement the rulers promised to coöperate in the preservation of peace, and, in case war should threaten, to consult together "in order to determine a common course of action."

Apparently secure on the east, Bismarck felt free to concentrate on his western neighbor. Austria had been willing to forget 1866, partly because Bismarck had given very generous terms after the Seven Weeks' War, but chiefly because the Dual Monarchy felt that peace was imperative. No such acquiescence in defeat could be expected from

France. For centuries France had been the strongest power on the Continent, and it would be strange if she meekly consented to the transfer of hegemony to the new German Empire. The tenacity with which the French had pursued their quarrel with England made surrender improbable, to say the least. In addition to the intangible question of prestige, Alsace-Lorraine in German hands was a symbol of French humiliation and defeat, barring the way to reconciliation. With the justice of the annexation we are not concerned, but it is well to remember that Alsace and Lorraine had once been German, and Germans never forgot that fact; as Bismarck said, they were waging war on Louis XIV. Further, had the French won the war, as they anticipated, by their own admission they intended to annex territory as German in sentiment as the "lost provinces" were French. This to discount our wartime prejudices. With the results of the annexation we are concerned, and here there can be no divergence of opinion. From 1871 to 1914 no French statesman dared to admit that Alsace and Lorraine were lost forever. The sentiment of *revanche* rose and fell in intensity, but it never died, and in a Europe of shifting diplomatic alignments, even when on the verge of war with England, France never agreed to confirm the Treaty of Frankfort. For this the Germans were, in a measure, prepared. They underestimated the tenacity both of the French and of the people of Alsace-Lorraine, but they anticipated French hatred for many years.

"Our task," wrote Bismarck, "is to see that France leaves us in peace, and to make sure that in case France refuses to keep peace, she shall have no allies." In the early 1870's he hoped to attain these ends by keeping France weak, since a weak France would not only be afraid to attack Germany, but would also have difficulty finding allies. In 1871 he had sought to guard against a revival of French strength by imposing a heavy indemnity. After peace had been concluded he supported Thiers against the monarchists; a French Republic, he believed, would be torn by internal strife and in bad odor with conservative Austria and Russia. The Dreikaiserbund further served to keep France "in quarantine" by binding the eastern empires to Germany.

The rapidity with which France revived frightened Bismarck. By the end of 1873 the indemnity was paid, the last German troops had evacuated France, and the French army was being reorganized on the Prussian model. The French themselves were thrilled at the success of their efforts. The unthinking spoke of *revanche* as immediately impending; speeches of Gambetta and poems of Déroulède acted like a heady wine on the volatile Parisians. In the spring of 1875 the French government brought in a new army bill. Its passage was facilitated by a campaign against Germany in the press. Across the Rhine, the chief of the general staff, Moltke, and other prominent Germans began to talk of the necessity for a "preventive" war, a war to crush France before she was ready to attack. On April 9 a German newspaper article entitled "Is War in Sight?" caused a panic on the Paris Bourse. Bismarck preserved an ominous silence. On the basis of the information we now possess, it seems certain that he had no desire for war and that he had not inspired the alarmist press compaign. On the other hand, he did little or nothing to quiet the agitation. Apparently he hoped the French might be bluffed into abandoning their new army law; to accomplish this end he was willing to permit the development of tension so severe that a misstep on either side might easily have precipitated hostilities.

His bluff was called by England and Russia. The French government had diagnosed the situation very accurately: "Bismarck wants us to believe that he wishes war," wrote the Foreign Secretary, "but he does not really want war." In order to profit by the sympathy which the German threats had aroused in other countries, the Quai d'Orsay feigned terror and begged England and Russia to hold Germany in check. Bismarck replied in a tone of injured innocence to the protests from London and St. Petersburg;

but, by a suspicious coincidence, the agitation in Germany
immediately ceased.

The war scare gave the first hint that a new balance of
power was gradually taking form in Europe. For over a
dozen years Bismarck had been able to work his will unhampered. While he was reshaping the map, appeals and
threats had come from Downing Street, but Bismarck had
taken the measure of the men directing British affairs, and
he brushed aside all interference. Discontent with the negative part played by their own government grew steadily
among Englishmen until 1874, when Disraeli, soon to become Earl of Beaconsfield, became Prime Minister, with
a large Conservative majority behind him. His electoral
campaign had been based on the need for a spirited foreign
policy. Britain's record among the stirring events of the
1860's, he maintained, had been a sorry one. He promised
a return to the spacious days when Britain commanded
and the world obeyed. The appeal of France in 1875 gave
Disraeli an opportunity to assert England's claim to a voice
in Continental affairs, an opportunity which he eagerly
seized. In Russia also the feeling was growing that Bismarck's power must be circumscribed. The Tsar had not
merely consented to Bismarck's earlier moves, he had given
active assistance by preventing other powers from intervening against Prussia during the war with France. Now,
Russia agreed with England that a strong France was
necessary to counterbalance the strength of Germany. In
St. Petersburg there was a shrewd understanding that the
possibility of a Franco-Russian alliance was an excellent
bogey with which to frighten Germany into compliance
with Russian wishes. The Dreikaiserbund continued after
1875, but its weakness had been revealed. In later years,
Bismarck's every reference to the war scare of 1875 was
accompanied by wrathful denunciations of the unnecessary
counsel of moderation offered by England and Russia. His
anger was probably at himself for the overconfidence which
had made him forget that France and Germany were not

isolated antagonists. He learned his lesson. Thereafter he
showed himself keenly alive to the fact that a new and delicate equilibrium existed in Europe, an equilibrium which
might easily be altered to the disadvantage of Germany.

3. THE NEAR EAST, 1875–1878

England and Russia could not retain their united front
for long. Events in the Near East soon revived the traditional antagonism between the two countries. In 1875 one
of the frequent rebellions against Turkish misgovernment
broke out in Bosnia and Herzegovina. For some months
the revolt ran the usual course of atrocity and counter-
atrocity. Then, instead of subsiding, it began to spread over
the Balkan peninsula.

Three powers, Austria, Russia, and England, claimed an
active voice in Near Eastern affairs. Austria and Russia
had in earlier centuries been allies in the task of beating
back the Turk. The rise of Slav nationalism made continued coöperation difficult. As early as the Crimean War,
Austria had shown herself hostile to further Russian advance. Then came the expulsion of Austria from Germany
and Italy and the division of the remaining Hapsburg possessions into two autonomous parts. Within the Dual Monarchy there were already millions of Slavs—in the north,
Poles, Czechs, and Slovaks; in the south, several groups,
divided by culture, language, and religion, but known collectively as Jugo-Slavs. The Croats, the most numerous and
the most highly developed culturally of the Southern Slavs,
were bound by strong sentimental ties to the Hapsburgs,
who had rescued them from the Turkish oppressor, and
who would, they hoped, redeem the remaining Jugo-Slavs
who were still partially or completely under the control of
the Sultan. Many non-Slavs within the Monarchy shared
the Croat ideal: now that expansion to the north and west
was barred, the Hapsburg domain should be extended south
to Saloniki, and a triple monarchy created in which the
Slavs would have an equal voice with the Germans and
Magyars. Against this policy the great noble houses of

Hungary fought tenaciously. Their rule was now absolute.
They were determined that the territory of Hungary should
be preserved intact. For them the problem of nationalities
was non-existent. Every one in Hungary was to be made a
Magyar, by force if necessary. By 1875 the harsh program
of Magyarization was already undermining the loyalty of
the Croats and creating in the Balkans a strong antipathy
to the Hapsburgs. Fear of the Magyars was probably sufficient in itself to deter Francis Joseph from an adventurous
Balkan policy. There was another consideration which
made him hesitate. Would not the addition of more Slavs
to the empire intensify Jugo-Slav nationalism and in the
end create a problem which would shatter the monarchy?
The Magyars seized on this argument and used it as a cloak
for their purely selfish motives. Having already suffered
from German and Italian nationalism, Francis Joseph
naturally feared to make any move which might increase
the disruptive forces which already existed in abundance
in his empire.

The alternative was vigorous defense of the *status quo*.
If it was dangerous to add more Slavs to the Monarchy, it
would be doubly dangerous either to permit Russia to dominate the Balkans or to allow strong Slav states to grow in
the peninsula. A strong Slav power in the Balkans, whether
controlled by Russia or not, must inevitably act as a magnet
which would attract the discontented Jugo-Slavs of Austria-
Hungary. In Vienna there were many who pointed out that
mere resistance to change could neither solve Balkan problems nor end the strife of nationalities in the Hapsburg
domain. The Magyars refused to listen; they were confident that the malcontents could be coerced into obedience
and loyalty. Francis Joseph supported the Magyars, not
only because he feared them, but also because a passive
policy appealed to his intensely conservative nature. So at
the Foreign Office on the Ballplatz it was decided that
change must be prevented, if possible. If change proved
inevitable, then the strategically important provinces of
Bosnia and Herzegovina must be acquired by the Dual

Monarchy so that neither Serbia nor Montenegro could secure a good outlet on the Adriatic.

During 1875 and 1876 Russia was willing to coöperate in the task of preventing territorial changes. Alexander II had his hands full with revolution at home and quarrels with England in central Asia; he had no desire for a quarrel with Austria. For their part, the Austrians were willing to coöperate in forcing the Sultan to grant reforms which would placate the rebellious Christians. England was requested to assist in exerting pressure at Constantinople. Disraeli held back. He was completely indifferent to the fate of the Balkan Christians—in fact, as people he preferred the Turks. Furthermore he was adverse to anything which would weaken the Sultan's power and make it easier for Russia to advance toward the Ægean. The coöperation of Russia and Austria also displeased him. So long as the three emperors were working in harmony, they were strong enough to defy England; if Austria could be separated from Russia, the Dreikaiserbund would disintegrate. Without openly showing his hand, therefore, he adopted a passive attitude which encouraged the Sultan to refuse concessions. Then, in the summer of 1876, news reached Europe of unusually atrocious massacres in Bulgaria. Gladstone at once embarked on a campaign of impassioned oratory, demanding that the Turks be ejected "bag and baggage" from Bulgaria. For a time he caught the public ear. Disraeli was forced unwillingly into support of the Austro-Russian program. In December, 1876, a conference was held at Constantinople, and a list of reforms was unanimously agreed upon. Unanimity came too late. The Sultan refused to believe that the conversion of his British ally to disinterested humanitarianism was sincere, and, after infinite procrastination, he refused the demands of the powers.

The Russian Pan-Slavs now demanded war. Alexander II did not want to fight. At the same time he could not allow the murder of Balkan Slavs to continue indefinitely. For three months the Tsar vainly sought some concessions which would save his face, but the Sultan could not crush the revolt and would not grant reforms, while Disraeli relapsed into his suspiciously passive rôle. Finally, in April, 1877, Alexander declared war on Turkey. Russia was soon joined by Montenegro, Serbia, and Rumania.

At first the war justified Moltke's prediction that it would be a struggle between the "one-eyed and the blind"; from July to December, 1877, the strong fortress of Plevna barred the Russian advance. During the long delay, Englishmen had time to recover from Gladstone's intoxicating oratory. The poor Bulgarian and the Terrible Turk were forgotten; now, the gallant struggle of the weak Turks against England's ancient enemy aroused the cherished British sporting instinct. When Plevna surrendered, and the Russian columns moved rapidly toward Constantinople, a wave of war feeling swept across England. Queen Victoria exhorted her trusted Disraeli to "be bold! . . . Pray act quickly!" In the music-halls, crowds went wild over the song which was to attain immortality as a symbol of hysterical, insane lust for war:

> "We don't want to fight,
> But, by Jingo! if we do,
> We've got the ships,
> We've got the men,
> We've got the money too!"

Disraeli was reassured. He was a shrewd politician, and he realized he had a "shouting, rather than a fighting majority" behind him; but as few outside England grasped the distinction, he felt secure in asserting the claim of England to European leadership. When the Russians approached Constantinople, a British fleet was dispatched to the Straits. For some weeks war was imminent as the Russian land forces and the British ships confronted one another. Then, on March 3, 1878, Russia and Turkey signed the Treaty of San Stefano.

The most important feature of the treaty was the creation of a large autonomous Bulgaria, stretching from the Danube to the Ægean, and from the Black Sea to Albania, including most of Macedonia and Thrace, and splitting

European Turkey into two parts. Serbia and Montenegro received independence and increases of territory. Bosnia and Herzegovina were to be semi-autonomous. Rumania fared badly. She had given Russia invaluable assistance during the war, but in return she was forced to cede Bessarabia to Russia, receiving, as compensation, independence and the worthless Dobruja territory east and south of the Danube. In addition to Bessarabia, Russia secured territory in the Caucasus region and northern Armenia.

England immediately protested. The Austrians were also indignant, since the Tsar had broken his recent promise to give Bosnia and Herzegovina to Austria in case of victory. England and Austria both feared the effect of a huge Bulgaria, under Russian control, stretching to the Ægean. The Russians had expected opposition to the treaty; probably they had taken more than they expected to keep, for the express purpose of having a surplus for bargaining. The Tsar's advisers were prepared to buy off Austria and England, but Disraeli refused to hear of such disreputable proceedings. He took the high moral ground that the integrity of Turkey had been guaranteed by earlier treaties which could only be modified by a congress of all the powers which had signed these treaties. Russian pride rebelled against the thought of being arraigned like a prisoner at the bar; again war threatened. Behind Beaconsfield, however, were the British navy and the Austrian army, while Russia was exhausted. Humiliated and angry, the Tsar gave way. In June, 1878, a most impressive galaxy of diplomats assembled in Berlin to reconsider the Treaty of San Stefano.

Ostensibly, Beaconsfield had insisted on the congress in order to preserve the sanctity of international agreements, but he arrived with his hands full of documents which belied his lofty arguments. An Anglo-Austrian agreement provided for the surrender of Bosnia and Herzegovina to the Dual Monarchy. An Anglo-Turkish agreement put Cyprus under British control so that England might be in a position to prevent further Russian inroads on the Turkish Empire and to supervise the reforms which the Sultan promised to make. Finally, an Anglo-Russian agreement laid down the main changes to be made in the Treaty of San Stefano.

Under the circumstances there was little to be done at Berlin except work out the details of the preliminary deals and give them international sanction. By the Treaty of Berlin, Bulgaria was greatly reduced in size and divided into two autonomous provinces of Turkey: Bulgaria proper, later given Prince Alexander of Battenberg as ruler, and Eastern Rumelia, with a Christian governor-general. Serbia and Montenegro got their independence and small additions of territory; Greece got a vague promise of frontier rectifications; Rumania, in spite of loud protests, received the harsh terms meted out at San Stefano. Russia kept Bessarabia, but lost part of her Armenian gains. The administration of Bosnia and Herzegovina and control over the neck of territory separating Serbia and Montenegro—the Sanjak of Novibazar—were entrusted to Austria. England retained Cyprus. Turkey promised, as usual, reforms.

Disraeli returned to England in triumph, saying, "I bring you Peace with Honour." Later events do not substantiate his boast. Nothing had actually been settled by this prolonged crisis when war seemed certain again and again. "No solemn international covenant has been so systematically and openly infringed and ignored, in part by the Signatory Powers themselves, as the Treaty which was concluded in Berlin in July, 1878, 'in the name of Almighty God.'" [1] At San Stefano the eternal Near Eastern question had been partially solved; at Berlin, Disraeli set aside the solution. He justified his stand by an appeal to vital British interests. Even here his judgment was to be challenged. Within a few years, Lord Salisbury, Disraeli's successor as leader of the Conservatives, was forced to admit sadly: "We backed the wrong horse."

[1] W. H. Dawson in *The Cambridge History of British Foreign Policy*, III, 143 (Cambridge, 1923).

4. THE AUSTRO-GERMAN ALLIANCE, 1878–1882

By all reports, Bismarck's temper at the Congress of Berlin was vile, and well it might be. The Near Eastern crisis had wrecked the Dreikaiserbund. All his efforts to make Vienna and St. Petersburg work in harmony had been futile; Austria had combined with England to thwart Russian plans. This was serious, but far worse was the effect of the crisis on relations between Berlin and St. Petersburg. Bismarck had sought to avoid committing himself, to play, in his own words, the "honest broker" whose object was to find a working compromise. The Russians were not satisfied. During the Franco-Prussian War Russia had prevented other powers from intervening against Prussia. Now Alexander II called for his reward, but Bismarck refused to compel others to keep out of the Russo-Turkish quarrel. Worse, he even refused to promise neutrality in case of an Austro-Russian war; if either power was decisively defeated, he said, Germany would be at the mercy of the victor. Almost certainly Russia would not have dared to defy the Anglo-Austrian combination even if Bismarck had promised neutrality, but the Tsar was looking for a scapegoat. When Russia was forced to tear up the Treaty of San Stefano at Berlin, the blame was laid at Bismarck's door; Alexander II referred to the Congress as a "European coalition against Russia under the leadership of Prince Bismarck." The defeat of 1877–1878 had greatly strengthened the enemies of the autocracy in Russia; anarchist outrages increased at an alarming rate; the Tsar was angry and panic-stricken. All his wrath was poured out on ungrateful Bismarck, who had forgotten Russia's services in "keeping the ring" during 1870 and 1871. On the commissions appointed to execute the Treaty of Berlin, Russian wishes were disregarded; again he saw the hand of Bismarck. Complaints, threats, poured into Berlin; "Cela finera d'une manière très sérieuse," said Alexander to the German ambassador in August, 1879.

"Do not compel me to choose between Russia and

Austria-Hungary," Bismarck had warned the Russian envoy at Berlin in 1878. Events of the following months seemed to make the choice imperative. Russia was angry and threatening; well-founded rumors of alliance negotiations between Paris and St. Petersburg reached Berlin; in Vienna a change of ministers was impending, and the new ministers might be sympathetic to a coalition against Germany. At the end of August, 1879, Bismarck met Andrassy, the Austrian Chancellor, at Gastein, and the two worked out the main lines of an Austro-German alliance. Francis Joseph was enthusiastic, but William I was difficult to convince. It was a full month before he reluctantly agreed to sign the treaty, which was consummated on October 7. The agreement, which was to be secret and was to remain in force for five years, provided that if either of the signatories should be attacked by Russia, the other must come to the assistance of the attacked party. If either was attacked by a power other than Russia, the ally was to observe at least benevolent neutrality unless Russia joined in the attack, in which case armed aid became obligatory. If danger of an attack by Russia became imminent, the Tsar was to be informed that the allies "must consider an attack on either as directed against both."

The wisdom of Bismarck's alliance with Austria in 1879 has often been challenged. The Austro-German alliance, it is argued, forced Russia into the arms of France, thus precipitating the very situation Bismarck wished to avoid, and leaving Germany tied to a moribund empire so weakened by internal dissensions as to be a liability rather than an asset. Let us try to envisage the situation as it appeared to Bismarck. His decision was not sudden, and it was backed by weighty arguments. Three considerations stand out in the lengthy despatches with which he tried to win over William I. First of all, he maintained that in every alliance there was a horse and a rider, and he did not wish Germany to be the horse. In more prosaic terms, Russia was strong enough to stand alone, while Austria was not. Size, location, and resources made it possible for the Tsar to pursue an independent policy. If Germany was allied with Russia, and if on any occasion Germany refused to support Russian policy, the Tsar could enforce submission by threatening to join forces with France. Francis Joseph could not afford to be so independent; only with German aid could he hope to thwart Russian ambitions in the Balkans. Neither could he use the threat of a union with France; Germany could reply by going over to the side of Russia. So long as Germany and Russia were not hopelessly estranged, therefore, Bismarck was confident that he could control Austria. A second consideration was the nature of the foreign policy of the two eastern empires. Russian policy was restless and aggressive, making for trouble not only in the Balkans, but also in the Middle East, where English and Russian interests were fundamentally opposed to each other. A Russo-German alliance would embroil Germany in every Russian quarrel, particularly with England. Austria, on the other hand, was a satiated state, desiring only the preservation of the *status quo*; her friendship need not involve dangerous obligations. Finally, England was no less anxious to prevent a further diminution of Turkish power than was Austria. This was important, for Bismarck had a great respect for British strength. In 1879 he even went so far as to put out feelers for an Anglo-German alliance. The suggestion came to nothing, but the English government welcomed the union of Austria and Germany. In a Europe dominated by five great powers, Bismarck wanted at least two friends for Germany. These he could have by alliance with Austria, but not by union with Russia.

But, continue Bismarck's critics, why any alliance at all? Were not Bismarck's fears of a Russian attack mere phantoms of a nervous old man's imagination? Would not the bitterness felt by Alexander and his advisers soon have passed, and therefore was not the sacrifice of Russian friendship needless? As a matter of fact, there was little danger of a Russian attack in 1879. Bismarck pointed to the massing of troops on the German and Austrian frontier, but it is very doubtful if he himself feared immediate war;

consciousness of Russian weakness must hold the Tsar in check. Not fear of an attack, but the old fear of a hostile coalition made Bismarck turn to Vienna. Furthermore, he hoped by the Austrian alliance to bring Russia to heel. So long as Germany was isolated, with a hostile France on her flank, the Tsar would strive to force compliance with his wishes. Once the German and Austrian emperors were bound together, Bismarck was confident that the Tsar's voice would lose its dictatorial ring.

Bismarck's confidence soon proved justified; Russian threats ceased when rumors of the impending alliance reached St. Petersburg. Alexander II was frightened by the thought of estrangement from Austria and Germany. Within a few months the Tsar was trying to revive the Dreikaiserbund. The negotiations moved slowly. It was quite evident that the Austro-Russian antagonism was merely suppressed, not dead. In the end, however, the same motives which had drawn the three empires together in 1872, namely, common desire for peace and hatred of liberalism, brought about renewed union. Austria had her hands full subduing the Bosnians she had rescued from Turkish oppression, while the assassination of Alexander II emphasized the need for united opposition to radicalism. Accordingly, the Dreikaiserbund of 1881 sought to heal the breach between the Near Eastern policies of Austria and Russia. All three powers promised neutrality in case one of the contracting parties "should find itself at war with a fourth Great Power," but this promise did not apply to a war with Turkey unless "a previous agreement shall have been reached between the three Courts as to the results of this war." No changes were to be permitted in the territorial *status quo* of European Turkey unless all three had agreed on a division of the spoils. Two exceptions were made to this provision: Austria might annex Bosnia and Herzegovina when she chose, and no opposition was to be made to the union of Bulgaria and Eastern Rumelia.

5. THE TRIPLE ALLIANCE

"You forget the importance of being in a party of three on the European chessboard," Bismarck once remarked to a Russian diplomat. "That is the object of all the Cabinets, and above all, mine. Nobody wishes to be in a minority. All politics reduce themselves to this formula: try to be *à trois* in a world governed by five Powers." With the revival of the Dreikaiserbund in 1881, Bismarck seemed to have improved upon his own formula. Austria was linked to Germany by a close defensive alliance; Russia had been drawn back into the German orbit. England was very friendly, "on the sound rule that you love those most whom you compete with least," as Salisbury put it in 1880. The strength of the Austro-German combination, with England as a "sleeping partner," was evidenced by the eagerness with which the smaller states courted Berlin and Vienna. Serbia and Rumania were chagrined at the meager rewards Russia had secured for them in 1878, and in their anger they decided to seek a new protector. By a treaty signed in 1881, Serbia promised to make no agreement with other powers without first securing the approval of Austria. In return, the right of Serbia to expand southward at some future date was acknowledged by Austria. Two years later, Rumania and Austria concluded a defensive alliance, to which Germany acceded. More important than the acquisition of these minor Balkan states, however, was the decision of Italy to join the Central Powers.

Both France and Italy had come away from the Congress of Berlin empty-handed. No one thought it necessary to placate Italy, but Salisbury had sought to allay French anger over the British acquisition of Cyprus by hinting: "How long are you going to leave Carthage in the hands of the barbarians?" Ever since 1875, Bismarck had been offering similar suggestions. His motive was obvious. By diverting the attention of the French to the colonial field he hoped to make them forget Alsace-Lorraine. The Paris government had no intention of forgetting 1871, but *revanche* was far off, and the acquisition of Tunis would give much needed prestige to the Third Republic. After three years of quiet preparation, one of the innumerable raids of Tunisian tribesmen into Algeria was made the pretext for establishing a French protectorate over Tunis. Tunis was theoretically a part of Turkey, and the Sultan, hoping for aid from other powers, tried to intervene. Italy, and apparently England, would have welcomed a chance to interfere but drew back when Bismarck came out squarely on the side of France. Bismarck had his reward. For four years the French were absorbed in colonial adventures, and Alsace-Lorraine seemed almost forgotten.

The French occupation of Tunis brought Bismarck another ally, but an ally Germany prized but little at first. Division of objectives, chaotic internal politics, and limitless ambitions only imperfectly chastened by obvious lack of power had already given Italy a bad reputation in European chancelleries. With unification had come a restless megalomania; as in the Renaissance, Italians were haunted by the memory that their country had once been the seat of a great empire. Italy must be worthy of her heritage, but her people were never able to agree on the proper way to prove their worth. One group, the Irredentists, wished to "redeem" the Italians still under Austrian rule, in the Tyrol and along the east coast of the Adriatic; some dreamed of converting the Adriatic into an Italian lake through the conquest of Albania; others looked across the Mediterranean to the north coast of Africa for the promised land.

Since Tunis was less than 100 miles from Sicily, and already contained a large Italian population, Italian imperialists had come to regard it as the logical nucleus for the great empire of which they dreamed. The action of France in 1881 dashed their hopes and aroused Italy to rage which was the more bitter because the Italians were not strong enough to fight. In Rome, many feared that worse might follow. The French maintained that Tunis should "logically" fall to them because of its proximity to Algeria, but the same logic would also give Tripoli and Morocco to

France. Conscious of their own impotence, Italian statesmen turned to Berlin for help. Traditionally, Bismarck's
support of France in 1881 has been attributed to desire to
estrange France from Italy. He undoubtedly envisaged this
result, but he did not regard it as a very important achievement. As late as the end of 1881 he argued against an alliance with Italy "because the unsettled and untrustworthy
character of the Italian policy could easily embroil Italy's
friends in difficulties." From the tone of his remarks, it
even seems possible that he wished to prevent a reconciliation between Vienna and Rome; if sure of Italy, Austria
might adopt a stiffer tone toward Russia. In the end he consented to an alliance, but during the negotiations he remained in the background, merely approving decisions
reached between Vienna and Rome. His one preoccupation
was to exclude from the treaty anything which would sanction aggressive designs of Italy or Austria.

Throughout the first treaty of the Triple Alliance, signed
May 20, 1882, this defensive purpose was explicitly affirmed. Austria and Germany agreed to support Italy if
France should attack her "without direct provocation." If
France attacked Germany, Italy was to help her ally. In
case of an attack upon one or two of the allies by two or
more great powers, the other ally, or allies, must give armed
assistance. In the case of wars not calling for aid, the allies
were to show benevolent neutrality toward each other. All
promised not to enter any engagement directed against any
member of the alliance. If war seemed impending, the
allies were to consult together. The treaty was to be secret
and to last for five years. A supplementary declaration provided that the alliance could not "in any case be regarded
as being directed against England."

Italy had petitioned for the alliance, but she came away
with the greatest gains. The mere fact of union with the
central monarchies gave her prestige and influence in international affairs. Both her allies must come to her aid in
case France should attack. The possibility that Austria
might try either to restore the temporal power of the Pope,

or to regain Venetia, was ended. The declaration of the preamble that one purpose of the alliance was "to fortify the monarchical principle" bolstered the House of Savoy against republican attacks. For Austria, the chief advantage of the treaty lay in the guarantee that she would not be attacked from the rear if involved in a war with Russia. In Vienna it was also hoped that the Irredentist movement would now die out. This hope was not realized, but at least the alliance prevented the Italian government from open support of the Irredentist agitation.

Because it endured until 1914, the formation of the Triple Alliance has come to be regarded as a momentous event in the history of prewar diplomacy. To Bismarck, however, Italy was merely another link, and that not a very strong one, in the network of agreements by which he was trying to prevent a disturbance of the *status quo* in Europe. He regarded France and Russia as the powers interested in disturbing the existing situation. Italy would be of some value in keeping these powers quiet. The fear that Italy might attack from the rear would make France hesitate to attack Germany; Russia could no longer count on Italian aid against Austria. Further, Austria and Italy both sought increased influence in Albania and Macedonia. Bismarck hoped to use his influence as dominant member of the Alliance to neutralize their conflicting ambitions and produce the stalemate he desired.

The conflict of alliance systems has seemed to many scholars the most important cause of the World War, and, since the Triple Alliance was the first durable union, Bismarck has been pictured as giving the first great push toward catastrophe. There is no doubt that the division of Europe into two armed camps made the diplomatic situation more tense and the peaceful solution of problems more difficult. The alliances were, however, symptoms of a more deep-seated trouble, namely, the conflicting ambitions of the European states. Alsace-Lorraine, the Balkans, and imperialistic ventures in Africa and Asia had all caused trouble between 1871 and 1882. In the last analysis, power had been

the deciding factor in the settlement of each of these im-
broglios. The moral, not only to Bismarck, but to all European statesmen, seemed obvious: make sure that when
trouble comes power will be on your side, power in the
form of guns and men, your own and those of your friends.
Bismarck sincerely regarded the Triple Alliance and the
subsidiary agreements with Serbia and Rumania as a
"League of Peace." He counted on being able to restrain
his allies from aggressive action, and he felt that France
and Russia would hesitate to challenge such a powerful
group of states, particularly since England was on friendly
terms with the allies. It is not strange, however, that the
very secret Triple Alliance should arouse alarm in Paris
and St. Petersburg, where the peaceful intentions of the
three allies did not seem as obvious as in Berlin. The very
structure by which Bismarck hoped to ensure peace suggested the formation of another "League of Peace" between
Russia and France.

CHAPTER II

THE FRANCO-RUSSIAN COUNTERWEIGHT, 1881–1893

CHAPTER II

THE FRANCO-RUSSIAN COUNTERWEIGHT, 1881–1893

I. GLADSTONIAN IMPERIALISM, 1880–1885

By 1882, Germany and Italy, the enemies of France, stood in alliance with Austria, the foe of Russian advance in the Balkans. A Franco-Russian union was the logical reply to the Triple Alliance. It took until 1894 to effect the union. Fear of Germany helps to explain the delay. After the Congress of Berlin, when the Tsar in anger sought an understanding with Paris, the French Foreign Secretary held back. "Bismarck has his eye on me. If a treaty were on the anvil he might reply with war." Bismarck was vigilant; whenever Franco-Russian relations became too intimate, a new German army bill was introduced. A second obstacle was divergence of political ideals. Russian nihilism and French liberalism seemed blood brothers to Alexander III; the Russian autocracy seemed a debased copy of their own detested *ancien régime* to French Republicans. Finally, and possibly of greatest importance, union was made almost impossible by confusion of objective in both governments. Should the fire of *revanche* be kept bright, or should German aid be sought in colonial disputes with England? Neither the French people nor the officials of the Quai d'Orsay could make up their minds which they hated more, Britain or Germany. The Russians were equally undecided. Some wished to concentrate on the Balkans and the Straits, defying Austria and Germany. Others advocated a temporary truce in the Near East so that Russia might be free to challenge England in the Middle East—Afghanistan and the Persian Gulf. For years the oscillations of French

29

and Russian policies prevented a lasting *rapprochement* between the two countries.

From 1879 to 1885 the idea of a Franco-Russian alliance almost disappeared from sight. Both countries were so busy quarreling with England that they had no time to think of European problems. These were the years when the new imperialism reached its first strident climax in Europe.

When, in 1876, Parliament reluctantly voted Victoria the title of Empress of India, most Englishmen saw in the act a desire to humor a whim of the Queen. For Disraeli, however, the title symbolized the beginning of a new British Empire, with India as its center. The ramifications of his dream were tremendous. Buffer states must separate India from the possessions of other European powers. British naval supremacy along the thousands of miles of water separating England and India must be uncontested. This involved not only the maintenance of an overwhelmingly powerful fleet, but also vigilant watch lest another power secure territory which might be used either to attack India or to cut the British lines of communication. The fate of Morocco and Zanzibar, no less than that of Afghanistan, was involved in the problem of Indian defense.

Disraeli's ambitious vision was frequently repudiated in theory by later British statesmen, but rarely in practice. Gladstone, for instance, was a "Little Englander." He regarded imperialism as not only inexpedient and dangerous, but also as downright immoral. Moreover, in 1880 Disraeli's "forward policy" was decisively defeated at the polls. The British electorate, wearied by six years of almost continuous friction in international affairs, turned once more to Gladstone, who promised tranquillity abroad and electoral and Irish reform at home. There is no doubt that Gladstone was sincere in his condemnation of Disraeli's adventurous policy. Nevertheless, the five years of Gladstone's second administration moved, for the most part, in the grooves marked out by his predecessor. Where Disraeli had gloried in an active imperialistic policy, Gladstone advanced on the same path complaining of the hard fate which forced him forward. Between 1880 and 1885 the British occupied Egypt, thereby beginning a twenty-year feud with France, came to the verge of war with Russia in central Asia, and quarreled with Germany over colonies.

The opening of the Suez Canal in 1869 shortened the sea route to India by 6,000 miles and therefore intensified British interest in eastern Mediterranean affairs. The Canal had been built largely with French and Egyptian capital, but in 1875 Disraeli made British influence paramount by buying the Egyptian shares from the bankrupt Khedive. Having checkmated France on the canal question, Disraeli turned his attention to Russia and in 1878, at the Congress of Berlin, not only barred Russian advance toward the Straits and the Ægean, but secured the strategically important island of Cyprus for England. The approaches to the Suez secure on the north, Disraeli turned his attention to Egypt. Theoretically Egypt was a Turkish province. Practically it was independent, under the rule of the spend-thrift Khedive Ismail. Since 1863 Ismail, with the assistance of European capitalists, had been piling the Egyptian debt to dizzy heights. By 1876 his credit was exhausted. Then came the customary procedure of a European receivership to protect the bondholders, the establishment of the international Caisse de la Dette. Bankruptcy also opened the way to foreign political control, and a quiet but bitter struggle began between France and England. Neither felt in a position to defy the other, so a dual control was established over Egyptian finances. As Lord Salisbury put it, since France was "bent on meddling" in Egypt, three courses were open. "You may renounce—or monopolize—or share. Renouncing would have been to place the French across our road to India. Monopolizing would have been very near the risk of war. So we resolved to share." The French, of course, maintained that it was the British who were bent on meddling in a region where French influence had been strong for a century. Neither the Khedive nor the Egyptian ruling classes looked kindly on foreign interference, and they were able to count on the religious prejudices of the Mohammedan populace to support them. To eliminate opposition, the British and French induced the Turkish Sultan to depose Ismail in 1879, but the new Khedive, Tewfik, was unable to resist the pressure of the Egyptian nationalists.

Such was the situation when Gladstone took office: Franco-British control over Egyptian finances, and a weak Khedive afraid both of the foreigners and of the nationalists, who were now ably led by an army officer, Arabi. During 1881 and the early months of 1882 the anti-foreign agitation increased, and the efforts of France and England to prevent the Khedive from joining the nationalists merely served to make Arabi a national hero. In June, 1882, riots began in Alexandria, and some fifty Christians lost their lives. The spread of disorder could only be checked by military intervention. Both powers realized that if they occupied Egypt they would certainly quarrel over the spoils. Since neither government thought Egypt was worth strained relations, both sought to turn the question over to the powers as a whole, by a conference at Constantinople. The conference moved slowly. Arabi used the interlude to prepare for the expected European invasion. Impatient at the failure of the conference to discover a solution, and fearful lest Arabi complete his defenses, the British struck out on a line of their own. In July, 1882, British warships bombarded the fortifications at Alexandria. As the French had foretold, the bombardment precipitated further disorders in Egypt. To restore order, British troops were landed; the landing of troops brought on clashes with the forces of Arabi. The English found themselves confronted with the task of conquering the whole country. The task was completed in September when Arabi was finally defeated at Tel-el-Kabir.

The French protested vigorously when the British abandoned the principle of international settlement of the Egyptian question by bombarding Alexandria, and during the campaign against Arabi the correspondence between London and Paris became increasingly angry. The British advance came at an inopportune time for France. Tunis was proving difficult to subdue, and in the Far East French troops were trying to wrest Tonkin and Annam from China. Already deeply involved in two military operations, the French did not feel strong enough to participate in the conquest of Egypt, but neither did they wish to see the Nile valley in English hands. To postpone the issue, the Paris government asked that the Dual Control be reëstablished. Gladstone refused, basing his stand on what seemed to him irrefutable arguments. He disclaimed any intention or desire to keep Egypt; his one object was to set up a stable government capable of maintaining order. The Dual Control had not accomplished this task; instead it had increased disorder in Egypt and caused friction between France and England. He was confident that the British agents would speedily secure peace and good government. Then the British troops would be withdrawn. The French were skeptical both of Gladstone's sincerity and of his ability to fulfil his promises. On the latter point their doubts were justified by later events. Despite Gladstone's best efforts, obstacles to evacuation persisted, even grew in number and complexity. With every delay French exasperation increased. By the time Gladstone went out of office in 1885 the Egyptian question had thoroughly embittered Anglo-French relations and created an antagonism which was to last until 1904.

The consequences of the quarrel over Egypt did not stop with tension between London and Paris; the events along the Nile affected the fate of far-off Afghanistan, where trouble had been brewing for many years. The history of the Middle Eastern question from 1868 to 1886 illustrates the difficulties of imperial administration. The vast reaches of central Asia were far removed from St. Petersburg. Communication was slow, and for months at a time the Tsar's ministers were out of touch with the military commanders who exercised almost complete authority in the East. Similarly, the London cabinet knew little of conditions in and around India, and the officials on the spot sometimes took action which embarrassed the home government in dealings with other powers. So long as the British and

Russian possessions were separated by a thick wall of savage and independent buffer states, the doings of irresponsible governors caused little trouble. After the middle of the nineteenth century, however, ambitious Russian generals discovered that fame and promotion could easily be attained by pushing the Russian frontiers southward. As the separating wall grew thinner, British uneasiness grew. When Samarcand was annexed in 1868, representations were made in St. Petersburg. The Tsar's ministers promised to halt the advance, but it continued nevertheless.

During the later 1870's, while Russian attention was concentrated on the Near East, there was little activity in central Asia. When France and England began to quarrel over Egypt, the Russians thought it safe to move again. Theoretically without orders from St. Petersburg, Russian troops moved southward, this time driving a wedge between Persia and Afghanistan. Jingoism appeared once more in England. By April, 1885, war appeared probable. The Russians were defiant, confident that fear of France would hold England back. As a matter of fact, the chief obstacle to war was the lack of a good battle-field. The British did not wish to fight in the wilds of Afghanistan or in Persia but showed a disposition to use the old Crimean battle-ground. To reach Russia's Black Sea ports, ships must be sent through the Straits, and the Straits were closed by a treaty which England herself had created. When the London government tried to evade the treaty by sophistical arguments, Bismarck interposed an emphatic veto. He had no objections to Anglo-Russian quarrels in central Asia, but he was determined that the Near Eastern question should not be reopened; the events of 1876–1878 were painfully fresh in his mind. Probably Bismarck's opposition was decisive. England gave way and in September, 1885, sanctioned the recent Russian conquests. Neither party expected the agreement to be any more enduring than the innumerable promises Russia had made earlier.

Bismarck looked on with satisfaction while the pacific Gladstone sank deeper into controversies with France and

Russia; Egypt and Afghanistan relieved the pressure on the
German and Austrian frontiers, and forced London, Paris,
and St. Petersburg alike to seek support in Berlin. Further,
the difficulties of England provided a favorable opportunity to pick up a few colonies for Germany. Bismarck disliked the idea of overseas expansion. He never ceased to
describe Germany as a Continental and satiated state. Colonies would be a useless expense, "like the silken sables in
the noble families of Poland, who have no shirts to their
backs." Imperialism accentuated friction with other states
—witness Egypt. Colonies, he argued, called for a navy to
protect them; a navy would divert money from the army
and would antagonize England. Nevertheless, during the
years 1884 and 1885 Bismarck acquired the bulk of Germany's colonial empire, at the expense of a quarrel with
England. His action is understandable only in the light of
German internal conditions. Elections for the Reichstag
were impending. Bismarck's economic and social policies
had raised formidable opposition. The demand for colonies
was strong, and a latent hostility to England existed among
large groups of the German people. Both overseas expansion and a quarrel with the British would increase the
chances of a government victory at the polls. The risk
seemed slight; England was too deeply estranged from
France and Russia to resist. So Bismarck decided to act
against his better judgment.

Bismarck turned his eyes first toward southwest Africa.
He asked the British if they claimed the territory which ad-
joined Cape Colony. The British were dilatory. They did
not want the land themselves; but they wanted no one else
to have it. Bismarck applied pressure. An anti-English campaign began in the German press. "I am in perfect despair,"
wrote the British ambassador from Berlin, "at Prince Bismarck's present inclination to increase his popularity before
the general election by taking up an anti-English attitude.
. . . He has discovered an unexplored mine of popularity in
starting a colonial policy, which public opinion persuades
itself to be anti-English." This interpretation was too one-

sided. Wherever the Chancellor turned for the colonies German opinion demanded, he met with English opposition, usually based on the proximity of the territory in question to some British possession. Cape Colony did not want the Germans in Angra Pequena; New Guinea and Samoa were close to Australia. There was some justice in the complaint that the British sought to set up a Monroe Doctrine for the whole world. When argument failed, Bismarck resorted to more drastic measures by supporting the French in Egypt. Gladstone immediately beat a hasty retreat, proclaiming "if Germany is to become a colonizing power, all I say is, 'God speed her!' She becomes our ally and partner in the execution of the great purposes of Providence for the advantage of mankind." To Bismarck, such statements were mere rhetoric, and he did not greatly prize the territory secured for Germany in southwest and east Africa; in the Cameroons and Togoland; and in far-off Oceania. The one bit of territory he really wanted, the island of Helgoland off the German coast, the British, despite his threats, had refused to surrender. Bismarck's immediate objective had been won: he had satisfied German opinion. It was a dangerous victory. The controversy left behind an undercurrent of bad feeling between England and Germany. As Bismarck himself once said: "Every country in the long run is responsible for the windows broken by its newspapers; the bill will be presented one day in the ill-temper of a neighbor."

Fate dealt harshly with Gladstone. He had come to office in 1880 promising an era of peace and tranquillity. Instead, his administration was filled with quarrels with the Continental powers. Then, just as he left office in 1885, two events rescued England from her dangerous position. In the southeast corner of Asia, French troops were defeated in an engagement with the Chinese. Discontent with imperialistic adventures had been slowly maturing in France. News of the defeat precipitated a cabinet crisis. For the next three years ministries rose and fell with bewildering rapidity, making a consistent foreign policy impossible. Of even greater importance for England was the revolution in

Eastern Rumelia on September 18 which brought about the unification of the two parts into which Bulgaria had been divided in 1878. The Tsar forgot his dreams of reaching the Persian Gulf and concentrated his attention on the Near East. Bismarck, faced with revived *revanche* sentiment in France and the probability of new Austro-Russian quarrels in the Balkans, became most conciliatory in his correspondence with London.

2. THE BULGARIAN CRISIS, 1885–1888

Between 1878 and 1885, England and Russia reversed their rôles on the Bulgarian question. At the Congress of Berlin, Disraeli handed back to the Sultan much of the territory the new state had received by the Treaty of San Stefano and divided the remainder into two autonomous provinces, Bulgaria and Eastern Rumelia. His action was ostensibly dictated by regard for the sanctity of treaties, but really by determination to thwart Russia's Balkan ambitions. Similarly, while the Tsar talked much of his generous desire to emancipate the Balkan Slavs from Turkish misgovernment, his real aim was to convert Bulgaria into a Russian satrapy. Calculations both in London and St. Petersburg were based on the premise that the Bulgarians, being Southern Slavs, would naturally gravitate toward their fellow-Slavs. That premise proved false. Past history had developed in the Bulgarian peasant venomous hatred for his Slav neighbors and passionate desire for national independence. Prince Alexander, who had been made ruler of the new state by the powers, quickly sensed the feelings of his subjects and coöperated with the popular assembly in repulsing all Russian efforts to dominate Bulgaria. The Tsar, furious at this ingratitude, resolved to punish his protégé. When the union of Bulgaria and Eastern Rumelia was proclaimed in 1885, Alexander III refused to sanction the violation of the Treaty of Berlin, and encouraged the Sultan to reëstablish Turkish control in Eastern Rumelia by force of arms. England promptly stepped into the protective rôle abandoned by Russia. Once it became apparent that a strong Bulgaria might serve as a bulwark against Russian control over the Balkans, the British forgot their concern for the sanctity of treaties and became enthusiastic about the right of the Balkan Christians to freedom and self-government. Under the circumstances, the Sultan decided to do nothing. Soon it was obvious, even in St. Petersburg, that efforts to redivide Bulgaria were useless. The Pan Slavs saw Russia's whole "historic mission" imperiled: Serbia and Rumania were already Austrian satellites; unless Bulgaria was brought once more within the orbit of Russia, by force of arms if necessary, Hapsburg hegemony in the Balkans was complete. Russia must be the protector of the little Slav brothers, even if the little brothers vehemently resisted "protection"! In September, 1886, Prince Alexander was terrified into abdicating, and the Tsar prepared to reëstablish Russia's supremacy in Bulgaria by force.

With the abdication of Prince Alexander the Bulgarian crisis became acute. So long as the Tsar merely sought to prevent the union of Bulgaria and Eastern Rumelia, Austria remained quiet, but when Russia determined to dominate united Bulgaria, Vienna protested vigorously and intimated that the entrance of Russian troops into the Balkans would be resisted. Both sides carried their complaints to Berlin. The Tsar maintained that Bulgaria had been designated as a Russian sphere of influence in the Dreikaiserbund, and that Austria, with the support of England, was trying to acquire complete control over the Balkan peninsula. The Austrians, and more particularly the Hungarians, argued that Russian success in Bulgaria would be the prelude to new Pan-Slav agitation aiming at Russian conquest, not only of the Balkans, b·t also of the Slav provinces of the Dual Monarchy; Austria had no Balkan ambitions, she merely wished in self-defense to check the Russian advance. In general we may say that both Russians and Austrians convinced themselves that they were seeking legitimate defensive objectives, but that each had good ground for suspecting the other of aggressive designs.

As far as the merits of the case were concerned, Bis-

EUROPEAN RIVALRIES
AND
PENETRATION IN ASIA
1840-1914

0   200   400   600   800   1000   1200
Scale of Miles

The European possessions are colored
according to the political status of 1914

Russian   Portuguese
British   Dutch
French   German

* *Important Treaty Ports in China, Japan
and Korea, with dates of opening*

MAX MAYER, THORNWOOD, N.Y.

NOTE: *The dates* (1557) *under names indicate
the acquisition of the territory or the
settlement of the locality concerned*

marck inclined to the side of the Tsar; he would have solved
the Balkan problem by giving the eastern half to Russia and
the western to Austria. Alexander III welcomed this arrangement—for the present. Austria refused, claiming that,
once Russia had secured her share, the Pan-Slavs would
clamor for the rest. Since Austria had rejected his solution,
Bismarck elaborately dissociated himself from her. The
Austro-German Alliance, he argued, was purely defensive.
A war to keep Russia out of Bulgaria could not be called
defensive. Over and over he asserted: "In Bulgaria, I am
Russian." "What is Bulgaria to us?" he asked. "It is nothing to us who rules in Bulgaria, or even what becomes of
Bulgaria. . . . We have interests which do not affect Austria, and Austria has interests which are far removed from
us; therefore each must go its own way."

Bismarck's actions did not square with his words. His
words were designed at once to restrain Francis Joseph
from precipitate action and to keep the Tsar from turning
in anger toward France. His actions, on the other hand,
made the defeat of Russia's Bulgarian policy inevitable.
The plain fact was that Bismarck was coming to feel more
dependent on Austria than he cared to admit. If he turned
his back on the whole Bulgarian question with the indifference he professed, Russia would stand her ground fear-
lessly. Then Austria must either fight and be crushed or surrender. In either case, anger at the desertion of Germany
would strengthen the already powerful group in Austria
which advocated a coalition of France, Austria, and Russia against Germany. The risk was too great to be run;
Austria could not be left to confront Russia unaided. On
the other hand, for Bismarck to appear openly on the side
of his ally, Austria, would be doubly dangerous. Almost
certainly a Franco-Russian alliance would be the result;
very possibly there would be war. For some time alarming
reports had been coming in from Paris about the activities
of General Boulanger, whose reforms were increasing the
efficiency and strength of the French army. Amid rising
clamor for *revanche,* cheered on by the army and the Paris

populace, this new "man on horseback" rode toward a dictatorship. The French appeared in the mood for war. If Alexander III met with the open opposition of Germany in the Bulgarian affair, he would also be pushed toward war. Now as never before Bismarck needed peace. The party battles in Germany were more intense than ever, and socialism was growing. Emperor William was nearly ninety; Crown Prince Frederick was ill, probably dying; Prince William was an untried and unstable youth. Bismarck's problem thus resolved itself into a formula which was easy to state but hard to solve: Russia must be forced to surrender without war and without open coercion from Berlin.

The key to the situation lay in London. There, Lord Salisbury, Disraeli's successor as leader of the Conservatives, was now Foreign Minister. In Salisbury Bismarck met a diplomat who was his match. Shrewd, patient, never permitting details to obscure the whole picture, seldom mistaking desires for realities, keenly conscious of the sordid frailties of humanity as represented in European chancelleries, passionately devoted to British interests as he conceived them, Salisbury was one of the greatest representatives of the aristocratic tradition in British statesmanship, a worthy descendant of his Elizabethan ancestors, Lord Burleigh and Robert Cecil. Salisbury realized that strong community of interests bound England to the Triple Alliance. He was reluctant to see Russian influence grow in the Balkans. The Middle Eastern problem, though temporarily quiescent, still loomed in the background. The British were embroiled with France over Egypt and numerous other colonial questions: Salisbury even confessed that "it is very difficult to prevent oneself from wishing for another Franco-German war to put a stop to this incessant vexation." Like Bismarck, however, Salisbury had no desire to head the opposition to France and Russia. Rather he hoped to push Germany and Austria to the front line. When the activities of Boulanger made a Franco-German war seem probable, the British press, apparently inspired by the Foreign Office, was at pains to make clear that if the Germans chose to march on France through Belgium, England would not feel called upon to intervene. Similarly, in the Bulgarian question, Salisbury spurred Austria to oppose Russia by giving vague assurances of British sympathy and moral support. It is possible that, as he maintained, the other members of the cabinet prevented him from making concrete promises. It is rather more probable, however, that Bismarck was correct in suspecting that the British wished to stand aside while the Triple Alliance bore the brunt of Franco-Russian hostility. For months Bismarck and Salisbury played a waiting game, each trying to force the other into action.

In February, 1887, Salisbury at last began to yield. By an exchange of notes, the British and Italian governments promised to coöperate in the task of preserving the *status quo* in the Mediterranean basin and the Near East. The British note carefully stated that "the character of that coöperation must be decided by them [the signatory powers], when the occasion for it arises, according to the circumstances of the case." Nevertheless, the notes represented a decided departure from the non-committal attitude England had earlier observed. In March, Austria gladly acceded to the agreement. At the end of 1887 the entente was given even greater precision when the three powers stated in detail the problems upon which they were prepared to coöperate. In this second exchange, all three agreed to oppose any change in the status of Bulgaria. Bismarck was jubilant. With England, Austria, and Italy united, France and Russia would be afraid to move.

Nevertheless, the balance of power in Europe was shifting. In 1879 Bismarck had felt that the alliance with Austria would hold France and Russia in check, while the British saw no need of any allies. As France and Russia grew in military power, the situation changed. The Mediterranean Agreements of 1887 indicated that Salisbury saw the need of friends, and the eagerness with which Bismarck sought British aid showed that he also felt uneasy. Italy was quick to realize that her bargaining power was improving. When the Triple Alliance was renewed in February,

1887, she obtained important concessions from both her allies. By a separate treaty, Austria admitted her to complete equality in the settlement of Balkan questions, agreeing that, if either made gains in the Near East, the other should be entitled to reciprocal compensation. Germany went even further, promising to support Italy in a war to prevent France from taking Tripoli or Morocco, even if Italy should start the war. Thus, by skilful utilization of the difficulties of her allies, Italy was able to place herself on an equal plane with Austria in the Balkans and to change her alliance with Germany from a purely defensive to a potentially aggressive instrument.

Despite the secrecy with which the negotiations for the Mediterranean Agreements and for the renewal of the Triple Alliance were conducted, the Russians knew that a coalition was being formed against them, and they suspected that Bismarck was its architect. The Russian Foreign Minister put the matter very neatly in December, 1886. He expressed gratitude for Bismarck's promise to support the Tsar in the Bulgarian question. "But," he continued, "His Majesty regrets that in practice the good-will of the German government is neutralized by the relations in which it stands with other powers whose action is precisely the principal obstacle preventing the reëstablishment of the salutary and legitimate influence which Russia claims in Bulgaria." The Pan-Slav press harped ceaselessly on German treachery and on the necessity for an alliance with France. When Bismarck complained of these tirades, the Tsar intimated that the anger of the press was not wholly unjustified. Alexander III could not, however, conquer his aversion to France. The rapid rise and fall of ministries, the adulation with which the Paris populace followed the antics of Boulanger, the shelter offered Nihilists and Anarchists, all confirmed the Tsar's mistrust of republicanism and convinced him that France would be a volatile, untrustworthy, and dangerous ally. He clung desperately to the hope that Germany might yet be separated from Austria and England. To effect this end, in the spring of 1887 he proposed a

Russo-German neutrality agreement to replace the Drei-kaiserbund, which the Bulgarian crisis had killed.

The offer placed Bismarck in a quandary. He was anxious to get some sort of treaty with Russia, but a general neutrality agreement would be in flat contradiction to the Austro-German alliance. He extricated himself by a characteristically bold maneuver. The terms of the treaty with Austria were communicated to St. Petersburg with the statement that Russian threats had brought into existence this alliance, which could not now be repudiated. As Bismarck anticipated, the communication angered the Tsar but also made him even more anxious to escape complete isolation. Discussion continued, and a compromise was effected on the question of neutrality. Each promised benevolent neutrality if the other should be at war, but "this provision shall not apply to a war against Austria or France resulting from an attack made upon one of these two Powers by one of the Contracting Parties." By other clauses of the treaty, which was signed on June 18, 1887, Germany promised to aid Russia in the tasks of restoring Russian influence in Bulgaria, preserving the *status quo* in the Balkans, and preventing the opening of the Straits. The treaty was to remain in force for three years.

The actual provisions of the agreement seemed to indicate that Russia had made the greater gains. The promise of neutrality if France should attack Germany was balanced by the German promise to remain neutral if Austria should attack Russia, while Germany received no compensation for support of Russian policy in the Near East. Bismarck, however, was content. For him, this was a "reinsurance" treaty, supplementing the Austro-German alliance as a guarantee against war on two fronts, and postponing the dreaded Franco-Russian union for at least three years. The treaty was also insurance against Austria. Bismarck was convinced that if Russia were permanently alienated from Germany, Austria would be in a position to make exorbitant demands on Berlin, as Italy was already doing. But was it not disloyal, thus to consort with his ally's bitterest enemy?

Emphatically, No, Bismarck replied to his critics. The Austro-German alliance was defensive. Since 1879 Austria's Balkan policy had become increasingly aggressive. Germany was not called upon to support this policy; rather, the growing ambitions of Austria made good relations between Berlin and St. Petersburg essential to prevent Germany from becoming completely dependent on Vienna. If Austria wished to pursue objectives not covered by the alliance of 1879, let her find other friends—England and Italy.

The Tsar had chosen Germany rather than France in return for Bismarck's promise of support in Bulgaria. What did the promise mean? A test came almost immediately after the Reinsurance Treaty was signed, when the Bulgarians offered their vacant throne to Prince Ferdinand of Coburg. The Russian government objected, and demanded German support, which Bismarck gave. Nevertheless, Ferdinand, accepted the throne, confident of Austrian and British backing. The Tsar then asked Bismarck to force Austria into acceptance of Russia's position. The Chancellor refused. He would back Russian action; he would not take the lead himself: "La parole est à la Russie." This interpretation of German obligations under the Reinsurance Treaty nullified the value of the agreement for the Tsar, who had expected Bismarck to compel Austrian assent to Russian control over Bulgaria. In anger, Alexander III massed troops in increasing numbers along the Galician frontier. The resulting tension produced a panic in Vienna. Francis Joseph begged for a promise of German support in the "inevitable" war, but Bismarck, mistrusting Austria no less than Russia, refused to commit himself. Instead, he cautiously but steadily pressed on Russia's weakest point, finance. First, German papers hinted that Russia was approaching bankruptcy; then the German courts ruled that Russian bonds were too risky an investment for trust funds; finally, the Reichsbank decided to exclude Russian loans from the Berlin stock-exchange. At the same time the entente between England, Austria, and Italy was being strengthened. France, awed by the formidable anti-Russian combination, rejected the

bellicose counsels of Boulanger and turned aside the veiled
suggestions for an alliance which came from St. Petersburg. After four months of uneasy waiting, the strain became intolerable, and the Tsar surrendered. On December
18, 1887, the Russian ambassador in Vienna announced that
Alexander would not fight to regain control over Bulgaria
and had no intention of attacking Austria. A few months
later, Boulanger disappeared from the scene. With the dictatorship apparently in his grasp, his courage failed, and he
fled to Brussels.

The long crisis had passed without war, but the Europe
of 1887 was not the Europe of 1885. In 1885 the problem
of Alsace-Lorraine had seemed half forgotten; Boulanger
brought it to the fore again. By 1887 the arrest of a petty
French official, Schnaebele, by overzealous German police
could bring two great nations to the verge of war. Bulgaria
had killed the Dreikaiserbund. The Reinsurance Treaty
formed a tenuous bond uniting Germany and Russia, but the
old friendship and confidence between the two governments
was gone. England had drawn close to Austria and Italy
in an entente which was dangerous to the Mediterranean
ambitions of France and the Balkan ambitions of Russia.
Few believed Bismarck's assertion that Germany was in no
way a party to the entente. The coöperation of England and
the Triple Alliance turned the thoughts of leaders both in
Paris and St. Petersburg more strongly than ever before
toward a Franco-Russian alliance. Bismarck had unwittingly pushed the Tsar toward France by closing the Berlin
exchange to Russian securities. The Russian government
always needed money; French capitalists were eager to satisfy the need. The Paris Bourse floated one loan after another on favorable terms, inevitably creating a strong bond
of union between the two countries. The proceeds of the
loans temporarily removed the most powerful guarantee,
namely, financial embarrassment, that Russia would pursue
a pacific foreign policy. Wild rumors began to circulate.
Galicia, Constantinople, and Afghanistan were all suggested as the theater of the impending Russian threat.

Both in London and in Berlin the situation caused alarm. The British prepared for trouble by the Naval Defense Act of 1889, which laid down the principle that the British fleet "should be at least equal to the naval strength of any two other nations." In the same year, Bismarck proposed that the Franco-Russian peril be met by an Anglo-German alliance, preferably a public one. Salisbury turned down the suggestion, ostensibly because Parliament might object, really because he was firmly wedded to a policy of isolation. It is impossible to discern clearly what further moves Bismarck planned. The information we have indicates that the growing self-assertiveness of Austria and the refusal of England to make binding commitments suggested the wisdom of closer relations with Russia, at least until the drift of events became clearer.

Bismarck was, however, no longer the sole arbiter of German policy. William II, who became German Emperor in 1888, was not fitted for the rôle of passive, acquiescent observer. On the other hand, Bismarck could not tolerate interference. The tentative, opportunist, almost instinctive way in which Bismarck groped through the tangle of events until he saw a path open before him could only be successful if unhampered. The young Kaiser believed that the Tsar was planning a military adventure and that war could be averted only by making obvious the determination of Germany to side with Austria and England. Bismarck controverted these views in language which was respectful but permeated by that tone of Olympian condescension which from time immemorial has irked the spirit of youth. Worse, he sought to avoid controversy by withholding information from William II. Enemies were quick to inform the Kaiser that he was being kept in the dark. On questions of domestic policy, Kaiser and Chancellor were also at odds. During the opening months of 1890 there was an explosive conflict of wills. In March, Bismarck was forced to resign.

3. THE FRANCO-RUSSIAN ALLIANCE, 1888–1894

Bismarck left Germany the most powerful state in Europe, but he left Germany scarcely more of a nation than she had been in 1871. Jealousies persisted between the states; the phenomenal growth of commerce and industry added new jealousies between town and country, capital and labor. No tradition, no ideal, transcended factional differences. German history dealt either with the international medieval empire, with tribal divisions, or with the states and cities. Nowhere, except in the generation just past, did it coincide with the limits of the new Germany. The rich cultural and intellectual heritage was local, not national, and had little to do with the Prussian spirit which brought unification. The Prussian spirit of efficiency, practicality, and obedience to authority did provide at least a veneer of unity. Viewed pragmatically, these qualities worked. They had produced the Empire, wealth and power, and therefore they were reverenced. But they were not Germany. Beneath the surface of German life there was a restless, unsure spirit. Arrogant boastfulness and nervous fear, criticism and flattery of other nations—gusts of contradictory feeling swept over the German scene, arousing bewilderment, alarm, and anger in neighboring peoples.

German political life was the mirror of the national instability. Bismarck was too much of an autocrat to give the Germans the political education they needed. He could not guide, he could not train, the Germans to develop political sense by sharing power with them. He recognized the problem but dismissed it as insoluble: the German never had been and never would be a political animal. Bismarck felt only contempt for his opponents in the Reichstag, and in their worship of him Germans came to share his contempt for the Reichstag. After his fall, when the deplorable results of the incapacity of the German people to control either themselves or their ruler became apparent, he denied that he had furthered the autocratic principle; but his whole record belied his words.

Within the government, the evils which followed inevitably from Bismarck's masterful nature became apparent after 1890. Under his great shadow other wills weakened. He instinctively and unconsciously demanded servants, not colleagues. So long as his capacious mind and firm will were in control, the evils of the system were concealed. The machine became paralyzed when he fell from power. Wilhelmstrasse became and remained a place of intrigue and of small minds. Nowhere else in Europe could a man like Baron von Holstein have influenced policy for sixteen years. Holstein had been one of Bismarck's tools. After 1890 he was the only important survivor of the old régime, and the untrained directors of the "new course" turned to him for counsel. A brilliant mind he certainly possessed; his memoranda are models of lucidity and cogency. He loved power, but he was a creature of the dark, afraid of publicity, afraid of responsibility, suspicious, jealous. Shut off from men and the world, he strove with undoubted patriotism to chart a safe course for German policy. His isolation from life, his morbid fears, his propensity for plot and intrigue inevitably distorted his judgment. Yet the amateurs who theoretically directed German destinies listened to him with fear and respect because he was the magician's disciple. Only when his advice had brought Germany to the edge of catastrophe was he dismissed.

It would be almost as unfair to blame Bismarck for the evils which appeared after his fall as it would be to accuse a pilot because an airplane ceased to function properly when his hands were forcibly removed from the controls. Only a genius and an autocrat could use Bismarck's methods; the tragedy was that William II aspired to play the autocrat, although completely unfitted for the part. He did indeed possess the more superficial qualifications: an engaging personality, an instinct for the dramatic, and a wide range of interests. These qualities were vitiated by others. Despite his restless energy, sustained effort bored him intolerably. He could not decide on a course and keep it; new interests distracted his attention before anything was accomplished.

Always emphatic, he was often equally enthusiastic about incompatible objectives. His craving for power made him suspicious of advisers with vigor of will and honesty of expression; but since he was primarily concerned for the appearance of power, subtle flatterers could dominate him. Bismarck had trained the Germans to habits of obedience; under William II obedience was perverted to Byzantine servility. Ministers must either follow blindly the vagaries of the Imperial will, prepared to accept the blame if failure resulted, or they must thwart the Kaiser's whims by obscuring their opposition in clouds of intoxicating incense which heightened William's vanity and made him so much the more difficult to control thereafter. As the years passed and the Kaiser's impetuous actions exposed Germany increasingly to ridicule and danger, uneasiness spread among all ranks of the German people. Occasionally there were explosions in the Reichstag. They accomplished nothing. German political life never recovered from the blight cast upon it by Bismarck.

The instability of German national life was scarcely noticed until the unexpected dismissal of Bismarck turned all eyes toward Berlin. Even in France and Russia, joy soon gave way to uneasiness. In 1871 European statesmen, used to weakness and division in the center of the Continent, had eyed the new military empire uneasily as an incalculable, dangerous intruder. During succeeding years they became accustomed to it, but less to Germany than to Bismarck. Much as they might fear, even hate him, they were forced to recognize his political genius and his steady judgment. They recognized also that, while he might set others at odds, at bottom he was a powerful bulwark of peace and the *status quo.* Suddenly Bismarck was unceremoniously pushed off the stage. European statesmen were confronted with the necessity of understanding the German people and the new Kaiser. Both defied their comprehension. The German people accepted Bismarck's dismissal without violent protest. That fact indicated complete docility, the non-existence of any public opinion. At the same time the violence with which

Germans expressed their opinion of other nations raised the suspicion that the government might be forced against its better judgment into an adventurous foreign policy. Unable to find conclusive evidence on which to base a firm conclusion, (foreign statesmen wavered between two opinions: German public opinion was thought of now as a negligible quantity, now as a decisive factor.) So as always to err on the side of safety, statesmen naturally listened to German opinion when it was more bellicose than Wilhelmstrasse, and disregarded opinion when it was on the side of moderation. Had they been more sure of William II, they would have felt less uneasy, but they were afraid of him also. By 1890 stories of his impetuosity, his dreams of Cæsarism, his delight in the workings of his great military machine, were already beginning to circulate. Longer acquaintance failed to reassure foreign observers. "The Emperor is like a cat in a cupboard," an English diplomat complained many years later, "he may jump out anywhere." No one knew who ruled in Germany; it was difficult to forecast German action in any given situation; it was impossible to discern the ultimate objectives of German policy. The question naturally arose: Did the restless and contradictory nature of German diplomacy conceal deep-laid plans? It is easy to see now that German diplomacy after 1890 was no more and no less immoral than that of other states, that it was merely more blundering. It is easy to see now that William II, despite his boasts and threats, desired peace. Nevertheless, statesmen in England, France, and Russia cannot be blamed for being fearful. They saw a restless, unstable people ruled by a restless, unstable emperor. They saw also the great German army, the best in the world.

William II was unprepared for the stir caused by his dismissal of Bismarck. Embarrassed and bewildered, the Kaiser hastened to announce that the old policies of loyalty to the defensive aims of the Triple Alliance and friendly relations with other European powers were to be continued. The only change was to be one of tone. Instead of the complications—"chicanery" was the word hinted at—of Bismarckian diplomacy, German policy was now to be simple, open, straightforward. The Kaiser's "simple" policy met with the hearty approval of his new advisers, who were, like himself, ignorant of international affairs. The new Chancellor, Caprivi, was a soldier, who confessed he felt as if he were entering a dark room when he went to the foreign office. Marschall, the Foreign Secretary, was distinctly mediocre in capacity and attainments.

The attempt of the three well-meaning amateurs who now controlled German policy to follow an open and conciliatory policy hastened the union of Russia and France. The Reinsurance Treaty expired in 1890. Negotiations for renewal began early in the year, with the approval of William II. As soon as Bismarck was out of the way, Holstein and other Foreign Office officials raised the argument that the treaty with Russia was incompatible with loyalty to Austria and England. If Russia should reveal the existence of the agreement, Germany would be accused of double-dealing. British friendship would be lost and the Triple Alliance weakened. There is much to be said both for and against Holstein's arguments. Historians are still divided on the question. William II and Caprivi were convinced, and they refused to continue the negotiations with Russia. Honesty alone dictated their actions, they declared. Germany was through with the tortuous ambiguities of the Bismarckian period. The Russians were skeptical, and when their efforts to secure a less inclusive treaty failed, the conviction took root in St. Petersburg that the Kaiser planned a new and anti-Russian orientation of German policy.

The growing intimacy between Berlin and London fostered Russian suspicions. By a treaty concluded in July, 1890, the colonial differences of England and Germany were settled, Germany receiving Helgoland in return for great concessions in Africa. William II, in fulsome speeches which alarmed his advisers, stressed the community of interests between the two countries. The British, hard pressed by France and Russia, responded with alacrity. When the Triple Alliance was renewed early in 1891, the English press was so enthusiastic that rumors of British accession to the alliance began to spread. A few months later the effusive welcome accorded William II when he visited England seemed to bear out the rumors.

While it is undoubtedly true that France and Russia were moving toward an alliance before 1890, it is also certain that the dropping of the Reinsurance Treaty and the conviction that England had joined the Triple Alliance helped to overcome the Tsar's scruples. Further, the actions of William II made the French more eager for an alliance. His program of international peace and friendship called for a *rapprochement* with France, but his clumsy overtures only succeeded in arousing the *revanche* party. In anger, the Kaiser became cold and threatening. The French appealed to Russia for protection, and the Tsar was willing to go part way. Shortly after the Kaiser's visit to England, the French fleet received an enthusiastic welcome at Cronstadt. The Tsar even stood with bared head while the Revolutionary "Marseillaise" was played. In August, 1891, he agreed to an exchange of notes defining the scope of the entente. The Russian note stated that the agreement was necessitated by "the situation created in Europe by the open renewal of the Triple Alliance and the more or less probable adhesion of Great Britain to the political aims which that alliance pursues." Article I stated that "the two governments declare that they will take counsel together upon every question of a nature to jeopardize the general peace." Under the second article, in case of threatened aggression, "the two parties undertake to reach an understanding on the measures whose immediate and simultaneous adoption would be imposed upon the two governments by the realization of this eventuality." This was all very vague, so vague that either party might desert the other in a crisis without actually violating the agreement. The French were dissatisfied, but Alexander III refused to be more explicit.

In fact, neither the Anglo-German *rapprochement* nor the Franco-Russian entente constituted a definitive alignment of the powers. For two years, until the fall of 1893, the international situation remained obscure. France wished to bind Russia more closely, and Germany would have welcomed the entrance of England into the Triple Alliance, but England and Russia held back. Salisbury believed in a policy of isolation, and Gladstone, who became Prime Minister once more in 1892, disliked Germany profoundly. The Tsar saw no reason for committing himself further to France. In his eyes the entente of 1891 had a negative value. He neither wanted nor expected war with Germany; he wanted to keep Germany neutral in case of an Anglo-Russian war. Fear that France would attack from the rear would make Germany reluctant to intervene. The very eagerness of the French for a more far-reaching agreement showed that they could be counted on for aid. French eagerness also raised the suspicion that, if sure of Russia, the advocates of *revanche* would be encouraged to start trouble with Germany. The French government sought to disarm the Tsar's fear by silencing all discussion of Alsace-Lorraine, but it was not until the Russians thought they had found a new use for their ally that they agreed to strengthen the alliance.

For many years the efforts of France to undermine the independence of Siam, which formed a buffer state between Burma and French Indo-China, had met with steady but ineffectual opposition from England. In July, 1893, Lord Rosebery, Gladstone's Foreign Secretary, decided to resist the French encroachments, by force if necessary. The French took an equally firm stand, and for a few days there was acute tension. Then Rosebery's Liberal colleagues forced him to surrender. The firmness of France in the face of Rosebery's threats made a deep impression in St. Petersburg. Through their control over the seas, the British had been able to impede Russian expansionist ambitions ever since the Crimean War. Might not a union of the French and Russian fleets imperil English maritime supremacy? This hope ended the coolness, almost aversion, which Alexander III had shown for France since 1891.

In October, 1893, a Russian squadron was sent to the

Mediterranean. When the vessels reached Toulon, the French people burst into hysterical rejoicing; the visit seemed a symbol that the long isolation of France was over. Three months later a military convention defining the scope of the Franco-Russian alliance was signed. This secret agreement, the terms of which were not known until after the Russian revolution of 1917, provided that: "If France is attacked by Germany, or by Italy supported by Germany, Russia shall employ all her available forces to attack Germany. If Russia is attacked by Germany, or by Austria supported by Germany, France shall employ all her available forces to fight Germany." If any of the members of the Triple Alliance mobilized, France and Russia were also to mobilize.

With the consummation of the Dual Alliance the Continent was divided into two rival armed camps. England alone of the great European powers remained outside the alliance systems. British statesmen spoke much of the "splendour" of their isolation, but in truth their position was none too secure. The actual terms of the Dual Alliance singled out Germany as the enemy, but the sending of a Russian fleet to the Mediterranean was an anti-British demonstration, and British interests clashed with those of France and Russia all the way from Morocco to China. Could England remain aloof from the alliance systems? If not, in which group could the protection of British interests be best assured? These questions were to trouble the London government for ten years.

The nightmare which had troubled Bismarck's sleep for twenty years was a reality. After apparently endless hesitation, France and Russia had united. Whether or not Bismarck could have prevented the union will always be a moot question. It is undoubtedly true that talk of an alliance was in the air in 1889 as a result of the Boulanger and Bulgarian crises. But there had been rumors of an alliance in 1879 also, and nothing came of those rumors. Furthermore, the Tsar had been willing to continue the Reinsurance Treaty in 1890, and he would scarcely have bound himself

to France while the agreement with Germany existed. So
the argument goes, back and forth. On one point Bismarck
was certainly mistaken. The dire results which he had
prophesied the alliance would bring to Germany did not appear for many years, possibly need never have come. Aside
from the inevitable hotheads, no one in either France or
Russia wished to provoke a war with the Triple Alliance.
Alsace-Lorraine and the Balkans were not forgotten, and
did not cease to influence events, but colonial rivalry now
held the center of the stage. England bore the brunt of that
rivalry. At no time after 1871 did the danger of a Continental war seem so remote as in the last decade of the nineteenth century.

CHAPTER III

THE END OF BRITISH ISOLATION, 1893–1904

CHAPTER III

THE END OF BRITISH ISOLATION, 1893–1904

I. ENGLAND AND THE CONTINENTAL POWERS

Standing alone after 1894 outside the European alliance systems, the British called England "the balance-wheel" of European politics. As the century drew to a close this expression was heard more rarely. The masses were, as everywhere, profoundly ignorant of foreign affairs, and trusted the government to protect the honor and power of Britain. Those at the top were less confident, and with every passing year they became more uneasy. They saw that English agriculture was in desperate straits; they saw that British commerce and industry were being hard pressed by German and American competition. The Franco-Russian alliance united the two traditional colonial rivals of England. Under the leadership of William II, Germany was embarking on a career of overseas expansion. Continental problems seemed almost forgotten; imperialism held the center of the stage.

In the race for colonies, France, Germany, and Russia sometimes collided with each other, but with England all three collided at every turn. The map tells only part of the story. In addition to the crimson patches, Continental statesmen must take account of British "spheres of influence," which Lord Salisbury once defined as "a sort of ear-mark upon territory which, in case of a break-up, England did not want any other Power to have." We may gain some comprehension of the portion of the world thus earmarked from the fact that one sphere of influence was the Persian Gulf, and another was the Yangtze Valley in China, a territory as large as Europe, excluding Russia, with a population of more than 200 millions. Even this is not all. In other regions, such as Turkey, Morocco, and northern China, Brit-

ish trade had long enjoyed a dominant position which would
be impaired if the Continental powers acquired political preponderance. Change in the status of these areas was opposed by England. In view of such pretensions, it is not
strange that Continental statesmen came to think of the
British Empire as "a huge giant sprawling over the globe,
with gouty fingers and toes stretching in every direction,
which cannot be approached without eliciting a scream."
Common, and usually unsuccessful, opposition to England
suggested the wisdom of a Continental coalition. The project was debated constantly and frequently seemed about to
become a reality. After 1894 it was the turn of Britain to
be haunted by the nightmare of hostile alliances.

Most well-informed Englishmen agreed that the situation
was dangerous, but there was no agreement on the way out.
Many Liberals hoped to supplant the traditional rivalry
with France by friendship. Strong cultural ties and common
devotion to liberal political ideals would, they hoped, provide a basis for union. While they were in power, from
1892 to 1895, the Liberals tried to be conciliatory. The
French interpreted these gestures as signs of weakness, and
became more self-confident in their opposition to England.
At the opposite pole from the Liberal Francophiles stood
those who wished a close understanding or alliance with
Germany. Several members of the Unionist ministry which
took office in 1895 were advocates of this solution of England's problems. Until the end of the century an entente
with Germany would undoubtedly have been popular with
a large, though diminishing, number of Englishmen. Beginning in 1898, Joseph Chamberlain, the Colonial Secretary in the Unionist government, made repeated overtures
for an alliance. Like the French, the Germans interpreted
his proposals as symptoms that England was losing her
nerve.

The leader of the Conservatives, Lord Salisbury, had
little sympathy with Francophiles or Teutophiles. Sympathies and antipathies had no place in his view of politics.
"Politics," he said, "is a matter of business." The cold

facts, as he saw them, were that "the French and German *people* both hate us; the Russian people do not." Since France was a democracy, there was no chance of lasting friendship between England and France until popular feeling changed. Germany was not a democracy. British and German interests were, he thought, much alike. Nevertheless, Salisbury soon lost hope of steady coöperation with Berlin; he was afraid to trust the unstable government of William II. There remained Russia, for the past two generations England's most persistent rival. Salisbury thought the rivalry unnecessary. The world was big enough for both. After 1895 he tried to effect a reconciliation, but the Russians, like the rest of the Continent, had convinced themselves that England was decadent and could be defied with impunity. Despite the failure of his efforts, Salisbury refused to admit that there was any reason for alarm. He was convinced that the Triple Alliance and the Dual Alliance were paralyzed by hatred of each other. Great provocation would be necessary to bring about union for common action against England. That provocation he never gave. When concessions were necessary to prevent a coalition of England's rivals, he made them; when the opposing forces were too strong, he held his peace and waited; when he felt sure no hostile combination was possible, he struck with devastating force. His faith in a policy of isolation remained unshaken to the end. During the darkest days of the Boer War he was imperturbable, convinced that England was safe behind chalk cliffs and battle fleet.

Until the outbreak of the Boer War, he was able to hold the cabinet in line with his views. As the international situation became more complicated and dangerous, the Chamberlain group grew increasingly restive. The anti-isolationists triumphed when age and ill health forced Salisbury to leave the Foreign Office at the end of 1900. An alliance was made with Japan, and an understanding was vainly sought with Germany. In 1904 the entente with France was concluded, and British isolation, for better or worse, became a thing of the past.

2. ENGLAND AND FRANCE, 1895–1899

Salisbury knew the French people hated England, but he thought they hated Germany even more. He realized that the Russian alliance would encourage the French to hold firm in any quarrel with England, but he was confident that Russia would, in a crisis, refuse to fight for French interests. His policy followed from these convictions. Where vital British interests were not involved, he sought to allay French hostility by generous concessions, but when the French ventured too far, he took an uncompromising stand, confident that France would give way.

It was hazardous to prophesy what France would do in any given situation. French public life was in confusion during the closing years of the century. Doubts followed hard on the first enthusiasm for the Russian alliance. The new Tsar, Nicholas II, seemed indifferent toward his ally. He and William II were close friends. Demands for loans came with embarrassing frequency from St. Petersburg. The French did not dare refuse these requests, but they were increasingly suspicious that their resources were being drained to further Russian plans which had no connection with French aspirations. Even more depressing were nasty domestic scandals—the Panama Canal affair and the Dreyfus case—which made French politics the butt of European jests. Humiliation and chagrin at the bad figure cut by France created a public temper which was dangerously irritated. Irritation was increasingly directed against England. Almost every year since the occupation of Egypt had seen some quarrel, great or small, between the two countries. Each episode left behind a growing residuum of hatred. Press wars gave expression to, and intensified, the antagonism. English journals made caustic comments on the moral and political bankruptcy of France; French newspapers flung back ugly retorts.

Backed, or pushed on, by public opinion, the French government pursued a colonial policy which was bound to lead to conflict. In Africa, the British had staked out claims to

most of the desirable coast lands, but France was established on the north, in Algeria and Tunis; and on the west,
at the mouth of the Senegal, along the Ivory Coast, and
north of the Congo. From these points the French pene-
trated inland, making treaties with chiefs, securing the
headwaters of important rivers, and cutting off colonies of
other countries from contact with the hinterland. The British protested each advance, but usually gave way; the des-
erts of Africa were of little value.

The situation became dangerous when the French showed
signs of pushing eastward to the Sudan. The upper reaches
of the Nile, although theoretically a part of Egypt, had for
a decade been a political no-man's-land, scourged by the
followers of the Mad Mahdi, a Moslem prophet. If the
French acquired the Sudan, their empire would extend
across Africa, from the Atlantic to the Red Sea, and because of their control over the waters of the upper Nile,
Egypt would be at their mercy. In 1895 it was rumored that
France planned an expedition to the Sudan. Even the Liberals, who were still in office, felt that this would be regarded in England as an "unfriendly act." The next year a
race began. Kitchener, with a large Anglo-Egyptian force,
pushed up the Nile; Marchand, with a small French force,
advanced from the west. The objective of both was the
Sudan. As every one knew, there would be an explosion
when they met. Efforts were made to find a working compromise while there was time, but these efforts failed. Although the treacherous waters of the upper Nile were little
more than a name to most Frenchmen and Englishmen, that
name had become a symbol of the accumulated bitterness
between the two countries.

In September, 1898, the *mauvais quart d'heure* arrived
when Kitchener reached Fashoda, where Marchand was
already encamped. Neither would leave without orders from
home, so there they sat while their governments decided
whether the Sudan was worth a war. The initial positions
of the governments admitted of no arbitrament except war.
Delcassé, the French Foreign Secretary, refused to recall

Marchand until French claims in the Nile valley were recognized. Salisbury announced that the Sudan had fallen
jointly to England and Egypt by right of conquest. He refused to argue or make concessions: Marchand was tres-
passing and must be recalled. More bluntly, Salisbury was
resolved on a decisive test of strength. War or unconditional surrender were the alternatives he offered. He was
confident France would surrender. While hope of recovering Alsace-Lorraine remained alive, France would not con-
sume her blood and treasure fighting England. Furthermore, he maintained, Russia would desert her ally. For six
weeks the issue was in doubt; then Salisbury's diagnosis
proved correct. As Clemenceau said: "The brutal fact is
that France cannot think of throwing herself into a war for
the possession of some African marshes, when the German
is camped at Metz and Strasbourg." The Russians hinted
that they were not yet ready to fight. Humiliated and angry,
the French ordered Marchand home.

At first war seemed only to have been postponed. The
correspondent of the *Daily Telegraph* reported that "the
feeling of rage and wild desire for revenge to which the
French press now gives expression exceeds in degree the
outburst of hatred which the loss of Alsace-Lorraine provoked against Germany a generation ago." Later it was to
become apparent that Salisbury's firmness had forced France
to make a definite choice of enemies and of friends, to end
the oscillation between *revanche* and hatred of England
which had hampered French diplomatic action since 1871.
Fashoda paved the way for the Anglo-French entente of
1904. For some time, however, the violence of French edi-
torial opinion obscured the real result. Many in England
feared France would welcome an opportunity to unite in
a coalition against Britain.

3. ENGLAND AND RUSSIA, 1895–1899

Salisbury did not feel able or willing to deal summarily
with Russia. He feared Russia much less, and at the same
time much more, than the rank and file of his compatriots.

Most Englishmen reared on memories of the Crimean War, fortified by the unforgettable stories of Kipling, saw Russia through a haze of fear, hatred, and disgust. The Bear was a horrible prehistoric monster, to be vanquished from time to time by the British St. George. Salisbury was exempt from the nervous paroxysm which each Russian advance aroused in England: on one occasion he advised his countrymen to calm themselves by consulting large-scale maps. He realized the fundamental weakness of the Tsar's Empire and saw no reason to bolster up a tottering structure like Turkey as a bulwark against the advance of Russia. At the same time he dreaded an armed encounter. The British army was small, and the great land mass of Russia was impervious to attack by the fleet, which, as the popular saying went, did not run on wheels. Salisbury would have been glad to purchase, by generous concession, an agreement which would obviate the danger of war.

As soon as he returned to office in 1895, Salisbury tried to dispose of that most thorny of problems, the Near Eastern question. Earlier, he had followed the Palmerston-Disraeli tradition of opposing the advance of Russia toward Constantinople, but he never completely subscribed to the policy. Ever-recurring and dangerous crises convinced him that the disintegration of Turkey was inevitable. He did not believe that the route to India would be menaced by Russian possession of Constantinople, and strategists were coming to agree with him. Finally, and this consideration seems to have induced him to act, affairs in the Near East disturbed domestic politics in England. At one moment, revulsion against Turkish cruelty led to demands that the Sultan's rule be ended; at another, fear of Russia overwhelmed humanitarian feelings. It was impossible to chart a consistent course in the face of such contradictory commands. In 1895 humanitarianism was for the moment dominant: Armenians were being massacred wholesale. Ignorant of the danger attendant upon isolated action in a region where the powers watched each other with morbid suspicion, public opinion called on the government to intervene. The Liberals were thrown out of office partly because they hesitated to step into the Turkish arena. As Salisbury said, he must do something if he was to hold his majority.

Probably, though not certainly, Salisbury was entirely honest in saying his only motive in opening the Near Eastern question was a desire to end the problem. Turkey, he maintained, was "too rotten" to last much longer; if Europe waited until the Sick Man passed away in a chaos of revolution, there would certainly be disputes, probably a war, over the spoils. Why not arrange to divide the inheritance before Turkey's death-throes began? The argument was sensible. Russia had been using it for half a century, but it sounded strange coming from London. Continental statesmen exhausted their ingenuity in an effort to account for the revolution in British policy. The general conclusion was that Salisbury wished to end the united pressure of France, Germany, and Russia on England's Imperial supremacy by diverting attention to the Near East, where the Continental powers were sure to begin quarreling with each other. This conclusion was probably unwarranted, but it was plausible. Salisbury's proposal met everywhere with a cool or hostile reception. For the first time, England had attempted to solve the problem which all knew held tragic danger for Europe; the British plan, like the earlier ones of Russia, foundered on the suspicions of the powers. Even Russia held back from the proposal, which she would earlier have welcomed. The Tsar was anxious to put the Balkans "on ice" for the present.

The Far East now monopolized Russia's attention. Earlier in the century the Russians had reached the Pacific and established a naval base at Vladivostok. In 1891 the Trans-Siberian Railway was begun. Plans were made for the conquest of the border provinces of China—Tibet, Turkestan, Mongolia, and Manchuria—and of Korea as well. Why the provinces were wanted, it is hard to say. Russia's Asiatic provinces were sparsely inhabited; her commerce demanded no new ports; her resources were needed for the internal development of her existing possessions. Here, as so frequently in Russian history, insensate and insatiable land-hunger seems the only force back of her foreign policy.

In 1895 Japan momentarily threatened the Russian program. As a result of a victorious war against China, the Japanese had, by the Treaty of Shimonoseki, acquired control over the Liaotung peninsula, with the magnificent harbor of Port Arthur dominating the approaches to Peking. Russia, aided by France and Germany, intervened and forced the Japanese to surrender their conquests on the mainland. The Russians, believing all opposition had been overcome, advanced confidently. Concession after concession was wrested from the weak and bankrupt Peking government in exchange for loans.

The Russians interpreted Salisbury's effort to open the Near Eastern question as an attempt to divert Russian attention from the Far East. The interpretation was only partly correct. English influence had long been supreme in Peking; England had almost a monopoly on the trade of northern China. The sudden and successful intrusion of Russia aroused resentment and fear in England. "If the panic that has seized the Lancashire cotton industry as to its Chinese markets goes on in this way," wrote a member of the cabinet, "we shall soon have the greater part of the mills stopped and their hands out of work." The government was called on to do something. Salisbury was reluctant to threaten when he did not mean to fight; such threats rarely produced positive results, and usually cheapened the value of future threats. Therefore, like a good business man, he tried to make terms with Russia. In 1895 he suggested a deal over Turkey. Undaunted by the rebuff he had received then, he tried again two years later.

The occasion was the seizure of a north China port, Kiauchow, by Germany. German influence was also growing in Turkey. Russia resented German intrusion into two areas she had reserved for herself. Salisbury decided to take advantage of this resentment. In January, 1898, he proposed an understanding over China and Turkey where "Russia and England are constantly opposed, neutralizing each other's efforts much more frequently than the real antagonism of their interests would justify." Might a "partition of preponderance" be arranged? Japan was also anxious to buy off Russia, offering a free hand in Manchuria in exchange for Korea. Here was a golden opportunity for Russia to realize the greater part of her ambitions without fighting. Aggressive advisers had the ear of the Tsar. The English and Japanese offers were rejected. As "compensation" for the acquisition of Kiauchow by Germany, China was forced to lease Port Arthur to Russia. Port Arthur not only put Peking at the mercy of Russia; it was also the gateway to Manchuria. The possibility of restraining Russia peaceably seemed more remote than ever, and the British showed their realization that a base for armed operations might be necessary by securing a lease on Weihaiwei, across the Bay of Chihli from Port Arthur.

Salisbury continued to hope that Russia could be restrained without involving England in war. There were at least three grounds for optimism: the attitude of Japan, the attitude of the United States, and the possibility that Russia might go bankrupt. If she felt victory possible, Japan would undoubtedly oppose the Russians. She had not forgotten the way her fruits of victory were snatched away in 1895, and her memory was painfully refreshed when Russia took Port Arthur, the very port of which Japan had been deprived three years before. The Japanese said nothing, but they were obviously arming rapidly. In the future they might be useful to England.

The Americans might also be induced to take an active interest in Chinese affairs. For years the British had been trying to eradicate the traditional American feelings of mistrust and dislike of England. The way had been paved by a graceful retreat on the Venezuelan boundary question, and a willing collaborator was found in John Hay, who came to London as ambassador in 1897. The Spanish-American War crowned British efforts with success. The Continental press was strongly anti-American, the British press almost solidly on the side of the United States. In order to heighten the value of their friendship, English diplomats dropped dire hints of an impending Continental alliance against the United States, under the leadership of Germany. As usual, German blunders, such as that of Admiral Diedrichs at Manila Bay, made a sinister interpretation of German motives possible. Hay wrote in July, 1898: "I have been under great obligation the last few months to Spring-Rice [a British diplomat], who knows Germany as few men do and has kept me wonderfully *au courant* of facts and opinions there. *Voilà l'ennemi* in the present crisis. The jealousy and animosity felt toward us in Germany is something which can hardly be exaggerated." Having conjured up the specter of Continental intervention, England rushed to the rescue. "Terrible as war may be," declaimed Chamberlain, "even war itself would be cheaply purchased if, in a great and noble cause, the Stars and Stripes and the Union Jack should wave together over an Anglo-Saxon alliance." Late in 1898 Hay became Secretary of State. He and President Mc Kinley were impressed by the possibilities for commercial expansion in the Far East, now that the Philippines were in America's hands. If European states extended their spheres of influence in China, American commerce would be hampered by hostile tariff barriers. To avert this peril, the American government sought to obtain recognition of the principle of equality of commercial rights. In 1899, Hay invited the powers to adhere to the doctrine of the "open door." England agreed; other states sent more or less sympathetic replies. Only Russia held back completely. How far would the United States go to prevent the partitioning of China? No one knew. After the war with Spain the American temper showed a strange mixture of blatant imperialism and ardent pacifism.

Most Englishmen feared that Japan and the United States would hesitate to challenge Russia, but for a time there seemed ground for hope that the Tsar would be forced by lack of money to abandon his ambitious plans. The hope was raised by a circular letter sent to the powers by Nicholas II in 1898, proposing an international conference to consider the questions of disarmament and the peaceful settlement of disputes between nations. At the time, the proclamation was generally regarded as a confession of impending bankruptcy. In reality, the Tsar's motives were idealistic, but that fact did not foreshadow any change in Russian policy: the unstable mind of Nicholas II could entertain dreams of world peace and world conquest simultaneously. The conference met at The Hague in 1899. With a unanimity which was almost enthusiastic, the proposal to discuss limitation of armaments was voted down. On the question of arbitration, France and Germany were skeptical. American and British insistence resulted in the creation of a permanent court of arbitration, but with powers so slight that its subsequent influence was negligible. In truth, the first Hague conference merely served to throw into glaring relief the fact that no great power was, at the end of the nineteenth century, prepared to permit the slightest restriction on its independence of action in the field of foreign affairs.

When it became apparent that the Tsar's pacifistic proclamation meant no falling-off in Russia's expansionist ambitions, disillusion with Salisbury's policy spread in England. After four years of effort, he had nothing better to show than a port England did not want. Russia was practically supreme in Manchuria; her agents were busy in Tibet and Korea. All efforts at compromise had failed, and, despite Salisbury's continued confidence, seemed bound to fail. Even within Salisbury's cabinet the conviction was strong that the alternatives were retreat before Russia or a firm stand in alliance with Japan and, if possible, Germany.

4. THE BEGINNING OF GERMAN WELTPOLITIK

Formerly, when hard pressed by France and Russia, England had sought safety in coöperation with the Triple Alliance. After 1895, England, Italy, and Austria would have been glad to continue the old relationship. Germany refused, partly because the old basis for coöperation had disappeared, partly because invincible mistrust of England prevailed in Berlin.

In seeking to win an alliance with England after 1890, William II had disregarded not only the traditional German view of British policy, but common sense as well. As late as 1889, Salisbury said plainly that England did not want an alliance. In spite of this warning, the Kaiser embarked on a policy which helped to push Russia into the arms of France but did not bring England into the Triple Alliance. After 1892, when the Liberals came into office, the Germans discovered their mistake. Liberalism was not merely a domestic party creed to Gladstone; it was a moral principle of universal validity. Austria and Germany, as conservative empires, were "foes of freedom." He refused to consort with them. Naturally, his aloofness caused alarm and suspicion in Germany, especially since it coincided with the formation of the Franco-Russian alliance. It never occurred to the Germans that they were to blame. Bismarck had taught them to see only hypocrisy in British liberalism, so they disregarded the simple explanation that Gladstone did not like Germany. They attributed the failure of their plans to British perfidy: England had set out in 1890 to separate Germany from Russia; the task accomplished, English friendship cooled. Further proof of British treachery was seen in Salisbury's attempt to dispose of the Near Eastern question in 1895. The reasons he gave for his changed policy were denounced as hypocritical. His real objective, according to the Germans, was to divert the attention of the Continental powers from the colonial field by making them quarrel with each other over Turkey.

It was Holstein's morbid imagination which found these explanations for the action of Gladstone and Salisbury. Fear that Germany might be made a cat's-paw "to pull English chestnuts out of the fire" became an obsession with him, an obsession which the whole German government came to share. While this mood prevailed, loyal coöperation was impossible between the two governments. After his rebuff in 1895, Salisbury sensed the situation and made no attempt to revive the cordial relations which had prevailed during his earlier administrations.

Another and equally serious barrier to a resumption of the older relationship was the abandonment of Bismarck's thesis that Germany was a satiated, Continental state. Germany's commerce was world-wide; her industry was gaining markets in Asia, in Africa, in the Americas. The "backward" countries were rapidly being partitioned; each acquisition was marked off for economic as well as political monopoly by the conquering power. William II and his advisers felt they must acquire colonies and spheres of influence commensurate with Germany's economic strength and population. To be sure, there was scarcely a corner of the globe which was not either actually or tacitly claimed by some one else. The United States stood guard over North and South America. England, France, and Russia stood guard over Asia and Africa, and while they might quarrel among themselves, they resented the intrusion of another contestant.

Nevertheless, the Germans hoped to make off with a share of the spoils. Their confidence grew out of the conviction that England and the Dual Alliance were enemies beyond hope of reconciliation. England, they believed, was not strong enough to cope with the united force of France and Russia; but the strength of the contestants seemed so evenly balanced that the German sword would be decisive if thrown on either side. "No one in Europe can accomplish anything without our help," exulted William II. The temptation was strong to take a definite stand. Sometimes he toyed with the idea of a Continental alliance to end British arrogance, but the French were never willing to pay the price he asked: recognition of the settlement of 1871. Sometimes he courted England: if the British were willing to join the Triple Alliance, he would take their side. Neither Britain nor France would meet the terms imposed, but the Germans were in no hurry. When the inevitable clash came, both sides would seek support in Berlin. Until then, concessions might be wrung from each contestant by the threat to join the opposition. The game was safe: the enmity between

England and the Dual Alliance was irreconcilable. Different
methods were to be used in dealing with each faction. The
Dual Alliance was thought to be stronger than England and
therefore less in need of aid. Furthermore, there was always
the danger that Continental problems might once more come
to the fore and deprive Germany of her position as balance-
wheel. Obviously, France and Russia must be conciliated.
Not so England. Blinded to present dangers by past triumphs, Britain had refused the friendly hand put forward
by William II in 1890, and persistently refused to recognize
her dependence on Germany. Kindness had failed; harsher
methods were needed. The Germans set out to coerce England into recognition of her precarious position.

At the end of 1895 the Germans thought they saw an
opportunity at once to teach England a lesson, and to
strengthen their position in South Africa. Trouble had long
been brewing between England and the quasi-independent
Boer states. William II watched the quarrel eagerly and
encouraged President Kruger to count on German support.
Then, in December, 1895, came news that Dr. Jameson was
advancing on the Transvaal with a band of armed followers,
determined to establish British sovereignty. Continental
opinion denounced the high-handed proceeding. At
Holstein's suggestion, the German government asked the
other Continental states to join in concerted opposition to
England. William II was in a bellicose mood, and wished
to make a show of force; but his advisers restrained him.
Even after it became known that the Jameson raid had
failed, the Kaiser insisted on making public his attitude
toward the raid. On January 3, 1896, he sent a telegram to
President Kruger congratulating the Boers on their success
in repelling the invasion "without making any appeal for
the help of friendly powers." The response of England was
prompt. Salisbury flatly denied the right of Germany to
interfere in the British quarrel with the Boers, and mobilized a squadron in the Channel to show his readiness to
accept the German challenge. Italian and Austrian sympathies were with England. France and Russia looked on with

frank pleasure. The project for a Continental union disappeared from sight. Salisbury's confidence that conflicting interests would prevent common action by the Continent was justified. By the middle of January, 1896, Germany stood humiliated and isolated.

The Germans were undaunted by their failure and proceeded apace with new and better-laid plans. The squadron mobilized by the British in answer to the Kruger telegram showed the difficulty of opposition to England without sea power. The German fleet was almost ludicrously small in proportion to the commerce of the empire. In 1897, Admiral Tirpitz was appointed head of the Imperial navy and instructed to remedy this defect. He was admirably fitted for the task. In addition to great executive capacity, he possessed the tact and strength of will necessary to influence William II. Above all, he was a clever and not too scrupulous propagandist. He flooded Germany with pamphlets, organized naval societies, encouraged research, and presented the issue to public opinion in a thousand ways. All his ingenuity was necessary, for the members of the Reichstag, trained in the Bismarckian tradition, were reluctant to add large naval expenditures to the already tremendous military budget. Tirpitz soon discovered that the easiest way to achieve success was by intensifying the dislike of England which prevailed in Germany. Undeterred by the danger of antagonizing the British, Tirpitz pointed the guns of the new navy at England. His campaign was successful; in 1898 and 1900 large construction programs were authorized. The second bill indicated England—"the adversary with the greatest sea power"—as the state against which protection was needed.

Not content with announcing that they intended to build a fleet which England would be afraid to challenge, the Germans invaded a field which Russia regarded as hers almost by divine right, the Near East. For years, Germans had been acquiring railroad concessions in Asia Minor. Now these projects were to be coördinated into one great scheme. The way was paved by a visit of the Kaiser to Turkey, where he dramatically announced himself the friend of the 300 millions of Mohammedans in the world. As a large proportion of these 300 millions were subjects of England, France, and Russia, his announcement caused some uneasiness. The immediate object of Germany was, however, obtained. Now that the British had forsaken him, Abdul Hamid was glad to have a new protector. He showed his appreciation in 1899 by approving the German project for a railroad from Constantinople to the Persian Gulf, the famous "Berlin-Byzantium-Bagdad" railroad.

The Kaiser was convinced that England and the Dual Alliance could not unite to oppose effectively his great program of expansion; but he knew that some opposition, possibly dangerous, was to be expected. To steer Germany through the troubled waters that lay ahead, the ambassador at Rome, Bülow, was brought back to Berlin and made Foreign Secretary in 1897. Bülow was incapable either of performing the difficult task entrusted to him or of persuading the Kaiser to abandon his too ambitious program. Bülow possessed intelligence and a ready wit which enabled him to shine in Reichstag debates, but these gifts were vitiated by ambition and lack of seriousness. During the dozen years he held power, his actions show no higher objective than the desire to remain in office and to slide out of each difficulty as it appeared. To retain the Imperial favor, he resorted to flattery which acted like heady wine on William II, who was already prone to grandiose dreams. To extricate himself from one dilemma, Bülow made concessions and promises which led to others, which he hoped to overcome in turn by his mental agility. "An oiled eel is a leech compared with Bülow," complained Tirpitz, with justice. For ten years Bülow drifted with the tide, without a policy of his own, accepting the policy laid down before he took office or following the plausible but disastrous advice of Holstein, condoning or abetting the vagaries of William II, always confident and giving confidence to others. Then, when disaster loomed so clear that it could not be concealed, he tried in a few months to repair the damage he had done, or permitted others to do, and paid for his temerity with his office.

During Bülow's first years, nothing seemed more remote than German isolation, nothing more probable than a clash between England and the Dual Alliance. In 1897, the murder of certain German missionaries enabled Germany to wrest from China a lease on the port of Kiauchow and commercial privileges in the Shantung peninsula. In 1898, England was forced to agree that, if financial difficulties compelled Portugal to mortgage her colonies, Germany would share in the spoils. In 1899, the partition of the Samoan islands gave Germany a base in the South Seas. Shipyards were busily constructing the fleet which was to ensure for Germany her "place in the sun"; in Asia Minor a path of steel rails was opening the way for commercial, and possibly political, expansion. Chamberlain in 1898 proposed an Anglo-German alliance; France seemed to have forgotten Alsace in her hatred of England; Kaiser and Tsar exchanged intimate notes in bad English signed "Willy" and "Nicky." Bülow promised his master he would soon be "the arbiter of the world." William tried to speed the day by intensifying the hatred between England and the Dual Alliance, and by half promising his support to both sides. With strange lack of imagination, the Kaiser failed to see that he was adopting the perfidious policy which he, filled with righteous indignation, accused the British of following. His speeches became increasingly exuberant, his metaphors more grandiose: the trident belongs in our hands; strike out with the mailed fist. What was the meaning of all this activity and boasting talk? In Paris, London, and St. Petersburg, even in Rome and Vienna, vague alarm appeared. Germany was getting on Europe's nerves.

5. THE BOER WAR AND THE BOXER REBELLION

By 1899 British faith in Salisbury's policy of isolation was fading; after 1899 it vanished. Fashoda, to judge by the bitter tone of the French press, had aroused implacable hatred of England; German diplomatic communications

were growing increasingly hostile; every spike driven into
the Trans-Siberian Railroad made Russia more arrogantly
self-confident. There were signs of revolt in Salisbury's
cabinet. In 1898 Chamberlain had, without the Prime Minister's authorization, suggested an alliance to the German
ambassador. The proposal came to nothing because the
Germans held back; but in negotiations over the Portuguese
colonies and Samoa, Salisbury was forced by the Chamberlain group to accept the German demands so that the way
might be kept open for an alliance. Then, in November,
1899, the quarrel between England and the Boers resulted
in war. The British entered light-heartedly into the struggle,
but a series of Boer victories brought rapid disillusionment
and fear which continued even after the tide began to turn
in England's favor. In the spring of 1900 a new danger
appeared. The hatred of foreigners, which had long been
growing among the Chinese, assumed violent form in the
Boxer Rebellion. The Peking government, after vacillating
for a time, joined the Boxers. Rioting spread through north
China; the legations were besieged; the German minister
was murdered. An international force took possession of
Peking and restored a semblance of order, but the situation
remained tense throughout the year. At any moment the
dismemberment of China might begin.

For the first time since Waterloo, the British were frightened. If the Boer republics were so hard to subdue, what
chance would England have, unaided, in a struggle with a
great power? Would the exposure of British military weakness tempt other powers to hostile action? The hatred which
British sea power aroused on the Continent was reflected
in the shouts of joy with which the Continental press hailed
every Boer victory, and in gleeful prophecies that three
centuries of British supremacy were ending in the ridiculous
anticlimax of defeat by a handful of farmers. Rumors of
impending intervention in favor of the Boers followed hard
on one another. Delcassé very confidentially said that Germany had proposed, and that France had declined, an alliance. The Kaiser confidentially told his English relatives

that Russia and France had suggested a coalition, but that he had refused to hear of any action hostile to England. Neither quite told the whole truth. The proposal for intervention had come from Russia; the Germans were willing to agree if France would publicly renounce the intention of regaining Alsace-Lorraine; the French refused to meet this requirement, and hence the negotiations collapsed. The British did not know the details. They were inclined to believe Delcassé, because he had not been caught lying to them as often as the Kaiser, but they did not greatly care who started or who rejected the project. The important fact was that there had been negotiations which might be revived later with greater success. The anti-isolationists became more insistent than ever that it was necessary to forestall a hostile coalition by buying off one of England's rivals before it was too late. The situation in the Far East added force to the arguments of Chamberlain and his followers. Russia obviously hoped to complete her control over Manchuria while China was distracted by the Boxer Rebellion. England, the United States, Japan, and Germany were anxious to preserve the *status quo,* but they were suspicious of one another. Like hunting dogs, they circled around the Russian bear, each afraid to make a spring for fear the others would hang back, afraid also that France might help her ally. No one in England had any stomach for a war with Russia while the British forces were locked up in South Africa, but Chamberlain believed a firm stand would avert war. To eliminate mutual mistrust, he advocated an alliance between England, Germany, and Japan.

Advancing age prevented Salisbury from offering effective opposition to his opponents in the cabinet. At the very beginning of the Boer War, Chamberlain made a public speech in which he called for the abandonment of isolation and maintained that "the natural alliance is between ourselves and the great German Empire." He got no encouragement from across the Channel; in fact, Bülow's reply in the Reichstag was chilling. Bülow was then trying to prepare public opinion for the second navy bill; the pro-Boer sentiment of the press was his best guarantee of success. He could not encourage the thought of an Anglo-German alliance while he was justifying the navy bill as protection against England. Bülow's snub silenced Chamberlain, but only temporarily. In October, 1900, bad health forced Salisbury to leave the Foreign Office. He remained Prime Minister, but left the direction of affairs more and more to his colleagues. The new Foreign Secretary, Lord Lansdowne, agreed with Chamberlain that England could no longer maintain her isolated position with safety. He also believed the best guarantee of safety in Europe lay in coöperation with Germany. In Asia he looked to Japan for support. During 1901 he tried to come to terms with both powers.

The negotiations with Germany were doomed to failure from the start. The Germans stood fast by the terms they had been making for the past decade: England must join the Triple Alliance. They believed anything less would damage, not improve, Germany's position. At the time, Germany was on good terms with Russia; alliance with England would necessarily turn that friendship into enmity. If the alliance were only a defensive Anglo-German agreement, the whole British Empire would be protected, but Germany would not be protected. If Russia wished to strike at Germany, she need only attack Austria. Germany must then aid Austria under the terms of the Triple Alliance, but England could remain neutral, claiming that Germany had not been attacked. It is impossible to tell how far Lansdowne would have been willing to go toward meeting the German position. Salisbury was still a force to be reckoned with. Hampered by his opposition, Lansdowne could propose nothing more definite than "an understanding with regard to the policy which they [the British and German governments] might pursue in reference to particular questions or in particular parts of the world in which they are alike interested." To the Germans, this sounded very like the entente which Gladstone had so lightly repudiated only a few years before. Their fingers had been burned once; now "it was a case of 'the whole or none.' " When Lansdowne decided that union with the Triple Alliance was "too big a fence to ride at," the negotiations collapsed, in December, 1901. Neither side took the failure very seriously. The Germans felt that their bargaining power would increase as England sank deeper in quarrels with France and Russia; the British felt an alliance with Japan would solve their problems.

The relations of England, the United States, and Japan between 1899 and 1904 show diplomacy in its most cynical character. Each mistrusted the others completely; yet they needed one another and must perforce coöperate. The Americans realized that "England is as great an offender in China as Russia itself," but for the time being the English were willing to support the "open door." The British feared the exuberant imperialism which developed in the United States after the war with Spain, but felt compelled to humor American wishes—concerning the Panama Canal, for instance. There was little love of Japan in either London or Washington, but Japanese ambitions might serve as a homœopathic cure for Russian ambitions. In 1901 a British diplomat argued that Japan should be permitted to seize Port Arthur as a guarantee "that there would be no reconciliation between Russia and Japan . . . The yellow danger would be kept in check by Russia, and the Russian danger by Japan." Roosevelt held similar views.

The Japanese knew why they were being courted, and they played their advantageous position in a way which showed that they had learned all the lessons European diplomats could teach. Negotiations for an Anglo-Japanese treaty began in 1901. At first the discussions between Lansdowne and Hayashi, the Japanese minister, made little progress. Japan insisted that the alliance be restricted to the Far East; England wished to include the Middle East. Japan wanted her claims to Korea recognized; England objected. The Japanese sent one of their leading statesmen to St. Petersburg with proposals for a settlement between Russia and Japan. His mission was a failure, but it frightened the British into agreement with the Japanese demands.

Under the terms of the alliance signed in January, 1902, if
either signatory should become involved in a war with one
power over China or Korea, the other promised neutrality.
Should, however, either be at war with two powers over
these areas, the other must join its ally. The special interests, political and economic, of Japan in Korea were recognized.

For a time it seemed that the alliance with Japan had
solved England's difficulties. Russia tried in vain to revive
the Far Eastern entente with France and Germany to offset
the Anglo-Japanese combination. The Germans politely ex-
cused themselves, saying that their interests in China were
economic and that the new alliance expressly guaranteed the
"open door." Delcassé reluctantly consented to a vague
declaration that the Dual Alliance was operative in the Far
East as well as in Europe; but he practically repudiated his
own words shortly afterward in a speech before the Cham-
ber of Deputies. In April, 1902, the Russians, finding
themselves completely isolated, promised to evacuate Manchuria within eighteen months. In May, 1902, the Boer War
was ended. Apparently the stormy diplomatic weather which
had prevailed since 1899 was about to give place to the usual
choppy seas. What move did Lansdowne contemplate next?
It was formerly believed that, after the collapse of negotiations with Germany, the British promptly turned to France.
The evidence we now possess does not substantiate the
traditional view. Rather, Lansdowne seemed content to
revert to the policy of isolation from the Continent, now
that fear of a Continental coalition had subsided. The French
hinted they would welcome an entente. Lansdowne turned
their offer aside.

In the summer of 1903 Lansdowne suddenly reversed his
stand and eagerly welcomed the French advances he had
earlier repulsed. The specter of a Continental coalition, so
recently banished, appeared in more threatening form than
ever before. England was convulsed by hatred of Germany.
The Germans were turning for safety toward the Dual
Alliance. To block a union of the Triple and Dual Alliances,

Lansdowne thought it necessary to make terms with France, and, if possible, Russia.

6. THE ANGLO-GERMAN FEUD

Antagonism between England and Germany had been growing, almost unperceived, for decades. Hatred took root first in Germany. Its seed was the Continental fetish: perfidious, hypocritical England, a country grown fat on the blood of neighbors who had been tricked into fighting her battles. The seed sprouted luxuriantly during the period of unification. British protests against Bismarck's methods, from the Schleswig-Holstein affair to the siege of Paris, were interpreted as evidence that England wished to keep Germany divided and impotent. In books, lectures, and seminars, the great nationalistic historians like Treitschke pointed to Britain as the sleepless, furtive enemy of a strong Germany, and of Europe. By the end of the century most educated Germans believed implicitly that ever since 1864 England had been on the enemy's side, and that she strove constantly to embroil the Continental nations in war in order to keep them weak. The dazzling triumphs of Bismarck led to worship of the qualities he affected—brutal frankness, naked strength, disdain of idealism and of disinterestedness. England's manners were at the same time moving toward urbanity, humanitarianism, gentleness. Cant, said the Germans, cant and symptoms of decadence resulting from too much ease and wealth. The old parasitic qualities, the old malevolent selfishness, continue to dominate British policy. So decided learned professors, and they lectured their English cousins on the error of their ways.

While censuring, the Germans resented censure. As a French diplomat once complained: "They are the most sensitive people in the world, and at the same time it would never enter into their heads that they could by any possibility be offensive themselves, although in reality they very often were." A plausible explanation for this lack of logic was offered by an unusually discerning German. "The majority of us Germans," he admitted, "cannot shake off the feeling that we belong to a parvenu nation, and therefore we are always on the lookout to see if any other nation is offering us some slight." William II was typical. He was proud, very proud, of the rich historical past and the present power of Germany; but it was not enough that he should recognize his country's worth. Others must also, and if recognition was not forthcoming he was filled with angry humiliation. At bottom he admired the English and craved their friendship and approbation. An enthusiastic reception in London made him exude good-will; a jeering cartoon in *Punch,* or a rebuff from the *Times,* and there were plenty of both, could arouse him to fury. To Queen Victoria he protested in his peculiar English that Salisbury seemed to care "for us no more than for Portugal, Chili, or the Patagonians." He was outraged by "the high-handed, disdainful treatment of ministers who had never even come over to stay in or to study Germany and hardly have taken the trouble to understand her people." At the end came the inevitable threat: "The government of Lord Salisbury must learn to respect and to treat us as equals; as long as he cannot be brought to do that, Germany's People will always remain distrustful, and a sort of coolness will be the unavoidable result." William II was more naïve than most of his subjects, and expressed his feelings of wounded pride with unique lack of sophistication, but similar emotions are at the bottom of much German raillery at England.

Neither Bismarck nor his successors did anything to cure this state of mind. On the contrary, Bismarck taught the Germans the perilous belief that if they were only nasty enough, England would come to heel. His violent treatment of Gladstone in the colonial controversies of 1884 seemed proof that harsh methods brought success, were the only means of attaining success when dealing with London. After 1890, in his desperate search for weapons with which to take vengeance on William II, Bismarck did not scruple to throw the enormous weight of his prestige on the side of the Anglophobes. In the columns of the Hamburg *Nachrichten* and other journals he harped constantly on the theme that William II had sacrificed Russian friendship to curry favor with perfidious Albion. The success of his campaign became apparent when the Kaiser tired of courting England and began opposing her. The Kruger telegram was the first act of William II to win almost universal approbation in Germany. Thereafter the hymn of hate waxed ever more loud and shrill. In every colonial quarrel British jealousy of Germany's growing strength was seen; navy propagandists preached now fear of an attack, now the hope of ending British arrogance. With the Boer War came the strident climax: to Germans, the attack of England on humble, God-fearing, peaceful Boers, showed the brutal rapacity of British policy. Bülow used and encouraged the hatred of Britain in order to secure the passage of the second navy bill. Even as he pressed the campaign, he was frightened, not of the force of German opinion—he had profound contempt for German public opinion—but of the effect this clamor must have in England. However, England needed Germany; and the future could be cared for in the future.

By 1900, hate was growing rapidly in England also, where public opinion, at least opinion of the large educated minority, was able to dictate policy. The rise of "the German menace" is hard to trace, because the views even of individual Englishmen did not form a consistent picture. At first, a larger or smaller part of the picture usually included such things as beer-gardens, bad smells, sentimental music, sugary domestic life, and the stuffy courts of princelings. This Germany was personified by a fat, good-natured, rather stupid-looking fellow, wearing shapeless clothes and accompanied by his *Hausfrau,* who looked for all the world like a large sack of flour with a string tied about its middle. The Germans indignantly asserted this was the whole picture of Germany as seen by England. Unfortunately for Anglo-German relations, it was not. Justly or unjustly, the methods by which Bismarck effected German unification caused a revulsion of feeling which was never completely overcome. Methodical brutality, trickery, and Machiavellian cleverness were always expected from Germany. While the

Conservatives were in office this mistrust made no great difference; they felt able to avoid pitfalls. The Liberals, on the other hand, felt themselves to be strong in character but weak in shrewdness; they gave the rulers of Germany credit for far more cleverness than any people ever possessed but denied them any moral rectitude whatsoever.

Sometime after 1880 a new German appeared: the trader. Soon British manufacturers and shippers were lamenting the inroads of Germans "in quarters where our trade formerly enjoyed a practical monopoly." Dispassionate observers recognized that the spread of the industrial movement made it inevitable that British economic supremacy should be challenged. In both countries the greatest industrialists thought friendly relations essential to their own economic interests. Such objectivity could not be expected from the manufacturer who watched with dismay the steady decline of his profits and the growing prosperity of his German rivals. In his exasperation he forgot that Germany was one of Britain's best customers and became convinced, with the *Saturday Review,* that every Englishman would be richer if Germany were wiped from the face of the earth. Naturally, he did not wish to feel that his rancor arose from jealousy, so he sought other reasons for disliking Germany. He was likely to indulge in the tasteless ridicule which infuriated the Germans. He pointed in alarm at the huge German army, forgetful of the huge British fleet. He, with Gladstone, felt that German autocracy was at once an anachronism and a menace to those blessings of human freedom which, he believed, a discerning Providence had planted in England, whence they were to spread to the furthermost parts of the globe.

Until after 1893 dislike of Germany was nebulous, undefined. England and Germany, except for brief interruptions, were close friends politically; that is, they had common enemies, and their interests did not clash violently. After 1893 the situation changed rapidly. The British could not adjust themselves to the fact that Germany was a colonial power. The rules of the colonial game took for granted established empires. New territory was built out from old, claimed because it was adjacent, or necessary for defense and communication. The Germans were just beginning. They could not conform to the rules of the game, because the territory around their existing colonies was already claimed by other powers. The Germans expected England to help them, partly because the British already had most of the choice parts of the world and could afford to be generous, partly because England was thought to need German aid against the Dual Alliance. The English had other ideas. They had nearly all the territory they wanted, so they tended to identify perpetuation of the *status quo* with "the general desires and ideals common to all mankind." If new spoils were to be divided, they wished to follow the old rules, which were favorable to them. Certainly, they had no intention of forfeiting what they thought their fair share. Each government refused to see the other's point of view. Friction inevitably resulted. The Germans became ever more violent in their efforts to force England to a realization that she must give way. The British came to feel that "the actions of Germany toward this country since 1890 might be likened not inappropriately to that of a professional blackmailer whose extortions are wrung from his victims by the threat of some vague and terrible consequences in case of a refusal."

The details of colonial quarrels were known only to the small, though influential, groups who moved in the highest political circles. The rantings of German newspapers and publicists, on the other hand, were known to all. After 1895, the *Times* became anti-German. It was the most powerful newspaper in England on questions of foreign policy, and the quotations it gave from Anglophobe German writings attracted more and more attention. The passionately, even scurrilously, pro-Boer attitude of German opinion aroused resentment which was the deeper because England's position was too perilous to permit its expression. At the end of 1901, when the war was practically over, all restraint vanished. For months a press quarrel of unrivaled bitterness raged despite governmental efforts to call a halt. In March, 1902, the German ambassador declared that he "wouldn't give two pence for Anglo-German relations." The governments remained calm, and late in that year sought to relieve the strain by coöperating in a naval demonstration against Venezuela. This merely widened the breach. The furious protests in England against any friendly dealings with "the Goth and the frightful Hun" were described by Lansdowne as extraordinary and outrageous.

Worse was to follow. In April, 1903, the full force of British hatred for Germany became apparent during the Bagdad Railroad negotiations. In the preceding year the Sultan had finally confirmed the concession for a railroad to unite Constantinople and the Persian Gulf and had promised large subsidies to aid the construction. In order to make the grant effective, the consent of other powers was necessary, because the subsidies were to come from an increase in Turkish customs duties, which were fixed by international agreement. Further, the Deutsche Bank, which was financing the road, felt that sufficient capital could be secured only if financiers of other countries were given a share in the under-taking. At first everything went smoothly; both France and England were disposed to coöperate. When, however, Balfour intimated in the House of Commons that the government was considering the German proposals favorably, vehement opposition was voiced not only in the press but also in Parliament. Every conceivable adverse argument, sensible and foolish, was played up; but it was obvious that sheer hatred of Germany was back of it all. Government and financiers alike scurried for cover; England refused to aid the railroad in any way. Shortly afterward Delcassé, possibly under pressure from St. Petersburg, also declined to participate. There is irony in the situation: British opponents of Germany had blocked an arrangement which would have permitted England, France, and Russia to oust the Germans from control of the road. Later the Germans were to be glad the negotiations had failed; but at the time they were alarmed and disconcerted. For the first time Wilhelmstrasse realized that there was danger of isolation.

Even yet the antagonism was not really dangerous. With tact on both sides the storm might have passed if the British scaremongers had not discovered a terrifying bogey in the growing German fleet. British hatred of Germany was not caused, as many maintain, by the fleet. Hatred existed before popular attention was drawn to ship-building activities across the North Sea. In 1903 the German navy was too small to alarm dispassionate Englishmen; even when the construction authorized by the German law of 1900 was completed, British supremacy would be overwhelming. Naval rivalry did not cause the quarrel: it intensified and made permanent the suspicion and fear which might otherwise have been overcome. As the British government knew, there was no reason for alarm in 1903; but in its already excited state British public opinion was easily thrown by the alarmists into hysterical fear of a surprise attack. The hold of the Conservative ministry on the country was weak. After resisting the popular clamor as long as it dared, the government was forced, apparently against its better judgment, to give way. At the end of 1903 the establishment of a new naval base at Rosyth in Scotland and the strengthening of the North Sea squadron were announced. Tirpitz had pointed his guns at England; the British naval front was now turned toward Germany. The calamitous race was on. What would Germany's next move be? The Kaiser had often threatened to join forces with France and Russia. English hostility offered him strong reasons for doing so.

7. THE ENTENTE CORDIALE

The Anglo-German quarrel came at an inopportune moment for Lansdowne. During 1903 it became apparent that Russia had been only temporarily chastened by the Anglo-Japanese Alliance. The more moderate of the Tsar's advisers were in favor of abandoning the forward policy until the Russian finances and army could be strengthened;

but the "Easterners" fought these "defeatist" ideas with tenacity and success. In March, 1903, Kuropatkin, the Minister of War, wrote: "Our Tsar has grandiose plans in his head to capture Manchuria for Russia and to annex Korea. He is dreaming also of bringing Tibet under his dominion. He desires to take Persia, and to seize not only the Bosphorus, but also the Dardanelles." Despite the promise of April, 1902, Russian troops were not removed from Manchuria. Instead, soldiers disguised as lumbermen began to penetrate northern Korea. Simultaneously, the activities of Russian agents in Persia, Afghanistan, and Tibet were redoubled. In an effort to force Russia to terms, Lansdowne, early in 1903, sharply asserted British claims to supremacy in the Persian Gulf. Later in the year his words were reinforced by a naval demonstration, designed to bring home the power of Britain to chieftains who might be inclined to listen to Russian blandishments. For the same purpose, the London government decided to send a military expedition to Tibet.

Despite their brave words, the British and the Japanese as well were anxious to prevent a war. The Japanese would have been willing to leave Russian influence paramount in Manchuria if Korea were left to them. In November, 1903, the British offered an entente on all outstanding problems. These offers were interpreted as signs of weakness in St. Petersburg. Disgusted, the Japanese decided on war.

As each passing month brought war between Russia and Japan nearer, the British became increasingly alarmed. They had anticipated nothing but profit from the alliance with Japan; when it was signed there seemed little likelihood that England would ever be called upon to fulfil her promise of support to Japan. By 1903 a world war was possible. Not only might France aid Russia: Germany might also, if there was anything in the persistent rumors which reached London. The old specter of a Continental coalition reappeared in more menacing form than ever before.

The French had earlier resisted all efforts to unite the Triple and Dual Alliances, because the friendship of Germany could be purchased only by acknowledging that Alsace and Lorraine were irretrievably lost. Since 1898, however, French and German newspapers had coöperated enthusiastically in execrating the British. Furthermore, in 1903 Lansdowne was faced with the alternatives of further estranging France or conciliating her. Cromer, the British agent in Egypt, reported that the financial fetters on the Egyptian treasury had become intolerable and must be removed. The Sultan of Morocco, a British puppet, was threatened by rebels; armed intervention was necessary if he was to be retained in power. Any effort to strengthen the British position in either Egypt or Morocco would provoke an outburst of feeling in France, possibly sufficient to obliterate the memory of 1871. Under the circumstances, Lansdowne decided to placate France, even at the cost of Morocco. An Anglo-French understanding would obviate the possibility of a Continental alliance, and thus lessen the chances that England would be forced to aid Japan against Russia. An understanding would also, the British hoped, "not improbably be the precursor to a better understanding with Russia."

Fortune had been kind to Delcassé. For five years he had waited patiently for the opportunity which came at last in 1903. Despite the Anglophobe tone of the French press, the whirligig of French politics, propelled by the Dreyfus case and the consequent rise of anti-monarchical and anti-militaristic feeling, made each cabinet more radical and less imperialistic. The radicals were so pacific that they speedily lowered discipline and efficiency in the army and navy. By conviction and by necessity the radicals were glad to avoid trouble with England. They also dreamed of an amicable understanding with Germany over Alsace-Lorraine; but their efforts to awaken enthusiasm for a compromise aroused the ire of chauvinists on both sides of the Rhine and thereby made *revanche* a live issue for the first time in many years. Delcassé was neither an idealist nor a pacifist. He was, in his own words, a practical politician; and practical politics, as he saw the situation, demanded that France keep out of the Far Eastern imbroglio, awake from her "Egyptian dreams," concentrate her attention on the gap in the Vosges, and wait for something to happen. In seeking an understanding with England, Delcassé's "practical" aims and the "idealistic" aims of the French ministry coincided. By 1903 both governments were anxious for an accord, but public opinion, particularly in France, was accustomed to enmity. The tact of Edward VII, and the popularity he had acquired in France when he was Prince of Wales, now proved invaluable. In May, 1903, he visited Paris. At first he was received coldly, but before he left the tone changed to enthusiasm. In July, President Loubet was warmly received in England. With the way thus prepared, negotiations proceeded rapidly to a successful conclusion.

The Anglo-French agreement of April 8, 1904, dealt with all the varied questions which had vexed relations between the two countries for generations: spheres of influence in Siam, British rights in Madagascar, French fishing rights in Newfoundland, West African boundaries, and other minor causes of trouble. Most important was the declaration by which France finally gave England a free hand in Egypt and received in return a promise that French action in Morocco would not be impeded by England. The French declared "that they have no intention of altering the political status of Morocco," and the British gave a similar promise in regard to Egypt. So much for the public façade. On the same day, Lansdowne and Cambon signed secret agreements promising diplomatic support in case England should wish to extend her control over Egypt, or France to advance in Morocco.

Was the entente aimed at Germany? No definite answer can be given. Widely divergent interpretations of the known facts are possible, even inevitable. Probably the negotiators preferred not to examine their own motives too closely; and few European statesmen, except possibly the Russians, ever talked in terms of aggression. Delcassé, through his confidant, Étienne, placed the negotiations on a strictly "defensive" basis, saying that "the most serious menace to the

peace of Europe lay in Germany, and that a good understanding between France and England was the only means
of holding German designs in check." This, however, is the
conventional language of diplomacy. It is unsafe to under-
estimate the importance of such language, because it deceives
not only the hearer, but also the speaker himself, and
enables him to act with all the fervor of moral righteousness. Nevertheless, some at least of the British Conservatives
were unable to prevent themselves from looking behind
Delcassé's stated motives, and what they saw made them
uneasy. Cromer, for instance, felt that "it is manifestly in
French interests that we should fall out with Germany,"
and that "one of the main attractions" of the proposed
entente for Delcassé was the hope of isolating Germany.
Almost certainly Cromer was right in thinking Delcassé
was looking for trouble. He was frankly an advocate of
revanche. He knew Germany was interested in Morocco; he
knew also that there would be trouble if France tried to take
Morocco without a previous agreement with Germany. He
bought off England, Italy, and Spain. He ostentatiously
avoided any discussion with Germany. It is difficult to escape
the conclusion that his attitude was deliberately provocative.

Delcassé was, however, not representative of France, not
even of the French government. Many Frenchmen swallowed the entente with a wry face. Hatred of England died
hard; Fashoda was still a painful memory. Even the dominant radicals were becoming suspicious of Delcassé. They
welcomed the truce with England because they wished to
keep out of colonial adventures and concentrate on internal
affairs, but they were equally anxious for peace with Germany. The army was disorganized by the efforts to end
aristocratic control over the officers' corps. Internal politics
were envenomed by the fight against clericalism. Above all,
no aid could be expected from Russia. The long-impending
war between Russia and Japan began in February, 1904. No
matter what its issue, Russia would be in no position to put
up an effective fight against Germany for many years to

come. Evidently Delcassé could count on little popular support if he tried to make trouble with Germany.

It is hard to decide what the entente meant to Englishmen. It was received with almost universal enthusiasm. Among some groups the enthusiasm undoubtedly had a definitely anti-German foundation: the *Times* exultantly rubbed in the isolation and the precarious position of Germany. On the whole, Englishmen seemed to be rejoicing at freedom regained. For years their country had been subjected to a cross-fire from Russia, France, and Germany. No escape seemed possible; concessions must be made to all. Now one enemy had made terms. The fear that France would aid her Russian ally in the Far Eastern struggle, and thereby force England into war, was dissipated. With France a friend and Russia thoroughly occupied with Japan, Germany would no longer dare to bluster and threaten. The nerve-wracking siege was over; Britain was free once more. So thought most Englishmen. Downing Street knew this view was too simple: states do not, like individuals, suddenly cease quarreling and become friends through generosity of spirit. There is not a shred of evidence that Lansdowne and his colleagues wished to form a coalition against Germany; there is every indication that they dreaded the thought of being embroiled in Continental rivalries. At the same time, Lansdowne could not help seeing the germ of a quarrel with Germany in the promise to help France get Morocco. The French were honest. They made no secret either of their determination to exclude Germany from any voice in Moroccan affairs, or of their expectation that England was to help them in this task. France had not so much chosen England for a friend, as Germany for an enemy. In all probability, France would remain loyal to her British "friends" only so long as they were willing to support her when disputes arose with Germany. This was not the freedom the English people believed they had gained; it was perilously close to servitude. Lansdowne realized the implications of the secret agreement over Morocco; the fact that he was willing to compromise British freedom of action so dangerously shows conclusively the anxiety with which he viewed the international situation.

For ten years, from 1894 to 1904, England had hesitated. When the Franco-Russian Alliance completed the division of the Continent into two rival groups, it seemed that England would now more than ever before hold the balance between these two groups. Unfortunately for British peace of mind, Continental problems fell into the background. Imperialism held the center of the stage. France, Russia, and Germany pushed forward relentlessly, confidently, into areas where Britain had formerly been supreme. Could England check the advance unaided? Salisbury believed she could. Until the end of the century he put up a gallant and, on the whole, successful fight. Many Englishmen did not share his confidence. They thought, even as things stood, that England's fight was a losing one. Worse, they feared a coalition of the three great Continental powers. Both to ease the pressure on England and to avert a hostile coalition, they wished to agree on a territorial settlement and on a common policy, with at least one rival. Germany refused to make terms; France consented. The price England had to pay was Morocco—not merely to abandon British claims, but to help France get Morocco. That promise might mean trouble with Germany. England was no longer free. She was, to an indefinite extent, bound to France.

England was no longer the balance-wheel, but the Germans had not succeeded in securing the position she had vacated. They had staked everything on the thesis that the conflict of interests between England and the Dual Alliance was irreconcilable. For a time their confidence seemed justified. By the Bagdad Railroad concession they opened the way for expansion in the Near East; naval bases were secured in China and the South Seas. Then the balance began to shift. France and England drew together, and announced their intention of completing the entente by reconciling England and Russia. The Germans knew the Anglo-French entente impaired their position. Isolation loomed ahead. Even the foundation of German Continental strength, the Triple Alliance, was growing weaker.

The waning prestige of Germany could be charted with almost mathematical accuracy by the drift of Italian policy. In 1898 the most bitter phase of Franco-Italian hostility was ended when the economic relations of the two countries, long a source of trouble, were adjusted by a commercial treaty. Two years later notes were exchanged very vaguely recognizing that Tripoli lay within the Italian, and Morocco within the French, sphere of influence. By 1902, Italy was playing fast and loose with both sides. Her growing intimacy with France was used to extort concessions when the Triple Alliance was renewed. The old treaty was continued unchanged, but by a separate protocol Austria and Germany promised to support Italian claims to Tripoli, while Austria gave assurances that a commercial treaty favorable to Italy would be negotiated. Almost simultaneously, Italy promised France to remain neutral, even if France "as a result of direct provocation, should find herself compelled, in defense of her honor or her security, to take the initiative of a declaration of war." Later in the year, by another exchange of notes, the earlier Franco-Italian agreement on Tripoli and Morocco was made more definite. During the two years following, Italy moved, step by step, toward the Anglo-French group, and away from the Triple Alliance. When President Loubet visited Rome in 1904, he was greeted like the ruler of an allied state. Little wonder that the Italian Foreign Minister later admitted he found the obligations of Italy to France and the Triple Alliance "difficult to reconcile"! The Germans were alarmed, but they did not despair. They continued to hope for a revival of the antagonism between England and the Dual Alliance which had been so profitable to Germany.

CHAPTER IV

TRIPLE ALLIANCE AND TRIPLE ENTENTE, 1904–1911

CHAPTER IV

TRIPLE ALLIANCE AND TRIPLE ENTENTE, 1904–1911

I. TANGIER AND BJÖRKÖ

Between 1904 and 1914 three rivalries grew portentously, overshadowing all lesser antagonisms, becoming so intertwined that when one quarrel ended in war, all Europe was at war. All three had their roots in the old conflict between determination to preserve, and determination to change, the *status quo*. Anglo-German rivalry was the clearest example of this conflict. England was satisfied; Germany was dissatisfied. England sought to restrain German expansion by sea power and by the entente with France and Russia. Germany sought to weaken Britain's mastery of the sea and to disrupt the entente. Franco-German antagonism was somnolent in 1904; by 1912 the "inevitable" war was freely discussed in both countries. In 1904 French nationalists were a discredited minority; in 1912 a nationalist ministry took office. The change is largely explained by the entente and by German opposition to the entente. French nationalism had waned partly because the people were prosperous and contented, but partly also because the French felt they could never fight Germany on equal terms. The nationalists, Delcassé in particular, began to take heart as soon as the entente was formed: British sea power would more than redress the military balance between France and Germany. Now Germany could safely be defied, be forced to acquiesce in whatever France decided to do. Delcassé and the nationalists did not have popular support until after 1905, when the Germans accepted Delcassé's challenge and set out to demonstrate, once and for all time, the futility of defying

99

Germany. The German methods infuriated the French and produced a lasting revival of hostility. In 1906 the Germans realized their mistake and tried to repair the damage. Their efforts failed. The antagonism steadily deepened. Austro-Russian rivalry was an old story. Earlier, opposition from the other powers had prevented the rivals from fighting. After 1907 that opposition steadily lost strength. France and England needed Russian support in their quarrels with Germany; the hostility of France and England made Germany feel increasingly dependent for support on her only loyal ally, Austria. The rulers of Austria and Russia were anxious to avoid war, but it is hard to see how there could have been any peaceful solution of the conflict between Slav nationalism and the determination of the Dual Monarchy to resist disintegration.

In the last decade of the nineteenth century an approximate balance of power had been created by the interaction of three groups, the British Empire, the Triple Alliance, and the Dual Alliance. This situation had been to the liking of Germany. By throwing the weight of their influence now on the side of England, now on the side of the Dual Alliance, the Germans had been able to wrest concessions from both the other groups. By 1904 a new alignment of the powers was taking form: England, France, and Russia on one side; Germany and Austria on the other; Italy, with a foot in both camps. The Germans feared that, if this new grouping became complete, German expansion would be blocked and that possibly Germany's existence would be threatened.

News that England and France were about to compose their differences and substitute coöperation for rivalry reached Berlin early in 1904. What was to be done? Bülow affected indifference when he publicly discussed the Anglo-French entente. Apparently he really thought a policy of quiet waiting was best, but he soon allowed himself to be forced into action by the Kaiser and Holstein. Holstein said, Smash the entente by force if necessary; otherwise Germany will soon be surrounded by hostile states. William

II said, Draw France and Russia away from England; unite the Triple and Dual Alliances. Bülow attempted to combine the policies of the Kaiser and Holstein. The result was the opposite of that intended; the Anglo-French entente was strengthened, and the task of uniting England and Russia was facilitated.

William II was confident that the Russo-Japanese War, which had begun in February, 1904, would enable him to turn the tables on England. Surely the Tsar must resent the flirtations of his French ally with England, the ally of Japan. Surely, if Germany showed sympathy toward Russia's eastern ambitions, the Tsar would welcome an alliance with Germany. Surely the Tsar would be able to force France to exchange her friendship with England for a German alliance. The path must be made easy for France. Let her have Morocco, said the Kaiser. If we oppose her there, hatred of Germany will revive. Holstein thought all this was wishful dreaming: across the path to a union of the Continent lay the insuperable barrier of Alsace and the Balkans. Furthermore, friendly gestures would merely convince France that Germany was frightened by the entente. He did not hope to win an alliance with France, but he believed the French could be made to see that the entente with England was not only useless but dangerous. The means to his end was Morocco. Refuse to let France take Morocco, he argued. England will give the French only diplomatic support. France will be forced to give way. Then she will turn against Britain and try to conciliate Germany. William II thought Holstein's program too dangerous; during 1904 the Kaiser refused to sanction any action against France in Morocco.

The Kaiser's own program proved not only dangerous but futile. At the end of 1903 he began to bombard "Nicky" with letters which were filled with abuse of the Japanese and their British allies, filled also with suggestions for a Continental coalition to restrain British greed and knavery. The Tsar's replies were friendly, but they skirted warily around the idea of an alliance. The Kaiser remained hope-

ful. In October, 1904, he saw his opportunity. At the start
of the voyage to the Far East, the Russian Baltic fleet met
a fleet of British fishing boats at Dogger Bank. The tremu-
lous admiral mistook the trawlers for Japanese torpedo-
boats and opened fire, killing many fishermen. There was
a storm of indignation in England. For a time "the betting
was about even as between peace and war." The Kaiser
promptly proposed a Russo-German alliance, and forwarded
a draft treaty to St. Petersburg. At first all went smoothly.
The Tsar was enthusiastic, his ministers acquiescent. Then
England and Russia agreed to submit the Dogger Bank episode to arbitration. Almost immediately the Russian attitude toward the German alliance changed. Conditions were
raised which Germany could not possibly accept. Finally,
even William was forced to admit that the prize had slipped
through his fingers.

The only result of his efforts was heightened tension between England and Germany. Calculated indiscretion in
St. Petersburg revealed to the British the Kaiser's stric-
tures against England and his eagerness for an alliance.
The anti-German chorus in the English press took on an increasingly vehement tone. Alarm in England led to alarm
in Germany; fear of a surprise attack was widespread.
On one pretext or another the scattered units of the German fleet were called to home waters. A remarkable situation! Each government argued: "It is ridiculous to think
we are meditating an attack. Since your fears are obviously
ridiculous, we can only conclude that your alarm is a mask
covering your intention to strike at us." As a matter of
fact, neither government, nor country, had the slightest desire for war. Yet the atmosphere had become so tense at the
end of 1904 that any trivial episode would apparently have
sufficed to precipitate hostilities. These were the two powers
which, shortly before, had been "natural allies."

The Kaiser's plan to unite the Triple and Dual Alliances
had failed; he was disillusioned and uneasy. Holstein had
been waiting for this moment. For months he had been
vainly arguing that force, not conciliation, was the way to

success. At the beginning of 1905 Bülow began to ply the Kaiser with Holstein's arguments: Delcassé's policy after Fashoda had made the entente possible; he had drawn Italy away from her allies; his opposition barred the way to a union of the Dual and Triple Alliances; if he fell, the "iron ring" which King Edward was forging around Germany would disappear. Morocco, continued Bülow, was the basis of the entente for France. A French mission had already, by the end of 1904, been despatched to Fez with demands for reform, obviously the first step toward a protectorate. Morocco was an independent country; by the Treaty of Madrid of 1880 the powers had agreed to respect the *status quo*; France was impairing Moroccan independence. Make her answer for her conduct at a conference of the signatories of the Madrid treaty. Holstein's legal case was good. He and Bülow realized, however, that the success or failure of their policy really depended on the interests and fears of the states which would be asked to participate in the conference. Here also they felt safe. Roosevelt had signified his interest in the preservation of the "open door" in Morocco: France excluded other countries from the trade of her colonies. Spain and Italy had, to be sure, been bought off by France, but they were jealous of their Latin sister. If they saw a good chance to humiliate her, they would forget their promises. Russia was exhausted; besides, the Tsar owed a debt of gratitude to the Kaiser for services rendered in the Far Eastern war. Austria would support her ally. Even England would offer no effective resistance. British commercial circles did not wish to lose the profitable Moroccan market; the Conservative cabinet was too weak and divided to take a decided stand; the British people were anxious for peace. France would be isolated. Alone, she would be helpless. The conference, then, would result in the humiliation of France, the collapse of Delcassé's policy, and the disruption of the entente.

Such was the picture Bülow painted for William II in the rosy colors he could use so skilfully. The Kaiser was fearful; possibly painful memories of the humiliation which had followed Holstein's similar plans to chastise England in 1895 and 1896 lingered in his mind. When Bülow persisted and promised an easy victory, he gave way, reluctantly and half-heartedly. In March, 1905, while on a cruise, he landed at Tangier and proclaimed the determination of Germany to uphold Moroccan independence. Then Bülow made public his plans for a conference of the powers. Undoubtedly, he said, something must be done to end the chaos prevailing in Morocco. At the same time, the independence of Morocco must be safeguarded. The French demands for reform, read in the light of statements by French statesmen and newspapers, would impair Moroccan independence. The French action was, therefore, a violation of the Treaty of Madrid. Germany proposed that the signatories of the Madrid treaty meet in conference for the purpose of inaugurating reforms which would restore order without jeopardizing Moroccan independence.

The Kaiser's dramatic speech at Tangier caused consternation in Europe. What was the German objective? There was a suspicious coincidence between Tangier and the collapse of Russian military fortunes in the Far East. Did Germany want war now that Russia was weak? Everywhere the proposal to call a conference was viewed with suspicion and reserve. The British, fearing the very existence of the entente was at stake, rallied vigorously to the support of France. There is no evidence that, as Delcassé later maintained, armed support was promised in case of war, but Lansdowne did wish the two governments to "discuss in advance any contingencies by which they might in the course of events find themselves confronted." Only the French acted as the Germans anticipated. The French, like all Continental peoples, had been taught to suspect England of using her allies as cat's-paws. They soon suspected, unjustly, that England wished to push them into war with Britain's dreaded rival, Germany. The French people did not care about Morocco. They wanted peace, and they were afraid. The storm of opposition to Delcassé broke, now that his policy had led to trouble. With discretion Germany

could have won a substantial victory. The French Premier,
Rouvier, offered an agreement on all questions, Alsace-
Lorraine of course excepted. Here was a chance to weaken
the entente. Bülow refused to negotiate. After further hesitation, Rouvier decided to sacrifice his colleague; Delcassé
was forced to resign. The British were furious. "The fall of
Delcassé," wrote Lansdowne, "is disgusting, and has sent
the entente down any number of points in the market."
Again, the Germans might have come off victorious had
they been willing to spare France the humiliation of appearing before an international tribunal. Again Berlin was ada-
mant, and Rouvier was forced to agree to a conference.

Germany had triumphed. Step by step the French had
retreated; now they had surrendered. William II breathed
a sigh of relief. He had doubted whether France could
really be clubbed into friendship; Rouvier's eagerness for
an understanding reassured him. The next step, he and
Bülow thought, was to attempt once more to unite the Continent. A few weeks after France gave way, Kaiser and
Tsar met at Björkö, in Finland. They had a pleasant time
working up moral indignation over British perfidy, especially over King Edward's passion for making "a little
agreement" with every one. Next morning, after more
tirades, the Tsar was persuaded that a Continental alliance
was the only way to block the evil designs of England. At
the proper moment the Kaiser produced a draft treaty providing for mutual assistance in case of attack and providing
also for the adherence of France. The Tsar hesitated; then
he signed.

Despite the atmosphere of melodrama and unreality surrounding the signing of the Björkö Treaty, despite also the
knowledge that Nicholas II was devoid of will-power, the
Germans did not doubt the validity of the treaty. The next
step was to bring France into the alliance. Morocco, Bülow
thought, would serve as a bait. A sense of victory pervaded
Wilhelmstrasse. To the Triple Alliance, Russia was now
added. Soon France must fall in line: she had seen the futility of resistance. "My dear Fatherland," exclaimed Wil-

liam II, "is at last free from the clutch of the Franco-Russian vise."

2. ALGECIRAS

In a series of rapid moves, from Tangier in March, to Björkö in July, 1905, the Germans had isolated England. The British counterattack began immediately. By October all the German gains were lost. Thereafter the Anglo-French entente grew daily in strength, and Russia began to think of a truce with England. The Germans had tried to gain too much. When Delcassé fell, both France and Russia wished a truce with Germany. The Germans were not satisfied with a truce; they wished an alliance. In grasping for that prize they lost everything.

The Tsar had concluded the Björkö agreement without consulting his ministers. When he told of his action, he was assailed by conflicting counsels. Some advisers, filled with hatred of England, were enthusiastic. On September 5, 1905, the Treaty of Portsmouth was signed. It registered the death of Russia's Far Eastern policy. Russia was forced to evacuate Manchuria, to surrender her lease on the Liaotung peninsula, including Port Arthur, to Japan, and to recognize the preponderant influence of Japan in Korea. A few days later came news that the British and Japanese had renewed their alliance and had extended it in two important ways. The scope of the alliance now included the "region" of India, as well as eastern Asia, and each ally promised aid to the other if attacked by one power, instead of two powers. Russia was, therefore, barred from expansion in the Middle and Far East, unless she cared to encounter armed opposition from both England and Japan. The logical answer, thought many Russians, was a Continental alliance. This group for a time was in the ascendant.

France was approached. The French government refused even to discuss the proposal to conclude an alliance with Germany. The refusal gave the anti-German advisers of the Tsar a hearing. They stressed the necessity of preserving the French alliance while Balkan problems were still unsolved. They said Germany would be a valuable ally only in case of a war with England and Japan, a war which Russia would be too weak to wage for many years. On the other hand, the British and Japanese were willing to make concessions in China and Persia. In the Near East the British could assist in holding back the Austro-German advance, and in blocking the Bagdad Railroad. Obviously, Russia could gain more in coöperation with England, France, and Japan than Germany would offer her. For a time, anger and humiliation over their recent defeat made the Russians hesitate. In October, 1905, interest triumphed over passion. The Tsar tried to be gentle: he said the Björkö Treaty could not go into effect just yet. The Kaiser saw through the veil of words and desperately appealed to the Tsar's sense of honor. "What is signed is signed! and God is our testator!" His appeal was unavailing. Thereafter the Russians treated the Björkö Treaty as non-existent, and the road lay open for an Anglo-Russian entente.

Germany had gone too far with France as well as with Russia. During the early months of 1905, the French blamed Delcassé more than Germany for the tension over Morocco. They knew he had provoked Germany. They did not care about Morocco, and they were suspicious of England. When Delcassé resigned, France breathed a sigh of relief. The trouble-maker was gone; now all would go well. The French were soon disillusioned. Germany insisted on dragging France, like an indicted criminal, before a conference of the powers. Angry and humiliated, the French accepted; but they had made their last concession. They began to realize that Morocco was not the real stake: Germany was trying to browbeat France into friendship. The French resolved to resist at all costs. Indifference to Morocco vanished; military preparation was pushed at breakneck speed. So far as the conference was concerned, the French were increasingly confident of success. England, by indirect threats, had frightened Italy and Spain: they would abide by their secret agreements with France. When Russia repudiated the Björkö Treaty, doubt as to her attitude disappeared. Roosevelt tried to be impartial, but the French ambassador, Jusserand, was a clever psychologist: the picture of a weak but manly France confronting a German bully was taking shape in the President's mind. The little powers did not count. France, it seemed, might command a majority at the conference called to humiliate her.

France no longer feared the conference: but what if Germany refused to abide by the decisions of the conference? If the Germans were really determined to have a decisive test of strength, defeat at the conference would force them to war as the logical continuation of their policy. If war came, what would England do? So far as we know, the French did not ask this question directly while Lansdowne, the author of the entente, held office. In December, 1905, the Conservatives resigned and a Liberal ministry was formed, with Sir Henry Campbell-Bannerman as Prime Minister. The Liberals had a reputation for pacifism, and the French became uneasy. They asked point-blank whether armed assistance would be forthcoming from England in case of a Franco-German war. Sir Edward Grey, the new Foreign Secretary, tried to hedge; but the French persisted. After some hesitation, Grey authorized the continuation of the discussions between the military and naval authorities of the two countries, which had begun under Lansdowne. At last, on January 31, 1906, he stated his views on the political question. He refused to make a definite pledge of assistance; he said that he had no power to give such a pledge. On the other hand, he let the French ambassador see clearly that, if war came, he would do everything in his power to bring England in and that he was confident of success. The French tried in vain to get a more definite commitment. Apparently, however, they were more content than they pretended. Thereafter they proceeded on the confident assumption of British aid.

When Grey finally gave the assurance France was seeking, the conference was already in session. It met at the beginning of January, 1906, in the little town of Algeciras near Gibraltar. The task of the conference was to devise means of reëstablishing order in Morocco without impairing Moroccan independence. It was an impossible task. The Moorish Sultan was bankrupt. He could not preserve order in his domain. European assistance, financial and military, was the only way of securing order. Unfortunately, the whole history of imperialism showed that European control over the police would eventually mean European political control. Moroccan independence would eventually become an empty phrase. No one knew this better than the Germans. Since their objective was to prevent France from acquiring Morocco, they must prevent her from acquiring exclusive supervision over the police. They made a whole series of proposals, but the French and British easily demonstrated that each suggestion sacrificed either order or independence or both.

What the French and British were really demonstrating was the impossibility of securing order without impairing Moroccan independence, but they managed to obscure that fact. The French argument was a triumph of lucid but specious logic. Germany said her interests in Morocco were economic. Very well. She might have representation in the international bank which was to regulate Moroccan finances; she might also ask the conference to pass resolutions guaranteeing equal commercial opportunities to all countries in Morocco. All France asked was the ending of the intolerable political chaos in Morocco, which hampered trade, made trouble along the Algerian frontier, and gave ambitious powers an excuse to meddle in Moroccan affairs. European control over the police in the ports was necessary for the preservation of order. A force drawn from all the powers would be inefficient, would lead to incessant intrigues, and eventually each power would come to regard the ports under its control as spheres of influence. It would be best, therefore, to entrust the police to France; France had officers trained for similar service in Algeria. To emphasize the international character of the police mandate, France was willing to share the task with Spain, the other power with territory adjacent to Morocco. As conclusive evidence of their pure intentions, the French were prepared to guarantee the independence and integrity of Morocco.

These arguments were a façade masking the determination of France to begin the "penetration" of Morocco, but they sounded plausible. Russia, as France's ally, and England, Italy, and Spain, because they had secret agreements with France, were glad to be convinced. More discernment might have been expected from Roosevelt, but apparently he was thoroughly taken in. Only Austria stood with Germany. For two months the Germans managed to avoid a vote in full conference, and hence their isolation did not become obvious. During this respite they tried desperately, sometimes by methods which were unethical even for diplomats, to break the solidarity of the opposition. As the conference dragged on, week after week, the delegates became restive at their confinement in overcrowded Algeciras. Every one hesitated to call for a vote. What would Germany do after her defeat was made evident? At last, on March 2, the British delegate summoned his courage. A roll-call was taken on the police question. Germany and Austria were alone, deserted even by their ally.

"Wenig erfreulich," said Bülow. What next? Holstein stood firmly to his original position. If France won, the entente survived and German hegemony was gone. Better disrupt the conference even if war followed. Holstein stood alone. Bülow had promised an easy victory. Neither the Kaiser nor the German people would sanction war. Like a player who sees the game is lost, Bülow swept his pieces from the table and surrendered. Holstein presented his resignation. To his discomfiture, it was accepted. The strange career of Germany's "Grey Eminence" was over. That much, at least, Germany had gained.

Superficially, the Treaty of Algeciras embodied the essentials for which Germany had been striving. The independence and integrity of Morocco were solemnly reaffirmed. The bank was international; the police were international. At the head of the police was an inspector, a Swiss, who was to make periodic reports to the powers. In reality, Germany had been defeated. The police in the ports were French and Spanish; each country was supreme in the area allotted to it by the secret treaties of 1904. Germany had neither expelled the French from Morocco nor got a foothold herself. At the conference assembled at the behest of Germany, Germany had been consistently outvoted.

3. THE ANGLO-RUSSIAN ENTENTE

Algeciras was humiliating, but it was only a symbol. The campaign upon which Germany had embarked so confidently had failed. France and Russia had not been drawn to the side of Germany. The Anglo-French entente not only survived: it was stronger than ever. Russia and England were already seeking a basis for agreement.

While the area of Anglo-Russian friction extended almost a third of the distance around the globe—from the Balkans to Manchuria—and while each country felt safe in opposing the other, there had been no hope of friendly relations. By 1906 the "danger spots" were fewer, and the disposition to quarrel had abated. The blood-letting of 1904 and 1905 removed fear of Russian control over China and Korea. British strategists had concluded by 1903 that Russian conquest of the Dardanelles "would not make any marked difference in our strategic dispositions." The Near East, therefore, receded into the background so far as the British government was concerned. There remained Persia, Afghanistan and Tibet. These still held explosive possibilities. The British were anxious to avoid trouble: an Anglo-Russian quarrel would strengthen German influence in St. Petersburg and weaken the entente with France. If amicable relations could be established between London and St. Petersburg, the danger of a Russo-German alliance would be obviated, and the three friendly powers, united in a Triple Entente, could call a halt if German ambitions went beyond "legitimate" bounds. There was some opposition in England. An understanding with reactionary tsardom was difficult to square with devotion to liberalism, and the task was made more complicated when the Russian revolution of

1905 was drowned in blood. Grey placated his conscience by assuring himself that Russia must inevitably move toward liberalism, particularly if united to the liberty-loving British and French; but the more doctrinaire Liberals were hard to convince. Many beside Liberals were skeptical or hostile. The Indian government, and most Englishmen who had come in contact with Russian diplomacy in the past, were convinced that Russia would never honorably observe a promise.

Grey was able to win over, or to silence, dissenters at home, but he had difficulty prodding the Russians into action. Throughout 1906 and 1907 it was hard to make the Tsar think of anything except his shaky throne. The revolution had intensified his natural sympathy with conservative Austria and Germany. He was reluctant to alienate his fellow-emperors by an understanding with England. Even the large anti-German group in his court was afraid that if the British offer was accepted, Germany might strike out in anger as she had against France in 1905. Russia would be too weak to resist. The war with Japan had exhausted the Tsar's treasury and decimated and disorganized his armies. Revolution had completed the demoralization of Russia. A long period of recuperation was essential.

Fear of Germany held the Russians back; fear of Germany also drove them on. The Balkans, after a decade of comparative calm, were once more in a state of turmoil. German influence was supreme in Constantinople, and the hated Bagdad Railway was being pushed on relentlessly. Even in Persia, German concessionaires were busy. Russia could not halt the German advance unaided; England was willing to assist in the task. Further, if the Turkish problem was to be reopened, peace in Asia was essential. The British offered generous terms in Persia; Japan was equally generous with Chinese territory. It seemed that Russia could not but welcome such an accommodating spirit. Nevertheless, the predatory instincts of the Russians combined with fear of Germany to hamper negotiations until Grey held out new and enticing bait.

Isvolski, the Russian Foreign Secretary, was a man of one idea. The dream of his life was to open the Straits, not to all the powers, but to Russia alone. During the war with Japan the Black Sea fleet had been useless; men and arms had to be transported from Black Sea depots to the Baltic and then back, around Europe, all because old treaties, forced on Russia after defeat, prohibited vessels of war from passing through the straits which joined the Black Sea to the Ægean. Isvolski thought it intolerable, a humiliating reminder of defeat and impotence, that the Black Sea ports and the Black Sea fleet should be useless to Russia in time of war. When he became Foreign Secretary in 1906, he made the opening of the Straits his great objective. In 1907 he injected the question into the negotiations with England.

Grey knew that the fate of the agreement with Russia probably hinged on his reply to Isvolski's soundings; as he also knew, British public opinion still mistrusted Russia, and would not be willing to see the Straits opened to Russia alone. Grey tried to steer his way between these two reefs. He asked the Russians to defer consideration of the Straits until later. British opinion must first be prepared for the change. Once an agreement over the Middle East was signed and Anglo-Russian friendship became obvious, public opinion would be less suspicious. It would be a mistake to complicate the Anglo-Russian discussion by consulting other states, Germany for instance. Personally, Grey said, he was in sympathy with the Russian desire to be able to use the Straits, and he would be glad to take the matter up later. Despite Grey's cautious language, Isvolski thought he saw victory ahead. He agreed to postpone the discussion until the consent of the other powers had been secured. He noted with pleasure that Grey did not object to the Russian proposal; this was "a great evolution in our relations and an historical event."

When the alluring possibility of a revision of the Straits settlement appeared, Russian hesitation ended. In the summer of 1907 agreements were signed with both England

and Japan. The treaty with Japan, signed in July, was ostensibly merely a mutual promise to respect the *status quo* in the Far East, but there were secret clauses defining spheres of influence in Manchuria. The two powers thereafter coöperated amiably in the task of keeping others out of the province. The Anglo-Russian agreement of August, 1907, had no secret articles. Both parties agreed to keep out of Tibet. Afghanistan was recognized as a British sphere of influence, but England promised not to change the political or territorial status of the country. The Persian settlement was the most important part of the agreement. After affirming their desire to preserve the independence of Persia and the "open door" for the commerce of all nations, the two governments proceeded to divide the country into three zones. The northern zone, which was the largest and most valuable, and contained Teheran and Ispahan, was allotted to Russia. The British zone was in the southeast. Economically it was of little value, but it included Bunder Abbas, at the entrance to the Persian Gulf, and the province of Seistan, the gateway to Afghanistan and India. Between the two spheres of influence was a large neutral zone, including the Gulf littoral. Each government claimed a special interest in the preservation of peace and order in its sphere. In regard to trade, the only expressed restriction was the promise of each government not to seek concessions in the zone allotted to the other. Nevertheless, their subsequent actions show clearly that, while the agreement of 1907 was worded so as to render protests by other nations impossible, England and Russia tacitly agreed to prevent Germany from obtaining a foothold in Persia.

The Anglo-Russian agreement received a tepid reception in both countries. Most Englishmen still thought in terms of the nineteenth century. They did not trust Russia. The old British policy of preserving Persian independence, it was said, had been abandoned. Russia, with Teheran in her control, would soon advance again. As the Liberals were fond of portraying England as the friend of small nations, Grey indignantly denied that Persia had been partitioned:

"Our agreement with Russia is a mutual self-denying ordinance recognizing Persian independence." It is hard to believe Grey really meant these words. Russia soon proved them false. The feeling of disgust which the thought of association with the Tsarist régime aroused in many Englishmen was kept alive by the brutality with which Russia suppressed all efforts of the Persians to extricate themselves from foreign domination. In Russia, also, the agreement of 1907 was unpopular. It was accepted as a necessary evil. Russia was too weak to oppose Britain and Japan; a truce was the safest course.

In the highest political circles the Anglo-Russian entente aroused something like enthusiasm. The Russian government was alarmed by the rapid spread of German influence eastward: England, France, and Russia together might be able to dam the flood. Isvolski hoped for positive benefits. "Who knows," he asked hopefully, "whether the pressure of events may not compel us once more to open the question of the Straits?" Here lay great danger. The conflicting aspirations and fears of the powers and of the Balkan states made changes in the Near East hazardous to European peace. Fear blinded the directors of the British policy to the danger. They welcomed the entente with Russia because it facilitated the task of restraining Germany, and because it practically eliminated the possibility of a Russo-German alliance. Therefore, as Russia soon perceived, the British government was willing to make great sacrifices to prevent the agreement from breaking down. Hypnotized by fear of a Russo-German alliance, the British actually welcomed the thought of a Russian advance. "I hope," wrote the British Undersecretary in October, 1907, "the developments of Russian foreign policy in the near future may show themselves in the Near East, where it will not be easy for Germany and Russia to work together." He got his wish.

4. BOSNIA

In 1906 the Dual Monarchy secured, for the first time in many years, a foreign secretary who possessed initiative and determination. During these years Europe had ceased to think of Austria as a great power. At best, she was thought of as a German satellite; at worst, as a dying state whose possessions would cause dissension among the powers. Count Aehrenthal took office resolved to demonstrate that Austria was capable of independent action. Indeed, he felt drastic action alone could prevent the death of the monarchy.

Jugo-Slav nationalism, stimulated by the Hungarian policy of forced Magyarization, was draining the strength of the Dual Monarchy like a cancerous growth. Formerly the Southern Slavs had dreamed of "redeeming" their more backward brothers in the Balkans; now they dreamed of being themselves redeemed by Serbia, the Piedmont of the future Jugo-Slav nation. Until 1903 Austria kept a tenuous hold on Serbia by protecting the members of the Obrenovitch dynasty against the hatred of their subjects. Then there was a palace revolution. King Alexander and his spouse were tossed out of the palace windows. A member of the rival Karageorgevitch family, Peter, took the throne. Leaders of the Radical party brought about the revolution; after 1903 they were the real rulers of Serbia. The Radicals frankly preached the ideal of "Greater Serbia," a Serbia which would some day include the Jugo-Slav provinces of Austria-Hungary and Turkey. Revolutionary propaganda was spread in Bosnia and Croatia. At first the Austrians did not take the agitation seriously, and set out to discipline Serbia by the usual method, the discovery of an epidemic of "political swine fever." Serbia's greatest export was pork; most of the pork was shipped to, or through, Austria. Ostensibly as a sanitary measure, but really as a punitive measure, the frontiers of the Dual Monarchy were closed to shipments of Serbian pork. Formerly this device had brought results; now it did not. The Radicals pretended to desire a truce. Actually, they prolonged the dispute as a means of intensifying popular feeling in Serbia against Austria. The "Pig War" dragged on, an inglorious repetition of the conflict of Francis Joseph with Cavour and Bismarck.

Aehrenthal was conscious of the danger to which the new Piedmont exposed the monarchy. He spoke confidently of "exterminating the Serbian revolutionary nest." But how? For two years he tried unsuccessfully to devise a plan of campaign. While he hesitated, the Young Turk revolution took place in June, 1908. The new rulers of Turkey announced their determination to strengthen the unity of the empire. Bosnia and the Sanjak of Novibazar, both under Austrian control, were still nominally Turkish provinces. Faced by a revival of Turkish nationalism, Aehrenthal decided to embark on no far-reaching schemes for the present. Instead, he would consolidate the existing situation by annexing Bosnia. Annexation would, of course, violate the Treaty of Berlin. Aehrenthal anticipated protests; there were always protests when treaties were broken. He did not expect effective opposition. The Berlin treaty had, after all, been disregarded so often, and Bosnia had, for all practical purposes, been a part of the Monarchy for a generation. The Serbians would undoubtedly cry out when they saw Slavic Bosnia passing irrevocably into Hapsburg possession; but Serbia was not a signatory of the Berlin treaty, and therefore had no legal right to protest. The Turks could be placated by giving them the Sanjak. There would undoubtedly be opposition from Russia; but Russia was weak, and Bosnia lay in what had traditionally been the Austrian sphere of influence. In earlier secret agreements Russia had sanctioned the annexation. Isvolski might be willing to make a new agreement.

Isvolski was quite willing to strike a bargain. He, like Aehrenthal, had been disconcerted by the Young Turk revolution. His Straits program rested on the supposition that Turkey would be too weak to resist when Russia demanded the right to send battle-ships through the Straits.

The Young Turks were beginning extensive military reforms. Isvolski thought prompt action was necessary. He was overruled by the ministerial council: revolutionary discontent at home must be stamped out before new foreign adventures were begun. Secretly, without telling the other ministers, Isvolski approached the Tsar. There was no danger, Isvolski said. British opposition had always been the stumbling-block; England was now willing to see the Straits opened. Austria was the only other formidable opponent. Aehrenthal was evidently planning to annex Bosnia. Why not strike a bargain? Without danger, without sacrifice, Russia could realize her old ambition to use the Straits, unhampered by humiliating treaty restrictions. The Tsar agreed. Isvolski confidently set out to secure the consent of the powers.

On September 15, 1908, Aehrenthal and Isvolski talked for six hours at the palace at Buchlau. Just what they decided is doubtful; within a few weeks each statesman was calling the other a liar. Up to a certain point their stories may be reconciled. Aehrenthal told of his plan to annex Bosnia and give the Sanjak to Turkey; Isvolski told of his plan to open the Straits to Russian war-ships. Aehrenthal requested that the Straits be opened to the other Black Sea states, Rumania and Bulgaria, as well as to Russia; Isvolski accepted the suggestion. Each promised to support, or at least not to oppose, the plan of the other. Here the stories diverge sharply. Aehrenthal claimed he told Isvolski that the proclamation of annexation would be issued in October; he would send notice of the exact date. Isvolski claimed not only that he did not expect early action, but also that he had told Aehrenthal the changes contemplated must be ratified by a congress of the powers who had signed the Treaty of Berlin in 1878. Almost certainly Aehrenthal's version is closer to the truth. Probably Isvolski expected that the annexation would take place late in October and that he would receive notice some time in advance. At any rate, he seemed in no hurry. From Buchlau he started on a leisurely tour to prepare Europe for the impending events. At the

beginning of October he arrived in Paris. There he learned
that the annexation was to take place immediately.

On October 6, Turkey was informed that Austria had
annexed Bosnia and Herzegovina. Europe was taken by
surprise. Even William II had not been warned in advance.
He was furious. German influence in Constantinople had
already fallen off; the Young Turks were liberals whose
natural sympathies were with England. The annexation of
Bosnia by Germany's ally would inevitably push the Turks
still further into the arms of England. His first impulse
was to dissociate himself from the Austrian action, but
Bülow reminded him that Germany could not afford to
make any more enemies. Reluctantly, William ranged himself on the side of his ally.

The British angrily protested against the Austrian action
as a breach of the Treaty of Berlin, and as a blow to the
prestige of the new Turkish government. England alone
of the great powers rejoiced when the Young Turks seized
power. England rejoiced because a very painful conflict between her interests and her humanitarian sentiments
seemed over. Until the last quarter of the nineteenth century, British influence was dominant in Constantinople,
and, through the favor their ambassador enjoyed, British
business men had a quasi-monopoly on economic concessions. By 1908, British influence over the Sultan had vanished, and the British got no concessions. Humanitarian
sentiment, which compelled the Foreign Office to be unpleasant about massacres, had wrought the change. The
history of British relations with Turkey after 1878 con-
stitutes one of the few clear examples of a national policy
dictated by idealistic feelings which were obviously opposed to selfish national interest. Inevitably, the sacrifice
was painful. The triumph of the Young Turks opened the
enthralling vista of interest and feeling united once more.
The Young Turks admired English institutions and sought
English advice and help; they disliked the Germans as conservatives and as friends of Abdul Hamid. The British
were sure the liberal Young Turks would give good govern-

ment and peace to the Near East; they hoped that conces-
sions would soon come to British merchants, and that the
Bagdad Railway might never be completed. Little wonder
England objected to any action which might discredit the
Young Turks in the eyes of their subjects. The Austrian
annexation of Bosnia would undoubtedly have this effect.
So would the Bulgarian declaration of independence which
was issued simultaneously with the Austrian proclamation.
There was no chance that the British would consent to a
third blow at Turkish prestige.

Failure to consider British sympathy for the Young
Turks was the first of Isvolski's fatal blunders. On learning that Aehrenthal had claimed his half of the bargain,
Isvolski hurried to London and begged for support on the
Straits question. He met with a cold reception. He reminded
Grey of his promises of 1907. He threatened to end the entente. All in vain. Then he asked for a written promise that
England would support the opening of the Straits to Russia alone at some future date. Grey would gladly have com-
plied with this request, but suspicion of Russia was still
strong in the cabinet. The most it would permit Grey to say
was that he recognized the necessity for some unspecified
change in the status of the Straits, a change to be made
in the future and only with Turkish consent.

Duped by Aehrenthal, disappointed by Grey, Isvolski returned to Russia. He was met with a storm of abuse. Isvolski had forgotten to consider Pan-Slavism. When the Premier, Stolypin, and the other ministers learned of the Buchlau bargain, they were horrified and indignant. To sanction
the annexation of Slav Bosnia by Austria would be treason
to the Pan-Slav ideal. The Tsar had approved of the bargain in advance. He tried to abide by the promise of support he had given Isvolski, but when Stolypin threatened to
resign, Nicholas gave way. The ministry ordered Isvolski
to oppose the annexation of Bosnia. Terrified by the reproaches of his colleagues, and by the violent denunciation
of the Pan-Slav press, Isvolski turned against Austria.
He denied that he had consented to the annexation. He

denounced the annexation as a flagrant violation of covenants sworn and sealed, as an injustice to Turkey, and as
an injustice to Serbia. Austria must answer for her conduct at a conference of the powers. Isvolski called on
France and England for aid.

Aehrenthal was astonished by the commotion, and he was
indignant at Isvolski's repudiation of the Buchlau bargain.
His first impulse was to publish a report of what had been
said at Buchlau. On second thought he held his hand: the
publication would discredit Isvolski, but it would anger the
Tsar. Under German and British pressure, Aehrenthal
chose a more sensible course. Direct negotiations were begun with the Turks, who agreed to recognize the annexation in return for a money payment. One justification for
opposing the annexation was removed. Aehrenthal admitted
that the Treaty of Berlin had been broken. He admitted
that the signatories of the treaty must sanction the change
before the annexation would be legal. He refused, however,
to submit the question to the free decision of a conference
of the signatories. Like Russia in 1878, and like France in
1905, he said it was humiliating for a great power to be
treated like an indicted criminal. As for Isvolski's third contention, that the annexation was an injustice to Serbia,
Aehrenthal refused to admit its validity. Here he would not
yield an inch, and with good reason. In all earlier agreements, Russia had tacitly admitted that Serbia was within
the Austrian sphere of influence. Now Russia claimed to be
the protector of Serbia. As the Austrians had always feared,
Russia was trying to dominate the whole Balkan peninsula.
If this move succeeded, Russia would soon be planning the
partition of the Dual Monarchy. Aehrenthal refused, therefore, even to discuss Isvolski's contention that Serbia was
entitled to compensation.

Many in Austria wished to go further. The Serbians,
encouraged by Russian sympathy, sent agitators into Bosnia
and massed armed bands along the Austrian frontier. To
hold the Serbians quiet, a large part of the Austrian army
was mobilized and kept under arms through the winter of

1908-1909. To keep such forces mobilized was expensive. War would be cheaper and more profitable, many argued. Merely to deny Serbia compensation for the annexation of Bosnia would be no gain. Now that the Serbians had Russia behind them, they would plot to disrupt the Monarchy more vigorously than ever before. The only solution was to wipe Serbia from the map, to annex most of the kingdom and give the remainder to Bulgaria. Russia was too weak to fight. Later, when Russia got stronger, this solution would be impossible, and the Serbians would be more provocative than ever. An opportunity like the present one would never come again. At first the argument of the war party was too bold for Francis Joseph. He was old; his long reign, extending back to the mid-century revolution, had been full of tragedy; he would die in peace. As the tension dragged on through the winter, and spring approached, however, the war party became more numerous and more insistent. Francis Joseph began to waver.

Isvolski should have surrendered. The prolonged crisis was dangerous to peace. Force alone could compel Austria to comply with his demands. He did not possess that weapon. England and France supported his contention that a congress must be held, but they were unwilling to espouse the Serbian claim to compensation. The Serbian claim had no legal justification, and neither England nor France cared to encourage the Pan-Slavs. In any case, neither the British nor French people would fight over this obscure Balkan question. Practically speaking, Russia stood alone, and Russia was so weak that war against Austria and Germany would be suicide. The failure of Isvolski's program was a foregone conclusion. Still he hesitated. While the Serbians blustered and talked of war, while the Russian Pan-Slavs preached war to the death against Germany and Austria, while England and France hinted more and more broadly that some decision must be made, Isvolski stood paralyzed, terrified by the knowledge that Austria might any day accept the Serbian challenge and declare war, even more terrified by the thought of the abuse which the Pan-Slavs would hurl at him when he surrendered.

In March, 1909, the Germans decided to force a decision. Winter, the best guarantee of peace, was nearly over. With the coming of spring, Austria and Serbia would almost certainly drift into war. What would follow no one could tell. It might be a war of all Europe. The British had at first held aloof, but a campaign in England for increased naval appropriations had been turned into a campaign of hatred against Germany. English neutrality could not be counted on. Germany decided it was time to intervene. A settlement was proposed to Isvolski. Serbia's demands for "compensation" were ruled out, but the Germans were willing to save Isvolski's face. He maintained that the annexation of Bosnia could not be legal without the consent of the signatories of the Berlin treaty. Very well. Germany would advise Austria to seek the approval of the signatories if Isvolski would secretly promise in advance to accept the request. Isvolski acknowledged the conciliatory purpose of the suggestion; he would give it his consideration. A week passed. Isvolski still did not reply. Bülow's patience was exhausted. On March 21 he wired the German ambassador: "Say to M. Isvolski . . . that we expect an answer—yes or no; we must regard any evasive, conditional, or unclear answer as a refusal. We should then draw back and let things take their course. The responsibility for further events would then fall exclusively on M. Isvolski." Thus pinned down Isvolski surrendered. Notes were duly exchanged. Serbia was forced to abandon her protests, disband the forces along the Austrian frontier, and promise to live on good neighborly terms with the Dual Monarchy in the future. The long crisis was over. It ended none too soon. On the eve of Russia's surrender, the war party in Vienna had succeeded in securing consent for mobilization against Serbia. After mobilization, war would not long have been deferred.

A parallel has often been drawn between the Bosnian

crisis and the crisis of 1914. It is true that on both occasions the central problem was the conflict of interests between Austria and Russia in the Balkans. In 1908 and in 1914 Austria was supported by Germany, and Russia had the support of France and England, while Italy stood apart. Despite these points of similarity, the disparate elements are more striking and fundamental. In 1908 the Vienna government was worried by Serbia's aspiration to be the Piedmont of Jugo-Slav nationalism; by 1914 fear of Jugo-Slav nationalism had created a desperate mood in Vienna. In 1908 Pan-Slavism was just waking from a twenty-year sleep; by 1914 the influence of Pan-Slavism was irresistible in Russia. The Bosnian crisis itself was a powerful stimulant to Jugo-Slav nationalism, to the Pan-Slav ideal, and to Austrian fear of these disruptive forces. Serbia's promise to be a good neighbor was worthless. Anti-Austrian propaganda did not cease. After 1909 it was merely driven underground, where it continued more vigorously than ever. Isvolski acquiesced in the annexation of Bosnia, but he was determined to secure vengeance. Even the Tsar, formerly so eager to have the friendship of William II and Francis Joseph, now felt that a conflict with Germany and Austria was inevitable.

In 1908 and 1909 Germany and Italy acted as they were to act in 1914. Germany already recognized her dependence on Austria and the consequent necessity for unquestioning support of Austrian policies. During the crisis, Moltke and Conrad, the German and Austrian chiefs of staff, had begun to concoct plans for common action in time of war. Hitherto Germany had refused to sanction joint plans for fear of encouraging Austria to expect German aid under any circumstances. Hitherto Germany had refused to promise support in case of an Austro-Russian war over the Balkans. Now Germany was forced to allow conversations which not only presupposed common action, but which also took for granted German assistance if Russia intervened in a war between Austria and Serbia. In 1908, as in 1914, Italy deserted her allies. Under the terms of the Triple Alliance,

Italy was entitled to compensation if Austria made gains in the Balkans. Austria refused to admit that the annexation of Bosnia altered the *status quo* in the Balkans and refused to give compensation. Italy, therefore, acted with the Triple Entente during the crisis. In 1908 and in 1914 the relations between Austria and her allies were much the same, but in 1908 the Entente was a shaky structure. Neither France nor England was prepared to support Russia to the point of war. Isvolski was disposed to blame Russia's "friends" for her defeat. He believed the Entente was potentially the stronger combination, but it lacked "firmness and cohesion." He was determined to remedy this deficiency, determined also to hasten the rehabilitation of the Russian army.

The foundations of European peace were undermined during the five tense months between October, 1908, and March, 1909. The truce between Austria and Russia was broken; Pan-Slavism and Jugo-Slav nationalism gained immeasurably in strength; Austria and Serbia became implacable foes.

5. ENGLAND AND GERMANY

Morocco revived Franco-German antagonism; Bosnia revived Austro-Russian antagonism. Anglo-German antagonism caused no dramatic crises; it was a slow poison. The basic causes of the antagonism were British satisfaction, and German dissatisfaction, with the existing distribution of power in the world. To preserve the existing conditions, Britain built her fleet and made the Entente with France and Russia. To change the existing conditions, Germany built her fleet, clung to Austria, and tried to disrupt the Entente. Each country strove to make its will prevail, but neither country was willing to face frankly the cause of the dissension. The British did not like to think themselves selfish, or unwilling to tolerate "legitimate" German expansion. The Germans did not like to think themselves aggressive, or unwilling to recognize "legitimate" British vested interests. Each tried to improve its own case by throwing blame on the other side. The British said Germany wanted to conquer the world. The Germans said England stimulated French *revanche* and Russian Pan-Slavism in order to compass the destruction of German commercial competition. Both governments honestly tried to effect a compromise, but both attacked symptoms of the disorder, not the disease itself. The British insisted that Germany give up her navy; the Germans insisted that Britain promise neutrality in case of a Continental war.

Britain was satiated. Her empire included about a quarter of the world, both in land surface and in population. Her trade empire was even larger. For protection, she had an invulnerable fleet. A great armada stood watch in the North Sea; in 1906 Britain launched a new type of battleship, the *Dreadnaught,* more powerful by far than anything else afloat. An empire of unparalleled size and wealth, protected by a fleet of incomparable size and strength—little wonder that Englishmen wished to perpetuate so enviable a situation. Englishmen did not stop here; few men do. Nearly all men, and groups of men, assume that what is good for them is good for the world, and that what is bad for them is bad for the world. Englishmen forgot their history and assumed that their supremacy resulted from the operation of a beneficent moral law. To challenge British supremacy was to challenge moral law. Could the Germans really be so wicked? Roughly speaking, the Conservatives believed the Germans were capable of this crime; the Liberals were reluctant to entertain such a thought.

The Liberals, who took office in December, 1905, wished to think well of the Germans. In part, this desire resulted from general optimism about the human race. There were other considerations. Liberals wished to preserve British freedom of action, to feel that the Continent, with all its quarrels, was far away. They retained the old insular conviction that all Continental statesmen were immoral and diabolically clever; all English statesmen, honest but slow-witted. Therefore, Englishmen could only be safe if, refusing to be seduced by honeyed words, they kept clear of binding commitments. The Liberals did not regard the

Entente as an entangling alliance: the agreements with
France and Russia merely settled colonial quarrels. Undoubtedly, England would have fought if war had come
over the Moroccan question. England had promised to help
France get Morocco; besides, the sight of weak France being
bullied by Germany had aroused the British sporting instinct.
Undoubtedly, if Germany tried to bully France again,
Britain would again come to the rescue. But Britain had no
alliance with France; the English people were free to make
the decision for peace or war when the crisis arose. As for
Russia, the agreement of 1907 was merely a colonial agreement. It was not an *entente cordiale;* Liberal England could
have no sympathy for Tsarist Russia. Even the colonial
agreement was none too popular; if Russia continued her
outrageous brutality in Persia, England might be forced to
declare the understanding at an end.

Most Englishmen agreed with the Liberals in their determination to preserve British freedom of action. Freedom of
action could not be preserved if German ambitions were a
menace to Britain and to the world. The Liberals were
anxious, therefore, to believe that Germany did not wish to
challenge British supremacy. The Liberals also wished to
think well of Germany because they wished to save money
on armaments. Here again the British identified their interests with the interests of mankind. When the first dreadnaughts were launched early in 1906, the British became, as
Grey said, "more supreme at sea than we have ever been."
If the armament race could now be halted, that supremacy
would be inexpensively perpetuated. Having no motive for
spending more on battle-ships, the English concluded that a
move for the limitation, even proportionate reduction, of
armaments would benefit every nation. The Liberals were
peculiarly interested in the problem, not only because they
thought themselves pacifists, but also because they had come
to office pledged to inaugurate extensive and expensive social
reforms. Unless expenditure on armaments was reduced, the
reforms would necessitate a burdensome increase in taxes.

The opportunity, without prejudice to British supremacy,

to save money and to further the cause of international peace appealed to the Liberals. When they took office they called for international reduction of military and naval expenditures. England would lead the way by building only three, instead of the usual four dreadnaughts during the next fiscal year. At first the Liberal hopes seemed justified. The German Reichstag did, to be sure, appropriate funds for dreadnaughts under the spur of the usual anti-British campaign; but instead of laying down the three keels called for by the Navy Law, Tirpitz began construction on only one. Encouraged, the Liberal Prime Minister, Campbell-Bannerman, announced his intentions of proposing limitation of armaments at the Hague Conference which was to meet in 1907. Then he was undeceived. The Germans threatened not to go to The Hague if reduction was to be discussed. The English persisted, but they got no support except from the United States, and their motion was defeated. They next discovered that Tirpitz had held back construction in 1906 only because he wished to study the technical problems which the dreadnaught involved. In 1907 he laid down five ships, the three for that year and the two held over from 1906. The British continued hopeful; they were still far ahead in the race. In 1907 they laid down three, and in 1908 only two, dreadnaughts. Far from following the British lead, Tirpitz secured an amendment to the Navy Law in 1908: from 1908 to 1911, four ships were to be built each year; thereafter, two.

The British were in despair. They realized that expenditures so large as to endanger their social reforms were inevitable if the Germans held this pace. In August, 1908, King Edward visited Germany. He was accompanied by Hardinge, the British Undersecretary, who made a last effort to win over William II. The conversation became heated. The Kaiser accused the British Admiralty of lying and Hardinge of ignorance. Hardinge persisted. "An arrangement ought to be found for diminishing the construction. You must stop or build slower." "Then we shall fight," retorted the Kaiser, "for it is a question of national honour and dignity." Hardinge flushed, and was silent. "You must always treat Englishmen thus," wrote William to Bülow.

The rapid—and repeatedly hastened—rate of German naval construction disillusioned those who wished to think well of Germany and gave a hearing to those who believed in the "German menace." Ever since the last years of the nineteenth century, a small but influential and rapidly growing number of Englishmen had believed that Germany was determined to dominate the world. The German army was by far the strongest on the Continent; Germany was building a great navy. These were the weapons with which Germany sought to accomplish her purpose. Germany would, of course, prefer not to use these weapons. If Europe could be reduced to vassalage without war, so much the better for the Germans. It was quite possible that France and Russia, terrified by the strength of Germany, might decide that the safest course was alliance with the tyrant. Once France and Russia were forced into an alliance, Germany could concentrate on preparation for the conquest of Britain. Isolated, Britain was doomed. She, like the Continental powers, would come under the yoke of Germany. Europe was once more confronted by a Louis XIV, a Napoleon. England must once more lead a crusade for liberty, must once more prevent the triumph of tyranny. If Britain acted wisely, the crusade would be bloodless. If the Germans found themselves confronted by overwhelming power, they would probably abandon their pretensions and peacefully admit that Germany was entitled to be only one of the free nations of Europe. Two battle-ships must be built for every one Germany built; the Entente must be made ever stronger, possibly welded into a new triple alliance. There was no other way to meet the German challenge. To hope for compromise was futile and dangerous, futile because Germany would interpret friendly gestures as signs of weakness; dangerous because, if Britain wavered, Russia and France would become frightened and would be tempted to "sell out" to Germany.

By 1908 many Conservative leaders, some newspaper publishers, and most of the diplomatic service, including practically the whole permanent staff of the Foreign Office, believed that the "German menace" was a reality. Earlier, British opinion had scoffed at this bogey. In 1908 a systematic campaign was begun to awaken the English people. The campaign was aided by the increases in the German building program. Germany was catching up, the Conservatives declared. Popular agitators portrayed the dangers of a German invasion in hair-raising fashion. The scare gradually took possession of the popular imagination. William II tried, with characteristic clumsiness, to disarm hostility. He wrote privately to Lord Tweedmouth, the first lord of the Admiralty, assuring him that Germany had no intention of challenging British naval supremacy. News of the letter leaked out; its contents were distorted. The Kaiser, British papers said, was trying, in his usual deceitful way, to hoodwink English officials. Later in 1908, the *Daily Telegraph* published an account of an interview with the Kaiser. William described himself as a friend of England, standing firm against his people's hatred of the British. He told how Russia and France had tried to unite the Continent against England during the Boer War, and how he had not only refused, but had drafted a plan of campaign which enabled the British to fight the war to a successful conclusion. The interview was a sincere gesture of friendship, but it was also a pathetic example of William's ineptitude. The British jeered at his protestation of friendship. They accused him of trying to sow dissension between England and her partners in the Entente. On the other hand, they believed his statement that the German people hated England.

By the beginning of 1909 the Liberals realized that an increase in naval expenditure was necessary. Many of the ministers thought four dreadnaughts would be enough. The Admiralty demanded six. To aid his argument, the first lord of the Admiralty hinted that Germany was secretly building even more ships than the law of 1908 authorized. His words sent a tremor of fear through England. Balfour, the Conservative leader, completed the demoralization of national common sense. By 1910, he said, Germany would be ahead, with thirteen dreadnaughts to England's ten. By 1912 Germany would, he believed, have twenty-five. Balfour's figures were fantastic—in 1912 Germany possessed nine, not twenty-five—but the British were in a mood to believe anything. "We want eight, and we won't wait!" The cry was heard over all England. Eight were voted.

Those who preached the German menace had won; but their victory was only partial, and it was precarious. The English people had been stampeded by the fear of invasion, but they were soon complaining once more against the size of the naval estimates. Hope of a truce with Germany revived. More important, even the navy scare had not shaken the popular determination to keep clear of entangling alliances. The fate of the Entente seemed more precarious than ever. On the one hand, both France and Russia were dissatisfied with the nebulous character of the Entente, and pressed for a precise statement of obligations. Flat refusal of these requests might convince the French and Russians that no dependence could be placed on British support in time of war. On the other hand, many Englishmen were impressed by the German argument that, so long as there was danger of an attack by the Entente, Germany must continue to build ships. Englishmen knew their country was not bound to aid France and Russia in time of war; why not obtain the desired naval truce by promising neutrality in case France or Russia attacked Germany? The question was hard to answer without implying that England *was* bound to her Continental "friends." Yet those who feared Germany were determined not to give a neutrality promise, because they feared the Entente would straightway collapse.

The lot of the British Foreign Secretary, pulled now this way and now that by conflicting currents of opinion, was not a happy one. In the Foreign Office, and in dispatches from ambassadors abroad, Sir Edward Grey was plied with arguments justifying belief in the German menace. In the cabinet meetings, most of his colleagues favored a naval truce with Germany, and insisted that Grey preserve British freedom of action unimpaired. Grey himself wished above all else to preserve international peace. He wished to deal honestly and straightforwardly with all nations. He was determined to give Germany "no excuse for saying that she is being cold-shouldered, isolated, or squeezed." He knew the English people wanted no binding commitments with other powers, and he felt he must carry out the popular wish.

At the same time he was afraid, afraid of Germany and of isolation. He believed from the moment he took office that Germany wished to dominate the Continent. He believed the Entente alone stood in her path. He believed that if England wavered in her loyalty to France and Russia, these powers would, in fear, make terms with Germany and become hostile to England for her desertion. Then Germany could settle her score with England without fear of attack from any Continental state. Obviously, thought Grey, the Entente must be preserved. France and Russia must not be permitted to doubt British loyalty.

Grey refused to recognized that his objectives were contradictory and irreconcilable. He was determined to preserve England's freedom of action, but the French demanded assurances of support. He was afraid to give, and afraid to withhold, assurance. His equivocal response to the French demand for a promise of armed assistance during the Moroccan crisis seems to have been framed so as both to satisfy France and to avoid the necessity of consulting the British cabinet. During the Moroccan crisis, Campbell-Bannerman reluctantly consented to military and naval conversations between the French and British general staffs. He was afraid a moral obligation to aid France would be created by such intimacy. The Prime Minister's fears had greater warrant when, after the passing of the crisis, the two general staffs continued to discuss plans for joint action. There is no evidence that he knew what was going on; and most of the cabinet members were in complete ignorance. The French were obviously counting with increasing confidence on British support. Grey was afraid to say plainly that British aid must not be taken for granted. He kept

silent. His silence encouraged the French; but it enabled him
to say he had not promised aid. Even Grey's most admirable
qualities, his love of truth and his sense of fair play, were
warped by the conflict between his guiding principles. He
demanded the same ethical standards in public and private
affairs. The diplomacy of no state could measure up to such
a standard, but Grey could not abandon his convictions without loss of self-respect. The inevitable result was distorted
vision. He focused the white light of moral indignation on
the sins of Germany, which were numerous enough. Unconsciously he shut out of his field of vision policies or actions
of the Entente powers which could not be reconciled with
his sincere devotion to honorable action.

On the one hand, fair play, honesty, love of peace, and
loyalty to the popular demand that freedom of action be
preserved; on the other, fear of Germany and of isolation.
Casuistry alone could unify these disparate elements. Once
embarked on the slippery path of casuistry, Grey slid in-
sensibly from self-deception to deception of his colleagues
in the cabinet, of Parliament, and of the British people.

While the British were convincing themselves that, in
perfecting means to perpetuate their imperial supremacy,
they were protecting Europe against tyranny, the Germans
were convincing themselves that, in seeking means to secure
a greater share of the imperial spoils, they were protecting
Germany from destruction. In 1900, when the Triple Alliance was strong and the British were quarreling with
France and Russia, the chances for German expansion
seemed excellent. By 1908 the chances of expansion were
slight. The Anglo-French entente shut Germany out of
Morocco. In 1907 an agreement between England, France,
and Spain to preserve the *status quo* in the Mediterranean
was hailed by the French press as a "Keep Out" sign for
Germans. In the Far East, Japan had understandings with
Russia and France and an alliance with England—more
"Keep Out" signs. In Persia, the British showed so much
determination to exclude German economic activity that
even Isvolski was alarmed. In Turkey, the British insisted

that the Bagdad Railway could proceed only after an understanding with the united Entente powers. The opposition
was growing; the Triple Alliance was losing strength.
Neither Austria nor Germany had any illusions about Italy.
Irredentism was growing. The French no longer made
appropriations for the defense of their Italian frontier; the
Italians made large appropriations for the fortification of
their Austrian frontier. The Triple Alliance was renewed
in 1907, but only because Berlin and Vienna felt that its
sudden ending would be too violent a shock to the European
balance. Germany and Austria stood alone. Bülow even
feared that Austria might make a "sudden swing" into the
English camp.

William II attributed the isolation of Germany to a
malevolent plot. Ever since the failure of his efforts to win
Russia in 1905, his febrile imagination had been haunted
by visions of encirclement and attack. By 1908 fear had
become an obsession. He refused to believe that England
was afraid, England with her great fleet. No, England and
her friends were trying to compass the destruction of Germany. "Now," he told his soldiers at Döberitz, "it certainly
seems as though they are trying to encircle us and hem us
in. We will be able to stand that. The German has never
fought better than when he had to defend himself on all
sides. Just let them come on. We are ready." The alarm cry
was skilfully taken up by Tirpitz's propagandists as a means
of securing larger naval appropriations. By 1908 the German people, like the English, had fallen victim to hysterical
fear. King Edward had only to visit Italy to drive Berlin
"stark, raving mad" with terror.

Bülow knew that there was no plot, that the purpose of
the Entente was to restrain, not destroy, Germany. Yet,
optimist though he was, the closing months of 1908 brought
him to a realization that the situation was very dangerous.
In September, a brush between the German consul at Casablanca and the French police angered opinion in both countries. In October, the Bosnian crisis began. Before Bosnia
was settled, the navy scare in England began. The Casa-

blanca affair showed that Morocco had so estranged France
and Germany that a trifling incident could throw the press
on both sides of the Rhine into paroxysms of rage. The
navy scare in England was symptomatic of the fear which
was driving the British into ever closer relations with France
and Russia. The Bosnian crisis showed that dependence on
Austria involved Germany in Balkan affairs; against their
will, the Germans might some day be dragged into war by
Austria.

Faced with the danger that Germany might be drawn
into war with the Entente powers, Bülow abandoned the
easy policy of drift which had kept him in William's good
graces for more than a decade. To hold France quiet during
the Bosnian crisis, he made concessions in Morocco. The
Casablanca dispute was turned over to the Hague Court.
Bülow then proposed a general agreement on Morocco. The
generosity of the proposal made the French suspect a trap;
reassured, they accepted with alacrity. By the agreement
signed in February, 1909, Germany recognized the political
preponderance of France in Morocco. In return, France
promised Germany a share in Moroccan economic concessions. The French had secured a good bargain; if they had
lived up to it, Morocco might never have been heard of
again. William II gladly consented to the agreement; he
had never cared about Morocco. He would have welcomed
a truce with Russia also, but Isvolski would make no terms
unless Germany abandoned Austria. If Germany would
promise neutrality in an Austro-Russian war, Russia would
promise neutrality in an Anglo-German war. Germany rejected this proposal without hesitation.

Bülow thought France and Russia were only potentially
dangerous antagonists. The German army could keep them
quiet, unless they felt confident of British support. If Germany was to be extricated from dangerous isolation or
equally dangerous dependence on Austria, England must be
placated. England could only be placated, he believed, if the
navy race was abandoned. Athwart the path to a naval
truce stood Tirpitz, and behind Tirpitz stood the Kaiser and

the most vocal elements in German public opinion. From the outset, Tirpitz had pursued a consistent policy. His objective was the establishment of a balance of power on the seas. The navy he was creating was to be an instrument of policy powerful enough to enable Germany to bargain on equal terms with England when disputes arose. The German navy was not to be as large as the British, but it was to be powerful enough to make England hesitate before seeking an armed conflict with Germany. Tirpitz was confident that his objective was attainable. Building costs were lower in Germany than in England. Conscript crews were paid less than enlisted men. The advent of the dreadnaught helped Germany. In the older types of vessels, Germany was far behind. In dreadnaughts the race started almost from scratch; England had only a few years' lead. Tirpitz was convinced that the British could not stand the strain of building two dreadnaughts for each one Germany built. He decided to quicken his pace; by the amendment to the Navy Law passed in 1908 he secured four ships each year until 1911. The Kaiser had been of one mind with Tirpitz ever since 1897. German public opinion, at first doubtful or hostile, had been converted to enthusiastic support by ten years of ceaseless and clever propaganda. Bülow, until 1908, applauded; then he tried to halt the Admiral's plans. Tirpitz had laid on the Foreign Office the duty of piloting Germany peacefully through the "danger zone," the years when Britain could easily cope with the young German navy. All would be lost if war came before the danger period was safely past. Tirpitz contended that the danger would pass within a few years. Bülow now said peace probably could not be preserved if the race continued. Further, he challenged the "danger zone" theory.

The naval race, Bülow argued, involved triple peril for Germany. Large naval appropriations meant less money for the army at a time when France and Russia were arming rapidly. Fear of Germany made England dependent on her partners in the Entente; France and Russia might, if confident of British support, feel strong enough to embark on an aggressive policy, in the Near East, for instance. Finally, the naval scare indicated that England might, goaded by fear and hatred of Germany, precipitate hostilities. Ship-building was dangerous; it was also futile, like pouring water through a sieve. Britain was rich; Britain was not forced to spend money on a large army. How could any one argue that Britain could not build twice as fast as Germany? Tirpitz denied that the fleet was the cause of German isolation. The other powers were jealous of German strength and enterprise. Fleet or no fleet, the jealousy would continue while German banks, manufacturers, and ships continued to challenge British supremacy. Britain was jealous, but the English knew what war would cost. Skilfully handled, Britain would not fight; but Britain would be more likely to fight if German naval power were slight than if Germany were a dangerous antagonist. As for British ability to keep ahead, the strain was already telling: the efforts to secure a truce showed that clearly.

For the first and last time of his career, Bülow persisted. He told the Kaiser that an agreement with England was necessary. William gladly consented to a political agreement, either a non-aggressive pact or, even better, an alliance. As for a naval agreement, Tirpitz would say what was possible. At the beginning of June, 1909, Bülow brought together the officials most concerned for a discussion of the question. All were in favor of a ship-building truce, except Tirpitz. Even he professed eagerness for an agreement, but it was obvious that he was really determined to continue the race, obvious that he was already contemplating further increases in construction. Behind Tirpitz stood the Kaiser. Bülow realized that negotiations would be futile. In the same month he resigned, ostensibly on a question of domestic politics. Possibly, as some maintain, he was unwilling to remain responsible for the naval rivalry. More probably he had lost the imperial favor now that he spoke hard truths instead of smooth flattery.

He was succeeded by Bethmann-Hollweg, an old friend of William II. Bethmann did not possess Bülow's quick intelligence, and he was irresolute as well as slow-witted. His knowledge of foreign affairs was slight. These defects were only partly counterbalanced by honesty and conscientiousness; indeed, his conscientiousness was almost a defect. He, like almost every one in the Foreign Office, disliked Tirpitz's naval policy and lamented the Admiral's influence on the Kaiser. Time after time William II accepted Tirpitz's views against the Chancellor's opposition. Yet Bethmann did not resign. He feared Tirpitz would be his successor. Blinded by ignorance and devotion to duty, Bethmann failed to realize that, while the responsibility for Tirpitz's policy was accepted by a Chancellor who was known to be a friend of peace and international conciliation, Tirpitz was stronger than he would be at the head of the government.

Bethmann, like Bülow, believed that the naval race was dangerous to peace, and that a truce would restore friendly relations with England. The new Chancellor wrested one concession from the Kaiser: if England would conclude a political agreement, Germany would build only three, instead of four, ships during the next few years. The Kaiser and Bethmann hoped to achieve very different objectives by this concession. The Kaiser's views are, as usual, hard to discern because he contradicted himself repeatedly. He obviously wanted a political agreement, if possible an alliance, with England; he obviously wanted to keep, and strengthen, his fleet. He convinced himself that both objectives could be attained. The whole Anglo-German quarrel had, he felt, grown out of the false British notion that Germany was aggressive. Apparently he believed that a short truce would bring the British out of this panicky condition and enable them to see how pacific Germany really was. This realized, England would no longer fear the German fleet. Instead, the English would abandon France and Russia, the true disturbing elements in European society, and ally with Germany. Then the British would actually encourage the growth of the German army and navy as guardians of peace. Bethmann had a very different picture

of the future in his mind. He regarded the truce as preliminary to the abandonment of the naval race. He thought
a reconciliation between England and Germany essential to
peace, and he thought that a permanent reconciliation could
be attained if Germany stopped building dreadnaughts, or
built fewer.

Obviously, the Kaiser's vision of the future was fantastic. It was improbable that a brief truce would dissipate
English suspicions; it was certain that new German building
at the termination of the agreement would revive and intensify hostility. It is by no means certain, however, that
Bethmann's ideal was workable. Practically, he was prof-
fering the surrender of Germany. If events moved as he
hoped, Germany would in future rely less on her own
strength than on English good-will to insure compliance
with her wishes in the field of commercial and political
imperialism. It is very improbable that the two countries
could long agree on what constituted proper British good-
will. The British were securely entrenched politically and
economically, in every quarter of the globe; the long pent-up
energies of the German people were expanding with explosive rapidity. When the Germans pushed into a British
sphere of influence or a market dominated by British traders, the British were bound to accuse the Germans of aggression, and the Germans were bound to accuse the British of
hostile obstruction. One dispute and then another might be
patched up, but even with the best will conceivable, the
British were going to be tempted some day to call a halt;
then the Germans would fall back on force, on their fleet,
once more. The race would recommence. It is hard to see
how there could be any other result so long as political and
economic imperialism were thought to be of paramount national importance.

Bethmann and the Kaiser agreed that the building truce
was to be made conditional on a political agreement. As
Bethmann explained to the British ambassador, the German
fleet was being built to protect German interests outside
Europe. If England was determined to aid France and

Russia in case they attacked Germany, and if England was determined to obstruct German expansion, then building must continue. If England showed that she would do neither of these things, he was sure friendly relations could be restored by the navy truce. Germany could take no chances on the question of British aid to France and Russia; the Anglo-German accord must contain a promise of British neutrality in the event of a Continental war. Germany could take chances, for a few years, on the question of Britain's attitude toward German expansion. If, during these years, harmonious coöperation were shown to be possible, Bethmann believed the Reichstag would be deterred by satisfaction with the existing situation from incurring the costs and the risks which renewed competition would entail.

The British were of two minds about the German proposal. The Foreign Office saw in the request for a neutrality agreement a plot to disrupt the Entente. Too weak to stand alone, France and Russia would undoubtedly make terms with Germany if England promised to stand aloof from Continental wars. According to Grey, the proposed Anglo-German agreement "would serve to establish German hegemony in Europe and would not last long after it had served that purpose. It is in fact an invitation to help Germany to make a European combination which could be directed against us when it suited her so to use it." Use it Germany certainly would. "If we sacrifice the other Powers to Germany, we shall eventually be attacked."

Grey's views met with opposition in the cabinet. The opposition is hard to trace because we lack precise information. It was sufficiently strong to prevent a flat refusal of Bethmann's offer; at times the Foreign Office officials even feared Grey might lose. Grey's opponents were inclined to accept Bethmann's gesture as a sincere effort to effect a reconciliation. They did not believe Germany wished to attack England or to dominate Europe, and they were appalled by the cost and danger of the naval race. The reply which emerged from the conflict within the government went far beyond what Grey and his advisers were willing to give, but

fell far short of the German proposal. England was willing
to negotiate on the basis of retarded German construction.
England was also willing to make a colonial agreement. The
request for a political agreement was not denied, but the
English pointed out that the Entente contained no commitments on general policy. France and Russia would feel
slighted if such engagements were made between England
and Germany alone. Although Bethmann remained eager to
negotiate after he learned the English terms, there was little
hope of a compromise. William II insisted on a precise
neutrality formula; those in the English cabinet who most
desired German friendship were also those who feared
binding engagements with Continental powers. What hope
there was Grey destroyed by dilatory tactics. During 1909
and 1910 English domestic politics were disturbed by conflicts between the two houses of Parliament over finances.
The hold of the Liberals on office was at times precarious;
there were two general elections. These circumstances enabled Grey to postpone the discussions with Germany again
and again, so that by the end of 1910 no progress had been
made.

The picture Grey drew of the international scene had
attractions even for his opponents in England. They liked
to think of England stretching her strong protective hand
over France and Russia, restraining arrogant Germany.
Unfortunately for Grey's peace of mind, Russia, and to a
lesser extent France, refused to play the parts assigned to
them. It had been hard to ignore Isvolski's part in precipitating the Bosnian crisis. After Isvolski left the Russian
Foreign Office to become ambassador at Paris, in 1910, it
was even harder to picture his successor, Sazonov, as a
frightened suppliant. Sazonov knew Russia was still too
weak for great adventures, but he felt that the antagonism
which existed between England and Germany might permit
Russia to extort a little blackmail from both sides. He knew
England feared that Russia might make an alliance with
Germany: England would, therefore, hesitate to oppose
Russian plans. Cautiously but confidently, Russian policy

became more active in Asia. When the British protested against the subjugation of northern Persia, Sazonov paid no heed; England needed Russia too much to risk a break. Britain, fearing Germany, must make concessions to Russia; Germany, fearing Britain, must also make concessions. When Sazonov accompanied the Tsar to Potsdam in November, 1910, he found Kaiser and Chancellor most conciliatory. The Potsdam conversation led to an informal agreement. Germany promised to keep out of the Russian sphere of influence in northern Persia and, more important, to hold Austria back from an adventurous Balkan policy. In return, Sazonov promised not to oppose the Bagdad Railway. Further, he gave assurance that Russia would not be a party to any aggressive action against Germany.

The Potsdam agreement put Grey in a quandary. He insisted that England must, in the name of all that was right and just, wage the good fight for European freedom. The fight required, he said, that England hold aloof from Germany out of loyalty to France and Russia. The Russians, however, had shown contempt alike for British wishes and for treaty obligations in their treatment of Persia. At Potsdam the Russians gave to Germany exactly those assurances which Grey had refused to give for fear of alarming Russia. Was not the picture drawn by Grey the reverse of the true situation? It looked very much as though England were clinging desperately to Russia for support, not Russia to England. Had England fallen so low that she must beg protection of Russia, and make humiliating concessions to secure that protection? If Russia could promise not to join in aggressive action against Germany, why could not England make a similar promise and secure a lessening of the armament burden? These questions were asked in England early in 1911. The opposition to Grey suddenly stiffened. A committee of the cabinet was appointed to supervise the negotiations with Germany. There was a disposition in the cabinet to meet the German view.

The German view had, however, changed. In 1909, after the Casablanca affair, the Bosnian crisis, and the British navy scare, William had been afraid, half-convinced that the "danger zone" could not safely be traversed. By 1911 fear was gone. At Potsdam the Tsar had shown himself eager to avoid trouble with Germany. France could not make trouble while Russia held back. The belligerent confidence which the British had shown during the navy scare had given place to timorous anxiety for an agreement with Germany. The German naval attaché at London reported that the debates on the naval estimates in Parliament had been despondent. Grey had spoken of the danger of bleeding to death in time of peace. There had been no mention of the two-power standard; the speakers had professed themselves content with a ratio of thirty boats to Germany's twenty-one. England was faltering, concluded the attaché. The Kaiser scribbled joyful comments over the dispatches. He was glad Germany had not surrendered as Bülow had wished. "They respect our firm will, and must bow before the accomplished fact! Now further quiet building." In 1912 the German building program fell to two ships a year. The Kaiser was certainly not going to reduce this number to placate England; instead, he would increase the program. On May 8, 1911, Bethmann was forced to tell the British that his earlier proposals must be withdrawn. He had nothing further to propose, but he would be quite willing to listen to anything England might suggest. Thereafter the negotiations quickly ran into the sands.

It is difficult to see how there could have been any result but failure. This is true not merely because it is always easier to separate nations than to knit the threads of amity anew. During the two years of discussion the fundamental issue had not even been touched: Is it possible to reconcile the interests of two powerful states, the one desiring to prevent change, the other bent on changing a distribution of power which it feels unjust? Each side approached the question obliquely. Obviously, Germany wished to weaken the Entente. To Germans this desire seemed natural: they wished to obviate the possibility of a combined attack. Englishmen thought Germany wished to disrupt the Entente so that her three rivals might be subdued in turn. To the Kaiser, England's efforts to make him give up his fleet were prompted by desire to see Germany helpless, bound to obey England. To Grey, the insistence of Germany on a large fleet was evidence that Germany wished to make England helpless, bound to obey Germany. Each could make out a good case; each had grounds for fear. Each changed and magnified the objective of the other. Neither was prepared to grapple with the problem which, unsolved, must bring the two greatest European nations to ruin.

6. THE SEARCH FOR A BALANCE OF POWER

During the early years of the twentieth century the will to peace was stronger and more nearly universal than ever before in modern history. Never before had the foundations of European civilization seemed so unstable. The defeat of Russia by Oriental Japan sent a tremor of hope through "backward" countries. From Morocco to China opposition to European domination became more determined. Was the revolt only transitory, or had the tide of imperialism definitely turned? In Europe itself things were not well. "Three hundred men, all acquainted with each other, control the economic destiny of the Continent," wrote a German industrialist in 1907. These 300, plus a few thousand others, realized that the great mechanism of finance, commerce, and industry was both unwieldy and delicate, hard to control even in times of tranquillity, reacting violently to the slightest political disturbance. Closely connected with economic instability was political and social instability. The shadow of revolution hung over Russia and Austria. Liberals in the west looked forward to these revolutions as the logical and too long-delayed conclusion of the great nineteenth century liberal movement. More discerning observers were fearful. They knew nineteenth century liberalism was bankrupt. The middle classes, the leaders of liberalism, had largely attained their ends in the western countries, and desired nothing better than the *status quo,* which gave them political power and wealth. The old liberal catchwords were still used, but they no longer enthralled the workers. Increasingly, the proletariat complained that the prizes in the political battles which they had helped to win had gone to the middle class. Discontent found expression in the rapid growth of Marxian socialism and in the increasing number and violence of labor disputes. The shadow of revolution was creeping westward. Imperialism was under attack; the European social and political order was under attack; credit, the heart of capitalistic enterprise, was notoriously subject to panic. Here was instability indeed! War would change instability into chaos. War would plunge Europe into the throes of revolution.

The doom which threatened Europe was seen more or less clearly by statesmen in every country. It was seen most clearly in England because England had the greatest imperial domain, the most highly developed industrial system, and the most active and powerful laboring class. It was seen by the ruling element of Russia, although the insatiable expansionist instincts of Russia fought hard against the moderation inspired by fear of revolution. In Germany, industry, commerce, and finance counseled moderation, but here too the desire for expansion was strong and untempered by weakness. Austria was coming to believe that even war might be better than slow disintegration. Italy was, as always, restless, restrained only by consciousness of weakness. In France the older philosophy still dominated. There was little fear of revolution. The proletariat was violent, but it was small and was more than counterbalanced by the great mass of conservative peasant proprietors. Neither industry nor foreign trade played a dominant part in the national economy. French finance made huge investments abroad, but the banks and the Bourse were more completely under governmental control than in any other European country. France wanted peace, but her rulers did not dread war with the same intensity as the rulers of England, Germany, and Russia, because the disruptive elements in French national life were less strong.

Despite the fact that Europe was filled with dread of

war, the organization of European international life still presupposed the acceptance of war as the final, decisive argument in disputes between states. Since on all important questions each state wished its own will to prevail, and since the interests of states were divergent, conflicts of interest were inevitable. In each conflict, victory went to the state which could mass the greatest force on its side. Armies, navies, and allies were instruments of national policy, instruments by which a state could make its will prevail against the will of other states. Armed forces were not intended primarily for use in war; they were to bring victory without war by forcing rival states to give way without an armed encounter. Only if both antagonists thought the issue vital, and only if the discrepancy of power was not overwhelming, did both stand firm. Then there was war. The ideal was power so great that other states would, unless desperate, invariably give way rather than fight. No state had ever attained that peak of strength. Occasionally Europe had been threatened by the hegemony of one state. Then the rest of Europe combined in opposition. For centuries the ideal of a "balance of power" had tempered the rule of force in Europe; but it had not prevented war, as the bloody history of Europe showed. A perfect balance of power, while theoretically possible, was actually unattainable. Inevitably, each country wished the balance weighted in favor of its own interests, since those interests seemed natural and just.

Englishmen, for instance, regarded their country as the traditional defender of the balance of power. They did not deny that their policy resulted from selfish interest. If any one state dominated the Continent, that state could concentrate on the building of a fleet to conquer England. At the same time, Englishmen felt that their policy furthered the cause of European liberty by preventing the growth of a single despotic state. British interest and European progress were alike served when England nerved the Continent against Louis XIV and Napoleon, or when England shielded the smaller states, like Holland and Belgium, from more powerful neighbors. Further, English sea power could only protect, and never menace, European liberty. England had no army with which to fight the huge Continental forces. Therefore, in insisting on naval supremacy, the British felt they were protecting a claim which no one but a potential world despot could protest. There was much in the English claim so long as the Continental states were preoccupied almost exclusively with European affairs, although England had certainly exploited her rôle of balance-wheel to acquire a rich colonial domain. In the twentieth century Englishmen still used the traditional arguments to justify their naval hegemony, but the new imperialism had demolished the premises upon which these arguments rested. Overseas colonies and overseas trade were now of major importance to the Continental states. So long as England was undisputed master of the seas, the colonies and trade of other countries were at her mercy. Furthermore, the increasing dependence of Continental states on non-European countries for products vital in wartime made the blockade a deadly weapon which England could use to enforce her will. The setting for international politics was now not Europe but the world. On that larger stage sea power provided opportunities for despotic rule such as Napoleon never enjoyed.

The Germans were quick to sense the situation. They realized that in every quarrel with England, German colonies and trade were, as Sir Edward Grey said, hostages for England to take. How could the bargaining power of England and Germany be made more nearly equal? Directly by building up the German fleet; indirectly by securing allies. William II tried both methods. His objective was not the destruction of England; it was the creation of a balance of power on the sea. His plan to unite the Continent failed, partly because England made timely concessions to French and Russian land hunger, but chiefly because France and Russia felt German hegemony on the Continent to be more dangerous to their interests than British maritime hegemony. Here again, self-interest had prevented understanding of the interests of other states. Blinded by his own satisfaction with the Continental *status quo,* and by his desire to change the *status quo* outside Europe, William II drove France and Russia to a decision which they had been reluctant to make. Despite his failure to win the Dual Alliance, the Kaiser was confident that Germany could, unaided, establish a balance of power on the sea. The navy scare of 1909 brought fear of Germany home to the English people for the first time. They ignored the justifiable elements in the German fleet argument. They forgot that the British fleet could seize and blockade. They saw only that Germany, the greatest military power, was challenging their naval supremacy, their bulwark against starvation and Europe's bulwark against despotism.

It was not only in Berlin and London that passion clouded reason. France had forgotten Delcassé's sins but remembered Germany's efforts to browbeat her into surrender. France watched for another insult, and prepared to meet it by strengthening her army. Russia could not understand Austria's fear of Serbia. Austria was desperate with fear of Pan-Slavism. In this atmosphere peace had but a poor chance of survival. Each side feared that the balance was turning in favor of the other. Each side piled more arms into the scales. So long as faith in arms as instruments of policy continued, the race must also continue until ended by war or revolution. The imagination of Europe recoiled from these alternatives. Statesmen labored to find some other solution, but they were afraid to abandon the weapon of force. They wanted no war, but what if war came and they were unprepared? To be sure, the masses everywhere were desirous of peace, but experience showed how weak a prop this sentiment was: desire for peace could change into bellicose fervor almost overnight. To be sure, the peace movement was growing, but only in England did the pacifists possess appreciable political influence. Even there, while the overburdened taxpayer might for a time heed the pacifists' plan for reduction of armaments, reaction followed. English pacifists held down ship-building for three years; the advocates of preparedness became strident in their warnings; in 1909 came the naval scare, and eight dreadnaughts. There were trouble-makers in every country: Russians who plotted dangerously in the Balkans; Austrians who preached war against Serbia; Pan-Germans intoxicated with dreams of conquest; Frenchmen who hoped to use Morocco as a means of stirring the embers of *revanche;* Englishmen who would block German expansion completely, who would sink the German fleet without warning. Every country had its firebrands. If they controlled one government, they could embroil all Europe. If any state felt confident of victory, would it not be tempted to heed aggressive counselors? The times were too dangerous for new and untried experiments. Force and the balance of power were dangerous guardians for peace, but they were the best Europe knew.

CHAPTER V

FROM AGADIR TO ARMAGEDDON, 1911–1914

CHAPTER V

FROM AGADIR TO ARMAGEDDON, 1911–1914

1. MOROCCO, 1911

At the beginning of 1911 Europe enjoyed an illusory feeling of security. In 1909 France and Germany shelved the Moroccan question. In 1910, Kaiser and Tsar compromised their differences and affirmed their desire for good relations. The Anglo-German naval negotiations bore no fruit, but both countries obviously wished peace. Something like a balance of power seemed achieved. Sir Edward Grey, surveying Europe, thought "there was nothing to bring the two groups of European Powers into conflict; and it could therefore fairly be said at any time that, though there were two separate groups of Powers, these groups were not necessarily hostile." In April, the idyllic vision was suddenly and permanently shattered. The despatch of French troops to Fez was announced; Morocco immediately became a live issue once more. War threatened. Before Morocco was disposed of, the second act began. In haste to claim her share of her bargain with France, Italy abruptly demanded Tripoli from Turkey. The demand was refused. In September, 1911, war began between Italy and Turkey. Seeing Turkey's strength drained by war, the Balkan states, with Russian encouragement, drew together. In October, 1912, against Russian wishes, they attacked Turkey. For ten months there was war in the Balkans—first between the allies and Turkey, then between the victorious allies themselves. In August, 1913, exhaustion forced the antagonists to make peace. Peace was merely a truce; disappointment, hope, hatred pervaded the air. The powers struggled to keep clear of the vortex of Balkan strife. In July and August, 1914, they were drawn in, one by one—all except Italy. She bided her time. Morocco, Tripoli, the Balkan wars, Sarajevo, followed one another in remorseless succession.

The Moroccan crisis of 1911 forms a record of blunders, French, German, and English blunders. The French made the first misstep. Under the Treaty of Algeciras, France was permitted to police certain ports. Between 1906 and 1911 other ports had been taken over in order to prevent native outbreaks against foreigners. The French "penetration" of Morocco was progressing. Meanwhile, the Franco-German agreement of 1909 remained practically inoperative. Both sides were to blame for failure to secure the harmonious action hoped for in 1909; but the chief obstacle was French nationalist opposition to German economic concessions in Morocco. Since they had not secured the economic advantages promised them, the Germans were unwilling to see France acquire complete political control. Once she had absorbed Morocco, France would be less inclined than ever to concede anything to German commerce and industry. While France and Germany talked and got nowhere, the Moroccans grew more restive. In March, 1911, there was a revolt. The French press urged the necessity of occupying the capital, Fez: the foreign residents of the city were in danger; they must be rescued; no one, not even Germany, could object to an effort to protect the interests of all civilized nations. The Foreign Minister, Cruppi, supported the project before the cabinet. He was asked about the attitude of Germany; he gave the impression that Germany would do nothing. The cabinet then approved the expedition. The troops started early in April, and arrived at Fez on May 21.

Whether or not the foreigners at Fez were in danger is debatable; that the attitude of Germany had been misrepresented by the French press and Foreign Office is certain. In March, when the expedition was first suggested, the Germans hinted that an understanding was advisable: once Fez was in French possession, public opinion on both sides would be aroused, and a compromise would be difficult. The French ambassador was evasive. In April, the German Foreign Secretary, Kiderlen, returned to the charge: "Be sincere, I pray you, and let us throw our cards on the table! When you are at Fez, you will not leave it." Again a dilatory response. Even after Fez had been reached, the French turned aside all hints from Berlin.

A vague uneasiness spread through European chancelleries. What was the French objective? The French press continued to reiterate its original theme: the troops will restore order; then they will retire. Europe was skeptical. "The experience of all European states, beginning with England," said the British Undersecretary, "shows that it is easier to occupy a city than to withdraw again." France had gone beyond her rights under the Treaty of Algeciras; there was little possibility that she could regain firm legal ground. Her partners in the Entente had not been consulted. They feared France had no definite program. Trouble was inevitable—in fact, had begun. As soon as the Spaniards heard of the expedition they suspected a trick to deprive them of their share of Morocco. They lost no time in sending troops—to suppress disorder.

Without diplomatic preparations, even spurning all offers to effect a quiet settlement, France had reopened the difficult Moroccan question. So far as the majority of Frenchmen, even of French ministers, were concerned, the action was taken unwittingly. Yet Germany had at least as much right to complain of the occupation of Fez as France had had earlier when England occupied Egypt. Those who inspired the press campaign in favor of the expedition, as well as those who prompted the foreign secretaries, Cruppi and de Selves—both novices in the realm of foreign affairs —cannot have been ignorant of the fact that they were steering France straight toward a test of strength with Germany. A small but active and powerful group of ardent nationalists existed within the French government. Increasingly intimate relations with England, together with the rapid growth of French and Russian military strength, heartened the nationalists and swelled their ranks. By 1911, Delcassé was back in the ministry. There is no evidence that he inspired French foreign policy, but there is every indication that from March to June, 1911, the Moroccan policy of France was directed by nationalists who, like Delcassé, concealed dangerous expedients behind plausible arguments.

Just as the French ministers, alarmed by the growing tension, began to think of compromise, Germany blundered. The German Foreign Secretary, Kiderlen, drew up a plan of action early in May. Kiderlen realized it was no longer possible to reconcile the independence of Morocco with the maintenance of order. He also knew that France and England would not permit Germany to secure part of Morocco. He was confident, however, that compensation could be secured elsewhere. He proposed to wait until it became apparent that Fez could not be evacuated within a reasonable time. Then he would send war-ships to some Moroccan port and leave them there until France came to time. He selected Agadir as a suitable port, because it was far removed from Gibraltar and therefore beyond England's vital sphere of influence. The Kaiser hesitated, then approved the program. The French reached Fez on May 21. Kiderlen waited a month. Again and again he hinted at the desirability of a compromise. Germany, he intimated, would be willing to see France get Morocco in return for territory in French equatorial Africa. "It must be a decent mouthful," he warned in June. No response came from Paris. On July 1, the German gunboat *Panther* appeared off Agadir. It was sent, the powers were told, in response to appeals for protection from German firms; it would leave when order was restored.

The *"Panther's* spring," intended to facilitate a settlement, made compromise more difficult. Caillaux, the French premier, was an advocate of Franco-German friendship. He had to contend with nationalist opinion in the ministry and at the Foreign Office. The nationalists described the *"coup d'Agadir"* as new evidence of German truculence; they would stand firm in face of this "insult." Traditional methods of diplomatic bargaining aided the nationalists. The country which first stated its terms would be at a disadvantage in the subsequent haggling. France, therefore, made no offer. Kiderlen was nonplussed. He had expected a speedy solution. The Kaiser was angry and impatient: "What the devil is to be done now? This is sheer farce; negotiating and negotiating, and never getting any further! . . . This kind of diplomacy is beyond my brain." In desperation, Kiderlen started the bargaining. On July 15 he asked for all the French Congo. The French ambassador was duly horrified. France might give part of the Congo. Even for that she would expect to get some German territory in central Africa as recompense. All this followed the usual formula, but the bargainers started very far apart. Suppose France refused to advance far toward the German position? Kiderlen, Bethmann, and the Kaiser discussed the question. The result was a decision for peace, no matter how little France offered. The recognition by France that some compensation was necessary, together with the decision of Germany that war must be avoided, opened the way for a settlement, although undoubtedly the road would be difficult at best.

So far the duel had been between France and Germany; their respective allies remained in the background. When the German gunboat arrived at Agadir, however, the British began to get uneasy; they were determined to prevent Germany from securing a naval base in Morocco. "Further developments," Grey warned the German ambassador on July 4, "might affect British interests more directly than they had hitherto been affected, and, therefore, we could not recognize any new arrangement which was come to without us." Here was a broad hint. England wished to be consulted. The Germans disregarded the hint. They thought it was safe to do so because they were not seeking Moroccan territory; they thought it was desirable to do so because France would yield more if England did not stand by her side. For the same reason that Germany wished to keep England out of the discussion, the French wished to bring

her in. Kiderlen's demand for the Congo gave them their
opportunity. Some one at the Quai d'Orsay was "indis-
creet"; the *Matin* published the German demand, without
the concessions Germany was willing to give. The nationalist outcry became shrill. The French government turned to
England, filled with trepidation. Germany was making demands French opinion would never concede. Where did
England stand? Grey acted with moderation. To France he
said: If the German demand is too high, make a counter-
offer before breaking off negotiations. He reminded Germany of his warning of July 4, and asked for a statement
of German intentions. Grey's actions greatly facilitated a
peaceful solution. Both contestants had been warned that
England desired moderation and compromise.

On July 21, the same day that Grey asked Metternich for
a statement of Germany's intentions, and before a reply
could be received from Berlin, David Lloyd George appeared at Grey's office in a state of great excitement. Lloyd
George had a reputation for radicalism and pacifism. He
was a consistent opponent of naval expenditures and an advocate of friendship with Germany. But now he was indignant: Germany had disregarded England's wish to be consulted about Morocco. He was to speak at the Mansion
House. He wished to warn Germany. He showed Grey
what he proposed to say. Grey gave his approval. That evening Lloyd George delivered his challenge.

"If a situation were to be forced upon us in which peace
could only be preserved by the surrender of the great and
beneficent position Britain has won by centuries of heroism
and achievement, by allowing Britain to be treated, where
her interests were vitally affected, as if she were of no account in the Cabinet of Nations, then I say emphatically that
peace at that price would be a humiliation intolerable for a
great country like ours to endure. National honor is no party
question."

The idea was an old one: fight or give way, but it ex-
ploded with terrific force over Europe, partly because diplomats traditionally spoke gently and in secret until there was

no hope of compromise, partly because the idea sounded new and ominous, expressed by a professed anti-militarist. National honor, that most delicate of subjects, was placed squarely in the center of the picture. The way to a graceful retreat, which diplomats always tried to keep open for each other, was closed. French nationalists were encouraged. Grey, Caillaux, and Bethmann, all anxious to find a peaceful settlement, found their task more difficult. Caillaux, fearing the stubbornness of the Quai d'Orsay, resorted to the dangerous expedient of negotiating through intermediaries with the German embassy, behind the back of his Foreign Minister. The Quai d'Orsay deciphered the German telegrams and discovered the ruse. Caillaux was forced to desist. If the Quai d'Orsay revealed his secret dealings with "the enemy," he was lost. He could now offer only the meager concessions the Foreign Office was willing to give. At first the Germans, maddened by the prospect of open defeat, were equally obdurate. French finance intervened. Short-term loans to Germany were recalled; German financial stability was threatened. Germany gave way. Even when Germany offered sweeping concessions, the French ambassador at Berlin feared the nationalists would prevent their acceptance. He asked Russia to exert pressure in Paris. The Russians, dreading war, were glad to comply. "We might," they warned, "support you if Morocco was at stake—even that would be difficult, but we could not stand by you over the question of a larger or smaller *pourboire*."

At the beginning of November agreement was reached. Germany gave France a free hand in Morocco, and secured in exchange a large, and worthless, tract in central Africa. German opinion was bitter. French opinion was moderately pleased, because Germany was displeased. While the French press was discussing the treaty with tepid enthusiasm, the Quai d'Orsay published the Franco-Spanish treaty of 1904. The French had thought they were to get all Morocco; now they found Spain was to get part. The nationalists cried out that France had been cheated. To maim a French colony at German behest was a humiliation acceptable only if

France was to get all Morocco. The reaction of public opinion threatened to block the treaty. Ratification was secured, but after a debate filled with animus against Germany. Caillaux was made the scapegoat. His secret dealings with Germany were revealed. He was thrown from office and branded a traitor. A new, a "national," ministry took office under Poincaré, a ministry determined to prevent further insults to French honor. No more would France yield to German threats. The interests of France were the interests of Europe, and of civilization. Compromise with Germany was compromise with evil.

Such is the strange history of the second Moroccan crisis. "France" marched on Fez, and rebuffed German efforts to open negotiations. Who constituted "France" is unknown; certainly few Frenchmen knew how it all started. "Germany" was Kiderlen, who devised a policy which proved to be based on false assumptions. "Germany" was not the German people, not even the Kaiser, who acquiesced unwillingly. Was England Sir Edward Grey, who feared and mistrusted Germany, yet sought moderation and compromise? Or was England Mr. Lloyd George, the pacifist turned jingo in a crisis? The crisis seems comic—its obscure origin, the question at stake, the conduct of the actors —all comic. The results were tragic. Tension between France and Germany and between Germany and England had been increased; the armaments race received new impetus; the conviction that an early war was inevitable spread through the governing class of Europe. Nor was this all. When the French marched on Fez they unwittingly reopened the Near Eastern question.

2. TRIPOLI AND THE BALKAN LEAGUE, 1911–1912

The Young Turk revolution did not bring about the rejuvenation and liberalism of Turkey. Instead, the process of disintegration was accelerated. As earlier in Western Europe, the nationalism of the Young Turks proved stronger than their liberalism. When their first efforts to win the loyalty of the non-Turkish Balkan peoples failed, the Young Turks resorted to coercion. Inexperienced, they made errors which even Abdul Hamid had avoided. Tax-collectors and governors were sent into the mountains of Albania. The Albanians had long enjoyed quasi-independence. The arrival of Turkish officials was an unwelcome surprise to them. They told the officials to leave; any who insisted on staying were killed. The Turks sent troops. The Albanians called a truce in their age-old blood feuds, and embarked with enthusiasm on a guerilla war which not only drained Turkish strength but encouraged the Macedonian bands to resume their atrocious activities—and brought the great powers on the scene once more.

Albania was a mountainous wilderness inhabited by primitive and warlike tribesmen; yet because of its position, Albania was a vitally important part of Europe. If Serbia and Montenegro got northern Albania, with a port on the Adriatic, their trade need no longer be dependent on Austrian railways and Austrian good-will. Instead, in time of war, they could offer the enemies of Austria the opportunity of blockading the Adriatic ports of the Dual Monarchy. Similarly, if Greece got southern Albania, with the port of Avlona, a naval power in alliance with Greece could dominate the whole Adriatic. Naturally, the two great Adriatic powers, Austria and Italy, were preoccupied with the fate of this strategic strip of coast-line. Both spoke defensively and thought aggressively. Austria pleaded the manifest danger to her safety which the possession of ports in the northern Adriatic by Slav states, protégés of Russia, would involve. Austria, or rather the military party in the monarchy, secretly hoped to secure northern Albania; then Serbia and Montenegro could be encircled, dominated, and eventually absorbed. Therefore Austria expended much effort and money to build up a sympathetic party among the Albanian tribesmen. Italy pointed to the fact that, since she had no good harbors on her southern Adriatic coast, she could not oppose a blockading fleet based on southern Albania. In reality, Italy coveted Avlona; its possession would give Italy incontestable mastery of the Adriatic and a base for further expansion in the Balkans. Therefore, Italian agents were busy in southern Albania. Both Austria and Italy realized the dangers of trying to effect an immediate conquest of Albania. They would quarrel over the spoils, and other powers would oppose their plan. For the immediate future, the allied rivals wished to preserve the *status quo* in Albania; if that proved impossible, Albania was to be made an independent state, and thus kept intact until the moment for action arrived.

The Balkan states, Turkey, and Russia realized the ambitions of Austria and Italy; they were also alarmed by the expansion of German economic influence in the Near East. The military power of the Triple Alliance seemed overwhelming. For common defense a Balkan union, supported by Russia, was thought advisable. The project was discussed, but across the path to success lay conflicting aggressive ambitions which, though temporarily held in check by fear, were very much alive. Not only had the Balkan states and Russia all staked out claims to parts of Turkey; the claims conflicted at many points. From 1908 to 1911 Russia vainly tried one expedient after another in her desire to find a combination which would block the Triple Alliance and preserve the *status quo* until Russia was strong enough to act.

Both sides were seeking defensive ends, for the present; both sides cherished aggressive plans, for the future. By the mental jugglery which is a commonplace in international relations, each state regarded its own aggressive ends as non-existent, because in abeyance. These eliminated, a simple and convincing argument resulted: our actions are dictated by defensive needs; our opponents are uniting against us and are trying to thwart our efforts; we know the opposing camp harbors aggressive designs beneath the cloak of defensive purposes; therefore, in uniting to resist our opponents, and in thwarting their efforts, we are resisting aggression. This attitude of mind prevailed in every capital; the prospect for a peaceful solution of Balkan disputes was not bright.

While the Balkan rivals watched the convulsive disintegration of Turkish power, the French marched to Fez.
Italian policy immediately became active. By balancing deli-
cately between her allies and the Entente, Italy had been
able to win secret recognition of her claim to Tripoli from
all the Continental powers. Austria and Russia had also
been forced to promise Italy a voice in Balkan affairs.
Would these paper promises be kept? Not from any affec-
tion her neighbors felt for Italy, certainly. The powers
thought it necessary to court Italy, but they regarded her
with suspicion, because she was untrustworthy, and with
contempt, because she was weak. Italy feared Austria and
Russia would force her to be content with Tripoli when the
dissolution of Turkey came. Better, the Italians were beginning to think, seize Tripoli now, so that other compensation could be demanded later. The advance of France in
Morocco convinced Italy that quick action was necessary.
France had promised Italy a free hand in Tripoli in return
for a free hand in Morocco. With Morocco hers, would not
France, eyeing the map, hunger to complete her north African empire by securing Tripoli? The Italians decided to
take no chances. Without even waiting for the usual excuse,
they called on Turkey to give them a protectorate over
Tripoli. When the Italian demand was refused, war began,
in September, 1911.

The war was a poor affair. The Turks themselves did
almost no fighting, but they refused to make peace. As for
the Italians, they found a desert hard to conquer; they demanded that Turkey force the Tripolitans to stop defending themselves. Despite the frightened protests of the powers, Italy entered the Ægean, occupied islands in the Dode-
canese, and threatened to attack the Straits. Still the Turks
remained obdurate; they threatened to close the Straits to
commerce if Italy approached the Dardanelles. The war
dragged on through the spring and summer of 1912.

The Balkan peoples and Russia watched the war, half
hopeful, half fearful. What next? Would Austria follow
the example of Italy, and, under the ægis of Germany, try

to settle her score with Serbia, or try to seize Albania?
Would the Turks try to furbish their prestige by a campaign against the Balkan states? Was Turkey about to collapse? Rumor followed rumor. The Russians decided something must be done. At the end of 1911, Russian diplomats
became active in every capital. The statesmen of other countries became confused and frightened: no one could understand what Russia was trying to do, because at least three
contradictory policies were being energetically pushed by
different Russian diplomats. Even to-day it is hard to follow the vagaries of those inveterate plotters, Isvolski,
Charykov, Hartwig, and Nekliudov. Many scholars make
much of Isvolski's activities during these months. He had,
it will be remembered, been appointed ambassador at Paris
in 1910. When the Tripolitan war broke out, he tried once
more to open the Straits question. Again his efforts failed.
The evidence we now possess suggests that, after this failure, Isvolski decided war was the only way to success, and
that he did everything in his power to hurry France and
Russia into war. When war came, he boasted: "C'est ma
guerre." Some scholars are disposed to give him a large
share of the dubious glory of precipitating the catastrophe.
It is probable that, in days to come, Isvolski's pompous
little figure will sink to less satanically grandiose proportions.

Far more important work was done by the Russian ministers at Belgrade and Sofia, Hartwig and Nekliudov.
These diplomats, with Sazonov's approval, created an alliance between the Balkan states. The task had been attempted before, but it had always broken down. Serbia,
Montenegro, Bulgaria, and Greece possessed insatiable appe-
tites and hungered for as large a share of European Turkey
as possible. The Russians succeeded in overcoming these
jealousies by pointing out the dangers attendant on continued rivalry. German influence was spreading in the Near
East; Italy hoped to secure southern Albania; Austrians
spoke of the conquest not only of northern Albania, but of
Serbia and western Macedonia as well. The Italian con-

quest of Tripoli might be the prelude to a united descent on the Balkans by the Triple Alliance. Turkey also was talking of war as a means of stamping out subversive agitation in Macedonia. While the Balkan states quarreled among themselves, they could be played off one against another; in the end all would lose. The Russians were undoubtedly sincere in urging, and the Balkan governments were undoubtedly sincere in heeding, these defensive arguments. The primary purpose of the projected alliance was to bar the road to the aggressive aims, real or supposed, of the Triple Alliance. A secondary purpose was to prevent Turkey from applying once more her old motto: Divide and conquer. Before the Balkan states could be welded together, however, it was necessary to sketch at least a partial division of the spoils which they hoped eventually to get. Otherwise suspicion and discord would speedily revive.

The nucleus of the Balkan league was an alliance between Bulgaria and Serbia, signed in March, 1912. The body of the treaty set forth the defensive objective: each promised to aid the other in case of attack; both promised to repel any effort by a great power to acquire territory in the Balkans. Aggressive aims were dealt with in a secret annex. If either wished to attack Turkey, the other must be consulted, and a common course of action devised. A tentative division of the spoils was outlined, leaving northern Albania and the extreme western part of Macedonia to Serbia. The rest of Macedonia, and Thrace, went to Bulgaria. A small contested zone was to be referred to Russia for settlement, if necessary. The Tsar was also appointed arbiter in any disputes which might arise between the allies. Two months later Greece allied with Bulgaria, but only for protection against a Turkish attack. No division of territory was agreed upon; indeed, such an agreement was impossible, since both desired the same area. Montenegro was already bound to Serbia by an informal but close understanding.

By May, 1912, the Balkan states south of the Danube were united on the principle of "the Balkans for the Balkan peoples," with Russia as protector. The union was designed for defense: as Sazonov said, to oppose the advance of Germany and Austria with a wall of bayonets. The existence of potentially offensive clauses does not disprove the defensive nature of the alliance. Everybody knew that one day Serbia and Bulgaria would claim Macedonia and would, if necessary, fight Turkey to get it. Unless the conditions under which the war was to start and the distribution of territory were settled, no alliance could have been made. At the beginning of 1912, Russia and the Balkan states were afraid of the Triple Alliance; the Balkan states were also afraid of each other and of Turkey. The alliance was designed to banish fear. Throughout 1912, most Balkan statesmen continued to desire peace. Among more venturesome spirits union did not merely banish fear; it also raised hope. It was the old story: an instrument designed for protection engendered the desire for aggression, and as fear weakened, resistance to aggressive counsels also weakened.

3. THE ENTENTE AND GERMANY, 1912

Morocco led to Tripoli; Tripoli led to the Balkan league, from which momentous consequences were to flow. The effects of the second Moroccan crisis did not stop here. The crisis modified relations between the western nations. In England and Germany, reaction from the imminence of war produced a powerful desire for reconciliation. In France, the result was exactly the opposite; the French under Poincaré began an energetic attempt to strengthen the Triple Entente in opposition to Germany.

In 1911, the German and British peoples realized for the first time the probability of war between their countries. Germany retreated, angry and humiliated. Tirpitz hoped to utilize this resentment. In 1912 the German building program fell to two ships a year; Tirpitz's propagandists urged the necessity for an increase in the program so that Germany might not be forced to surrender in future to England. Opposition immediately appeared, opposition more strenuous than ever before. Not merely pacifists, but leaders of industry, finance, and the army as well, attacked Tirpitz. Germany, they argued, had been building ships for over a decade. England was still safely ahead, and England had become an enemy of Germany. Germany, meanwhile, had become perilously isolated. The Triple Alliance was no alliance. Austria and Italy hated each other. Italy had deserted, and Austria had given only wavering support to Germany, during the Moroccan crises. Without consulting Germany, Austria embarked on dangerous policies in the Balkans, and Italy fought Turkey. Realizing that Germany was isolated and dependent upon them, Austria and Italy might yet drag Germany into war. On either side of Germany were the French and the Russians, arming rapidly. Germany spent money which was needed for the army on ships which had no effect except to ensure British hostility. It was time to curb Tirpitz, argued an increasingly large and powerful group in Germany. William II was forced to heed the opposition, but he raised the same condition as in 1908: England must first promise not to help France and Russia in a war against Germany.

Simultaneously, opposition to Grey's policy was growing in England. In 1908, England had been brought to the brink of war over Bosnia; in 1911, war threatened over Morocco. The British cared little about either Bosnia or Morocco. England had promised to help France get Morocco; France now had Morocco. That promise was fulfilled. England and Russia had promised to preserve Persian independence. Russia had broken, and was breaking, that promise. In 1911, the Persians made a desperate bid for freedom. They brought in a young American, W. Morgan Shuster. They gave him practically dictatorial power. He set about his task with such energy that he threatened to be successful. Russia sent an ultimatum: Shuster must leave. The Persians appealed to England for help. None came. In January, 1912, Shuster left, and the world laughed. England, the home of humanitarianism, at that very moment abusing the Belgians for the horrors of their rule in the Congo, England a party to the strangling of Persia! Englishmen writhed under scornful taunts. Feeling against Russia rose, and with it rose desire to end the feud with Germany. That quarrel healed, England could turn her back on the Continent and devote her energy and her money to her empire, to Ireland, and to Lloyd George's program of social reform. Lloyd George himself, all jingoism forgotten, pressed for a friendly understanding. As Chancellor of the Exchequer, and as leader of the reformers, he hated the thought of spending money for ships. Grey held back, fearful for the Entente, and convinced that Germany would demand much and offer little. He was overruled by his colleagues. In February, 1912, the Minister of War, Haldane, was sent to Berlin to discover if agreement was possible.

Haldane arrived full of hope. He was a warm admirer of Germany, the Germany of philosophers and artists he had known in his student days, and he was anxious to heal the quarrel between the two countries. Conversations with the Kaiser, Tirpitz, and Bethmann dampened his hopes. It was evident that counsels in Berlin were divided. Bethmann and Tirpitz were pulling against each other. The English negotiator was uncomfortable between the two. He was further embarrassed by the Kaiser's impetuous eagerness to settle things at once. Haldane was neither a naval expert nor a diplomat. Realizing his deficiencies, he put the bulky copy of the Navy Bill which was given him into his pocket unread. Tirpitz explained the bill. At present, a large part of the German fleet was out of commission, while recruits were being trained. To remedy this defect the formation of a new squadron was necessary. The Reichstag would be asked for three new ships and for increases in personnel. If a political agreement was reached, the building of the ships might be deferred for a few years, but the increases in personnel must be made at once. Haldane refrained from discussing details, but he said plainly that any political agreement would be "bones without flesh" if Germany increased her program. "Indeed, the world would laugh at the agreement, and our people would think that we had been fooled." The Kaiser was depressed; then he dismissed the subject, saying that the political agreement was the important thing. That attained, concessions on ship-building would be easy. Haldane was unconvinced, but agreed to map out a political program. Possible bases for a colonial agreement were discussed, but the most important result of the long conferences was the tentative draft of a neutrality formula. The third clause was the most important: "If either of the high contracting parties becomes entangled in a war in which it cannot be said to be the aggressor, the other will at least observe towards the Power so entangled a benevolent neutrality."

Haldane returned to London. Long and confused negotiations then began between the two governments. Records of these negotiations have been published and minutely analyzed by scholars. Nevertheless, much still remains in doubt. In Berlin, Bethmann and Kiderlen were willing to give up the new Navy Bill if England would promise neutrality in case of a French attack on Germany. In London, some members of the cabinet were willing to proceed on this basis. In Berlin, Tirpitz fought to save the substance of the Navy Bill, even at the cost of the political agreement. In London, Grey and the permanent staff of the Foreign Office were unwilling to make a binding promise of neutrality under any circumstances. The position of William II is dubious. He strongly desired both the Navy Bill and the promise of neutrality. Which he would have chosen had he been forced to choose never became known.

Haldane's report of his negotiations in Berlin strengthened Grey's hand. Those who wished an agreement with Germany were motivated in large part by desire to reduce expenditure on naval armaments. After examining the German Navy Bill which Haldane brought with him, the Admiralty reported that the estimates must be greatly increased even if Tirpitz made the concessions he promised. The purpose of the Navy Bill was to keep the fleet in constant readiness for war. Tirpitz had carefully offered concessions which would not impair this purpose. Therefore, whether the bill went through modified or unmodified, the

British home fleet must be in constant readiness to parry a surprise attack. For the present, this strength could only be secured by bringing home the Atlantic or the Mediterranean fleet. Since it would be dangerous to leave the Atlantic or the Mediterranean permanently unprotected, new vessels must be constructed to take the place of those brought home. The advocates of conciliation were disheartened. Could greater concessions on the building program be secured from Berlin? The Foreign Office took up this approach with enthusiasm; for weeks the political agreement almost dropped out of sight.

William II was furious. With his usual tendency to exclude unpleasant facts from his field of vision, he forgot Haldane's warnings about the effect of naval increases and remembered only the tempting discussion of colonies and the neutrality formula. After Haldane left Berlin, the discussions within the German government centered almost entirely around the political agreement. The wording suggested by Bethmann and Haldane was thought to be too vague. The word "aggressor" was hard to define. A more precise expression was needed. England must promise neutrality "should war be forced upon Germany." While William's imagination was grasping at new advantages in the political field, England shifted the discussion back to the fleet. With customary petulance, the Kaiser angrily decided to bring the negotiation to an end by presenting the Navy Bill to the Reichstag. There was a sharp crisis. Bethmann threatened to resign if the bill was introduced. Tirpitz threatened to resign if the bill was abandoned. The Kaiser hesitated.

In London, Metternich pleaded for some action on the political question. There were discussions in the cabinet. On March 14, Grey conveyed the decision to Metternich: England would promise not to make, or join in, an "unprovoked attack" on Germany. This was less than Haldane had offered; the word "neutrality" was carefully omitted. The negotiations had reached a deadlock. Each side waited for the other to make concessions. In the end, Tirpitz's strong will triumphed over the timorous Bethmann. The Navy Bill was introduced and passed in the spring of 1912. England appropriated funds to build two ships for each one Germany built, and prepared to call home the Atlantic fleet.

So ended the last and most determined effort of two great powers to find some solution for the problem of security other than the solution of force. The desire to bridge the gulf separating them persisted in both countries. In an effort to lessen antagonism, negotiations were begun on specific colonial questions, but these discussions did not touch the root of the difficulty. Indeed, it might be argued that they did more harm than good by encouraging each government to hope that the other might desert its allies in a crisis.

Those who had hoped that the Haldane mission would lead to agreement thought that the system of alliances was dangerous to peace. By 1912 the French had reached the opposite conclusion. They doubted if peace could be preserved, but they were convinced that safety, whether in peace or in war, could be attained only by converting the Entente into an alliance. The second Moroccan crisis intensified the revival of nationalism which had begun under Delcassé. Agadir, like Tangier, was interpreted as a deliberate German affront, intended to humiliate France. Few Frenchmen would admit that France was even partially to blame for either crisis. Nearly all Frenchmen were proud of the intransigent attitude of the Quai d'Orsay in 1911. Instinctively France braced herself to meet the next German "insult." Arms and allies had enabled France to win; in arms and allies Frenchmen put their trust. Great military reviews were held, crowds gathered to see and cheer. The army, the guardian of French honor, was idolized as in the days of Boulanger. The press ceaselessly extolled the virtues of "the policy of equilibrium," which would preserve peace by establishing a balance of power. France wanted peace, but peace with honor. The honor of France had suffered much from the "barbarians" across the Rhine. It would suffer no more. France, after forty years of weakness, was herself again.

It was dangerous to speak so much of honor. National honor was the most inflammable of all the subjects with which diplomats dealt. It was dangerous to interpret the desired balance of power as a balance which would always enable France to have her will when disputes arose; unconsciously many Frenchmen did interpret the policy of equilibrium in this manner. Above all, the revival of *revanche* was dangerous to peace. It made no difference that the Alsatians no longer wanted "redemption" if redemption meant war; France refused to hear. The old phrases of Gambetta and Déroulède were intoned with new fervor. Probably most Frenchmen were unconscious of the strident tone which was becoming increasingly prevalent in the press and in public speeches. Convinced that France had suffered much at the hands of Germany, desirous of vengeance for old wrongs, confident that vengeance was possible, never doubting that Germany would try to regain her hegemony, the articulate elements in French national life seemed to anticipate with little sorrow, sometimes even with joy, what they were coming to call "the inevitable war."

Poincaré, who became premier in January, 1912, was the embodiment of the national revival. His ideals were the ideals of Gambetta, but in character and personality he was the antithesis of the earlier patriot. Passionate his nature certainly was, but the passion was cold, and rigorously held in check. He had none of the spontaneous warmth of feeling which made Frenchmen love statesmen like Gambetta and Clemenceau. Poincaré was more closely akin to Richelieu. Mind and will were his weapons, a mind powerful and exact, a will tenacious to the point of stubbornness, so strong that other wills collapsed under its pressure. With these weapons he inspired respect, even awe, but rarely love. France turned to him in 1912 because he perfectly represented the dominant mood.

Poincaré was a Lorrainer who through a long public

career had never wavered in his determination to reverse
the verdict of 1871. At the same time, he was not a fire-
brand. He knew France was not prepared to fight in order
to recover Alsace-Lorraine, and he knew what hazards war
would entail. For both reasons he was opposed to a provocative policy. Nevertheless, Poincaré was sure war would
come, and speedily. War would come through German
provocation. For over a generation Germany had dominated Europe. The formation of the Triple Entente ended
her supremacy, but Agadir showed that Germany was not
prepared to surrender her hegemony peacefully. There
would be other incidents. One of these would end in war.
Poincaré did not falter at the thought of war, and he was
determined that France should not falter. If French resolution weakened, the crisis would merely be hastened. The
Germans would again become brutally arrogant, and France
must either sink to the level of a minor power or fight for
the right to make her voice heard. To restrain Germany as
long as possible, and to ensure victory when the inevitable
war came, France must look to her defenses. She must bind
her allies more closely to her, she must keep her armed
forces at the peak of efficiency, and she must keep the flame
of courage burning brightly. "We must," said Poincaré in
a great speech at Nantes, "maintain all of the patience, all
of the energy, all of the pride of a people which does not
desire war but which nevertheless does not fear it."

Poincaré did not believe that France could cope with
Germany single-handed; the Entente must stand united in
face of the impending danger. Solidarity had not existed
in the past. Members of the Entente had embarked on dangerous policies without warning to the others; desertion
had been frequent in time of crisis. Poincaré set out to
remedy these defects. He soon found, however, that the
tide was against him. All the powers except France were in
a hesitant, indecisive mood in 1912. The dangers of the
international situation were obvious to all, but the first impulse of statesmen was to seek safety in isolation, to avoid
friction by direct discussions with statesmen in the opposing

camp. Relations between the Kaiser and the Tsar had been growing more cordial since 1910; the Haldane mission showed the existence of groups seeking a reconciliation between England and Germany. At first, Poincaré fought in vain against these tendencies. He succeeded in negotiating a naval convention with Russia, providing for discussions between the two naval staffs. In August he journeyed to St. Petersburg and tried to impress the necessity for solidarity on the Tsar and Sazonov. Sazonov heartily concurred, but the visit did not banish from French minds the fear that, in a crisis, Russia might refuse to fight.

With England Poincaré had no better luck. He was relieved when the Haldane mission failed, but there was no guarantee that a new effort to reconcile England and Germany might not succeed. The Entente was entirely too nebulous a bond. Possibly, he thought, British alarm over the new German Navy Bill might be used to advantage. In April, 1912, Cambon approached the British Undersecretary: "The French Government were convinced that an opportunity would be seized, perhaps not this year, but possibly the next year or the year after, by Germany to create some incident which would arouse public feeling on both sides of the frontier, and which would, viewing the temper in both countries, very probably lead to war . . . In these circumstances M. Poincaré considered that it was necessary to take stock of the position of France, and to see on what outside assistance she could rely when the moment arrived." Could he "count upon" England? The blunt question was as bluntly answered: the British were not disposed "to tie their hands."

Poincaré's efforts to strengthen the Entente showed a paradoxical and significant result. Russia was united to France by an alliance which bound Russia to aid France in case of a German attack; England was bound by no obligation to aid France. Yet the slender evidence we possess suggests that the French felt more confident of British than of Russian aid. The explanation of this paradox lies in the French estimate of the relative dependence of Russia and

England on France. Russian military strength was growing; Russia might feel strong enough to stand alone. Furthermore, the Tsar had never quite broken his friendship
with Germany. If a Franco-German war came, Russia
might be induced to remain neutral in return for concessions, either in the Near East or at the expense of Austria.
The French were, therefore, fearful lest Russia desert.
That fear made the French reluctant to restrain Russian
ambitions in the Balkans, as the Russians fully realized.

England, on the other hand, was afraid of Germany.
Tirpitz and the Kaiser had put a powerful weapon into
Poincaré's hands. The reorganization of the German navy
authorized by the bill of 1912 forced England to strengthen
her North Sea forces. The Atlantic fleet, which had its base
at Gibraltar, was brought home. The Mediterranean fleet
moved from Malta to Gibraltar. These moves ensured supremacy in the North Sea, but left the Mediterranean, a vital link in imperial communication, unprotected. In time of
war Austria and Italy could close the short route to India.
The British wished France to move her Atlantic fleet from
Brest to the Mediterranean. Churchill, the first lord of the
Admiralty, was reluctant to make a direct request. He
pointed out to Grey "how tremendous would be the weapon
which France would possess to compel our intervention, if
she could say, 'On the advice of and by arrangement with
your naval authorities we have left our northern coasts defenseless. We cannot possibly come back in time.'" Poincaré realized the advantageous position France occupied.
England wished to preserve her complete freedom of action; she also wished the French to move their fleet to the
Mediterranean. Poincaré was determined that England
should not realize both her desires. Through the summer
and autumn of 1912 the French fleet remained at Brest.

During his first months in office, Poincaré was fighting
against the prevailing current. He believed safety lay in
Entente solidarity. England and Russia held back. Both
were reluctant to incur the risks which a promise of
common support might entail, both also felt that a sharp

division of Europe into two hostile camps would be hazardous to peace. Poincaré feared he would not be able to win Russia to his views: Russia did not feel dependent on France. He was confident of overcoming English hesitation: England needed both military and naval assistance from France. Unwittingly, Tirpitz and the Kaiser had provided the means for strengthening the Entente, the Entente which they wished above all else to weaken.

4. THE BALKAN WARS AND THE POWERS, 1912–1913

The fate of the two great alliance systems hung uncertain in 1912. In both camps there were dissension and an inclination to seek safety by avoiding too much intimacy with allies. The whole theory of a balance of forces, Triple Alliance and Triple Entente neutralizing each other, was under attack, except in France. The outbreak of war in the Balkans set two mighty forces in opposition. On the one hand, the imminence of a general war impelled allies to close ranks for safety; on the other, a valiant effort was made to set the ideal of the European concert above the ideal of loyalty to allies.

All through the summer of 1912 the Balkans were unusually disturbed. The powers watched, paralyzed. The inability of Turkey to restore order in Macedonia and Albania was obvious. There were the usual demands for reform, but even the most optimistic had no faith in this often-tried and always unsuccessful panacea. In September, Sazonov became frightened. The Balkan states, which he had expected to be docile tools in his hands, were getting out of control, talking of immediate war against Turkey. He called on the powers to intervene. Suddenly informed that a serious crisis impended, European chancelleries hurriedly tried to stave it off. At Poincaré's suggestion, Russia and Austria were instructed, as representatives of the powers, to dissuade the Balkan states from war and to give them warning that the powers would not consent to territorial changes.

The decision of the powers was made known on October 8, 1912. On the same day Montenegro declared war on

Turkey. Serbia, Greece, and Bulgaria immediately joined Montenegro. Turkey hastened to make peace with Italy, but to the surprise of every one, including the allies themselves, Turkish power collapsed. The climax came at the end of October, when two battles brought the Bulgarians within twelve miles of Constantinople. In Macedonia, Thrace, and Albania only a few forts held out. It was obvious that the powers would be unable to fulfil their threat to prevent territorial changes. The fate of Turkey in Europe was settled.

The Near Eastern question was by no means settled. Austria thought her very existence was threatened. The Balkan allies were allies of Russia. Austria saw herself caught in a pincers. Only Rumania broke the line of Russian power, and Rumanian loyalty was wavering now that Russia was in the ascendant. The pressure of the pincers, unless forcibly relaxed, must crush the Monarchy. The Serbs, encouraged by the Russian minister at Belgrade, were already pointing to Austria as the next victim. The subject races were stirring expectantly. In desperation, Austria thought of war against Serbia. Troops were mobilized. Then Austria hesitated, partly in fear of the troops Russia was mobilizing in reply, partly because of the old hopeless feeling that war against Serbia, even the annexation of Serbia, would aggravate rather than solve the Jugo-Slav problem. Finally, Austria decided to be content with minimizing the dangers of the new situation: the Adriatic coast of Turkey must form part of a new Albanian state; under no circumstances would Montenegro or Serbia be permitted to obtain ports on the Adriatic. Italy, because she hoped some day to secure the Albanian coast, and Germany, to strengthen her allies, supported Austria.

Russia and France opposed the Austrian demands. When Poincaré proposed that the powers prevent territorial changes, he thought the Turkish army stronger than the allied Balkan forces. The Balkan states victorious, he advanced a new formula: the victors should be allowed to make what disposition they would of their conquests. In theory his proposal was compatible with Austrian terms, because the Albanian chieftains had proclaimed their independence of Turkey. Practically there was a conflict. Montenegro was besieging the town of Scutari in Albania; Serbia was occupying the northern, and Greece the southern, part of Albania. All three refused to leave. The Albanians could not expel them. Austria threatened to intervene.

The powers at first inclined to a test of strength. As evidence of united purpose, the Triple Alliance was renewed on December 5, 1912. Poincaré rallied so vigorously to the side of Russia that he seemed more unyielding than the Russians themselves. The exact nature of Poincaré's views in 1912 is still in dispute among scholars. It is probable that if Russia had become involved in war over the Balkans, he would have made every effort to bring France to her assistance, no matter how the war started.

Poincaré was encouraged to regard the prospect of war with more equanimity than formerly, because the Balkan crisis had forced England's hand. Grey feared war might come, and that England might have to participate. He disclosed his fears to the cabinet, and for the first time told of the conversations which had been taking place between the military and naval staffs of France and England since 1905. He also set forth the danger of leaving the Mediterranean unguarded. The tenor of the cabinet discussion is not definitely known. Evidently some members continued to maintain that British freedom of action must be preserved. Others felt that the French demand for a written definition of the Entente must be accepted. The result was the very ambiguous compromise embodied in notes exchanged by Grey and the French ambassador on November 22 and 23, 1912. The notes began by stating that consultation between the general staffs "does not restrict the freedom of either Government to decide at any future time whether or not to assist the other by armed force." It was agreed, however, that "if either Government had grave reason to expect an unprovoked attack by a third Power, or something that threatened the general peace, it should immediately discuss with the other whether both Governments should act together."

Both Poincaré and the British ministers who wished to avoid entangling alliances were satisfied with this statement. It is difficult to understand why the latter were satisfied. Despite the explicit statement that England's hands were free, they were bound. France moved her fleet to the Mediterranean. Could England, in the promised consultation, refuse to protect the defenseless coast of France? Could England in cold blood say: "We recognize that you are threatened by an unprovoked attack; despite the intimacy of our relations, we will stand aside"? It is hard to think so. Of course, if France were the aggressor, or had provoked attack, the English might even refuse to discuss coöperation. The way war came would probably be decisive, as the French realized. They scrupulously avoided actions which English opinion might regard as aggressive, and they ceaselessly impressed on Russia the importance of forcing Germany or Austria to make the first openly warlike move.

In December, 1912, Triple Alliance and Triple Entente stood more solidly opposed to each other than ever before. Yet the crisis passed without war. A combination of three factors ensured for peace a precarious existence: the vacillation of Berchtold and Sazonov, fear of public opinion, and Anglo-German coöperation.

The directors of foreign affairs at Vienna and St. Petersburg were hesitant men who shrank from irrevocable decisions. Berchtold, who had succeeded Aehrenthal at the Ballplatz, was a weakling, a charming, refined, and indolent courtier, not a statesman. His colleagues bombarded him with conflicting counsels which his lazy mind had not the energy to analyze or understand. He started on one course, dropped it when difficulties appeared, and tried another. Sazonov was not so frivolous a man as Berchtold, but he was bewildered by the intricacy of the problems which his unruly Balkan protégés forced on him. Both Berchtold and Sazonov thought the fate of the Balkans important enough to risk a war, but there was no clear issue at any given time. Events moved quickly past: was it this event that controlled the sequence, or would it be the next one? Neither man dared to grasp a position and hold it without compromise.

The wavering, incalculable course pursued by Russia and Austria was harassing for their allies, who must prepare public opinion in advance of war. If war came, Grey and Poincaré felt that England and France must, to preserve the balance of power, aid Russia; the German government, for the same reason, thought Austria must be supported. On the other hand, the man in the street did not understand the intricacies of the balance of power. If war came, the immediate cause must be one which the popular mind could interpret as vitally important, and, above all, as defensive. Otherwise, a united front could not be presented to the enemy. This would be a fatal handicap under modern conditions of warfare. Whether the fate of some unknown Balkan town would constitute such a cause was very doubtful indeed. Therefore both Austria and Russia were repeatedly admonished to move carefully and to avoid taking a firm stand on obscure issues. Fear of repudiation by public opinion operated all through 1913 as a powerful deterrent to rash action.

This uneasiness concerning public opinion and the lack of strong leadership at Vienna and St. Petersburg were negative supports of peace. Positive support came from England and Germany. British public opinion was unmoved by the fate of this or that part of the Balkans; such issues seemed trivial compared to the catastrophic consequences of war. In Germany there was little realization of the danger which Serbian ambitions entailed for Austria: Serbia was so small; Austria, so large. Even Bethmann did not understand the disruptive nature of Jugo-Slav nationalism. Since they had no vital interest in the questions in dispute, and since, as highly industrialized states, the shock of war would do them irreparable harm, England and Germany took the lead in forcing compromises on Austria and Russia. The problem was to force Austria to acquiesce in the triumph of Russian policy in the Balkans, and to force Russia to accept restrictions on that victory. Obviously, Austria was asked to make the greater sacrifice. In practice, the German task was made easier by the fact that conflicting counsels produced a state of almost complete paralysis in Vienna, while the British task was complicated by the eager enthusiasm of the Pan-Slavs, who, confident of Russian strength, resented the slightest concession made by Sazonov.

To facilitate compromise, the British and Germans forced the convening of a conference of ambassadors at London in December, 1912. During the winter the conference successfully disposed of the thorny Albanian question. Austria and Italy succeeded in securing the Adriatic littoral, from Montenegro to the shore opposite Corfu, for the new state; Russia secured most of the disputed area of the interior for Serbia. Other and smaller problems were solved. As Grey said later: "The details with which we dealt were insignificant—in themselves mere sparks. But we were sitting on a powder magazine." In May, 1913, the European concert seemed to have attained its goal when Turkey and the allies were forced to make peace. Turkey abandoned all her European possessions except a small triangle between Midia on the Black Sea, and Enos on the Ægean. Turkey and Albania were now eliminated from the picture. The only remaining task was for the allies to divide their conquests.

This task they were unable to perform peacefully. The creation of Albania cut into the share earlier allotted to Greece and Serbia; Bulgaria, on the other hand, had obtained more than had been anticipated in the eastern part of the Balkans. Serbia and Greece demanded compensation for their losses and Bulgaria's gains. The Bulgarians refused to make concessions; instead, they attacked the Serbians and Greeks in June, 1913, in an effort to expel them from Macedonia. Scenting spoils, Rumania and Turkey attacked Bulgaria.

Again the fear of war threatened to spread over Europe. Austria had hoped to neutralize Serbia's increased strength by an alliance with Bulgaria. Now Serbia was despoiling Bulgaria. Serbia was becoming larger and more dangerous; Bulgaria was being weakened. Austrian hesitation momentarily vanished. Berchtold said Austria must prevent the crushing of Bulgaria. He appealed to Germany and Italy for assurances that they would support Austria if Russia tried to interfere. Instead, he received urgent advice to do nothing. Bethmann refused to admit that Austria's vital interests were involved. Armed intervention against Serbia would mean a European war. Germany was not prepared to risk war by supporting Austria in a policy which Germany thought unwise. Thus admonished, Berchtold subsided unhappily, and held his hand while Bulgaria was crushed. Peace was made at Bucharest in August. Bulgaria was shorn of nearly all the territory she had gained by her victories in the first Balkan war, and also of a broad strip between the Black Sea and the Danube, which Rumania took.

5. THE BULWARKS OF PEACE DESTROYED, 1913-1914

Another crisis had passed without war. Peace had been effectually protected by hesitancy at Vienna and St. Petersburg, by regard for the indifference of public opinion in the western nations to Balkan affairs, and by the efforts of England and Germany to set the ideal of the concert of Europe above the ideal of loyalty to allies. All three of these bulwarks of peace had, however, been weakened during the crisis, and they were weakened still further by the persistence and spread of disorder in the Near East during the year following the Peace of Bucharest.

England and Germany had, by their coöperation at the conference of ambassadors in London, succeeded in putting out many sparks. They had not been able to destroy the powder magazine upon which, as Grey said, Europe was sitting. Moreover, there was no guarantee that a spark might not escape their vigilance and produce the dreaded explosion. All governments decided it would be wise to get ready for the worst by strengthening defenses and preparing public opinion. The two processes were closely interrelated: already restive under the burden of armaments, the peoples of Europe could be induced to take on new burdens only by inflammatory arguments. Who began the new armaments race is a much discussed and futile question. Confronted by the imminence of war, every government discovered that new expenditures were needed to put defenses in readiness. Germany increased the number of men called to the colors each year and, by a capital levy, accumulated gold for her war reserve. France extended the term of service to three years and thus increased not only the efficiency but also the peace-time strength of her army. Further, France made loans to Russia for the express purpose of building strategic railways to the German frontier. Russia increased the already stupendous size of her army. Other powers made proportionate increases. In general, it is safe to say that every government increased the military burden to the limit public opinion would sanction when vigorously prodded. It has been estimated that the *increases* in military budgets during the year 1913 totaled about $250,000,000. The net result was that the relative strength of the powers remained substantially unchanged.

Undoubtedly the campaign for the three-year service law in France was the most vigorous of all. It began at the beginning of 1913, when Poincaré was seeking the French presidency. His election was opposed by many political leaders because he was thought to desire war. To destroy the force of this argument, his supporters stressed the disastrous consequences which must follow if France weakened in her loyalty to her allies, or in her determination to stand firm when Germany became provocative. Poincaré was swept into office on a wave of patriotic enthusiasm. At the end of January, 1913, the new premier, Briand, pledged himself to strengthen French military defenses. The campaign for the three-year service law then began in earnest and continued, aided by every possible appeal to French fears and hopes, until the law was passed in August. From these facts some scholars conclude that Poincaré was eager for war. That conclusion cannot be substantiated. Poincaré thought war in the immediate future was practically inevitable, because he thought Germany could not restrain what he called her arrogant aggressiveness. Poincaré almost certainly would have advocated following Russia into a flagrantly aggressive war, because he thought France would be in a precarious position if she lost the Russian alliance. Undoubtedly Poincaré was confident that France would win when war came, and that Alsace-Lorraine would be recovered. Nevertheless, the evidence we possess indicates that Poincaré, like all statesmen of his generation, thought war an evil which should be shunned if possible.

The campaign for increased military budgets inflamed public opinion and made it less likely to oppose war, if war came. One bulwark of peace was weakened. A second was also under attack. England and Germany wished to continue coöperating in efforts to preserve peace. To preserve and strengthen the improved relations which coöperation had produced, the two governments discussed the colonial questions at issue between them. By the summer of 1914, agreements had been reached concerning the Bagdad Railway and the colonies of bankrupt Portugal. Superficially, relations were improving; actually, both governments were weakening in their resolution to restrain their allies. Both were subjected to a steady stream of reproaches. Forgetting their own doubts and hesitations, the Austrians blamed Germany for the growth of Serbian power: Vienna angrily contrasted the loyal support France gave Russia with the delays and concessions Germany forced on Austria. Russia, on the other hand, blamed England for insisting on the creation of Albania. From the creation of Albania followed the quarrel among the Balkan allies and the break-up of the union by which Russia had hoped to bar the eastward expansion of Austria and Germany. The Entente, lamented Sazonov, was divided; therefore the firmly welded Triple Alliance was victorious.

England and Germany were both worried, fearful of losing their allies. They were also tormented by the suspicion that the real way to ensure peace was to overawe the opposition by a firm, united front. "I do not know," wrote Sir Arthur Nicolson, the British Undersecretary, to the ambassador at St. Petersburg, "how much longer we shall be able to follow our present policy of dancing on a tight rope, and not be compelled to take some definite line or other. I am also haunted by the same fear as you—lest Russia should become tired of us and strike a bargain with Germany." German statesmen were haunted by similar fears. Both in London and Berlin there was a disposition to end the prolonged strain by definite and final support of the alliance system. "I am convinced," Nicolson wrote again, "that if the Triple Entente could be converted into another Triple Alliance, the peace of Europe would be assured for a generation or two." This prospect was more tempting than dancing on a tight rope.

Finally, and most ominous for peace, both Vienna and St. Petersburg were feeling increasingly the necessity for decisive action. The Peace of Bucharest did not bring peace, scarcely even a truce, to the Balkans. No one was satisfied with the results of the wars just passed, or convinced that these results were final. Greece and Turkey were still quarreling over the Ægean islands. Bulgaria was determined to take vengeance on her late allies. The Albanians were showing complete incapacity for self-government. The Greeks, Serbians, and Italians were making plans to seize parts of the new state when it collapsed. Serbia and Rumania, their thirst for conquest stimulated by victory, were talking of the inevitable struggle with Austria. No sooner had he signed the Treaty of Bucharest than the Serbian premier remarked: "The first round is won; now we must prepare for the second, against Austria."

Instability spread east, into Asiatic Turkey, where Armenians, Greeks, Arabs, and other subject peoples hoped to emulate the Balkan states. It seemed improbable that Turkey, in her weakened condition, would have the strength to repress the disaffected elements; it was certain that the subject peoples could not govern themselves. A new field for intrigue was opened. Within the government of every great power there was discussion of the gains which must, or might, be secured when the crash came. The Russians even debated the possibility of a sudden seizure of the Straits. All the discussions ended with the same conclusion: it would be difficult, probably impossible, to divide Asia Minor without war. War was undesirable; therefore, the life of Turkey must be extended as long as possible. The mistrust between the powers was so great, however, that each suspected the others of trying to appropriate part of the plunder before the final division came. Russia was especially sensitive, because she coveted the most hotly contested prize, the Straits.

The tense atmosphere, which was fraying the nerves of statesmen, led to two episodes, both trivial in origin, both momentous in effect. Serbia, unable to restrain her eagerness, occupied parts of western Albania in 1913 "to restore order." Austria asked the London conference to oust the Serbians. The conference took no action; every one was heartily sick of disputes about Albania. Austria asked the Serbians to leave; they made excuses. Berchtold, with the sudden decisiveness of a weak man, launched an ultimatum in October, 1913, demanding that the Serbians leave within eight days. Germany, confronted with a *fait accompli*, reluctantly agreed to support Austria, even if Russia intervened. The Entente powers began by denouncing Austria for abandoning the ideal of the European concert. When it became apparent that Austria was in earnest, England and France drew back. Russia was forced to tell the Serbians they must surrender. In high dudgeon, the Serbians evacuated Albania. Vienna drew a disastrous conclusion from this success. For a year, Austria had made one concession after another out of fear of Russia. Confronted by the Austrian ultimatum, Russia gave way. Vienna concluded it would be safe to repeat the performance. Russia, on the other hand, complained that her allies had deserted and had once more permitted Austria to win a diplomatic victory.

A month later came the Liman von Sanders affair. It resulted from Turkish efforts to stave off collapse. In order to rebuild their shattered government, the Turks sought European assistance. France was asked to take charge of the gendarmerie; England, the navy and civil service; Germany, the army. All agreed. In November, 1913, it became known that the German general, Liman von Sanders, was to have command of a model army corps at Constantinople. Sazonov immediately became excited. He was adverse to any strengthening of Turkish military power, because he wanted no effective resistance when the day came for Russia to seize the Straits. He particularly objected to the presence of Liman at Constantinople. He suspected Germany was planning to secure a grip on the Straits. He determined to block Liman's mission, and called on France and England for aid. The French welcomed the possibility of demonstrating Entente solidarity; Grey was reluctant to intervene against Germany. He was won over by the argument that command of the forces at Constantinople would give Germany control over the Straits when war came. A vigorous protest was drafted for presentation to Turkey.

The German government was surprised and embarrassed by the Russian outcry against Liman's mission. Wilhelmstrasse had never anticipated objection, especially since the Tsar had been told of the projected mission early in 1913. The Germans would have been glad to effect a compromise, but the affair had got into the newspapers. The Russian press angrily denounced this blow prepared in secret against Russian influence at Constantinople; Germany was called on to surrender or face the Entente united in battle array. It was difficult to retreat before this outcry without giving the impression of a humiliating defeat. Germany turned to England for help, and pointed out that the English Admiral Limpus had exactly the same power over the Turkish fleet that General Liman had over the army. This was news to Grey. When he had verified the German contention, he refused to join in the protest to Turkey. The defection of England opened the way to compromise. Liman remained at Constantinople, but he gave up the direct command over troops.

Sazonov was furious at the failure of his plans. Again England had permitted the Triple Alliance to win. The Entente was useless. The British became alarmed, so alarmed that they abandoned the reserved attitude which they had so far shown toward Russia. In the spring of 1914, Grey visited Paris. Poincaré expressed concern: could something not be done to restore the confidence of Russia in the Entente? He suggested naval conversations similar to those which were taking place between England and France. To his delighted surprise, Grey agreed. Discussions looking to a joint plan of action were immediately begun. Although no definite decisions were reached, the fact that conversations were taking place encouraged Russia to count with greater confidence than formerly on British aid.

The spread and intensification of unrest in the Near East made both Berchtold and Sazonov jumpy, likely to confront Europe with sudden moves. Both men were shaking off the restraints which fear of desertion by their allies had imposed. In the spring of 1914 they strove frantically to build up support in the Balkans. Sazonov's purpose was defensive: to rebuild a Balkan alliance capable of preventing Austria from interfering in the Balkans. Undoubtedly Sazonov hoped for positive gains in the future. Undoubtedly he moved more confidently because the military authorities now said that Russia was in a position to face the prospect of war with Germany. Nevertheless, Sazonov did not want war. For the present he wished only to consolidate the gains Russia had already made. To accomplish his task, he was forced to encourage the Balkan states to hope for gains at Austria's expense. To Rumania he held out the prospect of winning Transylvania. Bulgaria could be won back to the Russian alliance only by the promise of the Macedonian districts Serbia had taken in 1913. Sazonov urged the Serbians to make concessions: Bulgaria would be a dangerous enemy to have in the rear when Serbia reached for the rich prizes of Croatia and Bosnia. The Serbs listened eagerly. They could not bring themselves to abandon Macedonia, but they were encouraged by Russian talk of war with Austria. In her campaign to win allies, Russia had another powerful argument—French money. The bankrupt Balkan states needed loans. France had money she was willing to lend in return for promises of political loyalty.

Berchtold watched the triumphant march of Franco-Russian diplomacy with anxiety made acute by consciousness of internal dangers. From the beginning of the Balkan wars, order could be maintained in Croatia and Bosnia only by the exercise of martial law. School after school was closed as a result of student strikes or riots. Subversive propaganda circulated despite the most stringent regulations. Youths banded together in revolutionary clubs linked by bonds so carefully concealed that they baffled all efforts to ferret them out. Austria was becoming the new "sick man" of Europe. To avert the doom which hung over her she struggled to neutralize the Serbian danger. The most drastic solution was the annexation of Serbia. Conrad, the chief of staff, thought this the only way out; but the Hungarian premier, Tisza, refused to hear of the acquisition of more Slavs. Berchtold thought Rumania and Bulgaria might be won by offering to let them partition Serbia when war came. The Germans laughed at this idea, and declared Rumania and Bulgaria could never be reconciled. What then should be done, Berchtold asked? Berlin counseled quiet waiting. The situation was bad, and no solution was obvious; but some favorable change might soon come. There was no immediate danger; there was nothing impending to cause war between the powers. Berchtold was unconvinced. Balkan affairs were going from bad to worse. Russia was winning. She could offer more, and she had French gold behind her. The Balkan states, seeing they had got their way in 1912, were convinced that Russia was a good protector.

The summer of 1914 found Russia confident and determined. In Austria, failure and fear had created a desperate mood. One lesson both had learned from the preceding two years: there must be no more yielding. The Balkan states, like Italy, were opportunists who knew their only chance of gain lay in alliance with the stronger side. The triumph of the Entente in the Moroccan crisis of 1911 had helped to convince Bulgaria that a Balkan league protected by Russia would be profitable. The success with which Russia staved off interference by Austria during 1912 and 1913 made Greece and Rumania turn to the Entente, despite the German sympathies of their rulers. Russia knew that, if the Entente received a setback, the loyalty of her protégés would waver. Austria knew that a diplomatic check would impair her already waning prestige. Therefore, no yielding. Vienna and St. Petersburg were both firmly resolved. Unfortunately, neither saw clearly the resolution of the other.

Sazonov was determined to consolidate and extend the gains brought to Russia by the Balkan wars; Berchtold was resolved to restore Austrian influence in the Balkans and, at all costs, to prevent the extension of Russian influence. One bulwark of peace, vacillation at St. Petersburg and Vienna, was gone. A second deterrent to war, the indifference of public opinion in Western Europe to Balkan affairs, had been temporarily removed by the armaments campaign of 1913. Chauvinism was for the moment dominant. A reaction against bellicose fervor and the burden of armaments set in early in 1914, but the reaction had not attained effective proportions by the beginning of summer. The third safeguard against war, the restraining influence of England and Germany, was losing its force, partly because of the growing recklessness of Russia and Austria, partly because British and German statesmen felt that allies must be supported or lost. The dominant element both in London and Berlin feared isolation more than war. French statesmen had been in that state of mind since 1912. The safeguards which had permitted the powers to surmount the Balkan crisis without war were, at least temporarily, in abeyance. In the summer of 1914 peace was at the mercy of an accident.

6. SARAJEVO, JUNE 28–JULY 23, 1914

On June 28, 1914, the Austrian heir-apparent, the Archduke Francis Ferdinand, was assassinated at Sarajevo, the capital of Bosnia. The assassins were Bosnian youths, but they had been able to bring their plot to a successful consummation only with the assistance of the Serbian terroristic society, Union or Death, more popularly known as the Black Hand. The Black Hand had grown out of a military cabal. Under the energetic leadership of Colonel Dimitrijevitch, an official of the Serbian general staff, it had become strong enough to dominate the Serbian army and to influence governmental policy. The objective of the society was the creation of a great Jugo-Slav state under Serbian leadership. To further its objective, the Black Hand extended its activities into Bosnia and stimulated the cult of terrorism and revolution which already existed there. To agents of the society the Archduke's assassins had told their plan. The agents secured arms from the Serbian government arsenals and gave them to the youths who, thus armed, were smuggled back into Bosnia along secret lines of communication maintained by the society. Almost certainly the Serbian premier, M. Pashitch, got wind of the plot; he gave the Austrian government no adequate warning. Why, it is impossible to say. Probably fear of the revenge which the society might take on him helped to keep him silent.

The plot succeeded because of assistance given by a powerful Serbian military clique, a clique whose objective could be reached only by the disruption of the Dual Monarchy, a clique, moreover, too strong for the Serbian government to control. Obviously, the Austrian government was correct in believing that the Serbian "revolutionary nest" must be extirpated if the Dual Monarchy was to be preserved. Whether or not the Dual Monarchy had a right to exist is beside the point: no state could be expected to admit it had not the right of self-defense.

All this is clear to-day; it was not clear in 1914. The Austrian government suspected, but could not prove, Serbian complicity in the crime. Therefore, in proceeding against Serbia, Austria could not make a clear case. The action was susceptible to an aggressive interpretation; it could be attributed to desire for expansion for the sake of expansion. This was the first disadvantage under which the Central Powers labored. The second was tardy action. The assassination aroused horror and indignation in Europe. The rejoicing with which news of the crime was received in Serbia, together with Serbia's reputation for violence, turned opinion momentarily against Serbia. Four weeks passed before Austria took action. During the interval the first emotional sympathy for Austria subsided. Pan-Slav loyalty to Serbia revived in Russia; both France and Russia recalled the value which Serbia possessed for the Entente.

The long delay resulted from the inability of the Austrian government to decide on a course of action. As in earlier years, opinions conflicted; but now Berchtold did not vacillate. He knew what he wanted: Serbia must be attacked and reduced to impotence; a part or all of her territory must be taken and divided among her neighbors, including Austria. At first Francis Joseph and the Hungarian premier, Tisza, thought Berchtold's program too adventurous. Berchtold persisted. For the first time in his career he now showed determination, persistence, and astuteness.

He first approached Germany. Without a promise of German assistance, war against Serbia would be suicide. Russian neutrality could not be counted on with certainty in any case; Russia was bound to intervene if Germany held aloof. On July 5 and 6, the Austrian ambassador and Count Hoyos, Berchtold's secretary, conferred with William II and Bethmann at Potsdam. How fully the Austrians revealed Berchtold's plans is still a matter of dispute. It is certain that they obtained a sweeping promise: Germany, said the Kaiser and Bethmann, would support Austria in any action she might take against Serbia, even if that action involved war with Russia. No attempt was made to set limits on Austrian action. Kaiser and Chancellor promised full support without reservation.

Why, after restraining Austria from action against Serbia for years, did William II and Bethmann suddenly abandon all attempts to hold Vienna in check? That question has never been satisfactorily answered. Undoubtedly, the Kaiser was profoundly moved by the murder of his friend, the Archduke, but that event cannot greatly have stirred Bethmann's feelings. There is no evidence that Bethmann tried to restrain the Kaiser. The murder did, apparently, bring home to the German government for the first time the dangerous nature of Jugo-Slav nationalism. Before 1914 the Germans steadily refused to admit that Serbia was a serious menace to Austria's existence. Sarajevo showed their error. Germany already felt dangerously isolated; she feared to lose her last ally.

Furthermore, while it is easy to see now that Germany had signed a blank check on which she must make terrible payment, that fact was not clear at the time. Germany promised support *if* Austria moved against Serbia and *if* Russia intervened. The magnitude of these reservations prevented the Germans from clearly envisaging the consequence of their promise. They doubted Austria's ability to reach a decision; she had vacillated so long. More strongly, they doubted Russian determination: would the Tsar really fight to save a nation of regicides, especially since Russian armaments were not yet complete? And would the French be willing to fight over Serbia? Above all, the Germans left England out of their calculations. They did not even state in detail why they thought it safe to disregard her. Anglo-German relations had been improving. England had shown herself persistently indifferent to Balkan problems. A war would be disastrous to English commerce and industry. The Irish question absorbed English attention. These considerations undoubtedly help to explain the fatal omission. All in all, it is safe to say that neither William II nor Bethmann really grasped the consequences of their act. No impartial student to-day believes their decision was prompted by a desire for war. Exactly what determined their decision, probably they themselves could not have said.

German support assured, Berchtold felt half his battle was won. Repeated conferences were held in Vienna. Berchtold said it was now or never. Internal disaffection was growing. Serbia, increased in power and self-confidence by the Balkan wars, was openly planning to seize the Jugo-Slav provinces. Rumanian loyalty to the Triple Alliance was being undermined by the hope of receiving Transylvania which Russia held out. Italian Irredentists were joining the hue and cry. Action must be taken now. In a few years it would be too late. When Russian armaments had been completed, Austria's enemies would close in on her. By that time Germany, impressed by Austrian weakness and the strength of the enemy forces, might have decided to end her unprofitable alliance with Austria. War even now was a desperate stroke, but better die fighting while there was a chance of success than perish miserably by slow decay. Send Serbia an ultimatum she cannot accept; attack when the demands were refused. Russia was not yet ready. Probably she would not fight. If she did, Germany would join Austria; Germany had promised to support Austria, come what might.

Which of these arguments had most weight, it is impossible to say. Taken as a whole, they proved convincing. By the middle of July the last opposition had been won over. During the following week the ultimatum was carefully drafted. The utmost secrecy was preserved. To throw the Entente off the scent, the leading ministers left Vienna.

Berchtold hoped to take Europe by surprise. His purpose was only partly realized. Rumors of an impending Austrian attack on Serbia began to spread almost as soon as unanimity was reached in Vienna. Sazonov took alarm. On July 18 he tried to avert trouble by a timely warning to the Austrian ambassador: "Russia would not be indifferent to any attempt to humiliate Serbia. Russia could not permit Austria to use menacing language or military measures against Serbia." This was frank enough. Two days later President Poincaré and the French premier arrived in Russia for a visit. The Austro-Serbian difficulty was discussed. Poincaré instructed the French ambassador: "Sazonov must be firm, and we must support him." Poincaré also was frank. "Serbia has very warm friends in the Russian people," he reminded the Austrian ambassador. "And Russia has an ally, France."

Rumor spread to Rome. The Italian government became restive, made inquiries. The German government urged on Berchtold the necessity of holding Italy in line by promises of compensation for any gains Austria might make. Berchtold was deaf to these suggestions, partly because he feared that the Italians, if informed, would betray his plans, partly because he did not wish to give any compensation. Thus ignored, the Italian government clearly intimated its views: Italy would not regard a European war, resulting from an Austrian attack on Serbia, as a defensive war; therefore, Italy would not feel called on to aid her ally. Whether Italy would remain neutral or join Austria's enemies remained obscure. Rome hinted its attitude woud be influenced by the "compensation" Austria offered.

During the July days of 1914, beneath the care-free, holiday skies, lines of battle were forming: Austria and Germany; France and Russia. Austria was determined to crush Serbia, come what might; Germany promised to guard the ring and prevent interference. France and Russia were determined to prevent any diminution of Serbian power; much less would they permit the practical extinction of Serbia. How serious was the determination of the antagonists? Each side hopefully thought the other was bluffing and would retreat before firmness; therefore war was not expected. What would happen when the firmness of both sides became apparent? Here was one dubious element. There was another element of uncertainty, closely related— England. Grey had said little, but he evidently thought trouble could be avoided by encouraging Austria and Russia to settle their difficulties without calling in their allies, as allies. What would England do if that method did not work? The Germans counted on her neutrality; the French and Russians on her aid. As for the British, they did not know what they would do.

On July 23, Austria threw down the gage of battle. At six in the evening the ultimatum was presented at Belgrade. The ultimatum began by setting forth the failure of Serbia to abide by her promises "to live in future on good neighborly terms" with Austria-Hungary. Rather, Serbia's "culpable tolerance" had permitted the growth of a subversive movement which culminated in the assassination of Francis Ferdinand. Serbia was called upon publicly to repudiate the anti-Austrian propaganda and to announce her intention to "proceed with the utmost vigor against persons who may be guilty of such machinations." In addition, Serbia was required to comply with ten specific demands. Of these, the following were most important:

"3. To eliminate without delay from public instruction . . . everything that serves, or might serve, to foment the propaganda against Austria-Hungary;

"4. To remove from the military service, and from the administration in general, all officers and functionaries guilty of propaganda against the Austro-Hungarian Government whose names and deeds the Austro-Hungarian Government reserve to themselves the right of communicating to the Royal Government;

"5. To accept the collaboration in Serbia of representatives of the Austro-Hungarian Government for the suppression of the subversive movement directed against the territorial integrity of the Monarchy;

"6. To take judicial proceedings against accessories to the plot of the 28th June who are on Serbian territory; delegates of the Austro-Hungarian Government will take part in the investigation relating thereto."

A reply was demanded by six o'clock Saturday evening, July 25.

7. THE COMING OF WAR, JULY 24–AUGUST 4, 1914

On Friday morning, July 24, Europe was greeted on waking by news of the ultimatum. Here, every one realized, was a crisis, a grave crisis. Generals, statesmen, rulers scurried back from vacations. Chancelleries became feverishly active. In the days following, activity became ever more frantic as the shadow of war loomed darker and nearer. Worn by lack of sleep, by efforts to follow the shifting scene, by dread of responsibility for war, worn to hysteria, grave self-contained statesmen contradicted themselves from hour to hour, talked wildly, did very foolish things. In the end, war came. A clear description of those days is impossible: the action is too swift and crowded; on important questions scholars are hopelessly at odds. For our purpose, it will suffice to tabulate the steps toward war and to indicate those parts of the crisis which influenced subsequent diplomatic history.

At the outset, both sides hoped for a peaceful solution. Austria and Germany demanded that the Austro-Serbian conflict be localized, and hoped that the Entente would hold aloof rather than risk war. The Entente pressed for a moderation of the Austrian demands, and hoped that, rather than fight the Entente, Austria and Germany would content themselves with a diplomatic victory which would preserve Serbian independence and territorial integrity. Russia was determined to fight if Austria tried to crush Serbia; France stood solidly with Russia. England refused to promise armed support.

Saturday, July 25. The Russians, to show their determination, began military preparations by proclaiming the "Period Preparatory to War." Sazonov continued to hope that Austria would compromise rather than fight; if these hopes proved false, the military measures would increase the chances of a Russian victory in war. Very secretly, in order to avoid the accusation of aggressive intent, France took precautionary military measures. In the evening, Serbia replied to the ultimatum. The reply was very conciliatory, although on many points there were reservations which made the concessions more apparent than real. The fact that the Serbians ordered mobilization before delivering the reply indicates that they did not expect Austria to accept Serbian terms. Finding that Serbia had not given complete acquiescence, Austria severed relations and ordered mobilization against Serbia.

Sunday, July 26. The nature, though not the exact text, of the Serbian reply and Austria's breach of relations became known. The British Admiralty ordered the fleet, then assembled for review, to remain concentrated. Germany, believing that the Entente would be less likely to intervene if confronted with a *fait accompli,* pressed Austria to declare war on Serbia.

Monday, July 27. Late in the evening, the Germans began to realize that "localization" was impossible. Russia and France would almost certainly fight. Worse, it was possible England might fight. Bethmann wired Vienna: the steady rejection of all proposals to compromise was making a bad impression. What did Berchtold think of the proposal to use the Serbian reply as a basis for negotiations, and what did he think of Sazonov's desire for direct Austro-Russian discussions?

Tuesday, July 28. Austria declared war on Serbia, in order, as Berchtold informed the German ambassador, "to cut the ground from any attempt at intervention." Optimism immediately vanished at St. Petersburg, where the conviction grew that a general war was inevitable. During the evening, conferences were held. Sazonov wished to mobilize against Austria alone. The military leaders said a partial mobilization was, for tactical reasons, impossible; they urged general mobilization. No decision was reached. In Berlin, the Kaiser had decided that the Serbian reply was "a capitulation of the most humiliating kind, and as a result, *every cause for war* falls to the ground." He proposed that Austria occupy Belgrade and hold it as a pledge until Serbia carried out the promises made in the reply. Bethmann was afraid to rein in Austria so suddenly. He pressed the Kaiser's proposal on Berchtold's attention, but timidly.

Wednesday, July 29. Alarm spread in Berlin. Reports of Russian military preparation were pouring in; England had sent her fleet to war station at Scapa Flow; Grey hinted plainly that England would be drawn in if France and Germany fought. From Vienna, no word. Bethmann sent telegram after telegram urging the "pledge" plan, and warning of the imminence of war; Berchtold refused to reply. Bethmann tried to avert English intervention by offering to promise not to take any of France's European territory. In St. Petersburg, the Tsar consented to general mobilization. Before the order was despatched, a telegram arrived from William II telling of his efforts to moderate Austrian demands, and asking the Tsar to avoid military measures which "would precipitate a calamity we both wish to avoid." The Tsar weakened, canceled the order for general mobilization, and substituted mobilization against Austria alone. The Russian military authorities were in despair; they had no plans for partial mobilization.

Thursday, July 30. Sazonov again urged the necessity for general mobilization. The Tsar hesitated: "Think of the responsibility which you are advising me to take! Think of the thousands and thousands of men who will be sent to their death!" Sazonov persisted. In the end, the Tsar yielded. Sazonov rushed to the telephone and gave the news to the chief of the general staff. "Now you can smash the telephone," said Sazonov. "Give your orders, General, and then—disappear for the rest of the day." In London, Cambon begged Grey for a promise of support. Grey promised to consult the cabinet. To avoid any chance of being called the aggressor, and in order to make a favorable impression on British opinion, France announced that her troops would withdraw ten kilometers from the German frontier.

Friday, July 31. Grey asked France and Germany for assurances that they would respect Belgian neutrality. France promptly gave assurances; Germany refused to answer. In Berlin, Russian mobilization became known. Germany ordered preliminary mobilization measures—"Threatening Danger of War"—and warned Russia that complete mobilization would follow if Russia did not suspend every war measure within twelve hours. To Paris, Germany sent a demand for a declaration of neutrality.

Saturday, August 1. General mobilization was ordered in France and Germany. Early in the day, France replied to the German ultimatum: "France will act in accordance with her interests." In the evening, Germany declared war on Russia. Italy announced her intention to remain neutral. The British cabinet remained divided. When Cambon renewed his plea for a promise of assistance, Grey could only say: "France must take her own decision at this moment without reckoning on an assistance that we are not now in a position to promise."

Sunday, August 2. In England, the cabinet wavered during the morning. At noon, the Conservative opposition presented a letter to Asquith demanding that England support France and Russia. On receipt of this letter the opponents of intervention in the cabinet began to weaken. In the afternoon Grey was allowed to tell Cambon that "if the German fleet comes into the Channel, or through the North Sea, to undertake hostile operations against the French coasts or shipping, the British fleet will give all the protection in its power." Later, at seven in the evening, Germany presented an ultimatum to Belgium: Germany must march through Belgium; if Belgium made no resistance, Germany would quit Belgian territory at the end of the war and make reparation for damage done; if Belgium resisted, she would be regarded as an enemy. A reply was demanded within twelve hours.

Monday, August 3. In the morning, Belgium rejected the German ultimatum, and appealed for aid to the other powers which had guaranteed Belgian neutrality. In the afternoon Grey spoke in the House of Commons. He reviewed the crisis, told of the conversations which had taken place in the previous years between the French and British staffs, reminded the House of Britain's obligations to Belgium, and urged the necessity for war. He was cheered. No vote was taken, but obviously Grey had the House behind him. That evening, Germany declared war on France.

Tuesday, August 4. News reached London that Germany had invaded Belgium. An ultimatum was despatched: by midnight Germany must promise to respect Belgium neutrality; otherwise, relations would be severed. That Germany would reject the ultimatum was a foregone conclusion. The British ambassador made a farewell call on Bethmann. The Chancellor excitedly lamented the British action: "Just for a word 'neutrality,' a word which in war time has so often been disregarded—just for a scrap of paper, Great Britain was going to make war on a kindred nation who desired nothing better than to be friends with her." At midnight, England declared war on Germany.

Such were the steps by which an Austro-Serbian dispute widened into a European war. To fix responsibility is impossible. For Serbia to work for Jugo-Slav unity was natural. The Jugo-Slav movement, stimulated by Serbia, with Russian encouragement, drove Austria to desperation; statesmen in Vienna felt they must fight to preserve the existence of the Monarchy. Germany, alarmed by increasing isolation, felt that Austria must be supported, both to ensure the continued existence of the Dual Monarchy, and to retain Austria as an ally. Russia and France saw in the Austrian action an attempt to reverse the verdict of the Balkan wars, and to establish Austro-German hegemony in the Near East. Such an alteration of the balance of power Russia and France refused to tolerate. Pan-Slav feeling made Russia toss caution to the winds; France had felt for two years that her very existence would be precarious if she abandoned Russia. England cared little about the Balkans; she would like to have kept clear of the whole imbroglio. But if she stayed out, and, as most Englishmen predicted, Germany won, German hegemony on the Continent would be complete; then the Germans could concentrate on the task of preparing to subdue England. In the unlikely event that France and Russia won, the situation would be no better. They would break the truce in their colonial rivalry with England. The die was cast before the Belgian issue arose; definite decision might have been shunned for a week or two, but probably not beyond the first French defeat. Belgium merely provided an issue over which men could wax enthusiastic. Protection of the balance of power might be a necessity; the balance of power was not something for which one could fight with enthusiasm.

No one wanted a European war, but the very methods by which Europe had sought to prevent war made for war. Allies and arms were thought necessary for security. Fear of impairing the loyalty of allies hampered energetic efforts for peace in 1914. Negotiations were further impeded by surreptitious military preparations which went on all through the crisis, intensifying apprehension and hastening the breakdown of diplomatic discussions. In the years since the World War there has been a disposition to conclude that all governments were guilty and all peoples were innocent. That conclusion has little meaning. All the actors in the mighty drama made mistakes, but each tried to do what he thought the interests of his country required. Since 1871 Europe had been seeking means to obtain both security and realization of national aspirations without recourse to war. The quest had failed. The responsibility for failure was collective, not individual.

In closing this tragic chapter it is necessary to examine certain elements in the history of the five weeks which attained importance later, particularly after the war. As the extent of the catastrophe became apparent, each side tried to clear itself from blame. When the Entente won, its thesis triumphed and became embedded in the Treaty of Versailles as an indictment against Germany. Blame for the precipitation of war was fixed on Germany because, first of all, Austria was thought to be a blind tool of Germany. Earlier parts of this narrative show how unjustified this conclusion was. On the contrary, Germany after 1906 felt dangerously dependent on Austria. Germany's case also looked bad because she was thought not to have put restraint on Austria during the crisis. To prevent the German people from seeing how Austria had pushed recklessly forward despite protests from Berlin, the German government was forced to suppress the evidence which showed how, after July 27, Austria had been urged to negotiate.

Further, there was the damning fact that Germany had been the first to declare war. In part, this count in the indictment arose from ignorance. After the war began, the Entente powers, by suppressing or altering some documents and forging others, carefully concealed the fact that Russia was the first power to order general mobilization. When the priority of Russian mobilization was finally proved, the argument shifted: Germany should have replied to mobilization by mobilization. There are two answers to that argument. Most statesmen and soldiers knew that general mobilization meant certain war. The Russians knew what they were doing, as the agonized protest of the Tsar attests. Furthermore, the Germans felt they would be defeated if they allowed Russia to complete her mobilization before war began. Russia and France, it must be remembered, possessed overwhelmingly superior man-power. The Russian army was thought to be a very powerful fighting force. In 1913 the French military authorities actually feared Russia was getting so strong that she would feel the French alliance was no longer necessary. The Germans were confident of victory, but only because they had speed to counterbalance numbers. The advantage of speed would be lost if Russia and France were allowed to mobilize. Then Germany would be forced to divide her forces and to encounter enemy forces greatly superior in number. Therefore, the Germans believed they could not wait; and France and Russia did not expect them to wait.

The last count in the indictment is Belgium. The invasion of Belgium was branded the greatest crime in history. A crime it certainly was, but treaties had been broken before, and they have been broken since 1914. In time of war every nation violates international law in the name of national necessity. The German plan of campaign had contemplated the invasion of Belgium ever since the beginning of the century. Invasion was thought to be necessary in order to attain speedy success. The eastern frontier of France was mountainous and heavily fortified; Belgium and northwestern France were flat and moderately fortified. To deal a stunning blow at France, in time to check Russia, Belgium must be invaded. The plan was an open secret. The building of a network of strategic railways to the Belgian frontier showed clearly the German purpose. Armed opposition from England was apparently not seriously anticipated. Belgian neutrality had last been prominently mentioned during the Boulanger crisis. At that time the British had shown a disposition to permit Germany to cross Belgium. From that time until 1914 no British statesman affirmed the determination of England to protect Belgian neutrality. Englishmen who attribute the entrance of their country into the war in 1914 to the violation of Belgian neutrality might well accuse British statesmen of culpable negligence.

The extent of German guilt is debatable. The extent of German stupidity was colossal. When nations break treaties they find excuses; excuses can always be found. Bethmann did not make excuses. He admitted Germany's guilt and in his agitation used the expression "a scrap of paper." A more terrible blunder no statesman ever made. What he said was known to statesmen. Even Lord Salisbury once publicly referred to treaties in similar words, but not during a crisis. Bethmann's words clung to Germany like the taint of leprosy and did the German cause incalculable damage. The paradox is that these words were spoken by one of the few statesmen who tried to act with the same regard for honor in public life as he did in private life, a statesman too honest to deny having used the words, as he might easily have done.

These observations on the crisis are not intended as an apology for German policy or action. The German contribution to European discord from 1871 to 1914 has been set forth in earlier pages of this narrative. The myth of Germany's sole guilt still distorts international thought and action. Therefore a discussion of the facts is necessary. The Germans also invented a mythical account of the origins of the war: since 1904 the Entente powers, led by England, had slowly been forging an iron ring around Germany; by 1914 the quarry was helpless; the Entente struck. Germans were taught, and are still taught, to believe themselves the innocent victims of a diabolical plot. The encirclement theory bears as little relation to truth as the theory of Germany's sole and deliberate guilt. Fear and suffering burned both myths indelibly into the minds of men, with tragic consequences for the world.

CHAPTER VI

WAR, 1914–1918

CHAPTER VI

WAR, 1914–1918

I. 1914: WAR MYTHS

The swift march of events at the end of July, 1914, overwhelmed public opinion in all countries. Even after the terms of the Austrian ultimatum became known on July 24, the imminence of war was not realized. Here was another crisis, exciting and dangerous. It would pass as others had passed. Then suddenly there was war; for the first time in a generation and a half, there was a European war. Russia, France, England, Serbia, and Montenegro aligned themselves against Germany and Austria. Armies were on the move. The Germans were in Belgium; the Russians were in East Prussia. For an instant, panic swept over Europe. Panic almost immediately gave place to a strange exhilaration. An intolerable strain seemed suddenly relaxed. War was an actual relief, relief first of all from what Matthew Arnold a half-century before had called "this strange disease of modern life,

> With its sick hurry, its divided aims,
> Its heads o'ertaxed, its palsied hearts. . . ."

Here was a single, a worth-while purpose, and man's first impulse was to rejoice. Millions echoed Rupert Brooke's exultant cry:

"Now God be thanked Who has matched us with His hour,
   And caught our youth, and wakened us from sleeping,
With hand made sure, clear eye, and sharpened power,
   To turn, as swimmers into cleanness leaping,
Glad from a world grown old and cold and weary."

Even those with sufficient knowledge and imagination to envisage what lay ahead rejoiced, while fearing. The years preceding 1914 had seen angry strife within every country, strife which threatened to disrupt the unity of national life. With the coming of war, internal discord was suddenly hushed. The people of every country were told that the war was a defensive struggle for national liberty and independence. With rare exceptions, men believed and rallied to the national cause. The Black Forest peasants and burghers who gathered on the Lorettoberg to stare at the Vosges where their sons were killing and being killed thought of the old, old story of French invasion which the chapel behind them commemorated. Across the valley of the Rhine, French peasants remembered 1870 and prepared to resist a new invasion. Englishmen thought of Trafalgar and Waterloo; Russians, of the long struggle of Teuton to dominate Slav. Even socialists forgot their hatred of "capitalist" wars; *this* war was different. The fact of war was almost universally lamented. Since there was war, men rejoiced at the national unity it had brought. "All that is best and noblest in the nation has risen to the surface; materialism, luxury, and selfishness have slipped from us, and each of us feels that we are better men and women than before." War redeemed, cleansed, nations as well as individuals. So men thought.

First panic, then confident exhilaration, then angry stupefaction. Europe had almost forgotten the nature of war; Europe had never known the horror of this new kind of war, which science and nationalism had combined to create. The magnitude of the struggle, the power of new engines of destruction, the endless roll of dead paralyzed the imagination. "We have lost our common human bearings, and all the old measurements of things are thrown away, and we have no new measurements; we are simply dazed." Why had this terrible thing been allowed to happen? What would be the end of it all? How might a repetition of this calamity be prevented?

The governments had answers ready for these questions. From the outset, the imperative necessity of creating and maintaining resolute determination behind the lines was appreciated by every government; in fact, many of the diplomatic gestures of the July crisis were designed to convince public opinion of the just and defensive nature of this or that governmental action. All governments insisted that the enemy had precipitated war without provocation. The initial pronouncements were followed by increasingly elaborate defenses, tracing the origins of the struggle back, usually to 1871, and always proving conclusively the sole and heinous guilt of the enemy. In their excited condition, men were glad to believe. With critical standards almost obliterated by passion, with opposing arguments either concealed by censorship or unheard in the tumult, with powerful engines of propaganda, official and unofficial, at its disposal, each government succeeded with ease in stamping its version of the facts indelibly on the public mind.

The German indictment was directed first against Russia, later against England. For years Germans had lived in fear of the great giant to the east, the giant whose fecundity added new millions every year to the hordes of "barbarians" who pressed harder and harder on the ramparts of civilization which Germany sought to defend. Afraid to attack Germany directly, the Germans argued, Russia began a flank attack in the Balkans, stirring her savage Serbian allies to attack, first Turkey, and then Germany's ally, Austria. When Germany insisted on the right of Austria to punish the murderous intrigues of Serbia, the Tsar refused to wait on the pacific efforts of the Kaiser. Instead, Russia began to mobilize her hordes. It would have been suicide to wait until this human avalanche was ready to fall. Russia had plotted with France the destruction of Germany; only by striking out before Russia was fully mobilized could Germany hope to escape the grip of the Franco-Russian vise.

Such was the official German argument in August, 1914: the war was a struggle of Slav to dominate Teuton, a struggle precipitated by Russia. France was indicted as the accomplice of Russia, but it is remarkable how little hatred, and how much sympathy, the Germans felt for France. Germans thought the desire of France to regain Alsace-Lorraine natural. Most intelligent Germans freely admitted that France had for centuries been the leader of western culture; and although twentieth century France was thought to be decadent, she was thought to be great because of the past. When the tenacious valor of France was proved beyond question by the courage of her troops, good-will persisted in Germany. Pity gave place to admiration. The desire for a reconciliation increased, reconciliation paid for, if necessary, by concessions in Lorraine. Even during the last year of the war, when the dominant military leaders were calling for "sanctions" at the expense of France, sympathy continued almost unimpaired. So far as the German people, aside from a small militant minority, were concerned, hostilities with France began only after the armed conflict ended.

The original German explanation of the war rapidly fell into the background after Hindenburg drove the Russians from Germany by his great victory at Tannenberg. England then became the enemy. The British declaration of war came as a shock to the German government and people alike. Tirpitz had taught Germans the importance of sea power. The sudden appearance of this new and most formidable foe aroused first terror, then blind rage in Germany. Why, when the Germans were fighting for their life against the barbarian Slav, did England strike out against her kindred? Because, replied historians and publicists, that is the English way. England, ever since the sixteenth century, had been the "Vampire of the Continent." Spain, Holland, France—the pages of history were strewn with the wrecks of empires, victims of British perfidy and jealousy, destroyed by Britain's sea power and by Continental mercenaries in British hire. Now it was Germany's turn to be destroyed by the encircling ring of powers Edward VII had created. But this time the plot would fail. This time England had met her match, and Germany would free the Continent from the menace of sea power which these islanders had wielded too long. The world could never be free until these arrogant traders and shopkeepers were made harmless. The war was a diabolical British plot in the old British tradition,

prepared by Edward VII, executed by Sir Edward Grey
—so Germans were taught and implicitly believed. In 1915,
Germany rang with Lissauer's "Hymn of Hate":

> "Hate by water and hate by land;
> Hate of the heart and hate of the head;
> We love as one; we hate as one;
> We have but one foe alone—England."

The leaders of Germany only half believed what they
said. They believed England had brought on the war; but
the "defeatist" idea that England would win again, as she
had won before, haunted their thoughts. The rulers of Germany could never quite free themselves from the thought
that sea power was decisive; oppressed by this fear, they
were to be led into decisions which ensured the defeat of
Germany.

History furnished Entente countries with an equally clear
and simple, but very different, explanation of the origins of
the war: history clearly showed that Germany had, after
long and careful preparation, deliberately and cold-bloodedly
attacked her pacific, unsuspecting, and therefore unready
neighbors. Austria almost dropped out of the picture, except
as a tool of Germany and as a decadent and immoral oppressor of nationalities. Austria, and later Turkey, both
degenerate empires, were fit allies of Germany, a military
despotism which could tolerate only slavish satellites. History showed that until 1890 German domination of the
Continent was complete; Europe trembled when Bismarck
spoke. After 1890 German ambition grew. The Kaiser
aspired to rule the world. When France, Russia, and England drew together to protect themselves and to save the
principle of national freedom, Germany tried to disrupt the
opposing union by trickery and threats. The Moroccan and
Bosnian crises were German blows for supremacy. When
the Entente refused to be bullied, Germany resolved on
war, chose the time, and struck. Power alone was good to
Germany. Honor, truth, and justice were unknown to the
German. To attain their purpose of conquering the world,
the Germans would stop at nothing, as the "rape" of

Belgium showed. Europe must once more fight for freedom. Europe must again repel the Huns.

Thus, by focusing attention on certain facts and ignoring others, by misrepresentation, and by substituting passion for thought, each camp saw the angels of light fighting in its cause, and the angels of darkness in the opposing camp. Germany forgot the saber-rattling and the blustering policy which had alarmed Entente peoples, forgot also the heavy responsibility German leaders bore for the outbreak of war in 1914. Entente peoples forgot their own spotted history: Russia's part in opening the Near Eastern question after 1908, and in precipitating hostilities in 1914; Serbian and Russian intrigues against Austria; the provocation which France had given Germany in Morocco; England's reluctance to see Germany receive a share of the imperial spoils commensurate with her wealth and population. Each side ridiculed the idealistic claims of the other. The Germans talked of their love of peace: the Entente hurled back the bellicose speeches of William II. The Germans talked of their chivalry: the Entente pointed to Belgium. Germans spoke of Ireland, of the Boer republics, of India, Persia, and Egypt, when England flamed with indignation at the invasion of Belgium. Would England, the Germans asked, have fought if interest had not been involved? The bloody history of imperialism was cited by Germans when the Entente called itself the friend of small nations. The Entente champions of liberty, with Russia as a partner! Each side saw only what it wanted to see. Self-criticism vanished. Credulity was boundless. Entente peoples read of Belgian atrocities—most of them invented—with fascinated horror; Germans read of exactly the same deeds, again fantastically exaggerated, committed by Russians in East Prussia. Both sides forgot there had been atrocities in every war. Myths appeared from nowhere, and overnight acquired the force of religious dogmas. Tolerance, skepticism, detachment became the vices of a coward and a traitor. The enemy ceased to be a fellow human being; he was diabolic. To suggest that he might again be a friend, to wish for peace on any

terms except the unconditional surrender of the enemy, was
to invite persecution. Mob passion unchained, the governments could not restrain its vehemence. No government in
Europe could have survived a compromise settlement at the
end of 1914. The terse estimate of British opinion made
by Walter Page, the American ambassador, would apply
equally well to other belligerent countries: "If any one
should talk about peace, or doves, or plowshares here, they'd
shoot him."

While the "home front" was being so solidly constructed
that parts of the original foundations have survived the on-
slaughts of post-war scholarship, the character of the war itself was undergoing revolutionary change. At the outset, expert and layman alike expected sure and speedy victory. The
French and Russians counted on a resistless advance against
the divided armies of Germany, until the Allied forces would
meet and dictate peace. The Germans planned two gigantic
enveloping movements. First, with Metz as the axis, there
would be a great swing through Belgium and northern
France, steadily outflanking the French armies, who would
in the end be surrounded and forced to surrender. Then a
similar maneuver would put Russia out of the combat. During August, September, and October, 1914, each side waited
for the anticipated dazzling success. Every government
reported great victories, but autumn passed into winter and
peace did not come.

We now know that both plans broke down. At Tannenberg, on August 27, Hindenburg halted the Russians and
hurled them back with terrific losses, but he did not succeed
in surrounding and capturing the Russian forces. The
French offensive in Alsace had advanced but a few miles
when it became necessary to send troops back for the defense of Paris. The Germans advanced almost to Paris, but
they did not outflank the French. From September 5 to
September 11 the issue hung uncertain during the Battle of
the Marne; then the Germans fell back. For two months
more there was confused movement in the west. In November, fighting died down, and the rival armies, munitions

exhausted, faced each other from trenches which extended over 600 miles, from the Channel to the Swiss frontier. That both sides had failed in 1914 is clear now; it was not known in 1914. The Germans celebrated Tannenberg as the delivery of Germany, and made a national hero of Hindenburg; the significance of the Marne was carefully concealed. Similarly, Entente governments made the most of German failure at the Marne, and censored reports of Tannenberg.

While every one watched fascinated the struggle in East Prussia and northern France, the theater of war was widening. On August 15, Japan ordered the Germans to leave the Pacific. When the demand was refused, the Japanese proceeded to conquer German posts in the Shantung peninsula and in the north Pacific islands. Australia and New Zealand conquered German possessions in the south Pacific and warned Japan away from that area. Once the German flag had disappeared from the Pacific, the Japanese ceased to play an active part in the war and concentrated their efforts on the task of extending their influence over China.

Far more important than the entrance of Japan into the war was the decision of Turkey to support Germany. Early in 1914, apparently, the Turkish government had decided that the territorial ambitions of Russia could be thwarted only with German aid. At the beginning of August a secret treaty of alliance was signed. The Turks were not yet ready to fight. For two months they quietly pushed military preparations, at the same time disarming Entente suspicions by incessant negotiations for a neutrality formula. The Entente was in a quandary. The preparations of Turkey were obvious. If they were allowed to continue, and Turkey eventually did intervene, the task of conquering the Straits would be difficult. Russia was eager to seize the Straits by a sudden attack: Constantinople was the only prize which would reconcile Russian opinion to the cost of the war. England, on the other hand, sought to prolong Turkish neutrality, arguing that the Mohammedan subjects of the Entente might rise in revolt if Turkey were attacked, and that the Turks might be able to endanger the transport of British troops from India to the west. To what extent the English attitude was determined by reluctance to add Turkey to the spoils of war is unknown. At the end of October the Turks suddenly closed the discussion by beginning hostilities against Russia in the Black Sea. The Russians rejoiced and hungrily planned rich conquests. England annexed Cyprus, and changed her "occupation" of Egypt into a protectorate in order to separate these territories from their Turkish suzerain.

Although the dreaded Mohammedan "Holy War" did not materialize and the offensive operations of the Turks uniformly failed, the entrance of Turkey into the war was a heavy blow to the Entente. Men and supplies which were badly needed in the west must be used for defense in the east, and there was a constant temptation, not always resisted, to deplete the western front still further by assuming the offensive in the Near East. During one of these "side shows," as Grey called them, General Townshend was surrounded and forced to surrender at Kut-el-Amara in April, 1916. This Turkish victory reverberated through the east and permanently damaged British prestige. Russia, however, suffered most from Turkish intervention. Turkey closed the Straits and kept them closed. Since Germany controlled the Baltic, Russia could now obtain supplies only through Archangel, which was ice-locked a large part of the year, or overland, thousands of miles, from the Pacific. Russia was not an industrial country, and after 1914 it became apparent that industrial power was of more importance than man-power in modern war. Russia was short of munitions from the first; by the beginning of 1915, the arsenals had one rifle for each twenty, or even twenty-five, recruits called to the colors. Although this appalling shortage, so disastrous to the morale of the troops, is largely explained by inefficiency and corruption, the closing of the Straits undoubtedly complicated the replenishment of depleted stocks.

2. 1915: HOPES OF VICTORY

The failure to achieve success during 1914 in no wise dampened the hope of victory. Both sides looked forward to the campaign of 1915 with confidence. While the rivals were locked in desperate combat on the Marne, in September, 1914, the Entente was changed to an alliance by the London Pact. England, France, and Russia agreed not to make peace separately, and to make common conditions of peace. Solidarity assured, the Allies expected complete victory. Man-power, industrial power, and sea power were all on their side. Sixty million Germans could not hope to win against the hundreds of millions in the Allied empires. Austria and Turkey were dismissed as negligible factors, weak in military power and divided by internal dissension. More important than man-power was sea power. At Scapa Flow, north of Scotland, was gathered the greatest armada the world had ever seen. While the German "risk" navy cowered behind Helgoland, afraid to emerge, Allied squadrons swept German commerce from the seas. Sea power ensured industrial supremacy to the Allies and threw the Central Powers almost entirely on their own resources, resources which could not suffice for long. For munitions, raw materials were necessary, materials which the Continent did not provide. Tremendous numbers of men were necessary for the manufacture of munitions, men Germany must take from her already smaller supply available for fighting. The Allies, on the other hand, could draw raw materials from all over the world, and neutral America could provide an endless quantity of munitions. Decidedly, Germany could not hope for victory.

In this optimistic mood, the Allied peoples and governments began to make plans for the impending peace. Every one accepted as fundamental the restoration of Alsace-Lorraine to France, and the acquisition of Constantinople by Russia. Englishmen took the acquisition of colonies for granted. In addition to these specific objectives, there were larger, more ambiguous aspirations, which were phrased idealistically, but which usually rested on the foundation of real or supposed self-interest. There was a universal desire to secure a stable and lasting peace. This desire was thought to necessitate three world changes: self-determination of peoples, the destruction of German militarism, and a league of nations.

Self-determination and the rights of small nations became popular rallying cries in England when Belgium was invaded. Soon afterward Russia appealed to the Poles to rise and win their freedom with Russian aid. Thereafter the resurrection of Poland became an Allied objective. Next, the subject races of Austria-Hungary received attention. The Serbians were encouraged to hope for the Jugo-Slav provinces; the Czechs and Slovaks, for a revival of the Bohemian kingdom; and the Italians and Rumanians, to secure their "unredeemed" compatriots. The subject races of Turkey were also promised freedom. The campaign was a great success. Encouraged by Allied propaganda, the subject races of Austria-Hungary and Turkey became increasingly restive. Austrian Slavs deserted to the enemy; Arabia, encouraged to hope for freedom by Colonel Lawrence, revolted against Turkey; the Armenians rose in a revolt which was subdued by a Turkish campaign of extermination.

The cry of "self-determination" weakened the enemy by provoking internal dissensions. The slogan also served as a tempting bait with which to entice neutrals like Italy and Rumania into the war on the Allied side in the hope of territorial expansion. Finally, self-determination placed a cloak of idealism on old imperial aspirations. This was especially true with the Russians, themselves the most flagrant violators of the principle blazoned on their banners. Polish "freedom" meant a Russian Poland to the Tsar. Many Poles suspected as much, and, led by Pilsudski, fought on the side of Austria. Austrian Poland had at least enjoyed cultural freedom, and much political liberty as well, before the war. Toward the other Slav provinces of Austria, Russian motives were not disinterested; the Tsar,

now as always, aimed at hegemony in the Balkans. The
Allies were no more disinterested in their sympathy for
those oppressed by Turkey. Secretly, a tentative division of
the spoils was arranged in March, 1915. Russia, the Allies
agreed, was to get European Turkey, including Constantinople, most of the coast on the Asiatic side of the Straits,
and part of the Turkish Black Sea coast. In return, Russia
agreed to recognize the claims France and England intended
to stake out in the Near East and to let England take the
neutral zone in Persia. Arabia was to be independent.
France consented to the agreement only after the Tsar had
given assurances about the settlement in the west.
Nicholas II was generous. "Take the left bank of the Rhine,"
he told the French ambassador; "take Mayence, take
Coblenz; go still further if you judge it useful." Thus reassured, Delcassé, now French Foreign Secretary, allowed
Russia a generous share of Turkey.

Next to self-determination on the Allied program came
the destruction of German militarism. What was meant by
German militarism is hard to say. When men said "the
German mad dog of militarism must be killed," they frequently saw a vision of Germans nailing Belgian children
to barn doors. More thoughtful and more generous men
meant that Germany was enslaved to a group of Prussian
junkers who were mad with the lust for power and military
glory. How the evil might be exorcised was also ill defined.
Some thought military defeat would unseat the militarists.
More usually, punishment and temporary or permanent
restraints on Germany were believed necessary. Englishmen
spoke of destroying German sea power and of shutting
Germany off from competition in the markets of the world
as protective measures. Frenchmen spoke of the permanent
destruction of German military power and of French domination of the Rhine country as protective measures.

When the peoples of the world had been freed and the
nightmare of German militarism had disappeared, the world
was to be reorganized. Some sort of league was to preserve
the peace. Here also men saw different visions. Some saw

a world commonwealth of equal nations. More frequently, the league was to be an organization of the victors united in a determination to retain the spoils of victory—in other words, an Entente permanently triumphant over a supine Germany.

It is impossible to separate the gold of idealism from the dross of material interests in the Allied program. All that can be said is that, as war passions became more intense, the desire to redeem the world was increasingly submerged in the fury of hatred. "They get more and more on edge as the strain becomes severer," wrote Page in June, 1916. "There'll soon be very few sane people left in the world." Throughout, the idealistic interpretation of the war as a crusade for world freedom and peace was strongest in England. Her Continental allies echoed the British program rather skeptically and were more inclined to regard the war as a struggle to preserve national unity against attack and to strengthen national power.

In Germany, too, thinking revolved about the problem of retaining the hard-won unity and strength of Germany and of increasing German safety and power after the war. The German people firmly believed victory would come, and speedily. The first fears of sea power seemed unfounded. The record harvest of 1914 averted hunger; the mobilization of industry by Walter Rathenau resulted in an adequate supply of munitions. The Russian giant was already wounded, and German armies held the rich industrial areas of Belgium and France as hostages. Even sea power itself might pass to Germany if the submarines accomplished what was expected of them. Soon the war would be over, and then the Germans would make sure that this attack by jealous neighbors would not be repeated.

The German government did not emulate the Allied governments in formulating a program. Publicists were, therefore, free to let their imaginations roam unhampered. The mass of conflicting programs may be classified roughly under four heads. Those who continued to regard Russia as the chief rival wished to erect a wall of buffer states to the east, including Poland and the Baltic provinces of Russia. Behind this wall of states, which would owe their existence to the Central Powers and would therefore be under German guidance, Germany would be safe from invasion. Industrialists and navy men were more preoccupied with sea power. Germany, they said, must have increased industrial power. Therefore, at least the mines of French Lorraine must be kept; if possible, more of the industrial area of northern France should be retained. To avert a blockade, some control must be kept over the Belgian ports: the proposals ranged from vague "guarantees" to actual annexation. The "freedom of the seas" must also be secured. Students of international law meant by this phrase immunity of private sea-borne property from seizure during wartime; the obvious difficulties of enforcing such a rule were the subject of innumerable arguments. Usually, Germans had little idea of what they meant by freedom of the seas, beyond the determination not to be blockaded again. The course which the popular argument took bore a striking resemblance to Tirpitz's propaganda, and seemed really designed to substitute German control over the seas for British control.

Two schools of opinion turned their eyes to the southeast. Both argued that Germany must be made self-sufficing and immune from blockade by securing a larger productive area. Some publicists argued that the Bagdad Railway would satisfy this need and urged the necessity for retaining and strengthening German interests in the Near East. Once the Bagdad Railway was completed, with arms stretching toward the Suez, the Red Sea, and the Persian Gulf, once Turkey was regenerated through the prosperity the railroad would bring, Germany would possess a rich commercial empire which no blockade could hurt. The "Middle Europeans," though they started with the same premises as those who saw salvation in the Bagdad Railway, advocated a very different policy. They would secure safety and strength by extending the old *Zollverein* idea. Just as the beginning of Germany had been a customs union, so Central Europe

should be united. The new union, like the old, would take
root and spread because it would be profitable. As a beginning, Germany and Austria-Hungary would unify their
economic life. Other states would soon see the great advantages of a large productive area without tariff walls and
would join also. Economic unity would give economic
strength. Economic peace would give political peace. Economic unity might even bring a loose political unity. Central
Europe would no longer be divided and exposed to attack.
It would be strong, rich, united—safe.

While Germans were busy redrawing the map in books
and by the beer bench, the German government said nothing
of war aims. The government was silent because Bethmann
and his colleagues, and the Kaiser in his calmer moods,
thought victory impossible to attain. The civil government
was in a painful predicament. The German people were
buoyed up by hopes of victory and expansion. The longer
the war lasted, the greater would be the prizes the German
people would demand as compensation for their suffering.
If those prizes were not forthcoming, feeling would turn
against the government. If the terms of peace might be
interpreted as defeat for Germany, the government would
almost certainly be overthrown. Doubt of victory gave early
to the German government a wavering comprehension of
the truth all governments were soon to see: defeat in this
war meant revolution.

The purpose of the Allies in 1915 was twofold: to widen
the battle-front which Germany must defend, and to split
the Teutonic alliance and renew free communication with
Russia by seizing the Straits. Both these objectives required
that the neutral states of southern and eastern Europe be
drawn into the war on the Allied side. Italy, as the only
neutral great power, was the most valuable prize. From
December, 1914, to the spring of 1915, a great diplomatic
battle was fought, the Germans striving to keep Italy neutral,
the Allies working to secure her aid. The Italians as so
often before, found themselves in the fortunate position of
being able to bargain with both sides. Salandra, the Italian

premier, set out to wrest the utmost advantage from this position. "Free from all preoccupations, prejudice and sentiment," he said, "we must have no other thought than exclusive and unlimited devotion to our country, to *sacro egoismo* for Italy." He had already made up his mind that the Allies would win, and that Italy would therefore gain most by siding with them; but he carefully concealed his decision, and permitted the rivals to bid higher and higher for Italian favor. What Italy wanted was the south Tyrol and the northern Adriatic possessions of Austria. For long, Vienna refused to make concessions; but, under pressure from Germany, this attitude was abandoned early in 1915. First meager, then larger and larger offers were made. The Italians steadily refused to commit themselves. Each offer was used to force new promises from the Allies, who were reluctant to grant the Italian demand for Dalmatian territory inhabited by Jugo-Slavs. The fact that Italy also claimed territory inhabited by Germans caused less concern. At last the Allies swallowed their scruples. "This," Balfour said later, "is the sort of thing you have to do when you are engaged in a war." By the Treaty of London, signed in April, 1915, Italy was to get the Tyrol up to the Brenner Pass; Austrian territory at the head of the Adriatic, including Trieste; Valona in Albania; a part of Turkey; and a share in the indemnity to be levied at the close of the war. The Italians had guarded well their country's sacred egoism. In May, Italy declared war on Austria.

During the winter of 1914–1915, Allied diplomacy was busy in the Balkans as well as in Italy, seeking to erect a barrier which would divide Turkey from her allies. Rumania was willing to intervene, but her price was too high. The Allies offered Hungarian Transylvania. Rumania demanded the huge semicircle enclosed within the rivers Theiss and Pruth. Anxious though they were to extend the battle-line, the Allies hesitated. Within the territory demanded by Rumania was the Banat of Temesvar, inhabited by Jugo-Slavs. Serbia was already angry and indignant at the way her interests had been sacrificed to Italy. Russia refused to hear of new injuries to the Slav cause. The Rumanians preferred to wait rather than compromise. They remained neutral through 1915, to the satisfaction of Austria.

Greece was valued by the Allies as a base for operations in the Balkans and against Turkey. To secure her aid the Allies offered tempting gains: southern Albania, Cyprus, and Smyrna. Venizelos, the Greek premier, wished to accept the offers. King Constantine refused, partly because of loyalty to dynastic ties with Germany, partly because he was sure Germany would win. Throughout 1915, the efforts of Venizelos to compel action kept Greece in turmoil, but though Constantine wavered, he never quite gave way. Again Allied diplomacy failed.

In Bulgaria, too, the Allies failed. This failure was serious, because Bulgaria occupied a strategic position on the flank of Serbia and Turkey. King Ferdinand leaned toward the Central Powers because of enmity toward Serbia. Again the Allies asked a sacrifice of Serbia: King Ferdinand must be kept quiet by giving him western Macedonia, which Serbia had won in the second Balkan war. Serbia resisted. Bulgaria opened negotiations with Germany, and in September, 1915, an alliance was signed. Bulgaria promised to attack Serbia when Germany gave the word. In return, Turkey ceded a strip of Thrace to Bulgaria. At the conclusion of hostilities, Bulgaria was to receive Serbian Macedonia. Further, if Rumania and Greece joined the Allies, Bulgaria was to secure parts of their possessions.

While Allied diplomacy was receiving a serious setback in the Balkans, Allied arms were suffering grievous defeat. The attack which Italy launched against Austria broke down with almost no gain; the English offensive at Neuve Chapelle was repulsed with terrible loss; the campaign against the Dardanelles, which went on through the year, was a spectacular failure. On the other hand, Germany marched from victory to victory. In May, a great offensive against Russia was begun. Through the entire summer, the Russian lines were subjected to a succession of stunning blows. The Russian generals, obsessed by obsolete theories, decided to duplicate the retreat of 1812 by turning the districts they were forced to abandon into a desert and by evacuating the civilian population. The result was horrible. "The immense stream of uprooted, desperate, suffering humanity rolls along the roads interfering with military traffic and completely disorganizing the rear of the army . . . men and women die by the hundred from hunger, exposure, and disease. The death rate among the children has reached a terrible height. Unburied corpses are left along the roads." By August, the retreat had become a rout. "Headquarters has completely lost its head. Contradictory orders, absence of a plan, feverish changes of commanding officers, and general confusion upset even the most courageous men."

In September the German offensive died down. Russia had lost Poland, Lithuania, and Courland. Worse, the morale of the Russian forces was irreparably damaged. The Tsar had assumed personal command of the army, hoping in this way to put new heart in the troops. His action merely redoubled the confusion. Nicholas II knew nothing of military affairs. His will was completely dominated by the empress, who, in turn, was dominated by the degenerate monk, Rasputin. More and more, Rasputin, stupid and hated though he was, became the real master of Russia. Ministers who resisted his influence, like Sazonov, were dismissed and replaced by sycophants and nonentities. Anger and resentment replaced the patriotic internal harmony of the early war days. Respect for the autocracy ebbed even among the nobility, and revolution was spoken of with increasing freedom.

Leaving Russia prostrate, the Austro-German forces turned southward against Serbia. The Allies hastily assembled a motley army and despatched it to Saloniki, where Allied headquarters were established, despite the protests of Greece at this breach of her neutrality. Before the Allies were ready to move, the campaign was over. In October, the Austro-German forces poured into Serbia from the north, and Bulgaria attacked from the east. The Serbians were overwhelmingly outnumbered. They retreated through the Albanian mountains, where the tribesmen took vengeance for old wrongs by killing every Serbian they could catch. The tiny remnant of the army found refuge in Corfu.

Even the censor could not fully conceal the disastrous failure of Allied arms in 1915. One hope only lit the pervading gloom: confidence that the United States would intervene as a result of the sinking of the *Lusitania* on May 7.

3. THE UNITED STATES AND THE WAR, 1914–1915

When the war began, the American people were completely bewildered. The desire to keep clear of the struggle was almost universal. Even those who later urged intervention most violently, such as Theodore Roosevelt, were for neutrality in the summer and autumn of 1914. Among those of German and Irish ancestry there was much sympathy for the Central Powers, but the violation of Belgian neutrality, the sufferings of that unfortunate nation, and the fact that Germany had been the first to declare war made a deep and lasting impression. The sentimental attachment for France, which dated from the American Revolution, strongly influenced opinion. During the early days of the war, President Wilson himself contemplated Germany policy with aversion. "He felt deeply the destruction of Louvain," wrote his confidant, Colonel House, on August 30, 1914. "He goes even further than I in his condemnation of Germany's part in this war . . . he was particularly scornful of Germany's disregard of treaty obligations, and was indignant at the German Chancellor's designation of the Belgian Treaty as being 'only a scrap of paper.'"

"Waging neutrality" proved difficult. Neutrals and belligerents have never seen eye to eye regarding the rules of naval warfare, but the inevitable controversies were complicated by the unusual violence of the war passions, which dominated statesmen as well as the general public in belligerent countries. Men who thought their cause the cause of right and justice refused to believe that any right-thinking neutral would object to actions which facilitated victory; indeed, the slightest sign of friendly spirit shown the enemy by a neutral, even a refusal to take sides, was construed as partiality for the enemy.

England, as the mistress of the seas, was the first seriously to infringe naval law. The fact that the German fleet dominated the Baltic prevented an effective blockade of the German coasts, and a blockade to be legal must be effective. England never proclaimed a blockade, but she sought to accomplish the same purpose by extending the contraband list. The rules for neutral commerce laid down in the British orders in council of November, 1914, already extended the list by including foodstuffs. This and other departures from earlier practice were justified on the ground that sea law was antiquated and did not take cognizance of modern conditions of warfare. Protests from shippers poured into Washington. Washington protested to London, objecting particularly to the British rules of search.

The British received the American protests with indignation. "What is felt here," explained Grey, "is that while Germany deliberately planned a war of pure aggression, has occupied and devastated large districts in Russia, Belgium, and France, inflicting great misery and wrong on innocent populations, the only act on record of the United States is a protest singling out Great Britain as the only Power whose conduct is worthy of reproach." The British felt fully justified, therefore, in refusing to heed the American protests. That American opinion saw no reason for taking part in European quarrels and that American protests against any acts which Germany had so far committed could scarcely have been reconciled with neutrality made no impression on the Allies. The Allies refused to admit that neutrality was justified when civilization was threatened, as they maintained it was by Germany. During the early days of 1915, a repetition of the quarrels of a century before seemed impending between England and the United States. American resentment was only beginning to take form, however, when it was swept aside by stronger feelings against Germany.

Germany also accused the Americans of unfairness. German soldiers were being killed by munitions provided by American firms. The United States was aiding those who sought to subjugate Germany. The anger was unjustified: an embargo on the export of munitions would have been unneutral. Germans refused to listen. "I do not think," wrote the American ambassador from Berlin, "that the people in America realize how excited the Germans have become on the question of selling munitions of war by Americans to the Allies. A veritable campaign of hate has been commenced against America and Americans . . . it would not surprise me to see this maddened nation-in-arms go to lengths however extreme."

To what length Germany would go was shown in February, 1915, when Germany announced that submarine warfare would be begun against enemy merchantmen. The American government became alarmed. The submarine, a new and relatively untried weapon, was not equipped to search vessels captured, and to make provision for the safety of passengers and crew, as international law required. A sharp warning was sent from Washington: Germany would be "held to strict accountability" if American lives were lost. The German reply was evasive. A period of uneasy waiting followed. On May 7, the *Lusitania* was sunk. Over 1,000 lives were lost, including over 100 Americans killed.

It is possible that President Wilson could have brought a united nation into the war had he chosen to act immediately. The indignation was practically universal. When, instead of calling for war, Wilson sought to obtain peaceful redress, feeling rapidly subsided west of the Appalachians. In the northeastern part of the country opinion remained permanently embittered against Germany, but in the Middle and Far West most people were glad war had been avoided. the people had left Europe to escape poverty or oppression. In the West, Europe seemed far away; a large portion of and the war was interpreted as a terrible judgment on Europe's sins. After all, why should 100 millions of people plunge into this catastrophe, sacrifice the blessings of peace, because 100 had been killed when they ventured into the scene of combat?

Despite the decline of feeling from the fighting pitch, American opinion remained in a state of chronic irritation during 1915. The German government, itself hard pressed by popular feeling, was slow to acknowledge responsibility; new sinkings produced new outbursts of passion; even after the Germans, in September, agreed to restrict the submarine activities, there were "accidents." Numerous plots to obstruct the manufacture of munitions were discovered. The Austrian ambassador was sent home for encouraging these activities. Slowly, imperceptibly, the desire for peace was undermined, and hatred of Germany spread. Allied propagandists assiduously encouraged anti-German sentiment. When the Germans first used liquid fire and poisonous gas on the western front in 1915, the horrors of these weapons were dramatically set forth, even while the Allies were endeavoring to copy and improve the German inventions. The execution of Edith Cavell by the Germans at Brussels was made much of, although the Allies had executed nurses under similar circumstances. Nevertheless, the Americans refused to fight. To the hard-pressed Allies, who confidently expected American aid after the sinking of the *Lusitania,* the disappointment was keen. Contempt for the United States grew alarmingly. "British opinion and the British government have absolutely lost their respect for us," wrote Page in September, 1915. The Americans had, to be sure, become more tolerant of Allied infractions of sea law. During 1915 the British whittled away neutral rights bit by bit. The Germans in their turn became excited and contrasted American acquiescence in Allied lawlessness with the harsh tone of notes to Berlin. The Germans refused to see that it was natural for the Americans to resent loss of life more than loss of property. By the end of 1915 American opinion was in a state of intense exasperation. The President was assailed by conflicting counsels. Some, a minority, wished to lay an embargo on the export of arms until England abandoned her unjust practices. Others, a minority, called for immediate war with Germany. For the most part, the President was merely called on to do "something"; what the confused American people really wanted no man could have fathomed.

While he was being abused for inaction, the President was acting in secret. At the end of 1915, Colonel House left for Europe armed with a proposal for peace: Wilson would, if the Allies consented, offer to mediate, and would support terms which would give the Allies substantial victory. Germany would be called on to restore the areas she had devastated, give Alsace-Lorraine to France, and consent to the establishment of an independent Poland. Russia was to receive Constantinople. The Italian-speaking districts of Austria were to go to Italy. Germany would receive compensation outside Europe. All the nations were to join a league which would prevent aggressive war. If Germany refused to make peace on these terms, Wilson would "probably" bring the United States into the war on the side of the Allies.

Despite the catastrophic defeats of 1915, the Allies refused to accept House's proposal. Why, it is impossible to say. One reason was undoubtedly fear lest, if the fighting were interrupted and the negotiations proved unsuccessful, the war-weary peoples would refuse to take up arms again. With the Germans in Belgium, France, Russia, and the Balkans, such a risk could not be run, especially since Wilson only said the United States would "probably" fight. This objection did not have a great deal of weight, because Wilson did not propose that hostilities cease before negotiations began. Another reason for the Allies' refusal was the fact that the strain of war was becoming so great that the tension could only be endured if everything except the thought of fighting was excluded from the mind. More and more, opinion was turning away from men like Grey, who retained some concern for the relative gains and losses of continued fighting, toward men whose only thought was to deal the enemy a "knock-out" blow, men like Lloyd George. "Great Britain will not come out of the war any the worse," Lloyd George assured House. Rather, he thought that habits of increased work "would add more than a billion dollars to England's wealth, and that untold millions would be saved because of the simple lives people will live from now." Finally, Wilson's terms embodied only a part, a small part, of Allied objectives. Russia wanted Poland not independent but Russian, and Russia wanted hegemony in the Near East. The Treaty of London promised Italy more than Wilson offered. France wanted not only Alsace-Lorraine but domination over the left bank of the Rhine, and supremacy in Western Continental Europe. England wanted uncontested maritime supremacy. Wilson wished to make surrender easier for Germany by giving her colonies. The Allies not only intended to keep Germany's colonies; in the spring of 1916, France, England, and Russia arranged for the almost complete partition of Turkey among themselves by the so-called Sykes-Picot agreements. Wilson had offered the Allies what they said they were fighting for. After the House mission, he realized that the war was, beneath the decorous covering of idealism, turning into a struggle for political power and imperial possessions.

In Berlin House found a great desire for peace, but not on terms which had any chance of acceptance. Bethmann could offer no more than the evacuation of Allied territories occupied by Germany in return for an indemnity. Defeated, House went back to America.

4. 1916-1917: THE UNITED STATES JOINS THE ALLIES

In 1915 the Allies had tried to break the enemy lines by direct attack in the west and at the Dardanelles. Both movements failed. The ease of defense and the difficulty of successful offensive action under modern conditions of warfare had been demonstrated. In 1916 the Allies fell back on the policy of attrition, the slow wearing-down of German strength by the blockade and by limited military action.

The blockade was strengthened by placing every product of importance on the contraband list. To prevent European neutrals from evading the blockade by buying American goods for their own use and exporting native products to Germany, these countries were placed on a ration, allowed to buy only limited quantities from abroad. Thus every possible leak was stopped. These tactics were eminently successful. In 1915 the German people were already beginning to feel the pinch of the blockade; in 1916 the shortage of foodstuffs and raw materials became painfully acute.

The policy of attrition worked less well on the field of battle, because the Germans themselves began a most spectacular campaign of attrition. Instead of a general offensive, the Germans chose one fort—Verdun. As a fort, Verdun was of little importance. As a symbol, it was all-important. A thousand years of history clustered around the name Verdun. If the fort fell, French morale would be badly shaken. The Germans knew France would make any sacrifice to hold so important a position. To wear down the French by forcing them to lose countless thousands defending Verdun and then take the fort and thereby break French self-confidence were the German objectives. The attack began in February. The ceaseless pounding went on into August. As the Germans expected, the French held on tenaciously despite terrible losses. But the fort did not fall. To relieve the pressure on Verdun the British began an attack on the Somme. In the east Russia launched an offensive. Rumania, too, was drawn in: the hard-pressed Allies accepted her terms. The Germans parried these thrusts, losing a few miles in the west, but conquering Rumania with ease. On the surface the campaign resulted in a draw, but the Germans had not taken Verdun. German, not French, morale was shaken. French resolution was stiffened.

Bethmann was in desperate straits. His hungry and discouraged countrymen clamored for renewed submarine warfare in retaliation for British violations of the law of contraband. Bethmann was convinced this would not win the war but would rather add the United States to the already overwhelming enemy forces. In March he yielded momentarily, but he drew back when a stiff protest came from America. Then he concentrated on the task of securing an early peace. All through the spring and summer he pressed Wilson to propose negotiations. In October, William II publicly urged peace to save Europe from ruin. The Allies did not respond. Finally, on December 12, Bethmann sent notes to the Allied governments. The Central Powers, he said, invited a discussion of peace. "They do not seek to crush or annihilate their adversaries . . . They feel sure that the propositions which they would bring forward . . . would serve as a basis for the restoration of a lasting peace."

The Allied governments vigorously repelled the German suggestion. Blind to the exhaustion of France by the Verdun defense, blind to the military paralysis and approaching dissolution of Russia, blind to everything except hatred of Germany, the Allies held firm in their determination to crush "the arrogant spirit of the Prussian military caste." Lloyd George had just become Prime Minister. He and Briand, the French premier, were resolved to deal Germany the "knock-out blow."

After the Allied position had been made clear, but before a definite reply had been made to Germany, President Wilson intervened. Throughout 1916 he had hesitated. The Allies had refused the offer he made early in the year, and Page warned him that American "peace talk" caused resentment in England. Nevertheless, Wilson felt increasingly that he must brave Allied displeasure. He and a large section of American opinion were losing the feeling that an Allied victory was imperative. In part this shift was a reaction against the moral claims of the Allies, a reaction facilitated by the taunts of cowardice and vile commercialism leveled at the United States by the Allies. The British said plainly that only a depraved nation would permit Wilson to say that the United States was not concerned with the "causes and objects" of the war. These insults caused resentment.

Nothing could shake the devotion of social leaders in the East to the Allied cause, devotion which had somehow become identified with good form. The American press made only scanty mention of the anti-American cartoons and writings which appeared daily in England and France. Nevertheless, enough was known to affect the views of men and women of moderate means who had formerly been in strong sympathy with the Allies. The shift was most pronounced among men who knew something of the Allies' material aims. Colonel House had been pro-Ally from the first, but in 1916, when Page alleged that Americans did not understand "the high purposes of the British in this war," House retorted: "We resented some of the cant and hypocrisy indulged in by the British; for instance, as to Belgium." Wilson reacted even more violently against Page's complaints of American blindness to the real causes of the war. "He spoke of England's having the world and of Germany wanting it," Page wrote bitterly.

Now that the depredations of German submarines had fallen off, the latent antagonism to England revived in the United States. British officials were peculiarly stupid in their treatment of Ireland after the Easter rebellion in 1916. The rebellion had been condemned, even by influential Irish-Americans, but the Draconian justice meted out by England sickened many who had no Irish blood. Feeling on the Irish question merged with and intensified resentment against the new blockade regulations. The "black list" of July, 1916, ordering British subjects not to trade with certain firms, including eighty American firms, suspected of trading with the enemy, was especially resented. Congress enthusiastically authorized the President to take retaliatory measures against infractions of neutral rights and voted a naval construction program of unparalleled size.

Wilson had no desire to run afoul of either England or Germany. In November, 1916, he was reëlected. The Democrats had adopted as their slogan: "He kept us out of war." Wilson interpreted his victory as a mandate for peace, but he knew America was bound to be embroiled if hostilities continued in Europe. Word came from Germany that Bethmann could not hold out much longer against the demand of the army chiefs and public opinion for unrestricted submarine warfare. If Bethmann yielded, America would have to fight. Wilson decided to act. On December 18, he asked the belligerents for a statement of their war aims, and pointed out that the statements of the rivals were virtually the same. "He confidently hopes," the note concluded, "for a response which will bring a new light into the affairs of the world."

The response was not encouraging. The Germans, while reiterating their desire for peace, said that direct negotiations between the belligerents seemed the best mode of procedure. The Allies responded on January 10, 1917. Stripped of idealistic phraseology, the note demanded the partition of Austria and Turkey, the unification of Poland under Russian control, Alsace-Lorraine for France, and an indemnity. Wilson refused to be discouraged. He pressed the Germans for an explicit statement. The Germans held back, saying that their demands were so modest in comparison with the Allied program that a public announcement would sound like a confession of defeat. Secretly, they said they were willing to accept what amounted to a restoration of the pre-war situation.

To force the issue, Wilson resolved on an appeal to public opinion. On January 22, he set forth his views of what would bring lasting peace. "It must be a peace without victory," he declared. "Victory would mean peace forced upon the loser, a victor's peace imposed upon the vanquished. It would be accepted in humiliation, under duress, at an intolerable sacrifice, and would leave a sting, a resentment, a bitter memory, upon which terms of peace would rest, not permanently, but only as upon quicksand. Only a peace between equals can last." In veiled guise, the whole speech was an attack on the Allied claim that civilization could be preserved only if the Allies won a complete victory. The appeal to public opinion was a failure. The speech was received with angry abuse by Allied opinion. As for the Germans, they had lost hope of peace when the Allies refused to negotiate and had resolved on a desperate bid for victory.

When the failure of the attack on Verdun had become evident, Hindenburg was made commander-in-chief of the German forces, with Ludendorff as chief of staff. Hindenburg was almost worshiped by the German people, but as commander he was something of a figurehead. Ludendorff was the real master. He possessed much military ability but even more self-confidence. His domineering will was not content with rule over Hindenburg; he soon set out to dominate the whole German government. During the fall of 1916 he steadily demanded a resumption of the submarine campaign. Bethmann secured a delay until the prospects of peace were explored. When the Allies rejected Bethmann's request for negotiations, Ludendorff returned to the charge. On January 8 and 9, a conference was held at Pless. The civil government opposed Ludendorff's demand: the United States would surely declare war. The army and navy chiefs swept this consideration aside. The United States had no army and only a small fleet. Before a force could be trained, the war would be over. The Admiralty promised to force England to bid for peace within five months. On the other hand, without the submarines, Hindenburg doubted if the western front could be held in 1917. "Things cannot be worse than they are now," he said. "The war must be brought to an end by all means as soon as possible." Appalled by the misery caused by the blockade, Hindenburg and Ludendorff underestimated the endurance of the German people and forgot that the Allies, beneath their boasting confidence, might also be weakening; forgot also the results, psychological as well as military, of adding a new and powerful enemy to the lists. These considerations the civil government should have had in mind, and it should have imposed them on the military, but the Kaiser and Bethmann, weak men both, could not stand up to Ludendorff's imperious will. Unrestricted submarine warfare was decided upon, to begin February 1. The decision made German defeat certain.

On January 31, 1917, Wilson was told of the German decision. On February 3 the United States severed relations with Germany. Wilson still hoped the Germans would revoke their decision. He still could not reconcile himself to war. War, he said, "would mean that we should lose our heads along with the rest and stop weighing right and wrong . . . Once lead this people into war and they'll forget there ever was such a thing as tolerance." Slowly the peace spirit died in Wilson and the nation. The discovery of German efforts to induce Mexico and Japan to attack the United States brought almost unanimous desire for war. On April 2, Wilson asked Congress to declare war. "Our object," he said, "is to vindicate the principles of peace and justice in the life of the world as against selfish autocratic power, and to set up amongst really free and self-governed peoples of the world such a concert of purpose and action as will henceforth ensure the observance of these principles . . . We have no quarrel with the German people. We have no feeling toward them but one of sympathy and friendship. It was not upon their impulse that their government acted in entering this war."

Thus the President spoke, and thus he and most Americans felt; but the Americans, like the Entente peoples and the Germans, could not hold to their ideals. Americans said they fought autocracy to bring about an era when the law of nations would be obeyed. In its official declarations, the American government continued to insist it was fighting the German government, not the German people. Nevertheless the American people soon saw all Germans through a mist of hate, saw all Germans as foes of the good and as lovers of evil. So it was also with law. The United States was fighting to uphold the rule of law, yet the Americans swept aside the restraints of international law as ruthlessly as ever the British or the Germans had done. "It took Great Britain three years to reach a point where it was prepared to violate all the laws of blockade," said a State Department official to the British Foreign Secretary, Balfour. "You will find that it will take us only two months to become as great criminals as you are!" After April, 1917, neutrals were forced to tolerate abuse of neutral rights such as had rarely been inflicted before.

To one of their promises the Americans did hold true. On April 2, Wilson said: "We desire no conquest, no dominion. We seek no indemnities for ourselves, no material compensation." The United States alone among the great powers failed to find in the war a stimulus to the appetite for territorial expansion.

5. THE DEFEAT OF THE CENTRAL POWERS, 1917-1918

Like drowning men, alternately buoyed up by wild hope and overwhelmed by black despair, the peoples of Europe struggled through the last two years of the war. The years may be roughly divided into three parts. Through the winter, spring, and early summer of 1917 Allied hopes were high, while the fortunes of the Central Powers sank. Then the rivals shifted positions. German resistance stiffened; "defeatism" reigned in Allied countries. In the summer of 1918 there was a sharp crisis, followed by the swift collapse of Germany and the triumph of the Allies. In a sense, the war became in 1917 a government war. The people of every country were exhausted, worn to the verge of collapse. Moreover, thoughtful men outside immediate circles of government looked above the battle and saw that Europe was approaching ruin. Any peace would be better than continued carnage. Those who controlled policy were not blind to the fact that the war was exhausting both sides. Few would echo the nonchalant hope of rejuvenated national life Lloyd George had expressed in 1915. Still, though all contestants would be exhausted, the victorious governments might hope to live; defeat meant revolution. In democratic as well as autocratic countries governments struggled for survival. Governments fought not only the foe but their own people. Engines of propaganda, suppression of military news and of peace proposals, and actual force were used in this struggle. From the beginning, governments had resorted to subterfuge and lies to hold popular opinion firm. In the first years of the war this task had not been difficult. In 1917 and 1918 the home front was as difficult to hold as the military front.

By the autumn of 1916 the courage of the Central Powers was shaken. During the early months of 1917 hopes of victory disappeared. The Austrian and German governments would have been glad to make concessions to secure peace. If defeat was certain, there was more chance of the people accepting it without revolutionary protests now than there would be later. Austria was the first to decide that concessions were necessary. The Emperor Karl, who succeeded Francis Joseph in November, 1916, was resolved on peace from his accession. Through Prince Sixte of Bourbon he established contact with the Allies in January, 1917, and announced his willingness to urge Germany to make peace. If Germany refused to surrender Alsace-Lorraine, he would make a separate peace. He would give a territorial outlet on the Adriatic to Serbia, and allow the Serbians to take northern Albania; Russia could have Constantinople; the Trentino would go to Italy, if Italy would veil the Austrian capitulation by giving an African colony in exchange. Germany protested and refused to follow Karl's lead; nevertheless, he persisted. Austria could not fight through another winter without revolution. France and England welcomed the possibility of eliminating Austria: Bulgaria and Turkey, cut off from Germany, would almost certainly surrender. Italy held back, insisting that a "white" peace which failed to bring all the territory Italy had been promised by the Treaty of London would mean certain revolution. Reluctantly the French and British closed the discussion in May. Austria was forced to fight on. To accept the Italian terms would provoke Austrian opinion to the revolution which Karl had hoped to avert by peace.

The German government refused to join Austria in offering concessions to the Allies, because the decision to

declare unrestricted submarine warfare brought renewed
hopes of victory and raised the flagging spirits of the German people. Winter passed into spring, and spring into
summer. The promised surrender of England did not come.
Instead, the United States had joined the enemy. Clouds of
dejection lowered once more over Germany. Disappointment
was the keener because the Admiralty had so confidently
promised victory. In July, 1917, the leader of the Center
party, Erzberger, obtained a copy of a despairing memorandum which Emperor Karl had sent to the Kaiser, setting
forth the plight of Austria. Erzberger had been a fiery
advocate of annexations, but the memorandum convinced
him that victory could not be achieved. He read the memorandum and stated his fears to the other directors of his
party, who agreed with his conclusion. News of the discussion spread. Everywhere the desire for peace, long suppressed by hope of victory, took possession of men's
minds. On July 19, the Reichstag, by an overwhelming
majority, approved a resolution calling for a peace of reconciliation, with no annexations and no indemnities. Secretly,
Bethmann went even further than the Reichstag. The Pope
was planning a peace appeal. The papal nuncio sounded out
Bethmann, who eagerly espoused the idea. To secure peace
he would even sacrifice part of Alsace-Lorraine.

Ludendorff, when he heard that the peace movement was
advancing unchecked, demanded Bethmann's removal. Peace
talk, said the military commanders, destroyed willingness to
fight, broke the fighting spirit. That there was something
in this contention was demonstrated shortly afterward by a
naval mutiny which took place at Wilhelmshaven. Further,
said Ludendorff, the German people might now call for
peace without victory, but once this peace was achieved
there would be a reaction, a feeling that the government
should have secured victory. Then there would be revolution. Therefore, the peace agitation must be suppressed and
the will to achieve victory revived among the people. To
achieve these purposes, the "defeatist" Bethmann must be
removed. The Kaiser, resenting interference by the generals

in civil affairs, refused. Hindenburg and Ludendorff threatened to resign. The Kaiser promptly capitulated. The new Chancellor, Michaelis, did not dare defy the Reichstag openly. He proclaimed himself in agreement with the July resolution—"as I understand it." Thereafter he and the military leaders worked to revive the hope and desire for victory. The collapse of Russia and the consequent opportunity for expansion to the east provided the needed stimulus.

Dejection was spreading in Allied countries also in the summer of 1917. While exulting over Verdun and over the German desire for peace, the Allies forgot their own weakness. In February, 1917, France and Russia confidently arranged a partition of Germany. Russia was given a free hand to do as she wished in the east. France was not merely to take Alsace-Lorraine, she was also to secure control over the rich Saar basin. The remaining German territory on the left bank of the Rhine was to be made into an independent state. In February, the Tsar was dreaming of conquest; in March, he was swept from his throne by the long-impending revolution. Even the Russian revolution did not alarm the French or the English: now that the Russians were free, they would fight better.

In the west, also, confidence ignored grave weaknesses. When Lloyd George was refusing to stop before giving the knock-out blow, British credit was almost exhausted. The purchase of munitions in the United States was financed by bonds, and Americans were becoming skeptical of Allied bonds. The entrance of the United States into the war saved the day, but by a narrow margin. No sooner was this danger averted than a new one appeared—starvation. In April, 1917, the U-boat campaign reached its height. Almost 900,000 tons of Allied shipping were lost. After April the sinkings fell off, but from April to June a total of almost two and a quarter millions of tons were sunk. How close the submarines came to achieving their end the English people were not told and did not suspect. Nevertheless, the acute food shortage partially revealed the danger. For a few months the English people got some faint idea of the misery which the blockade was causing in Germany.

France also received a rude shock. After Verdun, General Nivelle massed his forces for a decisive blow. When his preparations were nearing completion, the Germans suddenly retired to a new, shorter, and almost impregnable line of trenches, the Hindenburg line. As they retired the Germans systematically devastated the area evacuated, and Nivelle was forced to begin his preparations anew in what was practically a desert. In April Nivelle struck. The Germans had divined his plan and repulsed the drive with tremendous losses. Confident of victory, the French found failure intolerable. The French army was demoralized; there were numerous mutinies. During the remainder of 1917 the French were incapable of action, and the British had to hold the front almost unaided.

War weariness threatened to paralyze Allied effort. Against the succession of disasters the governments could point to but one success, and that none too glorious. King Constantine was driven from his throne by Allied bayonets, and Venizelos placed in power. Greece could now serve as a base for operations in the Balkans. In the Near East, too, there were small victories, but these made little impression on public opinion in Allied countries. One event alone could have revived hope of victory: news that American soldiers were in the battle-front. Pershing and the American government refused, however, to allow the brigading of Americans with Allied troops. A separate American army was slowly being formed, but at the end of 1917 the Allies were beginning to despair of help from the United States. The Americans were not yet in the war, and Russia was going out. All the efforts of the revolutionary government to rouse the tired masses to a "war of liberation" failed.

The demand for a revision of war aims as an essential prerequisite to peace became acute in France and England. In Paris, Caillaux was editing a defeatist newspaper whose message was rather advertised than silenced by many blank columns, eloquent of the censor's pencil. On November 28,

1917, the *Daily Telegraph* printed a letter from Lord Lansdowne, the author of the Entente Cordiale. "We are not going to lose this war," wrote Lansdowne, "but its prolongation will spell ruin for the civilized world." To secure peace, he argued, some abatement of the Allied demands was necessary; more moderate terms must be offered in order to encourage the peace party in Germany. The official voice of Russia was added to the voice of individuals in the west. On October 20 Russia appealed to her allies, asking that they accept the principle of no annexations and no indemnities. The appeal was unanswered. In November the Bolsheviks seized power and immediately repeated the appeal. Again, no answer. In December, Russia signed an armistice with Germany.

Throughout 1917 the Allied governments resisted the defeatist agitation. Representatives of French and British labor-unions were prohibited from attending a labor conference held at Stockholm to discuss peace. When, in August, the Pope publicly appealed for peace and suggested terms which amounted to a return to the status before the war, Wilson replied for the Allies: "We cannot take the word of the present rulers of Germany as a guarantee of anything that is to endure." This reply satisfied the French and British governments but not the people. Few intelligent Europeans, whether in public or private life, believed either that an imperial government must be untrustworthy, or that a democracy could not break faith. The clamor for a restatement of war aims continued.

In January, 1918, Lloyd George yielded, after a practical ultimatum from the trade-unions. In his new statement the fiery indignation of a year before was gone. He still maintained that Germany deliberately started the war and that Britain had been taken by surprise, and therefore had been "quite unprepared." But Britain was willing to forgive that crime. "Germany has occupied a great position in the world. It is not our wish or intention to question or destroy that position for the future." Lloyd George's territorial demands were also moderated by a year of disappointment. There must be a "reconsideration," whatever that word meant, of the Alsace-Lorraine question. Austria was no longer to be partitioned; now, the subject nationalities were merely to get self-government. Italy was to get only the lands inhabited by those of her own "race and tongue." Turkey was to retain her possessions in Europe, including Constantinople, and most of the Near East, but the subject nationalities in the Near East were to get their freedom.

Lloyd George's speech did not mean much. It was studiously vague, and it was delivered only on the insistence of the trade-unions. His nimble mind accepted ideas easily and as easily abandoned them. Different times would bring different words. Across the Channel there was a leader who disdained to placate opinion even by soft words. Clemenceau became French premier at the end of 1917. Blind patriotism and firm determination to win dominated this old foe of Germany. He set out to eliminate defeatism and to recreate confidence in victory. And after victory, he promised revenge.

It was to President Wilson, rather than to Lloyd George or Clemenceau, that moderate opinion in France and England turned for encouragement. On January 8, 1918, the President set forth what he called "the only possible" program for a lasting peace:

1. Open covenants openly arrived at; in the future, no secret treaties.
2. Absolute freedom of navigation upon the seas, except when the seas were closed by international action to enforce international agreements.
3. The removal, as far as possible, of all economic barriers.
4. Adequate guarantees given and taken that national armaments will be reduced to the lowest point consistent with public safety.
5. An impartial adjustment of all colonial claims, with the interests of the subject populations receiving equal weight with the government seeking title.
6. Evacuation of Russian territory; opportunity for Russia to determine her own political development.
7. Belgium to be evacuated and restored.

8. Evacuation and restoration of French territory; the wrong done in 1871 in the matter of Alsace-Lorraine should be righted.

9. Readjustment of Italian frontiers along clearly recognizable lines of nationality.

10. Autonomous development for the peoples of Austria-Hungary.

11. Evacuation and restoration of Serbian, Montenegran, and Rumanian territory; Serbia accorded free access to the seas; the relations of the Balkan states to one another determined along historically established lines of allegiance and nationality.

12. A secure sovereignty for the Turkish portions of Turkey; autonomous development for the other nationalities now under Turkish rule; the Straits permanently open to trade.

13. An independent Polish state should be created which should include the territories inhabited by indisputably Polish populations, and which should be assured a free and secure access to the sea.

14. A general association of nations must be formed under specific covenants for the purpose of affording mutual guarantees of political independence and territorial integrity to great and small states alike.

There was much that was vague in the Fourteen Points speech, much, too, that ran directly counter to the secret treaties. Nevertheless, this speech and other pronouncements of the President revived the flagging idealism of the Allied cause and rallied the weary peoples to new efforts. Seeing the stimulating effect of Wilson's words, the Allied governments vaguely endorsed his interpretations of the purposes for which they were fighting.

In Central Europe, too, Wilson's speech had profound effect; rather it had two conflicting effects. Unperceived, Wilson's words drew the screws of fighting courage. The visions of a new world order, when peace and good-will would reign, an order attainable if Germany made only slight territorial concessions, and if Germany revised the form of government which lack of success was already depriving of glamour—this vision of peace unconsciously stole into German minds and weakened the determination to hold out at all cost. The conscious effect was very different. Through the autumn of 1917 the German government fought to raise the faltering national spirit. The refusal of the Allies to heed the Pope's plea and France's constantly reiterated demand for Alsace-Lorraine offered the opportunity for an appeal to the deep-seated dread of return to the divided impotence of pre-Bismarckian Germany. "The quarrel for which Europe is gradually being transformed into a rubbish heap is the future of Alsace-Lorraine," declared the Foreign Secretary in October. "What we are fighting for—and shall fight till the last drop of blood—is no fantastic conquests; it is the integrity of the German Empire." Germans were fighting to preserve their country; their foes were fighting for conquests. Because their purpose was to live, the Germans would hold firm; because the enemy's purpose was conquest, the foe would weaken. The development of defeatism in Allied countries aided the German government's campaign. The moderation of the Allied terms of January, 1918, was exultantly contrasted with the demands of a year before. The Allied demand for conquest was weakening; hold firm, and the unity of Germany will soon be assured.

Self-preservation was not enough, the government thought. The Germans must have hopes of conquest to carry them through until peace was attained; the government must be able to point to definite gains if it was to survive the reaction after war. The collapse of Russia opened the way to at least a foretaste of victory. In December the Bolshevists agreed to an armistice and asked for a peace based on the principle of no annexations or indemnities. The Germans agreed to accept these terms if the Allies would also agree. When the Bolshevik appeal to the Allies went unanswered, the Germans still held in theory to the proposed basis. But, said the German delegates, Poland, Lithuania, and the Baltic provinces desire their freedom, under German protection. Trotzky protested: the Germans were pursuing old imperialistic aims under the guise of self-determination. When the Germans refused to yield, the Bolsheviks simply declared the war was over, without a treaty. The advance of a German army into Russia brought the Bolsheviks to terms. At Brest-Litovsk in March they accepted the German demands. At the same time, Rumania capitulated. By the Treaty of Bucharest, Austria received small strategic frontier rectifications, while Bulgaria took the Dobruja. Rumania was allowed to compensate herself by taking Bessarabia from Russia.

The Germans were dazzled by the prospects Brest-Litovsk and Bucharest offered: a chain of dependent states, barriers against the Russian advance, fields for commercial expansion. To hold these prizes, victory must be won in the west.

The iron will of Ludendorff had rallied the Germans once more, first to defense, then to win victory. He knew that victory must come soon. Germany's allies were almost paralyzed. In Germany, hunger would soon destroy the revived war spirit. From across the Atlantic, thousands of fresh American troops had come, and hundreds of thousands were preparing to come. Ludendorff was persuaded by all these dangerous elements to risk everything on a final effort to break through. In October, 1917, he made his first move. Like an avalanche, Austrian and German troops fell on the Italian lines. There was a confused retreat. Tremendous quantities of stores, a quarter of a million troops, a rich province—all these the Germans got. It was a glorious victory, but Ludendorff had not broken through. Celebrated as a victory, the advance to the Piave was a failure. Italy remained in the war.

In March, 1918, came the great effort. First, the British were assaulted at St. Quentin, and fell back almost to Amiens. Two weeks later the left wing of the British line was forced back. At the end of May, the whole French line was attacked. For a month and a half the French retreated, back to the gates of Rheims. Everywhere the Allied lines bent; nowhere, or only momentarily, did they break. Like some caged animal seeking freedom, the German forces hurled themselves, now against one part of the encircling barrier, now against another. The barrier always yielded, and always remained unbroken, barring the road to freedom.

On July 15, Ludendorff once more hurled his exhausted forces against Rheims. For the first time the Allies held. Encouraged, Foch began a counter-attack with his fresh reserves, including, for the first time, large American forces. The Germans began to fall back, slowly at first, then more and more rapidly. On August 8, "the black day of the German army," the first break appeared in the German lines. The retreat became a rout: on August 13, Ludendorff told the Kaiser the war was lost. In the Balkans and in far-off Asia Minor other Allied drives began. At the end of September exhausted Bulgaria surrendered. When he heard the news, Ludendorff lost his nerve and called for immediate peace.

Ludendorff's demand for peace became known and produced a complete revulsion of spirit among the German people. During the summer of 1918, influenza had swept over famished Central Europe, producing horror akin to that inspired by the great medieval plagues; still the Germans had continued to hope. The Allies had sent airplanes, balloons, secret agents, to scatter subversive pamphlets, promises of an easy peace. Revolts began in Austria. By September 15 Emperor Karl was begging the Allies for peace. Still the German people, buoyed up by Ludendorff's promises, had hoped. Abruptly, Ludendorff said the war was lost. Despair replaced hope. The "home front" crumbled away. Weary, disillusioned, the German people thought only of peace and of Wilson's promises of mercy.

At the beginning of October negotiations began. As a preliminary, the Kaiser replaced the reactionary ministers by a liberal cabinet headed by Prince Max of Baden. The new ministry proposed to Wilson that an armistice, a truce, be made for the purpose of drawing up a treaty of peace based on the Fourteen Points. Two days later a similar appeal went out from Vienna. The reply to Austria was swift and crushing: conditions had changed; the subject nationalities must have independence. To Germany, Wilson reiterated his old contention: the imperial government could not be trusted honestly to respect its promises. Practically, Wilson demanded a revolution. Ludendorff quickly grasped this fact and called for a new effort. There could be no new effort. To suggest the prolongation of war would mean revolution. His commands defied, Ludendorff angrily resigned. For once, Hindenburg refused to follow his mentor and remained loyal to the men who had fought for him.

Events moved faster. On October 28, a naval mutiny at Kiel heralded the impending revolution in Germany. On October 31 Turkey surrendered. On November 3 Austria obtained an armistice by agreeing to allow the subject nationalities to determine their own fate. Germany, torn by dissension, stood alone. On November 5, the Allies, through President Wilson, announced their terms: they agreed to make peace on the basis of the Fourteen Points, with two reservations. Complete freedom of action was reserved on the question of freedom of the seas; and Germany must promise to make reparation "for all damage done to the civilian populations of the Allies." Three days later the Allied commander made known the terms upon which an armistice would be granted for the purpose of negotiating the peace treaty. The terms were designed to prevent Germany from renewing the struggle. In the west, German forces must retire beyond the Rhine. In the east, the treaties of Brest-Litovsk and Bucharest must be canceled and all occupied territory evacuated. Large quantities of military stores and the whole fleet must be turned over to the Allies.

Germany was in turmoil. Revolution swept on unchecked. On November 9 a socialist republic was proclaimed. The Kaiser, after thirty years of rule, was forced to abdicate and to find safety in ignominious flight to Holland. A few days later Emperor Karl ended his pathetic two years of effort to preserve the Hapsburg monarchy. The new Socialist and democratic government of Germany accepted Foch's terms. On November 11, at eleven in the morning, the armistice began. After fifty-one months of struggle, against overwhelming numbers from the first, against most of the world before the end, the German people gave up. Friend and foe alike must pay tribute to the courage and the intelligence which enabled this nation of sixty-five millions to fight, almost unaided, against foes so numerous and so powerful, against the terrible force of sea power as well. These fifty-one months had taken a heavy toll of the world's strength. Over eight millions of men were killed. Many more than that number were swept away by the plague of influenza; countless millions were maimed in body and in spirit. The structure of western civilization was shaken, how seriously we do not know. The men and women who greeted the armistice in a delirium of relief, though they might be the same individuals, were different Europeans, and Americans, from those men and women who saw war descend on Europe in August, 1914.

CHAPTER VII

THE PEACE OF PARIS

EUROPE
IN 1929

Scale of Miles

0 100 200 300 400 500 600

The new Baltic and Central European states are shown in a light tint

MAX MAYER, THORNWOOD, N.Y.

Longitude   West   0°   Longitude   East   10°   from   Greenwich

© The Century Co., 1932

CHAPTER VII

THE PEACE OF PARIS

I. THE PRE-ARMISTICE AGREEMENT

In 1871, after a decade of rapid change, the map of
Europe settled into a definite pattern. Thereafter colors
shifted from time to time in the Balkan peninsula. Aside
from this corner, and aside from a few patches—Switzer-
land, Holland, and the other small states—the map consisted of large irregular splashes of color. From London,
from Paris, from Berlin, from St. Peter___rg, from Rome,
from Vienna and Budapest, lines vi___ and invisible
radiated, binding each stretch of terri___ to the capital.
For a generation and a half this bold, ___e pattern remained fixed. Outside Europe, the patt___ fted rapidly.
The area of European domination wid___ il the eastern hemisphere seemed but an extension ___ European
peninsula.

At the end of July, 1914, the map began to ___ con-
vulsively. In 1917 it became simplified as ne___ ___re.
A diagonal band ran south and east, from the ___ish
Channel and the Baltic, across the face of Europe down
into the Near East—the domain of the Central Powers.
Against this narrow band pressed almost all the rest of
the world, a Grand Alliance of twenty-seven states, great
and small, with the oceans of the world as a uniting high-
way. No sooner had the simplification become complete
than it began to disappear. At the end of 1917 the eastern
sustaining wall of the Grand Alliance gave way when
the Bolshevists sued for peace. Undeterred, the Alliance
pressed forward until the band of the Central Powers was
broken by defeat in November, 1918. Thereafter the map

of eastern Europe became as if drawn on water. Within the great land mass of Russia, stretching across Europe and Asia, competing armies and peoples fought, some for supremacy over the whole, some for separate existence. The empire of the Hapsburgs was pulverized into quarreling fragments. The proud edifice reared by Bismarck was in ruins. East of the Rhine, for thousands of miles, the only common force was hunger, hunger resulting from the disintegrating effect of war and revolution on the complicated economic system, hunger resulting from the strangling grip of the blockade. Outside this stark, hateful area there remained the Grand Alliance; but now that victory had come, the Grand Alliance threatened to break up into antagonistic parts.

How might the map be once more securely drawn? How might the world resume the comparatively orderly existence violently interrupted in 1914? How might the world have assurance that there might never be another such catastrophic struggle? Men pondered these questions after they lost the first delirious joy of relief from war. A host of plans, some fantastic, some claiming the verification of experience, were offered to cure the world's woes.

The pre-armistice agreement between the Allies and Germany had already established a contractual basis for the settlement with Germany, a peace based on "Wilsonian" principles. Democracy, nationalism, and a world commonwealth were the three cardinal points in Wilson's program. The first two were essential prerequisites to the third. Wilson pinned his faith to the "common man." Autocracies were irresponsible; the whims of an individual or a class dominated policy; those whims might call for war. Free peoples, unlike autocrats, would be loath to draw the sword. The world must be made safe for democracy, Wilson declared: the crash of thrones in Europe seemed an answer to his command. The plain people, it appeared, had triumphed. One evil was vanquished.

Autocracy had been an evil and a danger to peace. No less evil and no less dangerous was the unwilling subjection of one people to another. Following on democracy there must be self-determination. Every people must be allowed freely to choose its own political allegiance. Nationalism must be carried to its logical conclusion. Specifically, Wilson called for the return of Alsace-Lorraine to France, for the revival of the Polish republic, and for the emancipation of oppressed nationalities in Austria-Hungary and Turkey. Here also the words of Wilson were heeded. On the ruins of Austria-Hungary new states were rising; their boundaries alone remained to be fixed. Germany had agreed to surrender Alsace-Lorraine, and had consented to the creation of a Polish state. In Turkey also, subject races were freeing themselves; but Wilson made a significant reservation with regard to these and other non-European peoples. There were, he said, many peoples which had not yet reached political maturity and which must, therefore, be guided by more advanced nations. Colonies should not be private possessions, they should be trusts held in the name of society as a whole; backward peoples were not to be subjects, they were to be wards. As for the great defeated enemy, Germany, Wilson repeatedly and definitely said that the German people, like all others, must have freedom and self-determination. Previous peace treaties, like that after the Franco-Prussian War, had sown the seeds of future wars by inflicting unjust terms on the vanquished. That mistake must not be made again. Germany must restore the areas devastated by her troops and must surrender Alsace-Lorraine and territory inhabited by the Poles. That was all. Germany was not to be discriminated against or cut off from the family of nations.

Self-determination, Wilson believed, would establish a new status which would satisfy, so far as was humanly possible, the legitimate aspirations of all nations. The next and greatest task was to devise methods of assuring every nation that the *status quo* would not be violently upset by some one state or group of states to the disadvantage of the others, and that any nation which found the *status quo* oppressive would be able to secure justifiable changes. The

pre-war generation had grappled with this double problem
but had found no solution except armaments and alliances.
The war, Wilson contended, showed that the solution ag-
gravated the disease. Alliances and competitive armaments
must be swept away. Nations, all nations, must league together, and by a solemn covenant assure one another of
support against aggression and of coöperation in the task
of making any needful changes in the existing situation.
Thus assured, free peoples would not arm or band against
each other.

During 1917 and 1918 Wilson tried to secure the acceptance of his program by the governments with which the
United States was associated in the war. To a limited extent he was successful. His speeches won applause in every
Allied country, especially in England. More and more Wilson became the leader to whom the exhausted peoples of
all nations turned for the hope of a healing peace. The
British government appointed a committee led by Lord
Phillimore to draft a plan for a league of nations; indeed,
the idea of a league had taken root in England before
America entered the war. In January, 1918, pressure from
the trade-unions forced Lloyd George to make a declaration of war aims very similar to Wilson's program.

Nevertheless, the Allied governments disliked and mistrusted Wilson's program. During the war they worked
out by secret treaties the main lines of a settlement based
on the right of the victors to dictate changes in the *status
quo,* and to make provision for their own security at the
expense of the vanquished. Japan was to receive the German possessions in the Pacific north of the equator, and
German rights in the Shantung peninsula. The British Empire was to inherit Germany's south Pacific islands. From
the end of 1914 right into the period of the peace conference, discussions went forward and agreements were made
concerning spheres of influence in Turkey. Most of Austria-Hungary and Albania was parceled out. Without the
knowledge of England, the French and Russian governments promised to support each other in any demands con-

cerning the fate of the western and eastern portions of
Germany. Having obtained all they wished, the Allies
counted for security on the weakness of the Central Powers
which would follow territorial losses, on the forcible limitation of German military and naval strength, and on
continued solidarity between the Allies after the war.

Obviously the peace program outlined in the secret treaties and understandings was incompatible with Wilson's
program. He was aware of the discrepancy. When Germany appealed to him for peace, he made a final effort to
secure acceptance of his views. The German appeal contained two distinct proposals: there was to be an armistice,
and peace was to be made on the basis of Wilson's
speeches, particularly the Fourteen Points speech. Wilson
has since been accused of halting the Allied armies before
the Germans were unquestionably beaten. That is not true.
The request for an armistice—that is, for a truce while
peace was being made—was turned over to the Allied military commanders for decision. They debated the relative
merits of a further advance and of an immediate truce
granted on terms which would make the resumption of
hostilities by Germany practically impossible. The American representative was for pushing on. Foch demurred:
"On ne fait la guerre que pour les résultats." The military
objective was to destroy the enemy's ability to fight. "If
the Germans now sign an armistice under the general conditions we have just determined, those results are in our
possession. This being achieved, no man has the right to
cause another drop of blood to be shed."

Wilson let the generals decide the terms of the armistice,
but the political leaders must decide whether or not peace
was to be made on the basis of the Fourteen Points. The
question was threshed out at a conference between Colonel
House, Lloyd George, Clemenceau, and Orlando, the Italian premier. The European Allies wished to reject the
proposed basis: they had not studied the Fourteen Points;
they did not wish to tie their hands. Wilson threatened. If
the Allies insisted on refusing, he would end the negotia-

tions with Germany and say publicly why he had ended them. The threat was alarming. If the Allied peoples found their leaders had refused to accept what seemed fair terms, there would almost certainly be revolts and mutinies. House further intimated that Wilson would withdraw from the war and make a separate peace. This would also shock Allied opinion and, more important, the Allied countries would be deprived of the financial assistance which they hoped to secure from America after the war.

The Allied leaders resented Wilson's threats. Nevertheless, they agreed to accept the proposed basis for the peace, with reservations. In all, four objections were made to the Fourteen Points. Of these, two were accepted. Clemenceau did not like the idea of a league of nations, but Lloyd George was indifferent and Wilson insistent. Clemenceau gave way, unconvinced. Lloyd George wished to extend the reparation demand. Wilson had called for the restoration of devastated areas, but England had no devastated areas. Lloyd George asked that Germany be forced to make reparation for all damages done to civilians, so that England might get a share of the payments. All agreed to that change. Orlando objected to the point which promised Italy the Italian districts of Austria-Hungary. Italy wanted more. Orlando said Italy would want lands rightfully hers, not only on linguistic, but also on economic, strategic, and historical grounds. Clemenceau overruled Orlando. The discussions concerned the treaty with Germany, not with the Dual Monarchy, said Clemenceau; the Italian arguments could be brought up later. Complaining and suspicious, Orlando gave way.

The fourth divergence of opinion threatened to disrupt the Grand Alliance. Wilson's second point called for absolute freedom of commerce upon the seas in time of war. In other words, sea power would be of use in time of war only to prevent invasion or to facilitate the transport of troops. Traditionally, the British justified their naval supremacy on the ground that England could be starved into submission by any rival with a stronger fleet. Wilson's proposal would banish the fear of starvation, but it would also prevent Britain from starving her enemies. Lloyd George objected. The British navy had, he said, just helped to save civilization by preventing trade with Germany. Wilson rudely swept this argument aside: there was no certainty that Britain's interests would always be those of civilization. "We are," he cabled House, "pledged to fight not only Prussian militarism, but militarism everywhere." A few days later the President became more plain-spoken. If the British refused to accept the freedom of the seas, they could "count on the certainty of our using our present equipment to build up the strongest navy that our resources permit." Lloyd George was equally vehement: "Great Britain would spend her last guinea to keep a navy superior to that of the United States or any other Power." The negotiators stared down the appalling vista of a repetition of the Anglo-German rivalry. Then the issue was pushed from sight. Freedom of the seas was eliminated from the agreement with Germany; Lloyd George agreed to discuss the question with the United States at the peace conference. As a matter of fact, Wilson did not raise the issue at the peace conference, probably because he trusted to the League of Nations to prevent wars in which questions of sea law would cause dissension between neutrals and belligerents.

With two reservations, one eliminating the freedom of the seas from the discussions with Germany, the other making more precise the reparation Germany must pay, Wilson's program was accepted as the basis for peace. The pre-armistice agreement formed a contractual obligation on the Allies. It may be argued that Germany must soon have surrendered unconditionally, but the fact remains that the Allies neither asked for nor received unconditional surrender. The validity of the pre-armistice contract is incontestable. Nevertheless, the situation was far from clear. Were the secret treaties invalidated by the agreement with Germany? Opinions differed on that question. Again, in accepting the Fourteen Points as the basis for peace with Germany, had the Allies accepted those points which dealt

with Austrian and Turkish problems? Since no reservations had been made on these points, except privately by
Italy, it would seem that they had been accepted. On the
other hand, Austria and Turkey had surrendered unconditionally. It was all very confusing. With the best will in
the world, there must inevitably be widely divergent interpretation of what had been promised. It speedily became
apparent that good-will could not be hoped for. Rather,
it seemed that the Allied peoples would repudiate the contract, even deny its existence.

2. THE POST-ARMISTICE REACTION

President Wilson believed himself justified in forcing
his program on the Allied leaders because he thought their
desire to effect a punitive, imperialistic peace was not
shared by the "common man" in Allied countries. After
the armistice, Wilson clung to this belief, but it was soon
obvious to most thinking men that the leaders were more,
rather than less, moderate than the people they represented.
While the conflict raged, and the issue hung uncertain,
Wilson's ringing declarations heartened men; the fighting
over, and victory won, Wilson's words lost their appeal.
The lofty edifice of idealism and self-sacrifice he had
erected was swept away in floods of hate, cynicism, and
nationalism.

Before the armistice, victory loomed ahead as a haven
of peace and plenty. When the war tension was suddenly
relaxed, men and women realized what the war had cost.
For the first time the dead were really dead. The toppling
load of debt, unnoticed before, became a nightmare. Overwhelmed, men forgot their dreams of an era of good-will
and became obsessed with blind vindictiveness. The reaction was naturally most intense in France and Belgium.
These countries had the invaders on their soil throughout
the war, and the devastated regions were piteous to see.
Germany had not been invaded, and the lasting effects of
starvation on the whole German population were not apparent. Germany, men and women believed, had started the

war. German fields, forests, and mines had escaped unscathed. There was a clamor for retribution. Let the Hun
suffer what we have suffered! Let us do to Germany what
Germany has done to us!

The demand for vengeance was universal. England had *good*
most to gain by a moderate peace. Politically, England had
feared Germany before the war because Germany threatened to dominate the Continent. That threat had now disappeared. Of the four greatest Continental powers, three
—Russia, Germany, and Austria—were in at least temporary eclipse. France stood in a position to dominate the
Continent as no power had done before. Clear-sighted men
saw that, with Russia in the throes of revolution and the
Dual Monarchy dead, British interest demanded the revival of German power to counterbalance the power of
France. Economically, also, Britain would gain by a revival
of prosperity in Central Europe. England lived by trade;
world trade was in chaos; England must suffer until order
was restored. These facts were obvious to a few men, but
the voice of calm counsel was drowned in the chorus of
hate. Vindictiveness found its opportunity when Lloyd
George decided to dissolve Parliament and have new elections. Still scarcely aware of the popular temper, he began
the election campaign by urging moderation. The voice of
the mob angrily repudiated moderation. Soon the cabinet,
fearful of defeat, lost its head. Englishmen had been told
Germany was responsible for the crushing load of debt:
Germany must pay. Disregarding the advice of economists,
Lloyd George fell in line. "They must pay to the uttermost
farthing," he averred, "and we shall search their pockets
for it." The Kaiser and his advisers had been denounced
as arch-criminals throughout the war. They must be punished, cried those whose sons had been killed; the supporters of Lloyd George promised to bring the Kaiser to trial.
Placated, the British gave the Coalition ministry an overwhelming majority—but the ministers were pledged to
hang the Kaiser and make the Germans pay.

The United States entered the war late. American man-power and American economic resources were not drained in the struggle. Nevertheless, former President Roosevelt was applauded when he called on the Allies to disregard Wilson and the pre-armistice agreement and to punish the Germans. The American Congress voted money for relief, but with the stipulation that no starving German child should get a piece of the bread or a bowl of the soup bought with the funds appropriated.

Hate dominated opinion in Allied countries. The leaders, even those who thought calmly, were afraid to withstand the popular clamor. In the armistice agreement the Allies promised to see that Germany had food. That promise was broken, and when the Allied blockade was extended to the Baltic, Germany was prevented from getting food in neutral countries. The winter of 1918–1919 brought more privation and starvation to Germany than any of the war winters. The armistice agreement was broken, and there was scant chance that the pre-armistice agreement, with its promise of a peace of reconciliation, could be kept. The decision to hold the peace conference at Paris, instead of in some neutral capital, meant that the delegates would be in the midst of a people made passionately vindictive by suffering. Before the conference met, France had secured general acceptance for the idea that the treaty must contain an "acknowledgment by Germany of the responsibility and premeditation of her rulers, which would place in the forefront the ideas of justice and of responsibility, and would legitimize the means of punishment and precaution against her."

Hate attacked the pre-armistice agreement as too lenient; cynicism poured ridicule over Wilson's program. The war had overtaxed man's idealism. The armistice ushered in a "hard-boiled" era. Nauseated by canting war propaganda, instinctively fighting to dull the edge of pain, bewildered by the complex problems left by the war, men sought refuge in scoffing at all the emotions and qualities which a few months before had seemed heroic and humane. The spread of cynicism was quick and insidious; ideals wilted

as under a blighting frost. No man was more easy to ridicule than Wilson. Bitingly irreverent comparisons between
Wilson and God Almighty, between the Ten Command-
ments and the Fourteen Points, were joyously repeated,
and always attributed to Clemenceau. No program was
more easy to ridicule than that Wilson had formulated. A
world made safe for democracy: statesmen ironically
pointed to the antics of the hate-maddened mob, statesmen
too timorous to risk their political lives by opposing the
popular will. Self-determination as the foundation of a
stable world order: the bloody anarchy reigning among the
ruins of the Dual Monarchy seemed a scathing commentary
on this text. Lasting peace and disarmament through a
league of nations: Utopia, men replied. Wilson sometimes,
and his pacifist followers incessantly, spoke of "sacrifice"
and of "humanity first." The words sounded silly. Men
and women had had enough of sacrifice, enough of feeding
on hopes; now they would grasp at tangible benefits, benefits seized at no matter what cost to other men.

Hate, cynicism, and what idealism men had left centered
in nationalism. "He had one illusion—France; and one
disillusion—mankind, including Frenchmen," Keynes
wrote of Clemenceau. The description, with the substitu-
tion of England or America for France, would serve to
describe millions of men and women. Wilson argued that
his program served enlightened national self-interest: the
contention was dismissed as false. Wilson argued that it
showed great faith indeed for a statesman, after the war
just past, to trust in arms or alliances for safety: the argument was shrugged aside. Arms and alliances might be
faulty protection, but they were better than utopian dreams
of a world commonwealth. Now, while the enemy was
helpless, the victors could make sure their supremacy. The
opportunity must not be allowed to escape. Now, when
German tyranny had been averted, national freedom must
not be surrendered to the tyranny of a league of nations.
On the one hand, a league would not provide security; on
the other hand, it would impair national independence.

Nationalism rebelled against the thought of purchasing an unwanted league at the cost of foregoing a victors' peace.

Security was peculiarly a French problem. There were forty millions of Frenchmen; there were over sixty millions of Germans. German industrial power far surpassed that of France. The Germans had held out for over four years against most of the world. In view of these facts, the French felt justified in elaborating a program of security. As direct protection against invasion, they wished to separate the left bank of the Rhine from Germany and to attach that area, directly or indirectly, to France. To weaken Germany and to strengthen themselves, the French insisted on annexing the highly industrialized Saar Basin. Parts of the Saar had been held for a time under Napoleon. Upon this fact the French based their claim to the whole district. To weaken Germany and to strengthen potential allies of France, the French wished to secure the maximum possible gains for the new states to the east of Germany, particularly Poland. Upper Silesia, with its mines and its industry, must go to Poland. With great tracts of agricultural land and Upper Silesia in Polish hands, with Alsace-Lorraine and the Saar incorporated in France, with the Rhineland cut off and under French control, Germany would be unable to hope for a war of revenge. Germany would be weak, and France would be incomparably strong. France would not merely regain the hegemony lost in 1871. Enlarged in territory and resources, with a chain of allies in the east who would be bound to her by fear of Germany, France would regain and perpetuate the supremacy Napoleon had won. The vision was more attractive to Frenchmen than Wilson's peace of reconciliation, or Wilson's dream of a league of equals.

Neither England nor America was worried about the problem of security. Tirpitz's "risk" navy was safely interned at Scapa Flow in accordance with the armistice provision, and no one thought Germany would ever get the ships back. Therefore England felt safe. Thousands of miles of ocean protected the United States. The security of these two nations might be endangered by a naval race between them, but this possibility was not yet seriously envisaged. A few Englishmen were worried about the strength of France, but such fears seemed almost indecent so soon after the common struggle to save civilization. Unafraid, neither England nor America saw need for the protection of an international league. England was indifferent, but America was hostile to Wilson's ideal.

American aversion to political dealings with Europe had slowly been overcome by exasperation at German submarine warfare. Germany conquered, the desire to keep clear of Europe revived. A century of isolation, tradition inherited from the American Revolution and the Napoleonic wars, the prejudices of immigrants who had left Europe in quest of freedom, the pharisaic conviction that all Americans were upright, honest men and all Europeans effete, unscrupulous tricksters—all these elements in American life help to explain the determination with which the United States turned away from Europe after 1918. The desire to return to a policy of isolation was stimulated by the Republican party as an effective weapon against Wilson and the Democrats. Since the Republicans controlled the Senate, and the Senate must ratify the treaty, it was dubious whether Wilson's program would be accepted by his own country.

Before the conference opened, Wilson's "plain people," both in America and in the Allied countries, had deserted him. A minority did, to be sure, continue loyal. When he arrived in Europe in December, 1918, he was cheered everywhere by rapturous crowds, but most of those who cheered so lustily were to become angrily hostile when his program balked their national interest. The post-armistice reaction made impossible the fulfilment of the pre-armistice contract. Whether the reaction could itself have been prevented had other men been in power, or had a preliminary peace been quickly made, will long be debated by students. The question is only of academic interest. The reaction was a fact, a fact which explains the peace treaties.

Before the peace conference assembled, the whole basis of the treaty with Germany had been changed, unconsciously changed. President Wilson told the members of the American delegation that they would be the only disinterested people at the conference. He, and nearly all his advisers, sincerely believed they were disinterested. They were not. No man could pass unscathed through the bombardment of war propaganda and the mass attack of hate. The very fact that they thought themselves disinterested prevented most of the American delegates, Wilson not least, from making allowance for their own prejudices. The other delegations were obsessed by hate of Germany to an even greater extent. At the beginning of its deliberations, the peace conference agreed that Germany was to be punished. No one seemed to realize the importance of this decision. The whole basis of peace was changed. The pre-armistice agreement contained no hint that Germany was a guilty nation to be punished by the victors. Moral condemnation and punishment accepted, the flood-gates were open. Any terms could be justified.

Under the circumstances, it is remarkable that harsher terms were not imposed on Germany. Three forces worked, directly or indirectly, toward moderation: the conflict of interest between England and France, desire to conciliate the United States, and fear of Bolshevism. Blinded by passion, British opinion would willingly have allowed France to do her worst to Germany. The French were quick to take advantage of this feeling. When their demands were resisted, they pointed to the bleeding wounds of France, or hurled the terrible epithet "pro-German" at their opponent. Lloyd George knew, however, that British interests would not be served by French hegemony. Wherever he dared, he resisted French plans. In this respect he was closer to Wilsonian ideas than was the President himself. Wilson had become infected more than he realized by the vindictive spirit, and he willingly consented to injuries to Germany which Lloyd George opposed because British interests would also be injured. Even Clemenceau could be moderate when urged by interest. Unlike most of his countrymen, Clemenceau did not think France could maintain her hegemony unaided. He was determined not to disrupt the Grand Alliance by breaking with England or America. In his efforts to preserve the Alliance he made concessions which in the end ruined his political career.

All the Allies were anxious not to alienate the United States. American financial assistance would be necessary during the period of reconstruction, and all the Allies owed large sums to the United States, debts on which they desired to secure easy terms of payment, if not cancellation. Fortunately for Wilson, the extent to which he was losing control over American opinion was not fully appreciated. In order to retain American good-will, the Allies were willing to make some concession to Wilson's views. Although the American delegates were not, as they thought, impartial arbiters, they were less biased than most of the other delegations, and they were not hampered by the necessity of giving spoils to get spoils, as Lloyd George was. Wilson and his advisers were, therefore, the most consistent opponents of exorbitant demands. Possibly a more astute negotiator could have won more from Wilson's advantageous position, but no one could have been more earnest and persistent in fighting for what he desired.

Bolshevism was, paradoxically, a friend of moderation. Germany could not compel observance of the pre-armistice agreement, but Germany could, if driven too far, make a vindictive peace hard to enforce. From Moscow, Lenin was preaching a new program for the world settlement. The Bolshevists proclaimed that the war had grown out of the defects and the evils of capitalist society. The way to salvation lay through the degradation of the old ruling classes, whether bourgeois or noble, and through the exaltation of those who had been exploited alike in peace and war—the workmen, the proletariat. Let the workmen of all nations join hands for the good of all. There would then be peace and plenty. To the famine-ridden multitudes of Central and Eastern Europe, the Bolshevist promise of harmonious peace to follow the extermination of the oppressors came as a message of hope, but of hope as the only refuge from despair. At heart all but a handful, even of the workmen, still believed in the old capitalism or the older agrarianism. It was hunger and hopelessness which drove men unwillingly to accept the teachings of Moscow. Early in 1919, Bavaria and Hungary embraced Bolshevism for a brief period; the White reaction came, swift and bloody, in both countries.

Bolshevism aroused horror and disgust among the leaders of the Grand Alliance. In large part their feelings were the natural reaction to a program which called for the extermination of the classes from which these leaders had sprung. The class reaction was instinctive and for the most part unconscious. The bloody anarchy which prevailed in Russia and wherever Bolshevism appeared gave a less interested and more universally human basis for hatred of Bolshevism. That class feeling was stronger than humanitarianism, however, was indicated by the fact that the ferocity with which Bolshevism was everywhere attacked did not, like the excesses of Bolshevism, arouse loathing for the oppressors and pity for the victims in capitalist countries. Bolshevism—that "foul baboonery of Bolshevism," as Churchill called it—was hated and feared. The infection was spreading, rapidly in parts of the Dual Monarchy and in Germany, to some extent in the rest of Europe. There were even traces of the disease, magnified by fear, in the United States. How might the disease be checked? Bolder spirits, like Churchill and Foch, urged an armed attack on Russia itself. Small Allied expeditions were sent, but the people at home were clamoring for demobilization, and soldiers who fought unquestioningly against Germany showed a reluctance to kill and be killed when transported to Russia. Indeed, many of the men sent on these "sanitary" expeditions became themselves infected with Bolshevism. Armed attack failed. The Allies continued to interfere in Russia, but the only result was to heighten the misery which hung over that land.

Bolshevism remained. Lenin was not able to secure the reorganization of the world by a dictatorship of the proletariat, but Moscow influenced the settlement. The Allied leaders, especially Lloyd George, saw that Bolshevism was embraced only when the alternative was despair. Fear that the German people might see only these alternatives before them undoubtedly moderated Allied policy and ensured the rejection of many punitive proposals.

3. THE PEACE CONFERENCE

In January, 1919, after what seemed interminable delay to the suffering peoples of Europe, the peace conference assembled in Paris. The city was filled by the delegates of the Grand Alliance and the experts they had brought with them. Representatives of every conceivable cause were there clamoring for a hearing. No peace conference ever faced more numerous or more complicated problems. Large parts of the world were without settled government. What was to be done about Russia? There was fighting through most of Eastern Europe; what should be done? Rumanian forces invaded Hungary; what was to be done? Italy seized part of Turkey; what was to be done? The armistice must be renewed; the disarmament of the enemy must be supervised; some relief must go to Central Europe to stem the tide of famine and disease. All this in addition to the task of drafting the peace treaties. It was no easy task, liquidating the war.

To prevent the conference from degenerating into a forum in which the delegates would talk themselves and the world to death, the great powers took matters into their own hands. All important deliberations were confined to the Council of Ten, consisting of the two chief delegates respectively of France, the British Empire, the United States, Japan, and Italy. Later even this mechanism proved cumbersome. Decisions were made by the Four: Clemenceau, Lloyd George, Wilson, and Orlando. Then Orlando went home in a rage. The Three remained. When the Ten, the Four, or the Three had decided, a plenary session of the conference was held. There Clemenceau ruthlessly pushed through the decisions already made. Nevertheless, progress was slow. Current affairs consumed endless time. Each problem must be examined by a committee of experts; the experts found agreement hard to achieve. Slowly, painfully, through four months, the conditions of peace were worked out.

Every one was impatient at the delay. "Instead of drawing the picture with big lines," complained Colonel House, "they are drawing it like an etching." The complaint was just, and the treaty suffered from the failure to sketch the main lines before proceeding to details. It is doubtful whether a different method could have been followed. An attempt to secure agreement on guiding principles at the outset would have revealed and hardened differences of opinion among the delegates. Every delegation had an inflamed public opinion at its back demanding the impossible. The popular demands could not be disavowed without a domestic crisis; they could not be insisted upon without disrupting the conference. The only way out was to whittle away differences, first on this question and then on that, in the hope that the final result would be accepted by the national parliaments. Wilson was the only delegate to defy opinion at home, and the United States was the only great power to refuse ratification.

A brief survey of the history of the peace conference cannot yet be written because the whole subject is still in the controversial stage. It will suffice for our purpose to analyze the terms presented to Germany and to indicate the way in which the more important decisions were arrived at.

The Conditions of Peace began with the Covenant of the League of Nations. The purpose of the League was "to promote international coöperation and to achieve international peace and security." Membership was to be granted immediately to the members of the Grand Alliance and to most neutral states. Other states, that is, the enemies of the Alliance, were to be admitted when their applications were approved by a two-thirds vote of the Assembly, in which every member of the League had one vote. In addition to the Assembly, there was to be a Council, consisting of the five victorious great powers and four other states elected by the Assembly. Routine work of the League was entrusted to a permanent Secretariat. The seat of the League was to be in Geneva. An initial duty was laid upon the Council: a plan for the reduction of armaments was to be formulated; the terms of this agreement were to be revised every ten years.

Articles 10–17 defined the obligations of members and the means of preserving peace. By Article 10, "the Members of the League undertake to respect and preserve as against external aggression the territorial integrity and existing political independence of all Members of the League." The League was immediately to take action in case of war or threat of war; each member had the right to call attention to conditions dangerous to peace (Article 11). Three methods were provided for coping with disputes between members, or between a member and a non-member: arbitration, judicial settlement, and inquiry by the Council. The classes of disputes suitable to adjustment by each of the first two methods were defined; provision was made for the establishment of a permanent court of international justice. Disputes not susceptible to adjustment by either of these means, and any dispute which threatened war, were to be dealt with by the Council. The decision of the Council in a dispute must be unanimous, excluding the parties to the dispute.

When a dispute arose, neither party was permitted to resort to war until three months after the League had made its decision or announced its inability to reach a decision. In practice, this meant that there could not be war for at least six months after a dispute arose, because the deliberations of the League could be prolonged over at least three months. War was absolutely prohibited in case one party to the dispute accepted the decision of the League. War was sanctioned, therefore, only if the League organs were unable to reach a decision or if neither party agreed to the

League proposal. Even in these two cases, hostilities could not begin for at least half a year after the dispute reached the League. Practically, if obeyed, these restrictions would obviate the possibility of war: even if the League could not reach a decision, and even if the solution proposed by the League were acceptable to neither party, it would be very difficult indeed to keep a nation at fighting pitch for six months.

A nation which resorted to war in defiance of the restrictions imposed by the Covenant "shall *ipso facto* be deemed to have committed an act of war against all other Members of the League." An economic boycott was immediately to be proclaimed against the offending nation, and the Council was to decide on, and carry out, military measures sufficient to compel the acquiescence of the offending state. In short, the combined resources of the League members were to be mobilized against any state resorting to war in violation of the Covenant.

Security was amply provided for. Provision was also made, though less explicitly, for altering the *status quo,* by Article 19: "The Assembly may from time to time advise the reconsideration by members of the League of treaties which have become inapplicable and the consideration of international conditions whose continuance might endanger the peace of the world." On the whole, the conference showed far greater concern for security than for means of altering established conditions. This was natural, since the Covenant was drafted by victorious states.

The treaty proper, containing the conditions which Germany must accept, forms a bulky volume. Territorially, Germany was, first of all, stripped of colonies. German Southwest Africa went to the Union of South Africa; East Africa went to England; Togoland and the Cameroons were divided between Britain and France. In the Pacific, German possessions south of the equator were divided between Australia and New Zealand; German possessions north of the equator went to Japan. All these territories were given out as mandates under the League of Nations.

German rights in the Shantung peninsula were acquired by Japan.

In Europe, Germany suffered substantial losses. France got Alsace-Lorraine. In addition, France secured ownership of the Saar coal-fields, while the Saar district was separated from Germany and placed under the control of the League. After fifteen years, the inhabitants were to decide whether the Saar should remain under the League, return to Germany, or go to France. Belgium secured a few small districts subject to a plebiscite which, held under grossly unfair conditions, went in favor of Belgium. North Schleswig was, by vote of the inhabitants, acquired by Denmark. In the east, Poland secured nearly all of Posen and most of West Prussia, including the "corridor," a neck of land which connected Poland with the sea and divided East Prussia from the rest of Germany. Danzig was made a free city, but economically it was subjected to Poland. In the conditions presented to Germany, Upper Silesia was also given to Poland, but the conference finally decided, under pressure from Lloyd George, to hold a plebiscite in the region. Most of East Prussia remained German, but the city and district of Memel were lost and were eventually presented to Lithuania. Altogether, Germany lost well over 10 per cent of her land and her inhabitants in Europe. This does not tell the whole story. With Lorraine, Germany lost three quarters of her iron ore; in the Saar and the parts of Silesia which later went to Poland was a quarter of Germany's coal. A considerable part of the industrial machinery of Germany was in these lost areas. The territorial clauses struck at the very heart of German industrial hegemony.

The economic clauses further weakened Germany. Article 231, the first of the reparations clauses, has become the most famous sentence in the treaty:

"The Allied and Associated Governments affirm and Germany accepts the responsibility of Germany and her allies for causing all the loss and damage to which the Allied and Associated Governments and their nationals have been subjected as a consequence of the war imposed upon them by the aggression of Germany and her allies."

The amount Germany must pay was left to be decided by a reparations commission of the Allies, who were to report by May 1, 1921. Germany, in other words, was asked to sign a blank check. The size to which the check might mount was indicated by the demand that Germany pay the equivalent of five billions of dollars before May 1, 1921. A considerable part of the five billions was to be paid "in kind." All of the larger German merchant ships, and half of the smaller, were to go to the Allies. All property which Germans had abroad was to be placed at the disposition of the Allies. This property consisted for the most part of docks, banks, and industrial enterprises of one sort and another. Finally, Germany promised to build ships for, and export coal to, the Allied countries: the figures are unimportant; they were speedily revised. "Sanctions" were provided for, in case Germany voluntarily defaulted. The permissible measures "may include economic and financial prohibitions and reprisals and, in general, such other measures as the respective governments may determine to be necessary in the circumstances."

Germany was disarmed with minute completeness. Conscription was prohibited; the general staff must be abolished; many forts, including Helgoland, were to be dismantled. The whole left bank of the Rhine, and the right bank to a depth of over thirty miles, were permanently demilitarized. The army was limited to 100,000 men enlisted for long periods of service; the navy was limited to a few boats manned by not more than 15,000 men. The number and size of guns were specified. Germany was to possess no submarines or military airplanes. Here again a sentence was inserted which was later to prove troublesome. Germany was required to limit her forces "in order to render possible the initiation of a general limitation of the armaments of all nations." The Germans have been reminding the Allies of that sentence ever since.

As a guarantee that the treaty requirements would be fulfilled, Germany was forced to agree to the occupation of the left bank of the Rhine by Allied troops. Germany was to pay the cost of the occupation. If the treaty was carried out, the Allied armies would be withdrawn in three stages, at the end of five, ten, and fifteen years. If, after withdrawal, Germany defaulted, the occupation might be renewed.

One section of the treaty never became effective, but deserves mention: that on penalties. William II was to be tried "for a supreme offense against international morality and the sanctity of treaties." He was to be tried by Allied judges, "thereby assuring him the guarantees essential to the right of defense." This conception of what constituted a fair trial illuminates the post-war intellectual atmosphere. Nearly all the well-known military and political leaders of Germany were also to be brought to trial. It is unnecessary to follow the stages by which these demands fell into oblivion. The only effect of this section was to rehabilitate discredited leaders in the eyes of the German people, who looked on the proposed trials as an insult to Germany.

Such in brief were the conditions of peace. The way in which agreement was secured on the more important provisions of the treaty remains to be described.

President Wilson insisted that the League of Nations be the first work of the conference. He knew there was little enthusiasm for the project and much opposition to it; unless brought into existence before the powers got what they wanted, the League might be shelved completely. His suspicions were undoubtedly well founded. None of the other leading delegates and only a few of the subordinate delegates, like Lord Robert Cecil and General Smuts, had much interest in the League. It is almost certain that the League would not have been created had it not been for Wilson's persistence. The President had another motive for forcing early action. The League would provide security by guaranteeing its members against aggression. The League in existence, he hoped French demands for security at the expense of Germany could be denied on the ground that security had already been obtained. This hope proved false. The Covenant was quickly drafted; its provisions gave every guarantee against aggression which words could give; it was readily adopted amid great applause at a plenary session. The very ease of the victory was disconcerting. Before the conference ended, it became apparent that most of the delegates regarded the League as the statement of a pious ideal, with about as much validity as the formula with which earlier peace treaties had begun: "There shall be perpetual peace."

There is an instructive contrast between the ready acceptance of the great clauses of the Covenant which imposed obligations and restrictions on the powers and the fight over the mandate question. From the outset, Wilson had the idea that colonies were in future to be, so to speak, wealth held in trust for society. General Smuts of South Africa, a stanch advocate of the League, had a similar idea: he suggested that districts taken over from the Dual Monarchy and Turkey be owned by the League and administered as mandates by the various powers. Wilson accepted Smuts's suggestion and applied it to the German colonies. The British Dominion representatives, including Smuts, vigorously resented this extension. New Zealand, Australia, and South Africa, themselves but recently emancipated from imperial control, insisted on colonies themselves. A colony held in fee simple, some one remarked, was becoming necessary for the self-respect of every state. Wilson was forced to compromise. He obtained recognition of the principle that the German colonies were to be mandates, but the terms of these mandates were so liberal as to be almost indistinguishable from absolute ownership. If the British Dominions, supported by Lloyd George, were thus resentful of any effort to limit their sovereignty over the notoriously unprofitable German colonies, what chance was there that the powers would abide by the severe restrictions on freedom of action imposed by the Covenant?

Wilson secured a shadowy victory on the mandate question. He was defeated on the question of disarmament. He and Lloyd George, both representatives of countries with small armies, labored indefatigably to secure the limitation of land armaments. The French enthusiastically welcomed the disarmament of Germany, but offered a hundred good reasons for preserving complete freedom for their own forces. They were too courteous to do more than hint at the fact that neither England nor America showed a desire, even a willingness, to discuss the limitation of naval power. In the end, the whole question of disarmament was left for the League to deal with at some future time.

The French attitude on disarmament foreshadowed Clemenceau's security demands. He asked what all France asked: acquisition of the Saar Basin and separation of the left bank of the Rhine from Germany. Against both these demands Lloyd George and Wilson took a firm stand. Lloyd George said flatly that he had no desire to create a new Alsace-Lorraine problem. The sessions of the Four grew stormy; on one occasion Clemenceau called Wilson a pro-German and left the room. The peace conference seemed on the verge of collapse, but Clemenceau was not prepared to lose his allies. Finding he could not win, he compromised. The Rhineland remained German; the Saar was placed under the League, with the probability that it would later revert to Germany. France got the Saar coalfields. French security was protected by the disarmament of Germany, by the demilitarization of the left bank and part of the right bank of the Rhine, by temporary Allied occupation of the Rhineland, and, above all, by an alliance with the United States and England. This alliance, which was signed at the same time as the peace treaty, provided that Britain and America must come to the assistance of France in case of a German attack. The compromise was attacked at the time and has been attacked since, but it is doubtful whether Clemenceau could either have surrendered more or secured more. He certainly went far beyond the wishes of his countrymen, who showed their feelings by refusing to elect him President of the Republic a few months later.

The united opposition of Wilson and Lloyd George prevented Clemenceau from securing the territorial changes in the Rhine region which French opinion demanded. In the eastern territorial settlement, Anglo-American solidarity broke down. Except where hampered by the secret Treaty of London with Italy, Lloyd George stood for a strict application of the principle of self-determination: "this human criterion should have precedence over considerations of strategy, or economics, or communications, which can usually be adjusted by other means." To create new "unredeemed" territories in place of the old, he argued, would be to inject a disastrous poison into the European system. The defeated powers were weak now, but they would regain their strength. Germany in particular could not be held in permanent subjection. It would be unjust to the newly created states themselves if they were given territory which would ensure the hatred of Germany. "Injustice, arrogance, displayed in the hour of triumph, will never be forgotten or forgiven." Therefore the terms must be such that the enemy peoples would, on sober reflection, recognize their justice. Otherwise, the treaty would make new wars inevitable.

Clemenceau attacked Lloyd George's position vehemently. The British, he said, wished to be charitable at the expense of other people. Of course Germany would hate the treaty, hate not least the clauses Britian insisted upon: reparations, and loss of her fleet, her colonies, her merchant marine, and her trade connections. The late enemies were bound to resent the presence of new states carved out of their domain. The way to ensure the safety of the new states was to make them strong, strong economically, strategically, and in population.

Because British interests would be served by a stable distribution of territory on the Continent, Lloyd George preached moderation; because the French wished to see France and her allies permanently triumphant over an impotent Germany, Clemenceau would disregard self-determination to get more land for the new states. Wilson stood for self-determination as the basis of a stable peace;

but instinctive sympathy for the new states, and instinctive desire to punish the enemy, led him to abandon that principle again and again. Always there was a reason: the desire to get a good economic or military frontier, the presence of a considerable body of the nationals of the new states in the disputed territory. But always these arguments were considered when they worked against the claims of the enemy. Against the opposition of Lloyd George, Wilson successfully supported the creation of the Polish corridor, because Poland needed an outlet to the sea, and because the Slavs were said to constitute a majority in the corridor. That the corridor split Germany into two parts, and that every German school-boy, studying the map, would rebel against that division made no difference. Against the opposition of Lloyd George, he gave Upper Silesia to Poland. He was unimpressed by the fact that Germany needed this rich industrial area which German brains had created and in which the Poles were largely farmers or laborers, employees of German industrial plants. Only reluctantly did Wilson consent, in the final revision of the treaty, to substitute a plebiscite for outright cession to Poland.

It was the same story when the fate of the Dual Monarchy was discussed. Without argument Wilson agreed to give the South Tyrol, with its hundreds of thousands of German-Austrians, to Italy. Millions of German-Austrians went to Czechoslovakia. Millions of Magyars were handed over to Czechoslovakia, Rumania, and Jugoslavia. In every one of these cases good reasons were advanced for the decision which was made, but the same arguments, when they favored Germany, Austria, or Hungary, were disregarded. The most flagrant violation of the principle of self-determination was the refusal to permit union between Austria and Germany unless approved by unanimous vote of the League's Council. Since France had a permanent seat on the Council, her vote could block the union. Here again the reasoning was strong. German strength would be greatly increased by the acquisition of Austria, and the enlarged

German state would surround a large part of Czechoslovakia.

Aside from the left bank of the Rhine, Wilson took no
stand on territorial questions which even Clemenceau could
brand "pro-German." The two dramatic battles which
marked the closing days of the conference were between
members of the Allies; the enemy had already been eliminated. Her late partner in the Triple Alliance dead, Italy
demanded not merely the gains promised by the Treaty of
London, but complete supremacy in the Adriatic. It is probable that Clemenceau and Lloyd George would secretly have
rejoiced had Wilson attacked the secret treaty; they were
willing, but not eager, to redeem the promises Italy had
wrung from the Allies in 1915. Strangely enough, Wilson
did not attack the treaty. He agreed to give Italy the Brenner Pass for her northern frontier, and thus deprived the
Tyrolean Germans of self-determination. He was more
reluctant to give Italy large numbers of Dalmatian Slavs,
but he acquiesced in that also. It was only when Italy went
beyond the London line and demanded Fiume that he rebelled. The arguments used by Orlando to justify each
successive demand in the Italian program were remarkably,
almost naïvely, inconsistent. Now the necessity of securing
a good strategic frontier was used to combat self-determination; now self-determination for Italians combated the
strategic interests of other states. Strategy, self-determination, history, economics—each in turn was used to slay one
of the others, always to the advantage of Italy. In the case
of Fiume, the city itself was Italian; the country about the
city was Slav; the city had the only good harbor which
could be given to Jugoslavia. When Orlando persisted in
demanding Fiume despite the opposition of the other members of the Four, Wilson publicly appealed to the "plain
people" of Italy. Infuriated, Orlando left Paris and returned to Italy, where the "plain people" received him as
a hero and castigated Wilson as an agent of the ex-Kaiser.
Orlando came back before the treaty with Germany was

signed, but the Fiume question was never settled by the conference. Eventually, Italy took the city.

While Orlando was sulking in Italy, it seemed that Japan might also leave the conference. The secret treaties gave German rights in Shantung to Japan, and Japan insisted on carrying out the treaties. China was a member of the Grand Alliance, and she insisted that German concessions in China should revert to the Chinese. American opinion, partly out of sentimental sympathy for the under-dog, partly out of dislike for Japan, supported the Chinese. Similar feelings prevailed in milder form in other countries. The Japanese not unnaturally resented the criticism of other nations, especially the insulting attitude of nationalistic newspapers and politicians in the United States. The question became one of prestige. The Japanese said they would give the members of the conference a promise to return German political rights in Shantung to China at a later date, but those rights must first be given to Japan by the peace treaty. Otherwise Japan would not sign the treaty. The Chinese said they could not sign if the rights were given to Japan. In this dilemma the Three gave way to Japan. The whole question was in itself of no great importance, but the anti-treaty press in the United States, by misrepresenting the facts, and by playing on American sentimentality, made the "rape of Shantung" a moral issue.

Discontent with the territorial settlement has since 1919 smoldered beneath the surface of European politics, flaring up only occasionally. Undoubtedly this discontent will assume greater importance as time goes on. Up to the present the reparations clauses of the treaty have proved more troublesome. It is important, therefore, to understand what was done at Paris, and why these things were done.

The reparations problem was a complex of two questions: How much *ought* Germany to pay? How much *could* Germany pay? There was another question, however, which ensured erroneous answers to the others, and which helps to explain much of reparations history: What is

$1,000,000,000? To think or speak intelligently about any sum of money, we must first relate that sum to our experience or our economic training. Only a few people can think in terms of billions. Most of us are as helpless in the face of such figures as we are when astronomers talk about the distance from the earth to the sun. Our imagination, without any mental yardstick, cannot visualize what the words symbolize. After the war, men thought they had a yardstick: the national debt of their own country. Debts were paid by taxpayers; debts during the war had mounted by billions; the taxpayers must pay these billions—unless the Germans paid them. Well, men said, let the Germans pay. That would be a pleasant and just solution. The debts were incurred in combating German aggression; if the Germans did not pay, the taxpayer would have to pay. The taxpayer thought he had sacrificed enough to save civilization. Against this delightfully simple solution the economists argued in vain. Balance of trade, balance of payments, German capacity to pay—all these abstruse and tedious subjects were simply ignored, not only by the "plain people" but by statesmen, even by great men of affairs. During the months following the armistice an already insoluble financial problem became further complicated by an artificial and false simplification.

How much *should* Germany pay? Theoretically, the question was merely one of legal interpretation and of bookkeeping. By the pre-armistice agreement Germany promised to pay for all damage to Allied civilians. Damage to civilians was a fairly precise term, not difficult to define. The problem of finding the total damage was a complex but not insuperable problem in bookkeeping. In practice, the situation was less simple. The French had inserted a "joker" in the armistice terms which seemed to permit the Allies to make any financial demands they wished. Did this invalidate the pre-armistice agreement? The British and French were inclined to argue that it did. Both Lloyd George and Clemenceau had, under the pressure of public opinion, promised to collect the whole cost of the war. The

American delegation tenaciously opposed the "war costs" cry as illegal and fantastic. After Germany had fought four years herself, she could not pay all that the other nations had spent on the war. After many bitter arguments the American delegation won. What Germany ought to pay was to be determined on the basis of the pre-armistice agreement.

It was, however, possible to "interpret" the agreement. This the ingenious General Smuts proceeded to do. Pensions and allowances made to the dependents of soldiers who fought in the war might be fairly included, he contended, because the soldiers became civilians now that the war was over. Again the Americans objected: pensions to troops could not logically be called damages to civilians. President Wilson, however, brushed logic aside and agreed to Smuts's proposal. It is difficult to believe that Wilson knew what he was doing. To be sure, the reparations bill with pensions included would be much less than it would have been had total war costs been demanded. M. Tardieu estimated the difference at something less than $200,000,000,000. Undoubtedly that is a great deal of money, but the money was non-existent. No person who was willing to think believed Germany could pay such sums. The economists realized that Smuts's "interpretation" accomplished all that the demand for total war costs would have accomplished. Reparations for pensions could be expanded to, and beyond, the limit imposed by common sense, what Germany *could* pay. The discussion must now shift, the economists said, from what Germany should pay to what Germany could pay.

How much could Germany pay? The more conservative economists made estimates of ten to fifteen billions of dollars. Lloyd George and Clemenceau turned away in disgust: this was a mere bagatelle. Obliging financiers, who should have known better, were willing to multiply the lower figures by ten. Even that was not enough. Clemenceau cut short the debate. It would make no difference how many billions were asked. French opinion would say he should have secured twice as much, and call him a traitor. The only thing to do was not to name any figure; then no one could protest, except the Germans. Lloyd George, remembering his election promises, enthusiastically approved Clemenceau's suggestion. The economists protested that any figure was better than indefiniteness, because the Germans would have no incentive to pay anything until they knew what the total sum would be. Lloyd George and Clemenceau refused to hear. To them, politics was an exact science, while economics was elaborate academic guesswork. The voice of politics must be heeded. Germany was forced to sign a blank check.

By May 7, 1919, the treaty was ready. At Versailles, in 1871, victorious Germany in the person of Bismarck gave terms to, and concluded a preliminary peace with, defeated France. The French had not forgotten. Now, in 1919, victorious France, in the person of Clemenceau, gave terms to defeated Germany:

"You have before you the accredited plenipotentiaries of all the small and great Powers united to fight together in the war that has been so cruelly imposed upon them. The time has come when we must settle our accounts. You have asked for peace. We are ready to give you peace.

"We shall present to you now a book which contains our conditions. You will be given every facility to examine those conditions, and the time necessary for it. Everything will be done with the courtesy that is the privilege of civilized nations.

"To give you my thought completely, you will find us ready to give you any explanation you want, but we must say at the same time that this Second Treaty of Versailles has cost us too much, not to take on our side all the necessary precautions and guarantees that that peace shall be a lasting one."

The German Foreign Secretary, Count Brockdorff-Rantzau, replied. He did not rise when he spoke. Like most Germans he was suffering from undernourishment, and his remaining strength was drained by a sense of the tragic significance of this scene for Germany. He did not rise because he could not. Unfortunately, he was too proud to explain. The Allies were angry and insulted because he spoke seated. Further, what he said outraged the Allies. He was not penitent, he was not humble. Instead, he defiantly denied the unique guilt of Germany.

"We have no illusion as to the extent of our defeat and the measure of our impotence. We know that the force of German arms is broken, and we are aware of the fury of the hatred which greets us. We are asked to assume the sole guilt of the war. Such a confession from my lips would be a lie. We have no intention of absolving Germany from all responsibility for the war; . . . but we expressly contend that Germany, whose people was convinced that it was fighting a defensive war, should not be saddled with the whole responsibility.

"Public opinion among our foes dilates on the crimes committed by Germany during the conflict. . . . Crimes in times of war may be unpardonable, but they are committed in the heat of the contest. The hundreds of thousands of non-combatants who have died of the blockade since the 11th November were killed in cold blood after the victory had been won. Think of that when you speak of crime and punishment. Only an impartial inquiry, a neutral commission before which all the protagonists of the tragedy can appear and for which all the archives are open, can determine the degree of responsibility of all the actors. For this we have already asked, and we repeat our demand.

"In this conference, where we stand alone, we are not without defense. You yourselves have given us an ally—the rights guaranteed in the contract on the principles of peace. The principles of President Wilson are binding on you, as well as on us."

When the German delegate had finished speaking, the meeting ended. The Germans began a study of the terms presented to them. On May 29, they submitted their reply. They challenged the conditions of peace from two points of view. The terms, they contended, were in violation of the "agreed foundation" fixed by the pre-armistice agreement. Further, the terms could not be carried out. With the best will in the world, Germany could not carry the burden imposed on her. "A whole people is thus asked to sign its own death-warrant."

To prove that the treaty represented a breach of contract the German reply quoted from the speeches of President Wilson in which he had said that the war was not against the German people but only against the Imperial government; in which he had professed his intention to restore Germany to the family of nations on equal terms and to confer on Germany equal privileges and responsibilities with other peoples in the League of Nations; in which he had promised a peace of reconciliation and justice; in which he had declared that "every territorial settlement involved in this war must be made in the interest and for the benefit of the populations concerned." Point by point the proposed terms were attacked, alike as unjust, unworkable, and inimicable to the lasting peace which all professed to desire. Germany should be admitted at once to the League of Nations. Germany accepted disarmament, if the other nations also disarmed. Germany should have colonies, as other nations had colonies, but Germany was willing to give up Kiauchow and take back her other colonies as mandates under the League. Germany was willing to give up Alsace-Lorraine, but she desired a plebiscite. The eastern territorial settlement was challenged almost in its entirety. The cession of Posen was agreed to, but Polish gains in East and West Prussia, especially the corridor and Upper Silesia, were attacked, as was the demand for Memel. On the other hand, self-determination was asked for the Germans of Austria and Bohemia.

The economic demands were denounced as intolerable. Indefinite, but obviously colossal, sums were demanded by the Allies, sums including categories not justified by the pre-armistice agreement. Further, the economic life of Germany was crippled, and the capital resources necessary for the payment of reparations were seized, so that Germany would be unable to make payments. Germany was prepared to promise a total sum of twenty-five billions of dollars, five billions to be paid by 1926. Germany would also make large coal deliveries to France and Belgium. Germany could make these payments, however, only if her capital resources were not impaired to the point where revived production was impossible. Upper Silesia and the Saar Basin, with their mines and industrial works, must be retained by Germany. Shipping must also be retained: Germany would build new ships to compensate the Allies for the boats they had lost. Colonies must be retained so that Germany could secure raw materials. In short, to pay reparations Germany must be allowed to retain capital necessary for production and must be given complete economic freedom. Finally: "The German Delegation renews its request for a neutral inquiry into the responsibility for the war."

The German arguments did not, of course, make the slightest impression on Clemenceau. President Wilson was also unaffected. The appeal to his own words merely irritated him. He examined the German contentions, but on the basis of proved German guilt—guilt, not of the ruling class, but of the nation. The terms, he contended, were hard, "but the Germans earned that. And I think it is profitable that a nation should learn once and for all what an unjust war means in itself." Starting from the premise of German guilt, he had no difficulty in proving to his own satisfaction that the terms were "just." The confidence of Clemenceau and Wilson was not shared by many American and British experts and, more important, by Lloyd George. Lloyd George was worried, not primarily by the thought of injustice but by the sympathy the German arguments had aroused in British Liberal circles and by fear that the Germans might refuse to sign. What if the terms were rejected? Would Germany go Bolshevist? Would the British people, who were already clamoring for complete demobilization, support an invasion of Germany? Lloyd George pressed for compromise. "On every question—disarmament, occupation, reparations, Danzig, Upper Silesia —he proposed inadmissible concessions," complained Tardieu. Clemenceau pointed out that such generosity sat strangely on the British delegate, who had secured, and held, all the prizes England sought: colonies, cables, ships, and, above all, the extinction of German naval and commercial rivalry. Lloyd George was embarrassed by this shrewd thrust, but he persisted nevertheless. In the end he secured a few minor concessions and one important change: the fate of Upper Silesia was to be decided by a plebiscite. Balked in his desire to secure terms which the Germans would find less onerous, Lloyd George turned to the task of strengthening his position at home. "If the Germans declined to sign and an advance by the Army was necessary," he said, "it might be necessary to stir up public opinion again to a certain extent." Therefore, he had one of his advisers prepare a covering letter for the Allied reply, controverting the German contentions concerning responsibility for the war and concerning alleged discrepancies between the conditions of peace and the pre-armistice agreement. Clemenceau and Wilson readily agreed with the argument that the peace terms were in harmony with the pre-armistice agreement. Wilson was somewhat dubious about the evidence used to fix the responsibility for the war on Germany. "The document had conveyed a slight feeling of inadequacy," he commented. "It would not prove satisfactory to the future historian." Nevertheless, he concurred in the indictment. This catastrophe, the Germans were told on June 16, this catastrophe with its millions of dead, its millions maimed, physically and spiritually, its appalling drain on the world's economic strength, had come "because Germany saw fit to gratify her lust for tyranny by resort to war." There would be no further discussion.

In Weimar, the Assembly and the cabinet had been discussing the treaty ceaselessly for over a month. The first impulse had been to refuse to sign. "It means the annihilation of the German people," declared the President of the national Assembly. "It is incomprehensible that a man who had promised the world a peace of justice, upon which a society of nations would be founded, has been able to assist in framing this project dictated by hate." During the weeks following, cooler men began to weigh gains and losses. To sign, said Erzberger and his colleagues of the Center, meant peace, and the chance for a new hearing later; not to sign meant a military invasion, Bolshevism, the triumph of the separatist movement. Those who opposed signing had no single argument. The demand that Germany "perish with honor" had great emotional appeal, but the more sensible opponents of signature justified themselves by saying that if the Allies took Berlin, they would find the expedition futile and expensive; in a short time they would consent to peace on honorable terms. Erzberger won. The Assembly agreed to sign on two conditions: Germany would not acknowledge sole responsibility for the war, and Germany would not allow accused German leaders—"the war criminals"—to be tried in foreign courts.

When the German conditions reached Paris, the Allies were in a mood to be more rather than less exacting. Clemenceau had just learned that the Germans had destroyed the French battle-flags captured in 1870, flags which were to be surrendered under the conditions of peace. More important, the German officers who had been left on board the interned ships at Scapa Flow opened the sea-cocks of the vessels on June 21. Tirpitz's great "risk" navy had been powerless to break British sea power, but Germans preferred that their fleet find refuge on the bottom of the ocean rather than pass to the enemy. Thus cheated, the Allies were filled with indignation. Clemenceau wished to retaliate by seizing the industrial district of Essen. Wilson and Lloyd George refused his demand, but they also refused the German demand for treaty changes. Unconditional acceptance by the evening of June 23 was demanded of Germany. Confronted by the Allied ultimatum, the Germans capitulated: "Yielding to overwhelming force, but without on that account abandoning its view in regard to the unheard-of injustice of the conditions of peace, the Government of the German Republic therefore declares that it is ready to accept and sign the conditions of peace imposed by the Allied and Associated Governments."

Clemenceau staged the scene. In 1871 the German Empire had been proclaimed in the Hall of Mirrors at Versailles.

Less than a half-century later, on June 28, 1919, the Hall of Mirrors was again crowded, this time by representatives of the Grand Alliance which had overthrown the German Empire. The Chinese alone were absent; they refused to sign a treaty which gave the Shantung concessions to Japan. When the stage was set, the Germans were admitted. The treaty was signed. It was a grand spectacle, too grand, Colonel House confided to his diary:

"When the Germans had signed and the great Allied Powers had done so, the cannon began to boom. I had a feeling of sympathy for the Germans who sat there quite stoically. It was not unlike what was done in ancient times, when the conqueror dragged the conquered at his chariot wheels. To my mind, it is out of keeping with the new era which we profess an ardent desire to promote. I wish it could have been more simple and that there might have been an element of chivalry, which was wholly lacking. The affair was elaborately staged and made as humiliating to the enemy as it well could be.

"After the signing we went to the terrace to see the fountains, which were playing for the first time since the war began. Aeroplanes were in the air, guns were being fired, and the thousands surrounding Versailles made a brilliant and memorable scene."

4. THE EASTERN SETTLEMENT

The treaty with Germany signed, Wilson and Lloyd George left for home. The main lines of the treaties to be imposed on the other enemy states had already been worked out; the details were left to other members of the Allied delegations. Bulgaria lost least, because the Second Balkan War had left little for any one to take. By the Treaty of Neuilly, signed in November, 1919, Rumania secured the last remnant of the Dobruja, Greece took the last remnant of the Ægean coast, and Serbia took some mountainous land along the western frontier of Bulgaria. Like all the other treaties, the Treaty of Neuilly contained the League Covenant and provisions for reparation and disarmament.

Austria, hungry and helpless, signed the Treaty of St. Germain in September, 1919. The Treaty of the Trianon

with Hungary was not signed until June, 1920. The delay
was necessitated by a series of unparalleled calamities. In
November, 1918, a liberal Socialist government was established in Hungary by Count Karolyi. Karolyi had little
popular support. His rule was hated alike by the great
landed Magyar magnates, who had formerly governed the
country, and by the radical proletariat. Rumors of the
terms which the Paris conference intended to inflict on
Hungary precipitated revolt which culminated in the seizure
of power by the Bolshevists under Bela Kun in March,
1919. A reign of terror was begun against the old ruling
class, and the Allies were defied. The Rumanians decided
to restore order: they were afraid of Bolshevism, and they
had old scores to pay off against the Magyars. A large
force invaded Hungary, occupied Budapest, and inaugu-
rated a reign of terror more fierce than that of the Bolshevists. The countryside was systematically plundered.
All moveable objects, from works of art and jewelry to food
and machinery, even including the beds and bedding from
hospitals, were shipped back to Rumania. The Four thun-
dered in vain from Paris; not until November, 1919, did
the Rumanians quit Hungary. Naturally the Magyars did
not forget this episode. The Rumanians gone, the aristocrats seized power and began the third, and most bloody,
terror. It was with this government of Bethlen and Horthy
that peace was made in June, 1920.

What happened to the once proud Dual Monarchy is best
told in figures. Austria before the war was a country of
over 115,000 square miles with a population of nearly thirty
millions of people. Austria after the war became a small
land-locked state, with six and a half millions of people
living within 32,000 square miles. Most of the people lost
had belonged to subject races, but some four millions of
German-Austrians were subjected to foreign rule. Hungary met a similar fate. In area, Hungary was reduced
from 125,000 to 35,000 square miles; her population was
cut from twenty-one millions to eight millions. Over three
millions of Magyars were given to other states. In one re-

spect the Hungarians escaped more easily than Austria:
they at least were left a rich agricultural territory. The
mountains and valleys of the new Austria, for all their
beauty, could not support a capital containing almost two
millions of people. Vienna had flourished as the administrative and cultural center of a great empire, but now the
city contained almost a third of the whole Austrian population. The Austrians, surrounded by hostile, strangling
tariff barriers, saw only slow death in store for their country. To avert catastrophe they sought inclusion in the larger
political and economic system of Germany. The Treaty of
St. Germain barred this escape. Austria was forced to
promise "to abstain from any act which might directly or
indirectly, or by any means whatever, compromise her independence"—unless the League Council gave its unanimous consent. The Austrians lapsed back into despair. The
Magyars did not despair. They were filled with the fury
of a race which, having itself proudly oppressed others
for centuries, suddenly finds itself oppressed. Germany had
been a great power for only half a century; Hungary had
been a great power for ten centuries. The Magyars were
resolved that the Trianon verdict should not long stand.
On great placards, and in their own minds, they inscribed
the words which still are seen: "No! No! Never!"

The oppressed were now redeemed and could oppress
others. M. Pashitch saw his dream of playing the part of
Cavour realized. Serbia had become the Piedmont of the
Jugoslavs. There was one difference: Cavour had merged
Piedmont in the Kingdom of Italy; Pashitch merged all
the Jugoslavs—Montenegro, Bosnia and Herzegovina,
Croatia, and the other South Slav districts of the Dual
Monarchy—into the Kingdom of Serbia. Jugoslavia was
an enlarged Serbia, ruled by Serbs. The South Slavs found
that they had not won freedom; they had merely changed
masters. They had, however, won national unity. In
Rumania, on the other hand, the minorities were of different stock. After the war, Rumania was in the fortunate
position of being able to take toll from friend and foe alike:

Bessarabia from Russia; Transylvania and other smaller territories from Hungary; the Dobruja, from Bulgaria. The enlarged Rumania, twice as large as before the war, contained minorities who together constituted a majority of the population. There were a million and three-quarters Magyars, over a million Germans, a million Jews, almost a million Ukrainians, and other smaller groups in a total population of seventeen and a half millions. "Self-determination" worked little better in Poland, where the minorities—Ruthenians, Jews, and Germans—made up almost a third of the total population of twenty-seven millions.

Minorities constituted an even larger proportion of the people of Czechoslovakia, but the situation here was mitigated by three elements. The Croats and Magyars in Jugoslavia, the Germans and Magyars in Rumania, and the Germans in Poland had attained a higher cultural level than their new masters. The Czechs, on the other hand, had a long and rich cultural history behind them. They were the equals of the Germans and the Magyars. Furthermore, Czechoslovakia included the chief industrial centers of the Dual Monarchy, so that the country was well off economically. Finally, the Czechs possessed in Masaryk and Beneš two of the ablest statesmen in Europe. Which of these factors was of most importance is debatable; the combination made Czechoslovakia the only stable, successful country in that litter of states which grew out of the ruins of the three empires.

In the other states self-determination intensified national egoism, ruthless ambition, hatred of neighboring peoples, and persecution of minorities. The Dual Monarchy had at least provided an economic unit of adequate size; the successor states replaced that unity by ruinous tariff walls. The "Balkanization" of Eastern Europe hampered economic development without providing political peace or even self-determination. The oppressed peoples were fewer in numbers, but they were more outrageously oppressed than ever. It is doubtful if a substantially different result could have been attained. Information regarding the complex problems of Eastern Europe was both fragmentary and contradictory; it was inevitable that war passions should lead the conference to look sympathetically on evidence which favored the new states and hurt the enemy. Furthermore, the power of the conference was limited. The inflamed nationalism of the newly emancipated peoples brooked no restraint; they were already occupying the lands they claimed; the Allies were unwilling to use armed force against the states they had just liberated. An effort was made to mitigate the injustice of the new boundaries by treaties providing for just treatment of minorities. There was scant chance that the emancipated peoples would forego the opportunity to oppress their former oppressors, but the treaties did give a legitimate sanction for mobilizing European opinion against flagrant oppression.

The Treaty of Sèvres with Turkey was not signed until August, 1920, and it never went into effect. The settlement was delayed because the Allies could not agree among themselves; the settlement was upset by aroused Turkish nationalism.

From the moment Turkey entered the war the Allies planned territorial conquests and feared quarrels over the spoils. To avert discord, secret agreements were made. Nevertheless, when the war ended, harmony had not been achieved. The entrance of Italy and Greece into the war and the withdrawal of Russia complicated the task of map-drawing. The British had procured the aid of the Arabs against the Turks by promising them independence; Arab claims conflicted with those of France. President Wilson threw the whole problem into confusion by saying he thought the peoples of the Near East should decide their own fate and by sending out a commission to ask the peoples what they wanted.

While the other Allies were circling around the map of Turkey hesitantly, Italy acted. The powers had proved strangely unresponsive to the Adriatic claims which Italy had advanced. Italy decided not to be forestalled in Turkey.

A pretext was invented for landing troops at Adalia. Greece now came forward. Venizelos persuasively urged that the old Greek empire in Asia Minor should be revived. The argument was attractive to men trained in the classical tradition. Greece was allowed to send troops to Smyrna. Twenty thousand landed in May, 1919, and avenged old wrongs by butchering the Turks they encountered. The massacre passed almost unnoticed in Europe, but it created a furor in the Near East. Turks were being killed by the despised Greeks. The Turks began to lose the apathy of defeat. The nationalist revival found a leader in Mustapha Kemal, the military commander in Asia Minor. While the Allies debated terms to be offered a supposedly helpless enemy, revolt spread through Anatolia and Syria.

The Treaty of Sèvres confined Turkish power to central Anatolia. Because no one knew what else to do with Constantinople, the city was returned to Turkey, but the Straits were to be opened and under international control. Greece was given all the rest of European Turkey, and was to control the region about Smyrna. As a "mandate," Syria was given to France; Palestine and Mesopotamia, now called Iraq, to England. The Arabs of the Hedjaz received independence. Conflicting claims to spheres of influence under the secret treaties had not yet been adjusted; France, England, and Italy were to settle these questions later. The capitulations and other old restrictions on Turkish sovereignty were restored; the powers would supervise the Turkish military and financial administration. At first the Turks refused to sign the treaty. Allied forces occupied Constantinople; Greek armies advanced through Asia Minor. The Turks signed, signed what would, if carried out, be a death-warrant for Turkey. Turkey would be a small Anatolian state ruled from Constantinople under the watchful eyes of the powers.

In theory, the whole force of the Allies guaranteed the execution of the treaty; practically, the Greek army was the only fighting force behind the treaty. In Angora,

Mustapha Kemal was in revolt against Constantinople and the treaty. Within three years he was to annihilate the Greek forces and dictate a new treaty.

Versailles, St. Germain, Trianon, Neuilly, and Sèvres —these five treaties form the Peace of Paris. Together, they represent an effort to pin down a map which had been badly blown about since 1914. What are the chief characteristics and tendencies of the new situation? No one could have answered that question in 1919; no one can answer it to-day. Of the political settlement two contradictory descriptions were given.

Self-determination was the starting point of the first. From this starting point, optimists and pessimists drew different conclusions. The age of the dinosaurs is over, said the optimists. The years from 1871 to 1914 saw the world dominated by imperialistic powers, too powerful to be controlled, afraid only of each other. The smaller states trembled, fearing that they would be crushed in the battle of giants. Between 1914 and 1918, three of the seven greatest powers were completely broken in strength; the other four were seriously weakened by the struggle. Now the states of small or medium stature would lose their fear. New states had appeared in Eastern Europe, natural allies of the lesser states of Europe and America. Individually too weak to hope for a successful imperialistic career, collectively strong enough to restrain the giants, the lesser states would guide the world, through the League of Nations, into paths of coöperation and peace. So thought the optimists. The pessimists thought self-determination could lead only to anarchy. "The more I think about the President's declaration as to the right of 'self-determination,' the more convinced I am of the danger of putting such ideas into the minds of certain races," wrote the American Secretary of State, Lansing. "The phrase is simply loaded with dynamite . . . What a calamity that the phrase was ever uttered! What misery it will cause!" According to this view, it was folly to think either that self-determination would cure the evils of national egoism or that the lesser states would be more pacific than the great powers. Self-determination meant that the history of the world would be a gigantic repetition of Balkan history.

Other students shrugged self-determination aside as inconsequential and argued that the war had really divided the globe into four great spheres of influence. Japan was supreme in the Far East; the United States, with its Monroe Doctrine, in the Americas; France, in Continental Europe and the Mediterranean. The Indian Ocean was the domain of the British Empire. In East Africa, from the Cape to Cairo, British possessions formed an unbroken line of red. Spheres of influence carried the line across Arabia, Mesopotamia, Persia, and Afghanistan to India. From India the line descended to the solid base of Australia. Unfortunately, the British Empire was weakened by the fact that the heart lay in the British Isles, close to the domain of France. Granted that the world really was divided into four spheres of influence, hopeful or despondent conclusions could be drawn. It might be that the world had now achieved stability. These four giants might adopt a "live and let live" policy; or the two Anglo-Saxon empires, more enlightened than the lesser breeds without the law, might enforce a peace based, as an Englishman said, on the open Bible. On the other hand, the World War might prove to have been only the first world war. Possibly a more spectacular struggle between the giants lay ahead. The struggle might end in common ruin, or, men said, looking apprehensively toward the giant of the western world, one power might triumph.

More cautious critics refused to rise to a judgment of the trend of history. They merely pointed out that this was not the peace men had longed for. The Germans had not been brought back into the family of nations: they had been branded as moral criminals and placed in subjection by a dictated treaty. The relations between the states of Eastern and Southern Europe were dangerously unstable, and few thinking men expected that the settlement with Turkey would last. The Russian problem had been given up in despair. The economic difficulties bequeathed by the war had not simply been ignored; they were intensified by the reparations clauses of the treaty. Against these shortcomings, some achievements might be set. French *revanche* was past; but would peace now be troubled by German craving for revenge? Many peoples had won freedom; but would the new states be able to live on tolerable terms with each other and with their former oppressors? Above all, there was the League of Nations. To that men pinned their hopes. It might be that when passions subsided, when the nations counted the cost of war, the League Covenant might become more than a scrap of paper.

CHAPTER VIII

THE HEGEMONY OF FRANCE

CHAPTER VIII

THE HEGEMONY OF FRANCE

I. INTRODUCTION

The task of writing the diplomatic history of the years from 1871 to 1919 is simplified by the fact that the outcome of the events described is known in advance. In 1871 a new *status quo* was established. Efforts to revise the existing situation began immediately. Year after year the struggle continued between the forces making for change and the forces making for stability. For a generation and a half the European powers adjusted without recourse to armed conflict the issues which divided them. In 1914 there was a crisis in which neither side was willing either to compromise or to give way. War followed, and after war a new *status quo* was established. A chapter in European diplomatic history had been completed; it was possible to write a description of the events which had led to the conclusion reached in 1919. A new chapter then began. We are to-day watching the events in the new story unfold themselves. As yet the outcome is uncertain. For that reason it is impossible to select with any assurance from the myriad happenings of each passing year those events which the historian of the future will choose to describe the evolution of European politics during our era. What seems important to-day may next year be forgotten, because the perspective will then have changed. The point of view from which men saw the post-war years in 1928 already seems distorted. In 1928 men thought they had, with long travail, climbed from the valley of despair to the mountain slopes whence the dawning of a new and happier age could be seen. In 1932 we are again in the valley; the visions of 1928 seem only a deceptive mirage. Black night seems once more closing over

Europe. Possibly men will soon be lifted to a more pleasing vantage point. Then the gloom which must pervade a story told in 1932 will seem as fantastic as the buoyant optimism of 1928 seems to-day.

The fact that any conclusions reached to-day may be invalidated to-morrow is no reason for dismissing the problem of understanding the post-war years with a despairing *non possumus*. If we are to influence the course of events, we must first try to comprehend the elements with which we must deal. We can at least analyze the situation, if we cannot with any certainty narrate the events which will lead to an unpredictable conclusion. Analysis, more than narration, now becomes our task.

Before the war, two opposing forces were at work in the world: science was welding the world into an economic unit; nationalism was dividing the world into hostile fragments. The war disrupted the economic structure; the peace treaties added new disturbing elements. Economic reconstruction was possible only through international coöperation. The war had, however, intensified nationalism throughout the world. Wilson had hoped to placate the spirit of nationalism by granting the right of self-determination. Freedom attained, he believed, the nations of the world would then unite to ensure the preservation of peace. Events belied his hopes. Self-determination was, of course, applied only to a limited extent at Paris. No attempt was made to liberate peoples held in subjection by the victors. On the Continent of Europe, nationals of the defeated powers were in many cases handed over to the victors in defiance of Wilson's precepts. Even the most complete application of the principle of self-determination would not, however, have ensured harmonious peace. Post-war nationalism was quick to hate and fear, but slow to forget and trust. Devotion to nationalism proved no bar to oppression, whether of minorities at home or subject races overseas. Nationalism would tolerate no restriction on national freedom of action. Nationalism blinded men to all except immediate national self-interest.

Nationalism, which at its birth seemed a glorious liberating force, threatened after the war to drag the world to common ruin. In politics and economics alike nationalism barred the road to the coöperation which was essential if the world was to have peace. Peace men ardently wished. The disastrous effects of war were too obvious to be ignored. Nevertheless, almost a decade and a half after the armistice, millions are starving in the midst of plenty, an impoverished world supports a burden of armaments greater than that which seemed intolerable in 1914, and the imminence of war is freely prophesied. To a more detailed analysis of the circumstances which have brought the world to this plight we must now turn our attention.

2. ECONOMIC DISLOCATION

The World War was terribly wasting, physically and spiritually; serious difficulty in effecting economic readjustment was inevitable. Men living after 1918 realized that the war had been costly, but the costs they counted were not those which possessed greatest importance. The men who had been killed or maimed, or who had died of disease, were lost to productive effort, but they were replaceable. The falling birth-rate of the war years was largely cancelled by the rise after 1918. The steel, the foodstuffs, and the other supplies devoured by war were produced during the war. They were, to be sure, purchased with the proceeds of loans, because governments find the task of compelling men to give money more difficult than the task of compelling men to give their lives for their country. So long as government borrowings were domestic, war loans constituted no insuperable problem; tax burdens could be so adjusted after the war that those who held the bonds must also pay the taxes with which the interest and principal of the public debt were paid. Foreign borrowings for war supplies raised graver problems which will be analyzed later. Concentration on the production of war supplies also left a legacy in depreciated plants. Factories, railroads, homes were wearing out and were not being replaced. Economists have estimated that the depreciation left Europe in 1918 with fixed capital about equivalent to that possessed in 1912. After 1918 repairs and replacements were quickly made; within a few years productive capacity was as great as if no war had taken place.

Loss of life and of the products of human effort was not the really dangerous legacy of the war. One may regret that human life and effort were not consumed for other ends, but the loss does not explain the post-war instability. The really dangerous economic results of the war may be summed up in one word: *dislocation*. There had been a serious dislocation of industry. War expanded productive capacity in what are known as the heavy industries—steel, ship-building, and textiles. When war and reconstruction ceased, these industries were left with a plant capacity far in excess of the world's needs. The overexpansion was concealed temporarily in some places by the appearance of new uses—steel for automobiles, for instance. In time the facts became apparent, and the resulting plethora of productive capacity in the "heavies" acted as a depressing influence on other industries. Trade connections had also suffered dislocation. While, for instance, British enterprise was concentrated on production for war, the British could not supply goods to South America and to the East. The shortage was overcome, partly by the growth of native industry, partly by expanded production in the United States and Japan. The war over, competition for these markets became acute. By the terms of the peace treaty, the Allies attempted to hamper competition from Germany by confiscating German property abroad, so that the Germans were forced to rebuild their commercial connections. Even with Germany thus hampered, the other industrial powers found foreign markets far too small to absorb the produce of their expanded industries. Indeed the market was, for reasons not immediately economic, smaller than before the war. Russia, paralyzed by revolution, could purchase little. Other revolutionary disturbances, in India, China, and elsewhere, involved many hundreds of millions of people and similarly restricted purchasing power.

The peace treaties added new difficulties. The economic, as well as political, unity of the Dual Monarchy was shattered, with disastrous economic consequences. The Austrian republic suffered most; indeed, the plight of Austria was similar to that which would confront New York if foreign and hostile states stretched along her southern and western borders. Austria suffered most, but the other succession states of the Dual Monarchy, and the new Baltic states, also suffered from the sudden contraction of, or change in, the political unit within which their economic life must exist. Similarly, to change highly industrialized areas like the Saar, Alsace-Lorraine, and Upper Silesia from one customs jurisdiction to another meant economic disturbance, alike to the areas in question, to the countries of which they had formerly been part, and to the nations in whose economic life they were now included. Economic nationalism completed what the war and the peace treaties had begun. Tariff walls and discriminatory customs regulations rose ever higher as new states and old, all over the world, set out to achieve the elusive goal of self-sufficiency, or to injure the economic life of a hated neighbor. Once begun, the tariff race had no apparent ending. Increases in one nation provoked increases in a neighboring state, increases which brought new retaliatory restrictions. Confronted by tariff barriers, international trade languished; competition for the few remaining free markets intensified, while within its fortified limits domestic trade vainly sought sufficient outlets for its products. On no count can the makers of the peace treaties be more justly indicted than for their failure to grapple with the problems raised by the dislocation of trade which resulted from abnormal war conditions, from revolution, from the creation of new states and the transformation of old states, and from the extravagances of economic nationalism.

In striving to understand the instability of post-war industry and trade it is necessary to take cognizance of elements like revolution and nationalism, which are more emotional or spiritual than material. The dislocation of credit is even more intimately tied to mental and emotional conditions. Before 1914 the capitalistic system of production and distribution had rested on the apparently stable foundation of credit. The building of factories, ships, and railroads, the production and purchase of goods, the needs of governments—all the multifarious transactions of a busy world moved so smoothly that few of those engaged in economic endeavor realized how more than a tiny part of the system worked. Men were confident that the machinery would work; only trained students and men of affairs knew that it was the fact of confidence which enabled the machinery to work. One must be confident of the future to purchase the securities of an industrial plant as yet unbuilt, to agree to deliver or receive goods months in the future, to purchase government bonds maturing decades in the future, or with no maturity date. Confidence might, of course, be misplaced. There were risks; a business house or a government might become bankrupt; occasionally there were business depressions and financial crises. The intelligent man took these contingencies into consideration, as a farmer would allow for drought or excessive rain. The system of national and international credit by which industry and trade were financed was, however, thought fundamentally sound and stable.

The war and the peace drastically altered the credit relationship between nations. More important, confidence in the new relationship was never completely established and at times seemed completely lacking. During the war, the European Allies were unable to produce by their own efforts the supplies needed for the struggle. Purchases were made on a colossal scale from other countries, particularly from the United States. These purchases were financed in part by the sale of American securities which had been owned by Allied nationals, in part by loans floated in the United States. The effect might be compared to a geological dis-

turbance which compelled a river to reverse the direction of
its flow. Before the war, large sums had flowed from the
United States to Europe for the payment of interest on
American bonds and stocks held abroad. Many of these
securities had now been sold to American investors by their
foreign owners; less money would now flow from the
United States. On the other hand, American investors had
purchased the securities of the Allied governments. Henceforth, money must be sent from Europe to the United States
to repay the interest on these loans, sums much larger than
Americans must pay on securities held abroad. The flow of
interest payments was reversed. The United States had
changed from a debtor to a creditor nation.

The change was both intensified and complicated after
the United States entered the war. By 1917 so many Allied
bond issues had been floated in America that the investment
market was about exhausted, while the need for American
munitions continued unabated. In this emergency the American government came to the rescue. American investors
were unwilling to buy Allied bonds, but could be induced or
forced to buy American government bonds. The Washington government floated Liberty bonds, and with the proceeds of these bonds paid for Allied purchases in the United
States. The Allied governments promised to repay the sums
thus advanced at a later date. England had, since the beginning of the war, been making similar advances to her Continental allies. When lending ceased some time after the
armistice, England was owed large sums by her Continental
allies, while all the Allied governments owed amounts,
which in the aggregate were a still larger sum, to the United
States government. These intergovernmental transactions
constitute what came later to be known as the war debts.
They were, of course, only a part of the financing necessitated by the war. In addition to intergovernmental debts,
there were the bonds sold by Allied governments to their
own citizens and to American private investors. Would the
governments be able to pay these obligations? The answer
was dubious. The existence of governmental debts of colos-

sal magnitude introduced an element of uncertainty into the credit world.

Reparations were closely akin to war debts in that they were a debt payable by one government to other governments. The connection became still more intimate when the Allied governments began to look to reparations payments for the sums necessary to pay the United States government. If it was uncertain whether the Allied intergovernmental debts could be paid, it was still more dubious whether Germany could be saddled with the task of paying for the Allied war debts and for the cost of reconstructing the devastated areas as well. Reparations, therefore, further unsettled confidence in the new financial structure of the world.

Uncertainty concerning the worth of intergovernmental debts, whether reparations or war debts, was inevitable, because two questions were involved which could not be answered. Had governments the ability and the willingness to collect by taxation the sums involved? The obligations might, of course, be commercialized; that is, the debtor governments might sell bonds to the investing public, and satisfy the obligations to the creditor governments with the proceeds. Investors would buy the bonds, however, only if they thought the investment a safe one, if they were confident that the tax receipts of the debtor government would suffice for payments on principal and interest. This question therefore comes back to taxation. The other question is: Granted that the necessary amounts were raised by taxation, were the governments able or willing to transfer these sums from their own exchequers to those of the creditor countries? These two questions must be considered separately for reparations and war debts.

The proportion of a nation's income which may be collected in taxes is theoretically determinable. The proportion of the tax receipts which may be set aside for debt payments is also theoretically determinable. Learned statisticians have, by awe-inspiring calculations which are unintelligible to the layman, proved again and again that the German government could accumulate large sums for reparations payments by taxation and lowered governmental expenses. Probably the statisticians are right. Nevertheless the large sums have not been forthcoming. Our statisticians explain that German taxes have been too low and governmental expenditures too high. Probably the explanation is correct. Cogent arguments may be advanced to prove that Germany could, if willing to make the necessary sacrifices, assume heavy reparations burdens.

The arguments of the statisticians do not, however, go far enough. The new German Republic was the child, not of hope and triumph, but of disillusionment and defeat. There was, to be sure, hope in Germany that the creation of the Republic would bring peace on the lenient terms promised by the pre-armistice agreement. Hope vanished when the conditions of peace became known. Thereafter the Republic commanded enthusiastic support from only a minority of the German people. This weak government found itself saddled with the duty of taxing the German people for reparations payments of colossal size. At best, people do not like to pay taxes. Taxes may be made palatable by hope of sustaining national well-being, or by fear, as in the case of appropriations for national defense. Even when thus made palatable, high taxes impair the popularity of the government; high taxes which are odious may lead to revolution. Taxes for reparations—for tribute, as the Germans put it—were odious. The government hesitated to risk revolution by imposing the necessary burdens. Furthermore, the supporters of the Republic were liberals and socialists, who demanded expensive social improvements. To refuse these improvements might drive the government supporters into the Communist camp. To tax for reparations raised the threat of revolt by conservatives who refused to admit the necessity for reparations payments; to cut governmental expenses in order to save money for reparations raised the threat of revolt by radicals who demanded social improvements. On the other hand, non-payment of reparations brought the German government face to face with angry and powerful creditors. Fear of creditors and fear of revolution—the government of the Republic fled from one only to be confronted by the other. The government dared not defy either. It temporized with both and hoped that time would bring a solution.

That Germany could stand a considerable tax burden for reparations payments was possible; that the German people could be induced to bear this burden was improbable. The same dilemma appeared when the so-called transfer problem was considered. Let us assume for the moment that the German government was successful in its search for funds with which to pay reparations. What was to be the medium of payment to the creditor countries—gold? Impossible. All the gold in Germany was only a small fraction of the reparations demands, and the gold in Germany was needed as support for the currency. Some means of payment must be found which would not draw gold out of Germany, because to draw gold out of Germany in large amounts would be to destroy the value of the German currency. Only two other methods were visible in 1920: Germany could make things for foreign peoples, or do things for them; Germany could pay in goods or in services.

An illustration may make clear the mechanism of payment. Herr Schwarz of Berlin, sells goods to the value of ten thousand dollars to M. Blanc of Paris. The German government owes money to the French government for reparations account. The German government pays Herr Schwarz his ten thousand dollars, and tells the French government to collect from M. Blanc, and to credit Germany's account. Result: Germany has paid ten thousand dollars on reparations, although no money has been shipped across the German frontier. The transaction would of course be more complex, but the principle would be unchanged. To pay the sum due on reparations account, the transaction of Herr Schwarz would have to be repeated hundreds of thousands of times. Germany must every year export in goods and services enough, not merely to counterbalance her imports, but enough to counterbalance both her imports and her reparations payments. If German exports did not suffice, the balance must be paid in gold. As we have already seen, exporting gold was out of the question.

Most experts refused to believe that German exports could be stimulated enough to counterbalance annual payments of $1,500,000,000 on reparations, and the Allies were asking for that much or more as late as 1921. The skeptics had strong arguments. Before the war, Germany had imported more goods than she exported; the deficit was balanced by payments due to Germany on investments abroad and on services. By the Treaty of Versailles, German investments abroad and the bulk of Germany's shipping were confiscated. Therefore, Germany could not count on returns from services to help balance her international payments. Merely to achieve a balance, without reparations payments, Germany must now export more goods than formerly, unless imports could be decreased. The increase of exports must be very great indeed if reparations were to be paid. The Allies lessened the possibility of a growth of exports by confiscating German branch banks, factories, railroads, and other industrial property abroad, by seizing German shipping, by demanding large amounts of coal and other raw materials, and by severing three of the most important industrial areas from the Reich. To cut away German connections with foreign markets, to force her to build anew her facilities for shipment, to take away essential raw materials like coal and iron, to transfer industrial areas to other states—these were poor ways to encourage German exports.

Thus handicapped, German exports must be increased at a time when revolutionary disturbances were making international trade more difficult, when tariff walls were rising, and when the competition for markets was keen. Germany could be successful in the competition only if her prices were lower than those of her competitors. Most of the raw material for German manufacture was imported; costs could not be cut down greatly here. Efficient management might produce reduction in costs, but American industry was a model of efficient production. Germany could not cut under

American manufactures by managerial savings. The return given to holders of capital stock and bonds might be reduced; this proved only temporarily possible. The only other element of cost on which savings were possible was labor. By reducing the wages and the standard of living of German labor, German goods might be made cheaply enough to compete successfully with British and American goods.

German exports could be stimulated, but neither the Allies nor the Germans were willing to pay the necessary price. Did the Allies want the world, including their own domestic markets, flooded with German goods? The answer may be found in the tariff walls which were raised in every country after the war. The answer may also be seen in the controversy over payments in kind. The German government offered to reconstruct the devastated areas with German products and German labor. French industry and French labor immediately protested, and payments in kind were restricted to products which did not seriously compete with French industry. Where, then, were German exports to go? Everywhere they must compete with the products of Allied factories, to the discomfiture and loss of Allied exporters. Furthermore, the Allies were haunted by the knowledge that the stimulus to German exports would be permanent. When reparations had been paid, Germany would possess an industrial plant and a control over foreign markets which would make Germany incomparably the greatest industrial power in Europe. The Allies would then be confronted by a Germany made strong by the reparations burden which had been designed to keep Germany weak. Truly, reparations payments placed the victors in an awkward plight!

To lower the standard of living of German labor was the only way to lower the cost of German products. German labor objected to shouldering the burden, and after the war German labor was in a belligerent mood. Here again the German government was confronted with the danger of revolution if it sought to satisfy the Allied demand for reparations. Funds for reparations payments could be secured only by a tax burden resented by all classes in Germany, and by curtailing social expenditures demanded by the radicals; the funds accumulated could be transferred only by driving the already low standard of living still lower. It was possible that taxation and economy would produce the needed funds; it was possible that a degraded laboring class might enable Germans to sell their products at a price low enough to overcome competition or tariff barriers, and in quantity large enough to pay reparations. It was possible that a reactionary government might have paid reparations, submitting to high taxes and forcing labor down to a subsistence level, because reactionaries might hope to gain in the end. Reparations paid, German industry would be powerful; German labor would be broken by long-continued exploitation; then the profits of industry would be great. What a reactionary government might welcome, however, a democratic government, which was dependent on popular acquiescence for continued existence, could not do. If German statesmanship since the war has not seemed impressive, that is partly because the rulers of Germany were forced to cope with a nation determined not to pay and with creditors determined to be paid.

The elements involved in the reparations question are complex, understandable only after serious and dispassionate study. Men after the war were unable to see the problem clearly. Hatred of Germany was strong; men were terrified by knowledge of what the war had cost; fools and demagogues concocted plausible arguments to prove that Germany could pay fantastic sums. To their lasting honor, there were a few men with ability to understand and courage to speak. J. M. Keynes's *Economic Consequences of the Peace*, a scathing indictment based on profound knowledge and expressed with great force and clarity, was published late in 1919. It encountered much ignorant and prejudiced criticism, but its cogent argument slowly made headway. For years, few men and fewer women could keep distinct in their minds the questions of what Germany could, and what Germany should, pay. For years, the crushing logic with which economists sought to demolish extravagant hopes went unheeded. Politicians, fearful for their hold on office, popular writers who knew the public would pay well to read what the public wanted to believe—these continued to flatter the hopes of uninstructed electorates. Ignorance, prejudice, fear, and downright falsehood all blocked the path to a sane solution of the reparations problem. In this confusion of counsel, the force of events determined the issue: slowly, protesting, men abandoned the wild dreams of 1918. It is possible, however, and one would like to believe, that the lessons given by Keynes and other students did help men to accept the inevitable with less cost in human suffering than would otherwise have been the case.

The absurdity of the hope for large reparations can best be appreciated by an examination of the contrast which was made after the war between Germany's failure to pay and France's prompt payment in 1871. The indemnity laid on France by Bismarck was both definite and small; payment brought tangible benefits. The Allies did not fix the total of Germany's liability until two years and a half after the armistice. During the intervening period the Allied peoples demanded extravagant sums which no nation could conceivably have paid. These demands deprived the German people of the incentive to pay anything: if they were to be forced to default in any case, why try to pay a part of an insurmountable burden? The sum fixed in 1921 was also too high, and by that time the German capacity to pay had been impaired by the seizure of capital assets such as investments, ships, and railroad rolling stock by the Allies. As a keen student of the problem said, the Allies, by seizing the capital assets of Germany and then demanding sums which could only be procured by earnings from capital, were demanding "a daily diet of golden eggs and roast goose combined." Seizure of capital destroyed capacity to pay; the fixing of a sum which could never be paid in full impaired the will to pay. The will to pay was further impaired by the lack of reward. France paid quickly in 1871 because by so doing the German occupation and the restrictions on French sovereignty were removed. No such incentive was held out to Germany until six years after the armistice. Then the Germans did try to pay, only to fall back discouraged when all promised benefits had been attained and when the payments again seemed beyond German capacity. There is no parallel between the French indemnity of 1871 and German reparations after 1919, because the Allies did their best to destroy German capacity to pay and German desire to pay.

The problems created by war debts, and the difficulties of securing payment, were much the same as those encountered in the reparations problem. War debts were a far smaller burden on the debtor nations. The funding agreements were made on the basis of capacity to pay, and it would be difficult to prove that capacity was fixed at too high a figure. Nevertheless, the human obstacles to payment remained the same. If reparations were tribute to Germany, war debts were blood-money to the Allied peoples, debts incurred in fighting a common battle to save civilization. No amount of argument could shake this conviction; argument merely strengthened dislike of America. On the other hand, just as the Allied peoples claimed that Germany must be held to her promise to pay, so the American people claimed that the Allies must honor their bond. Just as the Allies insisted on payments which could only be made in goods and then did their best to hamper German exports, just so did the United States pass tariff laws high even for America and demand payment on debts which could be paid only in goods. Like reparations, the war debts heightened uncertainty, animosity, tension; and while the resulting load of misery was not commensurate with that occasioned by reparations, undoubtedly the existence of war debts impeded sane consideration of reparations.

The economic difficulties resulting from the dislocation of industry, trade, and credit were further complicated by currency inflation. During the war every government yielded more or less to the temptation to pay its way by issuing paper money unbacked by gold. As always, two results followed. In domestic trade, prices rose; people with fixed incomes found they could buy less; wage increases were demanded; debts were incurred and purchases made in terms of new prices. In foreign trade, the paper currency of each nation fluctuated: no longer related to gold, the currency had a value corresponding to the probability, or improbability, of a resumption of gold payments. Both the rise in prices and the fluctuations in exchange value produced uncertainty and strain. When, after the war, governments sought to return to the gold standard, there was new strain. Prices fell. Men who had accustomed themselves to reckoning values in terms of inflated prices were forced to adjust themselves to a new situation. Few citizens of any country understood what was happening. When prices rose, those with fixed incomes found themselves poor, while those whose products sold at the higher prices, like the farmers, rejoiced and increased production. When prices fell, the rôles were reversed. In both cases there was an outcry from those whose condition was worsened. When deflation was carried to completion, as in the United States and England, farmers and laborers felt that the fall in prices had been unjust; they became hostile to the "money barons" at whose door they laid their woes. Where inflation was carried to completion, as in Germany, those with fixed incomes found their investments worthless; impoverished, they became discontented, even rebellious. Everywhere currency inflation left a legacy of social discontent. Another legacy was impaired confidence. Having once seen governments slip away from the gold standard, men feared new inflation. Gold reserves were nervously watched. A fall in the reserve, even idle rumor, sufficed to produce a panicky demand for gold, which was then hoarded. States with strong gold reserves used the threat of a sudden withdrawal of credits invested in weak countries as a club with which to extort political concessions. It is impossible to analyze fully the causes of currency instability. Suffice it to say that the hysterical fear of new inflation and the resentment caused by both inflation and deflation added materially to the general economic dislocation.

Social unrest was both a cause and a result of economic instability. Before the war, the middle classes in Europe and America, long accustomed to power and to the conviction that power was rightly in their hands, were being increasingly subjected to pressure from the extremes of the social hierarchy, the very rich and the very poor. Nineteenth century humanitarianism and the need for political allies made the middle classes mildly sympathetic toward the demands of labor. In the years immediately preceding the war, small capital and organized labor combined to check the increasing concentration of wealth. The war produced a change. The growth of colossal aggregations of wealth was hastened; the necessity for uninterrupted production made governments acquiesce in the demands of labor for higher wages. The middle groups, on the other hand, were hard hit. Inflation progressively lowered the economic position of those who lived on the returns from investments; salaries rose much more slowly than either wages or prices.

After the war, deflation began. Deflation was, however, nowhere complete. In England and America prices remained high; in France and Italy inflation continued after the war, and the currency never recovered more than a fraction of its old value; in Germany the old currency was repudiated. Those with investments were, therefore, ruined in Germany, impoverished in France and Italy, and worse off than before the war in England and America. The salaried groups also had ground for complaint: salaries, slow to rise with prices, were slashed more rapidly than prices fell after the war. Even the small capitalist joined the ranks of the "new poor" as the growth of large-scale production lowered prices to a point where the individual producer or distributor could no longer compete. The great middle class, long accustomed to comfort and security, found itself increasingly deprived of both. Labor and large capital, however, were better off. Organized labor clung tenaciously and aggressively to gains made during the war; the massing of capital into fewer hands continued. Angry and bewildered, to a large extent ignorant of the forces at work, the middle class fought to retain its position, its wealth, and its power. Individuals adopted different courses, but by and large the middle class abandoned its alliance with labor: labor, aggressive and rising in the social scale, threatened to destroy the social and economic prerogatives which the middle class regarded as theirs by immutable and natural laws. Socially at least, the middle class had more in common with the possessors of great wealth than with labor. To a large extent, the middle-class revolt against the concentration of wealth collapsed; the middle and upper groups joined in concerted opposition to labor.

For our purposes, the plight of the middle class is important because of its connection with nationalism. Through long exercise of power, the middle class had come to regard itself as the representative of the nation. Itself menaced, the middle class came to feel that national safety was menaced; in defending its prerogatives, the middle class thought itself defending the state. The assumption was made plausible by the international character of socialism and, above all, of communism. From Moscow came propaganda frankly hostile to the existence of national states: Bolshevik Russia became the bugaboo of the propertied classes in Europe and America, as revolutionary France had once been to its neighbors. To be sure, communism had but little hold on labor in Europe, and still less in America; but the liberal reformer, who before the war might have been honored as a worthy citizen, was now painted red and thereby transformed into a traitor. The effort to fortify existing social and economic institutions by identifying them with national safety was, of course, nearly always unconscious. That fact does not detract from the importance of the effort. Whether or not the attempt could long be successful is also beside the point. The effect, at least temporarily, was to intensify nationalism by giving nationalism the support of strong economic interest. The power of the middle class was shaken, but it was not broken. The middle class had always been zealous for national honor. Zeal was redoubled by the precarious political, social, and economic position in which the middle class found itself after the war. The war accustomed men to violence; war propaganda made hate and intolerance seem, not despicable, but admirable. Armed with hate and intolerance, not scrupling at the use of violence, sure that its interests were those of the nation, the middle class battled for self-preservation. In the struggle ideals like democracy and personal liberty, which the middle class had formerly regarded as sacred, were ruthlessly sacrificed. In the field of foreign affairs national egoism became the highest virtue.

Never before had the world been confronted with economic problems so numerous and so perplexing. Never had the necessity for coöperation and compromise been more essential; but never had coöperation and compromise been more difficult. The French people insisted that Germany must remain economically weak: otherwise, Germany would be strong enough to fight. The French people insisted that Germany must pay reparations: otherwise, France must pay for German aggression. It did no good to tell the French people that a weak Germany could not pay. The French people lost their tempers and became still more unreasonable. In insisting on a tariff of prohibitive height and on debt payments which could only be made in goods, the Americans were equally unreasonable. Again and again we find nationalism impelling men to cling stubbornly to irreconcilable alternatives, refusing to surrender either and in the end losing both. The economic maladies which affected the post-war world could only be solved if men were willing to sacrifice immediate national interests for the attainment of common well-being. Nationalism prevented men from making the necessary sacrifices. Therefore the maladies persisted and grew in virulence. Men clung to the fetish of nationalism while industry and commerce languished and while hunger drove millions to desperation. The evils of the situation were obvious, but men refused to admit that the evils resulted from their own short-sightedness. Instead, they blamed other nations. Nationalism was nourished by the misery it was creating.

3. THE DISSOLUTION OF THE GRAND ALLIANCE

Just as men craved economic well-being, which national-ism made impossible to attain, so men craved peace, which nationalism jeopardized. During the war, men welcomed the vision of a harmonious world which Wilson had described. Wilson asked for a reconciliation between the warring peoples; then all nations were to coöperate in the task of adjusting differences which might arise in the future. The peace conference was to establish a stable world order; stability achieved, the League of Nations was to prevent the growth of instability. Wilson's program was based on the assumptions that men desired peace before all else and that they would recognize the necessity of coöperation and con-cession to achieve a lasting peace. These assumptions were unwarranted. Men wished peace, but they also wished to protect what they thought to be national interests. Methods of establishing and maintaining peace which ran counter to national interests were unhesitatingly rejected. In assuming this attitude men did not admit that they showed indiffer-ence to the preservation of peace. Peace purchased at the cost of national sacrifices was not peace; it was subjection to tyranny. Every nation, therefore, insisted that the real way to secure a lasting peace was by the method which coincided with its interests. Practically, what was done was to disguise the pursuit of national interests as concern for world peace. The disguise made the task of establishing a stable peace more complicated than ever: national egoism was, so to speak, sanctified by identification with the cause of world peace.

The peace conference did not establish a stable world order. It did not even attempt the task. The changes were all made at the expense of the Central Powers. The Peace of Paris was a settlement dictated by the victorious Grand Alliance. The first condition of Wilson's program had, therefore, not been fulfilled: the warring peoples had not been reconciled, and stability had not been achieved. Wilson did secure the second part of his program, the League of

Nations. The League was, however, condemned to at least temporary impotence by the very conditions under which it was created. The League from the outset was forced to cope with the problems of a disturbed world. It must not merely prevent the growth of discord; discord already existed in every quarter of the world. Furthermore, many nations felt that the League was not, from their point of view, the correct instrument for the preservation of peace. The defeated powers, which were not admitted to membership, regarded the League as the organization through which the victors sought to perpetuate their ascendancy. The stronger powers, like Britain and America, were unwilling to assume obligations in order to secure a protection of which they did not feel in need. To Russia the League seemed a capitalist conspiracy against communism. Founded when world affairs were in chaos, regarded with indifference, skepticism, or dislike by a large part of the world, the League threatened to die amid abuse and ridicule, as the Holy Alliance had died a century before.

The western peoples were not content to abandon as hopeless the task of organizing the world for the preservation of peace. The French had felt from the outset that the League was too ambitious a project. They had, therefore, sought to stabilize the new *status quo* by continuing the Grand Alliance. The refusal of the United States Senate to ratify the Anglo-American treaty guaranteeing protection to France deprived the French of this weapon. The French then fell back on the old system of Continental alliances. Like their old alliance with Russia, the new alliances had to be bolstered with loans and with aid in quarrels which only remotely affected French interests. The French felt aggrieved that the task of preserving the peace in Europe was left to them. They labored indefatigably, but with only partial success, to force other powers to assume part of the burden, whether through the League or through regional agreements such as the Locarno Treaties. The British and the Americans were, like the French, relatively content with the existing distribution of power in the world. Unlike the

French, they felt strong enough to perpetuate their hegemony unaided. Therefore, they denied the efficacy of treaties
of guarantee as aids to the preservation of peace. Instead,
the Anglo-Saxon powers advocated reduction of armaments. France steadily opposed their efforts, on the ground
that, in default of treaties of guarantee, arms alone enabled
her to preserve the peace and security of Europe and of
France. The Germans and the other defeated powers contended that no scheme for the preservation of peace could
have merit until the victors retraced their steps and replaced
the Peace of Paris by the peace of reconciliation promised
by Wilson. The French interpreted the German demand for
a revision of the treaties as the first step in the process of
restoring German hegemony in Europe. Having just rescued
Europe from German tyranny, the French argued, France
could not run the risk of reviving that tyranny. Therefore,
the French insisted on enforcing the Treaty of Versailles to
the letter, even those parts of the treaty which were unen-
forceable.

Disarmament, guarantee, revision—these three words
were endlessly reiterated. Each method of ensuring peace
was advocated as the one best for the world. In fact, each
was best for the immediate national interest of the nation
which advocated its acceptance. New words, new gestures,
but the old pursuit of national interests—that in brief is
what most post-war diplomacy shows forth. The desire for
peace was strong and articulate, but nationalism was far
more stridently vocal. The noisy clamor of nationalists
almost invariably drowned out, not merely those who
preached peace as an end in itself, but also those who urged
that national interests were best served by sacrificing tangible but transient interests to secure more lasting benefits.
In politics, as in economics, nationalism deprived men of
their reason. What the nationalist willed to believe he believed, even though all the evidence available showed the
belief to be false.

Fevered nationalism combined with the economic ills of
the world to make the post-war years an era of unprec-

edented violence in international affairs. Empires rose and fell almost overnight; a nation seemingly invincible to-day might to-morrow be helpless in the grip of financial panic. To reduce the story to even a semblance of order it is necessary to make a purely artificial division of the earlier years. Our primary concern is Europe. On the Continent of Europe events were largely dominated by the collapse of the Grand Alliance. The fortunes of the three great powers which tried to withdraw from European affairs will be described first. The efforts of France to build a new system for the protection of the *status quo* can then be described without interruption.

England in 1914 and the United States in 1917 were forced unwillingly into a war which they felt was not of their making. The war over, both nations resolutely turned their backs on Continental Europe and tried to forget the Continent and its quarrels. Ignorant of the real origins of the war, both peoples had accepted the official explanation that it was necessary to curb the German lust for world domination. Well, Germany had not merely been beaten, but permanently disarmed; subject peoples had been liberated. Surely, peace and harmony would now reign in Europe. Instead, old antagonisms persisted, and new ones appeared. Still there were huge armies, armies paid for with money that should have been given to Britain and America as payment on war debts. Not only were victors and vanquished threatening war over tiny patches of land; even liberated peoples were fighting, Czechs against Poles, Rumanians against Jugoslavs, fighting for a miserable half-dozen villages. The Continental peoples were incorrigible; they had learned nothing from the terrible holocaust just past; they could not see the waste, the tragedy, of war. If, deaf to argument and example, these people continued their butchery, they must be left to slaughter each other to extinction. Only, concluded the British and the Americans, in future we will keep clear; we at least are responsive to the dictates of experience and conscience. The reaction began in England and in the United States on the morrow of the armistice. Immediate demobilization was demanded by public opinion. The governments hesitated to disband these millions of men who formed so admirable an instrument of national policy. The pressure became irresistible; the great armies were disbanded. By the time the peace treaties were signed, the armies of Britain and America had once more dwindled to insignificant size. France refused to emulate this admirable example: voices in England and the United States lamented that militarism, killed in Germany, had risen to new life in France.

The British government was in an embarrassing predicament. At Paris, Lloyd George had struck a tacit bargain with Clemenceau. France received Continental hegemony and an Anglo-American treaty guaranteeing France against German efforts to upset the *status quo*. In return, Britain secured hegemony in the Near East. The American Senate refused to ratify the treaty of guarantee. This action relieved Britain of her obligations under the treaty. France tried in vain to induce the English to negotiate a new agreement without American participation: the British people were only too glad to be rid of an unwelcome entanglement in Continental affairs. Lloyd George was unable to fulfil his bargain with Clemenceau; now he must count on French opposition in the Near East.

At the end of the war, British military power was supreme in western Asia. Russian and German power was broken. France was willing to exchange favors in western Asia for favors in Europe. Italy need not be considered. England did not dare herself enter the Ægean for fear of arousing the jealousy of her allies, but Greece, bound by ties of interest and sentiment to Britain, was anxious to built an Ægean empire. For a time all went well. The Treaty of Sèvres gave Britain mandates over Palestine and Iraq. The independent Arab states fell within the British sphere of influence. Persia was forced to accept a British protectorate in 1919. Control over Afghanistan was strengthened. Greece controlled the European and Asiatic coasts of the Ægean. Constantinople and the Straits were demilitarized and therefore at the mercy of the British fleet. Disraeli's dream had become a reality. The British Suez Canal was flanked by British Egypt and Palestine. The Persian Gulf was a British lake. Gone was the Bagdad Railroad; the riches of Mesopotamia were now for Britain. Without a break, British power swept from the Cape to India.

Intoxicated by the war spirit, the ruling caste of Britain had grasped too much. The English people, weary of war, compelled the government to demobilize the armies with which the new imperial domain was held. The world economic crisis, which began late in 1920, hit Britain with great force. As Britain weakened, she felt the force of the weapon which had served so effectively against the Central Powers during the war. The cry of self-determination had been heard in Asia. By 1921 nationalist revolts had broken out from India to Egypt. The Bolsheviks, willing to further patriotism when patriotism opposed imperialism, encouraged the rebels. The British quickly regained the sober wisdom traditional in their history and made terms with the nationalists. Persia was evacuated in 1921; Egypt was given qualified independence in 1922; Afghanistan became completely independent.

The Turks remained to be placated. War had broken out between the Turkish nationalists, led by Mustapha Kemal, and the Greeks in June, 1920. The Greeks advanced steadily for a year until they were within 200 miles of Angora. There the Turks held. The Greeks could not advance; the Turks would not make peace. A year passed. During the year, the precarious unity which the Allies had maintained in their dealings with the Turks broke down. First Italy, then France, made terms with Angora. Britain and Greece were isolated. In August, 1922, the Turks attacked the Greek lines. Within a fortnight Smyrna was recaptured; the atrocities which had marked the Greek occupation were repaid with interest. The Turks turned north, toward Constantinople, where an Allied force was in occupation. The British government wished to fight.

Instead, the Italian and French forces at Constantinople took ship and left the British to face the Turks unaided. Mustapha Kemal was a shrewd statesman. He realized that the British were now concerned only to extricate themselves from their Near Eastern adventure without too great a loss of prestige. He agreed, therefore, to an armistice with Greece. In November, 1922, an international conference assembled at Lausanne to make new terms with Turkey. It took eight months to reach an agreement. The Turks were in no hurry; they were strong, while Greece was exhausted, and England was eager to get clear of Near Eastern affairs. The Turks stated their demands and waited until their terms were accepted.

The Treaty of Lausanne, signed in July, 1923, gave the Turks the national state they sought. The boundaries in Europe were substantially the same as before the war. In Asia Minor, the old frontiers with Russia and Persia were secured, while the southern frontier now ran due east from the Mediterranean, north of Syria and Iraq. Within this restricted area, Turkish authority was supreme. There was no indemnity or reparation; even the old capitulations were abolished. The problem of minorities received a most drastic solution. Greeks resident in Turkey were forced to leave; Turks resident in Greece must also leave. No more terrible indictment of nationalism is conceivable. Families by the thousand were forced to leave the land on which their ancestors had lived for centuries, to break associations which were as precious as life. All because Greek and Turk could not live peacefully in the same land.

British national imperialism had encountered Asiatic nationalism and had been forced to retreat. Might one conclude from this fact that the rise of nationalism in the so-called backward countries was making nineteenth century imperialism out of date? Possibly, but it is too soon to say. The opposition of other powers had also helped to balk the British plans; the episode might merely be the old clash of rival imperialisms, repeated with the precipitate violence characteristic of the post-war years. Finally, it should be noted that the British people had refused to support the plans of their leaders. The failure of these plans might be ascribed to the same reluctance to undertake new responsibilities which had led England to attempt withdrawal from Continental European affairs. Which of these three elements contributed most to the result is uncertain.

Turning from Britain to America, we find the same desire to escape from the complexities of the post-war world. Fighting in a common cause had suppressed, but not extinguished, American mistrust of Europe. With the armistice and the return of the troops, mistrust revived, stronger than ever before. Closer acquaintance had not enamored the American soldier of European ways. General Maurice relates a chance conversation with an American soldier. "I said: 'Well, how did you get on with the British?' No Hollywood star has ever registered contempt more satisfactorily as he replied: 'The British! Why them suckers drink tea!' " If the British drank tea—and spoke with an English accent—the French had still stranger ways, ways which, being strange, must be bad. The inherited sentimental fondness for the French came off very badly as a result of the comradeship in arms. No, the Americans had seen enough of what they thought the effete and wily, even immoral, ways of Europeans. Once home, American boys were going to stay home. Enough of crusades, enough of saving the world; enough of lending money and of winning wars for ungrateful allies. It was high time to think of America first, first and last. One lesson Americans had learned: a nation which possessed little military or naval strength also possessed little influence in the council of nations. The naval program which had been adopted in 1916, but suspended during the war, was taken up again with almost frantic energy after the armistice. America was rich; America would build a navy second to none; then America would live to herself, strong in her isolation.

The inchoate but powerful mistrust of Europe and the

desire for isolation found support in the ranks of the Republicans, who had a majority in the Senate. The Republicans professed to see in the League of Nations a menace to American ideals and institutions. How far their attitude was dictated by conviction, and how far by political expediency, is debatable. Senators like Mr. Borah undoubtedly believed that, in every bargain with a European state, the honest and homely, but simple, very simple, Americans would be worsted. The League of Nations was in his eyes no better than an instrument for the permanent subjugation of the United States. It is more difficult to believe that Senator Lodge, who led the Republicans during the debate on the treaty, was sincere. He knew enough of Europe not to be afraid; he had advocated the creation of a league of nations, until Wilson espoused the idea. Probably Lodge, and most other Republican senators, hesitated to examine their position too closely. The opportunity to discredit the work of a Democratic President was welcome, particularly a President who had been as dictatorial and as careless of senatorial sensibilities as Wilson. At the same time, popular opinion was undoubtedly uneasy about the League of Nations, fearful lest America be permanently embroiled in the quarrels of Europe.

When Wilson returned from Europe in the summer of 1919, the campaign against the treaty was already in full swing. Except in German-American and in advanced liberal groups, the terms imposed on Germany met with little criticism; feeling against Germany was still strong. The Shantung question occasioned an anti-Japanese campaign which further impaired the difficult relations between America and Japan. It was on the League, however, that opposition centered, and especially on Article 10 of the Covenant. The United States, it seemed, must protect the territorial integrity and political independence of every member of the League, must be prepared to sacrifice American men and money whenever a quarrel broke out anywhere in the world. This objection could be met in one of two ways. It might be argued that, if the United States really was resolved to sacrifice men and money, no nation would dare attack the independence or territory of another nation. On the other hand, it might be argued that Article 10 was, for the present at least, not to be taken seriously. Events showed that the second argument was correct: none of the stronger nations was prepared sincerely to accept the obligations or the limitations on national freedom of action imposed by the Covenant. Wilson could not see this obvious truth. Convinced that the world needed above all else some means of preventing a repetition of the war just past, and that the League provided the needed means, he insisted that the Covenant be accepted in good faith.

When it became apparent that the Senate would insist on reservations which weakened the force of the Covenant, Wilson carried his case to the people, to the "common man." In September, 1919, he set out on a tour of the country, intending to speak directly to the citizens of every section. Earlier in his career Wilson had used this method of attack successfully. What the result would now have been is dubious. Wilson was already exhausted by the prolonged negotiations at Paris. On September 25, in the midst of his appeal to the people, he collapsed. For the remaining year and a half of his administration he was a helpless invalid, cut off from contact with the world. Wilson silenced, his opponents had the field to themselves. In November, the Republican majority proposed ratification of the treaty, with reservations which greatly diminished, so far as the United States was concerned, the obligations and restrictions of the Covenant. For ratification, two-thirds of the Senate must concur. At Wilson's behest the Democrats voted against ratifying the amended treaty. In March, 1920, a final effort was made. Again the Democrats prevented ratification. The Treaty of Versailles was dead, so far as the United States was concerned. With it died the treaty by which the United States guaranteed aid to France in the event of a German invasion.

"The defection of America was a disaster the ultimate responsibility for which must be borne by the American nation . . . On the day America withdrew, the wave of reaction which President Wilson had bravely faced in Paris and in Washington leaped forward. We are still struggling with it. May we live to forgive America." This is the considered judgment of Salvador de Madariaga. The judgment commands respect; for Madariaga is one of the few students of international problems whose thinking is judicially compounded of idealism and sober intelligence. Undoubtedly the defection of the United States did facilitate the triumph of short-sighted nationalism. The American action is, however, understandable. The smaller neutral and victorious powers accepted the Covenant because it offered them a security which they could not attain by their own strength. When France, England, and Japan accepted the Covenant, they did so because the League constitution was embedded in the Treaty of Versailles, and the treaty contained tangible political and economic benefits for them. France, in her search for security, came later to support the League with enthusiasm, but in 1919 it cannot be said that these three powers sincerely accepted the responsibilities of the Covenant. The United States, on the other hand, acquired nothing of importance from the treaty with Germany, while the obligations of League membership were stressed to the American people, not only by foes of the treaty but by Wilson as well. Wilson urged that America would profit not only from the greater security which the League would afford against attack but also from tranquillity in the world as a whole. The opponents of the League argued that America could attain security unaided and that the problematic advantages of a tranquil world were more than offset by restrictions on national sovereignty. The reservations proposed by the Senate were designed to prevent the League either from compelling or from preventing American action without American consent. Similar reservations were tacitly taken for granted by the other great powers. Without securing the advantages which the Treaty of Versailles contained for the other great powers, the United States, as represented in the Senate, was willing to go as far toward acceptance of the Covenant as they were. Wilson was unwilling to accept these reservations because they changed the League from an authoritative to an advisory body. In grasping at all, he lost all. Had the United States joined the League with reservations, it is difficult to believe that the nationalistic desire for isolation would have triumphed as completely as it did after 1920.

All ties with the Allies cut, the United States made separate peace treaties with Germany, Austria, and Hungary in 1921. Thereafter, the American people stood proudly, even disdainfully, isolated, surveying the troubled affairs of Europe as from a lofty height. Fear of contamination by alien ideas helps to explain the hysterical fear of Bolshevism and the merciless hounding of all suspected of possessing radical views during the "Red Scare" of 1920. A year later, Congress passed an emergency law drastically curtailing immigration. America was no longer to be the melting-pot, the refuge for the oppressed of all nations. America was now to be "one hundred per cent American." The new president, Warren G. Harding, gave the watchword for the new era: "normalcy." In foreign affairs, normalcy meant the return to an earlier and happier day when Americans had been able to forget that Europe existed. The return to normalcy sometimes had a ludicrous aspect. Having rejected the League, Americans refused to admit that the League existed. As most of the long-established international scientific, administrative, and humanitarian activities became associated with the League, the task of participating in these activities without acknowledging the existence of the League became increasingly difficult for the American government. Nevertheless, the rather absurd effort continued for several years.

America had kept clear of European entanglements, but there were two problems which must be solved before that blessed state could be achieved when foreign affairs might safely be forgotten—the Far East and armaments. While the World War was in progress, Japan sought to extend her influence on the mainland of Asia. In 1915, China was forced to agree to the substance of the so-called Twenty-one Demands, which, if executed literally, would have given Japan a protectorate over all China. In 1917, Russian power collapsed. Japan had now no serious rival in northern China; indeed, Japan now began to think of bringing eastern Siberia within her sphere of influence. American and Japanese troops occupied Siberia for the purpose of opposing the Bolsheviks; when the American troops were recalled early in 1920, the Japanese remained. The Treaty of Versailles gave Japan the German north Pacific islands and Kiauchow. Japan had unofficially promised to restore Kiauchow to China, but the promise was not legally binding, and the terms upon which restitution would be made had not been specified. By 1920, Japan possessed Kiauchow and Port Arthur and therefore dominated the approaches to Peking; southern Manchuria and Inner Mongolia were definitely Japanese spheres of influence; the Twenty-one Demands gave Japan vague but extensive influence in China south of the Great Wall; eastern Siberia was occupied by Japanese troops. The Japanese navy was growing with great speed. In 1921 naval appropriations made up a third of the total budget. The newly acquired German islands were potential naval bases. With a great fleet operating behind a screen of island bases, Japan could parry the efforts of other powers to interfere with her plans in Asia.

The ultimate objective of Japan was uncertain; on the basis of existing information it is most reasonable to conclude that Japan had no carefully worked-out plan. Japan was undoubtedly filled with imperialistic ambition, made acute by overpopulation and inadequate natural resources. Undoubtedly Japanese hopes soared high when the war left eastern Asia unguarded by other powers. The very extent of Japanese activity suggests, however, that Japan was guided by ambition alone, unchastened by thoughtful study of what was possible. Events showed that the grandiose hopes of Japan were built on quicksand. The brutal methods used by military commanders aroused national sentiment in

China and Russia. An economic boycott in China hurt Japanese trade; the inhabitants of Siberia rebelliously preferred Soviet to Japanese rule. The depression of 1920 ended the wartime prosperity which had enabled Japan to support heavy military and naval burdens. Japanese imperialism was collapsing of its own weight by 1921.

The United States was not content to let events run their course. In the interest of trade, the Americans had for two decades been trying to preserve the integrity of China; Japan was endeavoring to secure a monopoly in at least northern China. The Philippine Islands lay exposed to the growing Japanese navy. Strong race prejudice against Japan, stimulated by immigration problems on the Pacific coast, existed in the United States. Advocates of large naval appropriations spread alarmist rumors in both countries. By 1921 the possibility of war was freely discussed.

At the same time, Anglo-American relations were becoming strained. Rebellion had broken out once more in Ireland, rebellion marked by barbaric atrocities. As usual, American opinion sided with Ireland. Naval propagandists not only seized upon the Irish issue, but hearkened back to the difficulties American shipping had suffered at British hands during the early years of the World War. The campaigns against Japan and England were fused by the existence of the Anglo-Japanese alliance. Now that Russia and Germany had disappeared from the Far Eastern scene, the alliance seemed to have no excuse for existence, unless it was directed against the United States. To be sure, England and Japan were, under the terms of the alliance, expressly relieved of the obligation to help each other in case of war with the United States. Might not this stipulation merely be a sham, designed to lull the Americans into a false sense of security? American opinion was in a mood to believe anything. The World War had lasted long enough thoroughly to arouse, but not long enough to sate, American emotions. As a result, the American temper was for some years nervous, irritable, unconsciously expectant of a new outlet for its pent-up energy. For a time the Americans seemed actually anxious to pick a quarrel with England and Japan.

They might have got their wish. According to traditional international practice, England and Japan would have drawn together for safety. Circumstances compelled all three governments to seek an amicable adjustment. In America the peace movement was strong, and American pacifists concentrated their efforts on the question of disarmament. With an economic depression in full progress, the pacifists found wide support. There was slight chance that appropriations could be secured for the big-navy program. Economically, Britain and Japan were in far worse plight. Japanese industrial life was prostrate; Britain was only less badly off. Statesmen both in London and in Tokyo realized that a naval race with America would probably be ruinous, while war would certainly be ruinous. England was in a peculiarly awkward position. Resolved to avoid war with America at all costs, England had no further use for the Anglo-Japanese Alliance. The alliance was obnoxious to the United States, and only less objectionable to British dominions in the Pacific, who shared American race prejudices. If the alliance could be terminated without offending Japan, the British would be well pleased.

Having decided that further competition would be too expensive, the three greatest naval and Pacific powers agreed to arrange a compromise. The American government issued an invitation to a conference to be held at Washington. In addition to England and Japan, invitations were sent to France and Italy, because they were naval powers, and to Portugal, China, Holland, and Belgium, because they had interests in the Pacific. There were two significant omissions. Germany was not invited, because Germany no longer counted as a naval or Pacific power. Russia was not invited, because the United States had not recognized the Soviet government. On November 12, 1921, the Washington Conference was opened.

During the conference, limitation of armaments was kept

persistently in the foreground. As the solution of the armaments problem hinged on the solution of Pacific questions,
these properly must be considered first. Two agreements
registered the defeat of Japan's ambitions. One, between
China and Japan, settled the terms for the restitution of
Kiauchow and the former German privileges in the Shantung peninsula to China. The other, signed by all nine
powers, guaranteed the independence and territorial integrity of China, and bound the signatories "to use their
influence for the purpose of effectually establishing and
maintaining the principle of equal opportunity for the commerce and industry of all nations throughout the territory
of China." The Anglo-Japanese Alliance was supplanted by
a Four-Power Pacific Treaty between Britain, France,
Japan, and the United States. The signatories mutually
agreed to respect one another's existing rights in the Pacific
islands. In case of a dispute between two of the signatories,
"the whole subject will be referred for consideration and
adjustment" to a conference of all the signatories. In case
of threatened aggression in the Pacific by any other power,
the signatories were to confer and to decide on the most
efficient measures for meeting the emergency.

With arrangements completed for the evacuation of
Kiauchow, with the principle of the "open door" for commerce recognized, with the insular *status quo* in the Pacific
guaranteed, with the four strongest powers bound to oppose
by concerted action any attempt at aggression in the Pacific,
and with the Anglo-Japanese Alliance ended, the conflict of
interests in the Pacific and in China was terminated, so far
as treaties could effect a solution. The way was now opened
for the limitation of armaments. At the beginning of the
conference, Secretary Hughes had made a definite proposal.
For the three greatest powers, he took existing strength in
capital ships as the basis for discussion. Existing strength
was calculated by taking into consideration the size, number,
and age of completed battle-ships and the amount of work
already done on ships still building. The resultant ratio was
approximately 6-5-3. Hughes proposed that all uncom-

pleted capital ships be scrapped, together with a large number of older ships; he would leave Britain with approximately 600,000 tons; the United States with 500,000; and Japan with 300,000. No further building might be done for ten years. Thereafter, existing capital ships might be replaced when they were twenty years old; but when replacements began, the three powers must keep within the following maximum tonnages: Britain and the United States, 500,000 tons each; Japan, 300,000.

Hughes's proposals were accepted practically unchanged, but only after an important concession had been made to Japan. The ratio of five to three obviously would give either Britain or America a decisive advantage over Japan in time of war. To counterbalance this advantage, all three powers promised not to build new fortifications within a specified part of the Pacific area. Without naval bases, the cruising radius of a fleet is short. The effect of the promise not to build fortifications was to make the Japanese fleet, on the one hand, and the British and American fleets, on the other, operate on what might be called different planes. Neither Britain nor America would possess bases from which an attack on Japan could be launched. Japan would be able to seize certain British or American possessions, such as the Philippines, but would not be able to strike at a vital part of the possessions of these powers. In short, Japan agreed to accept a fleet markedly inferior in size to that of Britain and America on condition that Japan be made practically immune from aggression.

Limitation and reduction were comparatively easy to agree upon between the three greatest naval powers. France and Italy offered greater difficulties. There was a flurry at the very beginning of the conference, when reduction of land armaments was proposed. M. Briand was immediately on his feet. If, he said, the other powers were prepared to promise France aid in case of attack, France would gladly abandon the burden of armaments; if France was to stand alone, France must decide what measures were necessary to ensure her safety. The subject of land armaments was promptly dropped by the conference. It was not dropped by American and British newspapers and publicists, who launched a sustained and indignant attack on French "militarism." On the question of naval armaments, France again came in for abuse. Since neither France nor Italy had built capital ships during or after the war, Secretary Hughes recognized that existing strength could not be taken as the basis for limitation. He proposed that France and Italy accept for the replacement ratio 1.75, that is 175,000 tons. Italy willingly accepted, because Italian resources would not support a larger program. France objected to accepting a ratio equal to that of Italy and so far inferior to that allotted the great naval powers. Under pressure from Britain and America, France gave way on the capital ship question, but refused to accept the ratio of 1.75 for auxiliary vessels. The French position wrecked all hope of limiting construction in the auxiliary categories. Again there was an outcry against French militarism. On this note the conference ended.

The Washington Conference is notable alike for its achievements and its failures. Pacific questions were at least temporarily adjusted; the tension in American relations with Britain and Japan was relaxed; the naval race had been halted so far as capital ships were concerned. These results were achieved at great cost. The Japanese delegates left the conference angry at heart. They had been forced to accept a ratio inferior to that of Britain and America. The question was largely one of prestige. Japan had achieved supremacy in the area where her interests centered; within that area lay valuable American possessions, gages of battle, so to speak; Japanese resources would not have sufficed to win a higher ratio had the race continued. The issue was one of prestige alone, but prestige is precious to nations. To fix ratios of armament seemed somehow like fixing the relative importance of nations in the world. Japanese pride was hurt. Japan at Washington had also been compelled to write off as a failure her imperialistic strivings of the years just past. Here again hurt pride was the real grievance. Japan's great imperial adventure failed because of Russian and Chinese nationalism and because Japanese resources were inadequate to sustain the burden. Reluctant to blame themselves, the Japanese blamed the United States, because the United States had compelled an open confession of defeat. Antagonism between America and Japan did not die. The Japanese remembered their defeat, and the outrageous affront to Japanese pride offered by the act excluding Japanese from the United States served to keep memory fresh. The possibility of further trouble in China remained. Japan had not surrendered all the rights acquired by the Twenty-one Demands. When these conflicted with the "open door" principle, which would win?

Anglo-American relations also had not been permanently adjusted. The treaty conferring dominion status on Ireland, signed in December, 1921, took the edge off one source of trouble. Another difficulty was temporarily removed when Britain funded her war debt to the United States in 1923. The navy question remained, and here the Americans wrongly thought they had a grievance. They took for granted America's right to a navy second to none in strength. When Britain accepted parity with the United States in capital ships, Americans took it for granted that parity in all categories had been conceded. The latter assumption was unwarranted. The British by 1921 were coming to doubt the value of the capital ship; therefore they accepted equality with America. In the other categories, the British, because of their world-wide empire, thought themselves entitled to a force superior to that of any other power. Since limitation of auxiliary vessels was blocked by France, the divergence between the British and American views did not become apparent. Later, when the divergence became obvious, the Americans felt cheated, and the course of Anglo-American relations was again troubled.

The French felt that they were being subjected to unjust criticism throughout the conference. America and Britain had refused to ratify the treaty guaranteeing France against a German attack. Since they were unwilling to accept responsibility for the preservation of peace in Europe, France thought that the United States and England had no right to determine what military forces were necessary to ensure French security. Instead, British and American opinion demanded that France drastically reduce her land forces and roundly abused France when the demand was refused. On the naval question also the French felt they had not been justly treated. They refused to admit that equality of population justified equality of naval strength; France, with a large colonial empire, was entitled to a larger fleet than Italy. Furthermore, as a great colonial power, and as a proud nation, France resented being forced into the category of a minor naval power, and resented still more being accused of militarism for refusing to submit to dictation. It is not overstating the case to say that the effect of the Washington Conference on French relations with England and the United States was disastrous, and that the conference contributed greatly to the quarrel which was brewing between France and Italy.

The Washington Conference brought into prominence two Anglo-American beliefs which have bulked large in the post-war years. Studying the origins of the World War, most Englishmen and Americans were disposed to attribute the war to secret diplomacy and the armaments race. Peace, they concluded, could be assured by the elimination of these evils. International conferences, meetings of leading statesmen for the adjustment of rival interests, were a characteristic feature of the "new diplomacy" which was to supplant the old secret methods. It may be doubted whether the new method was an advance. Before each conference met, the issues were thoroughly discussed in the press. The desires of each country became apparent. Once public opinion had hardened in support of a particular program, compromise became difficult, if not impossible. Compromise seemed a sacrifice of national interest. While the conference was in progress, the press closely watched the course of the debate and reported the proceedings much as battles had been reported, as a victory for this side or a defeat for that side. If, in the interests of harmony, compromise was attempted, there was a great popular outcry, which brought a denial that anything had been, or would be, conceded, to the rival combatants. Differences of opinion, dragged into the open, were accentuated. Almost every conference left a legacy of bad feeling. In every case where a conference was even partially successful, the foreign offices had secretly gone over the ground beforehand and achieved substantial agreement. As a means of dramatizing harmony already attained, conferences have been useful. As a means of securing agreement by friendly discussion between heads of state they have failed—not only failed but made future agreement more difficult.

In addition to open diplomacy, the English-speaking peoples have advocated disarmament, by which they meant limitation of armaments. Arms are an expensive waste of money, runs the argument. Arms do not give security; instead, competition in armaments breeds the fear and mistrust from which wars spring. Agreements for the limitation and reduction of armaments would end the competition, banish fear, and therefore make war less likely.

The French have consistently combated the theory that reduction of armaments would further the cause of peace. Granted, the French argue, that arms do not banish fear, the converse is not proved. Arms are a symptom; the disease is insecurity. At the present time, the only way in which a nation can obtain security against attack is by the possession of military force. Reduction of armaments, even the total abolition of arms, would not suffice to banish fear. The real way to banish fear is to provide firm guarantees against aggression. If the military resources of the whole world, or even of a few great powers, would automatically come into play against a nation guilty of aggression, then aggression would be futile, then the fear of aggression would vanish, then the burden of armaments could be lessened. Until such guarantees have been received, no nation will disarm—least of all Britain or America. There is, the French contend, a great deal of cant in the prayers offered

up by the English-speaking peoples for the conversion of
Continental nations to the paths of righteousness. Themselves immune from attack by land, Britain and America
would have conscription abolished and armies drastically
reduced in size. Britain and America would reduce naval
armaments—but always with the reservation that their fleets
must remain the largest in existence. Naturally, reduction
which does not impair supremacy is preferable to more
costly supremacy. When Britain and America propose a
reduction of naval armaments which impairs their supremacy, then their devotion to peace will be demonstrated. So
far, the French conclude, just two facts have been demonstrated: Britain and America wish supremacy at the lowest
possible price, and they wish to preserve their freedom to
use that supremacy in any way they may desire.

The attacks of France on the Anglo-American position
have force, as the history of the Washington Conference
shows. Reduction of naval armaments, as between Britain,
America, and Japan, proved possible only *after* political
questions in the Pacific had been settled, and *after* provision
had been made for continued coöperation for the prevention
of aggression in the Pacific. When the political conditions
which might produce war were adjusted, then there was no
reason for a naval race. Furthermore, Japan agreed to be
content with a fleet smaller than those possessed by Britain
and America only *after* Japan had made certain that the
strong powers would be unable, for lack of naval bases, to
attack Japan. Fear of aggression removed, Japan could be
content with a smaller force. On the other hand, adjustment
of the political difficulties between France and Italy in the
Mediterranean was not attempted at Washington. France
was, therefore, unwilling to accept equality of naval armaments with Italy. Partial equality was accepted by France,
but only after Anglo-American pressure, which the French
resented.

So far the Washington Conference substantiates the
French claim that reduction of armaments is only possible
when security has been attained. The conference proves

more than that, however. France, Britain, and America used different methods, but all three, under the cloak of concern for the welfare of mankind, were trying to perpetuate conditions favorable to themselves. America and Britain possessed the largest navies in the world. These navies gave them an overwhelming voice in the settlement of international disputes. Therefore, England and the United States favored proportionate limitation of naval armaments. Unless they quarreled with each other, either country could enforce its will on all other states, while naval supremacy continued. A more enviable situation could not be imagined: power, supreme and unrestrained. France also was satisfied with things as they were, territorially. But France viewed the future with apprehension. On the Continent, many states refused to accept the verdict of the peace treaties. Above France towered the strength of Britain and America. Lacking confidence in her ability to perpetuate the *status quo,* France sought to enlist the aid of Britain and America. The latter powers, confident in their own strength, saw no reason for sacrificing their freedom of action. There was irony in the situation. Would America have been so enthusiastic in 1890 for reduction of naval armaments on the basis of existing strength? Would France have been so enthusiastic for perpetuating the territorial *status quo* in 1913? France, Britain, and America all forgot the past and assumed that world affairs were static and were ordered for the best interests of mankind. That was not true. Nations wax in strength, as the United States had grown; and their power wanes, as Austrian strength had waned. Those at the peak of power can envisage no greater boon for the world as a whole than the continuance of things as they are; efforts at change are called aggression and are opposed with righteous fervor. Other states, like Japan, Germany, and Hungary after the war, feel themselves oppressed; defense of the *status quo* is to them tyranny; change is called justice, the means to a lasting peace. Neither the Anglo-American nor the French proposals for the pacification of the world took cognizance of the forces making for change;

disarmament and guarantees against aggression, as put forward by their sponsors, would perpetuate the *status quo*.

4. REPARATIONS AND SECURITY, 1919–1925

In 1871, Continental hegemony passed from France to Germany; by the Treaty of Versailles, France regained Continental hegemony. The circumstances under which these results were achieved were very different. The victory of Germany over France in 1871 was decisive. In the Great War, Germany was conquered by a coalition which included six great powers and a score of lesser states. This difference made the task of French statesmen far more difficult than that which Bismarck had faced. Bismarck felt compelled to keep France isolated; isolated, France could not challenge Germany. After 1918 it was practically certain that Germany could, if allowed to recover her strength, defeat France in war; France, not Germany, now needed allies. Germany must be kept weak, and France must have allies: these have been the guiding principles of French diplomacy since 1918.

Clemenceau thought he had achieved the necessary security by the Treaty of Versailles. The German army and navy were permanently reduced to insignificant proportions; the Rhineland was permanently demilitarized. Allied troops were to garrison the Rhineland for fifteen years—for longer, if Germany had not fulfilled the conditions of peace. Germany was economically weakened by the loss of industrial resources and by the reparations burden. Germany would be too weak to attack—if these provisions were enforced. Clemenceau did not feel that France could, of her own strength, keep Germany under permanent surveillance. He counted on the continued existence of the Grand Alliance, and especially on the Anglo-American treaty of guarantee for aid.

Clemenceau's plans were wrecked by the revival of desire for isolation in America and Britain. The United States felt able to cut all political ties with Europe. Britain sought to obtain her share of the spoils distributed in the Treaty of

Versailles, and at the same time to escape all obligations. The treaty of guarantee was allowed to lapse when it failed of ratification in the United States Senate. Able statesmen like Lord Robert Cecil were sent to the League of Nations meetings at Geneva, but the British frequently declined to ratify the work of their representatives, and in every way sought to minimize the obligations imposed by the Covenant. The Anglo-French entente continued and found expression in numerous meetings to concert a common policy; but the French did not want an entente which left Britain free to act or not to act in a crisis. France wanted Britain to accept the obligation to sustain the new *status quo,* by arms if necessary. This obligation the British refused to accept. The French soon had other grounds for reproach. British statesmen showed a disposition to placate Germany by leniency in interpreting the Treaty of Versailles. When, in March, 1920, Germany sent troops into the demilitarized zone to suppress a Communist revolt, France occupied additional territory as a protest against this violation of the treaty. The British condoned the German action and protested sharply when the French troops advanced. The French were alarmed. If one violation of the treaty could be justified, another and still others could be condoned, until the treaty became a dead letter. Even more alarming was British indifference to the Eastern European settlement. From the days of the peace conference, Lloyd George refused to believe that the new states could hold territory coveted by Germany and Russia. Since he was convinced that change must come eventually, he was disposed to believe that the sooner changes were made, the better it would be for all concerned. The French once more saw the beginning of a movement to destroy the peace treaties. Their fears were confirmed after the world economic depression began. In 1921 British opinion perceived that Britain could not prosper while a large part of Europe, especially Germany, was in economic chaos. The reparations question was the most obvious cause of the bankruptcy toward which Germany was heading. The British urged, therefore, that reparations payments be sus-

pended until German strength revived. The French resisted:
the Treaty of Versailles must be executed. The divergent
views of France and England proved impossible to reconcile. By 1923 the entente was temporarily broken.

Before the Treaty of Versailles came into effect in January, 1920, the French realized that they would be hard
pressed to enforce obedience to the treaty. Germany was
unreconciled to defeat. The armed assistance of America and
Britain could not be counted upon. The French set out to
devise new guarantees to protect the *status quo;* these will
be described later. France also set out to convince the Germans that resistance was futile; in this task France achieved
temporary success, though at terrible cost.

There were in France two opinions as to the correct way
of dealing with Germany. One was that represented by
Poincaré and supported by the conservative elements in the
country. The France of Poincaré and his followers was
dominated by a mood strangely compounded of confidence
and fear, hate and religious exaltation. France had stood
firm through four years with the invader on her territory,
and France had won: victory filled the French with buoyant
confidence. French territory had been devastated and French
man-power drained: France hated the Germans for the
misery and the losses of the war. French resistance had
been strained to the breaking point; France had won only
with the aid of allies who had now deserted her; the population of France was still far below that of Germany.
Therefore, the French were afraid. France, the France of
Poincaré, felt she had conquered no ordinary foe, but the
foe of freedom and civilization. The Germans were savages
who must be kept in subjection. It was not French hegemony
which must be protected; it was civilization, of which France
was the guardian. To this task the French dedicated themselves with holy zeal. They expected aid, aid for the struggle
against barbarism, not merely for France. When the aid was
not forthcoming, when her actions were criticized or opposed, France saw civilization betrayed. Such were the
views of French nationalists. Most Frenchmen responded at

times to the nationalist exhortation and when thus aroused were ready to strike out in rage and hate against Germany.

There was another France, a France which asked only to be safe. When not frightened or angered, most of the people of France realized that Germany could not be exterminated, and that to hold a rebellious Germany in forcible subjection permanently would be expensive and difficult, if not impossible. The parties of the left held to these facts. Increasingly, Aristide Briand became their spokesman. Briand was premier in the terrible year of Verdun, and, he said later, he was convinced that France must not and could not go through another such ordeal. He was not prepared to surrender the position France had won, but he denied that the position of France could be preserved by bayonets alone. Time, he believed, would give other guarantees to France. The map of Eastern Europe had been completely redrawn; the new states must have time to acquire stability and strength. Time would dull the edge of war passions and enable France, Germany, and the rest of the world to see that peace was their greatest need. The need for peace recognized, coöperation and mutual concession in the interests of peace would follow. All this would come in time—if the time could be had.

A similar cleavage in popular opinion was appearing in Germany. When the armistice was signed, the Germans were in a humble mood. A profound reaction began against the materialism and worship of power which had dominated German life since Bismarck. In search of new standards, Germans reached back to the older traditions of their history, to art, music, philosophy, and literature. In this atmosphere, the national assembly met—met, significantly, at that center of liberal culture, Weimar. Then came the conditions of peace. With one voice the Germans declared they had been tricked and betrayed. They had surrendered their arms on the agreement that the Fourteen Points were to serve as the basis for peace. That agreement, they maintained, was violated by the treaty, unless, as the reparations claims implied, Germany had deliberately forced Europe into war. If Germany had committed this crime, then it might be just to decree that Germany was not fit to possess colonies, that Germany could not be trusted with arms, that Germany should be forced to pay tribute, and that Germany must lose all territory which would be taken under the principle of self-determination, but should not gain when the principle worked to her advantage, as in the case of Austria. The Germans vehemently denied that they were worthy of such punishment. They did not claim, at least for some years after 1919, that Germany bore no share of the blame for the coming of war; they argued that responsibility rested on both sides. Further, they contended, it was unfair to indict a whole nation for matters of state of which most Germans had known nothing, and it was still more unjust to punish children who were unborn when the war started. To the German people, the treaty had no moral justification; its only sanction was force.

Momentarily, some Germans thought relief might come through the League, even though Germany had not been admitted to membership. That hope soon vanished. The Germans protested to the League against the manner in which the plebiscites were conducted in Eupen and Malmédy; the protests were disregarded. The Germans protested against the efforts of the French representative on the Saar commission to bind the Saar economically and politically to France; the protests were unheeded. The League Council gave the most valuable districts of Upper Silesia to Poland. The League commission on disarmament talked and did nothing. The League, Germans concluded, was only a means to perpetuate the helplessness of Germany. The old game of force was to go on, but played with loaded dice. Germany, having been tricked into surrendering her arms by false promises, was to be kept helpless, helpless not merely to regain her losses but also to protect herself from her heavily armed neighbors.

Against the thought of permanent subjection to force the German spirit rebelled. Yet the Allies had overwhelming force at their disposal. Subjection was both intolerable and inescapable. This was the tragic dilemma before the German people; but the human mind cannot believe in the existence of such a dilemma. What individual Germans have done ever since the war is confusedly to insist that one alternative must be true and the other false. In 1919 only those Germans who were most miserable were prepared to insist that the condition of Germany was intolerable, but escapable. These were the very lowest classes, who believed that communism would furnish an escape, and the aristocracy, who could not believe that the Germany they had known, the Germany in which their power and position were supreme, was gone forever. Both of these groups resorted to terroristic tactics in order to compel acceptance of their views. Hating each other, poles apart in every other respect, the Communists and the reactionaries were agreed in believing that the Republic must be overthrown; for the Republican leaders insisted that the subjugation of Germany was inescapable but tolerable, because temporary.

The Republicans maintained that the power of the Allies was absolute. If Germany revolted, the horrors of invasion, probably of partition, must be undergone. The position of Germany would then be worse than before. On the other hand, the Republicans believed that if Germany submitted, time would bring freedom. The very harshness of the Versailles settlement would in the end compel revision when the fury of the victors abated and they could see what they had attempted to do. War passions would only subside, however, if the Germans submitted, and if by loyal efforts to fulfil the treaty they showed that it could not be fulfilled. Time would also show the injustice of the treaty. The Allies justified the treaty on the assumption that Germany had been guilty of causing the war. The falsity of that assumption could, the Republicans argued, be demonstrated. To show that Germany was not guilty, the government threw open the archives to historical students and began the publication of diplomatic documents bearing on the origins of the war.

Time must be gained—time to show that the treaty could

not be fulfilled, time to show that the treaty was unjust, time to allow war passions to cool. The majority of the German people unenthusiastically accepted the Republican program. The first election under the new constitution showed marked gains for the extremists, but the government was able to suppress without difficulty the Communist and reactionary revolts which took place in 1919 and 1920. Despite these successes, the position of the government was precarious. The government based its policy of fulfilment on the contention that conditions might be worse if the Allies were defied and might become better if Germany submitted to the Allies. If the latter hope was not realized, if the plight of Germany became worse, more and more Germans would go over to the extremists.

Whether time would have reconciled Germany and France, as the moderate parties in both countries hoped, is very dubious indeed. To Germans, reconciliation implied the consent of France to substantial changes, territorial, military, and economic, in the Treaty of Versailles. To Frenchmen, reconciliation implied the acceptance by Germany of the Treaty of Versailles without substantial change. In any case time could not be had: the reparations question refused to wait on time for solution. The citizens of each country, disregarding the reservation that time was necessary, made reparations the test of desire for reconciliation; using this test, each country easily satisfied itself that the desire for reconciliation was non-existent in the other country.

The Germans saw only the incontestable fact that the Allies were demanding more than Germany could possibly pay. From this fact the German nationalists concluded that the real purpose of the Allies was to weaken Germany still further; reparations, like disarmament, were to keep Germany weak and thereby perpetuate the artificial hegemony of France. The German governmental policy of fulfilment served the purposes of those who would keep Germany in chains. Fulfilment meant, not liberation, but a lessened chance of liberation, argued the German nationalists. There was some truth in the argument. French nationalists were as much concerned to render Germany impotent as they were to collect money. The German government was in an awkward predicament. The only way to convince the Allies that the reparations claims of the treaty were economically unworkable was by a sincere effort to pay; otherwise, the Allies could claim that failure resulted from German bad faith. On the other hand, the policy of fulfilment was full of danger, danger that the Allies would refuse to moderate their demands and danger that the German people would revolt.

The French government was in an equally difficult position. The French people saw only the incontestable fact that the Germans were not paying to the limit of their capacity. From this fact French nationalists concluded that the real purpose of Germany was to repudiate reparations. If the Germans were successful, two results would follow. One part of the Treaty of Versailles would be broken; the Germans would then proceed to attack other parts. Already the task of disarming Germany was proving difficult. If the Germans won on reparations, they would next concentrate on arms, then on the occupation of the Rhineland, then on the territorial settlement. Eventually France would be confronted by the old saber-rattling Germany. Further, if Germany did not pay, France must pay for the fruits of German aggression: war debts and the reconstruction of the devastated areas. To moderate the reparations demands would, therefore, strengthen German desire and capacity to overthrow the Treaty of Versailles and weaken the capacity of France to prevent Germany from once more dominating the Continent. There was some truth in the argument of the French nationalists: the German nationalists did regard the attack on the reparations clauses as the first battle in the struggle to overthrow the Treaty of Versailles. The French government, if it attempted to lessen the burden of reparations, had no guarantee either that Germany would honor the new agreement or that French opinion would permit a readjustment.

In these circumstances, the French, German, and British

governments tried to temporize. The Allies, in terror of their own people, were afraid to take the initiative in proposing reduction. The Treaty of Versailles stipulated that the total of reparations must be fixed by May, 1921, and that prior to that date the Allies would consider any offer Germany might make. The Allies tried to get an acceptable offer from Germany. A settlement proposed by Germany would obviously have a stronger guarantee of payment than one imposed on Germany. To secure this advantage Allied opinion might be content with a smaller sum. The German government, fearing that a large offer would precipitate revolt in Germany, never came forward with acceptable proposals. The Allies were forced to wait until the Allied Reparations Commission fixed the total liability for reconstruction and pensions. The sum fixed was 132 billions of gold marks, or thirty-three billions of dollars. There was little possibility that such an amount could be paid by Germany. To bring the payments within reasonable limits and at the same time to prevent a popular outcry in Allied countries, the French and British governments decided that Germany must deliver three sets of bonds, called A, B, and C. Payments on the principal and interest of the A and B bonds, totaling about $12,500,000,000, were to begin at once. Payment on the C bonds was deferred until it should become apparent that Germany could bear the burden—that is, the C bonds would probably turn out to be waste paper.

The scheme was a clever one and might have worked had not the Allies demanded the payment of $250,000,000 within twenty-five days. This was the last and greatest of a series of similar errors. Ever since 1919 economists had been urging that, before large reparations payments could begin, Germany must have time to repair the damages which the war had inflicted on her industrial structure. The Allied governments were afraid to heed these warnings: public opinion demanded immediate payments. The German government made the payments demanded so far as it could, just as it accepted, after an ultimatum had been received from the Allies, the terms of May, 1921. But the German government knew that there would be a revolution if the attempt were made to raise such sums by taxation. Like all desperate governments, the German government had resort to the printing-press. The result was a foregone conclusion. The currency was inflated to meet each payment; each issue of paper marks drove the paper money lower in value, so the next payment required still greater amounts of paper money. With each new issue, domestic prices went higher, slowly when inflation first began, then faster and faster. Wages lagged somewhat behind prices, salaries far behind, while returns from investments remained unchanged. This process had been going on since 1920. The payments demanded by the Allies in the second half of 1921 caused the first really precipitous fall—in one month the mark lost half of its value.

At this rate Germany would soon be bankrupt. The government informed the Allies that a breathing space was necessary. Lloyd George agreed. British industry was stagnant and could not revive until the buying power of the Continent revived; Continental buying power could not revive while currencies were in chaos and credit relationships were in a state of complete uncertainty. Lloyd George succeeded in convoking a conference at Cannes in January, 1922. He succeeded in convincing Briand that there must be a moratorium on reparations payments, and that a conference to effect the economic reconstruction of Europe was necessary. To placate French fears, Britain was prepared to make a new treaty of guarantee with France. Briand was willing to negotiate, but French opinion was not. Briand had just returned from the Washington Conference; there his pleas for security had been rebuffed and France had been condemned for refusing to be coerced by Britain and America. France saw her security under attack. Britain and America demanded that France give up her means of defense; Britain demanded that, since the Germans did not like reparations, reparations be abandoned. In return, Britain was willing to promise aid if Germany attacked France. No! France would protect herself, and she would force the

Germans to obey the treaty. Briand was repudiated. Poincaré became premier.

Poincaré was forced to concur in the partial moratorium arranged at Cannes. Further than that he refused to go. He pointed out that German factories were busy, that there was no unemployment in Germany, that the night life of Berlin was the most extravagant in Europe. He failed to see that these were signs of a diseased condition. With the mark sliding, always sliding, money lost its value almost overnight. It was folly to save. Money must be spent before it became worthless. So the Germans spent all they had. Poincaré also pointed out that part of Germany's troubles resulted from the flight of German capital. Germans were investing their money abroad, particularly in America; they were doing this, Poincaré maintained, in order to cheat France. Again, Poincaré mistook a symptom for the disease. It was folly for Germans to buy German securities repayable in marks. Naturally Germans bought American currency and securities; these were not depreciating in value. Of economics M. Poincaré showed lamentable ignorance, but it is probable that he wilfully blinded himself.

Poincaré saw only one thing: Germany was in revolt against the treaty. Poincaré would hear of only one remedy: Germany must be crushed. Germany was, indeed, in revolt; but it was the economic folly of the reparations settlement which enabled the German nationalists to compel abandonment of the policy of fulfilment. Poincaré was to find that he could crush a helpless Germany, but that he could not collect what was not there to collect. He had to wait a year before he could try the experiment, because the moratorium barred the Reparations Commission from declaring Germany in default. During that year Lloyd George tried vainly to avert the consequences of the reparations clauses which he had helped to frame. The European economic conference he had summoned met at Genoa in April, 1922, but it was a farce, a tragic farce. Poincaré refused to attend. Lloyd George's slippery tactics aroused the mistrust even of the Germans and the Russians. Fearing he was playing them off one against the other, the German and Russian delegates met at Rapallo and concluded a treaty of commerce and friendship. News of the Treaty of Rapallo threw the Genoa conference into a flutter: the vanquished were uniting. The conference adjourned, nothing accomplished. A few months later the British overthrew Lloyd George in disgust at his failures both in Europe and Asia. The new Prime Minister, Bonar Law, took up the task of restraining Poincaré, with no better success. In December, 1922, the French delegate succeeded in getting the Reparations Commission to declare Germany in default on timber deliveries. The default was almost ridiculously unimportant. As the British delegate angrily declared: "Since, in the tenth year of the war, Troy fell to the stratagem of the wooden horse, history recorded no similar use of timber." The British had one weapon left. They declared that Germany could not be punished for default without the unanimous consent of the Allies. Poincaré brushed the argument aside.

In January, 1923, French and Belgian troops occupied the Ruhr, Germany's most valuable industrial area. Poincaré said that the occupation would continue until reparations were paid; apparently he meant the whole reparations bill. His purpose, he declared, was "to obtain the good-will of Germany." Undoubtedly that was his purpose: if Germany could be convinced that it was useless to fight, then France and Germany could be very good friends. Whether he failed to realize that no self-respecting nation could accept good relations on such terms or whether he thought the Germans unfit to possess self-respect is uncertain. The fact that he believed good relations could be purchased by methods like the Ruhr invasion is, however, a good example of the temper of post-war nationalism. The Germans could not fight; neither could they surrender. They resorted to passive resistance. All reparations payments were stopped. All German officials, managers, and industrial workers in the Ruhr ceased work. They were fed by the German government. A new war, bloodless but terrible, began. To appreciate what happened in 1923, one must have traveled in France and

Germany then. One must have seen the still-devastated provinces of France and learned from Frenchmen of the fear and hate which drove them on to conquer at all costs. Then one must have seen the German government and the German people fighting, with nothing but will-power, against what they thought slavery. The mark was slipping too fast for the German government to collect by taxation the sums necessary to feed the Ruhr workers. The printing-presses worked faster. One million, two million, a hundred million marks to the dollar—it was maddening, trying to spend marks before they became worthless. There could be but one end. By September, 1923, the German government was bankrupt. The mark was worthless. Resistance could not continue. Contrary to the expectation of German nationalists, France would and could compel German submission. The Stresemann government abandoned passive resistance; the Ruhr must submit to France.

Germany had been beaten to her knees. Poincaré had won. He had not, however, collected reparations. Instead, he had driven Germany into bankruptcy, and thereby jeopardized the future collection of reparations. The French grumbled; they had wanted money as well as submission. Soon they were frightened. Ever since the war the French budget had shown a deficit, which had been met by loans. The French government had promised that these loans were to be repaid out of reparations receipts. Now the possibility of securing reparations seemed remote. It was doubtful if the French government could repay all it had borrowed. French loans and French currency began to depreciate. France was going the road Germany had gone.

Faced with discontent and a shaky credit structure at home, Poincaré lost his intransigence. For two years Britain and America had argued that the problem of reparations must be approached as a problem in economics, not politics. In November, 1923, Poincaré agreed to an expert inquiry into the situation. He insisted on concealing his retreat: the experts were to find means of balancing the German budget and of bringing home the German capital which had been

sent abroad. The other governments consented to this subterfuge. The world was treated to another of the farces
made necessary by the delicate sensibilities of post-war
nationalism: the commission which must unravel the reparations tangle received instructions from which the word
reparations was carefully excluded! There was one other
comic aspect of the commission. The United States had
found that it could not prosper in a troubled world. Therefore, American delegates sat on the commission. But the
myth of isolation was maintained. The American delegates
were "unofficial."

The commission lost no time in getting down to its real
business. A committee was, to be sure, appointed for the
purpose of determining how German capital could be
brought home and kept there. The committee reported what
all economists knew: the only solution was to make Germans
feel that their investments would be safe at home; that
necessitated financial stability, which necessitated a solution
of the reparations question. Similarly, the German budget
could not be balanced until reparations payments were
brought within reasonable limits. Therefore the budget committee, which was headed by General Dawes, plunged without ado into the reparations question.

The political and economic conditions which prevailed
when the experts began their deliberations in January, 1924,
precluded a definitive solution of the reparations question.
Germany was prostrate. The old mark was worthless. In
November, 1923, a new currency, called the *Rentenmark,*
was created. Theoretically it was backed by a mortgage on
German land and industrial plants. Practically there was no
backing: the German government did not have possession
of the assets which it professed to mortgage. The German
people were glad, however, to have a currency of any kind.
Temporarily the new mark circulated at par, but if confidence in the government was shaken, the new mark would
go the way of the old. The end of inflation brought frenzied
spending and manufacturing to an abrupt stop in Germany.
Trade was limited to the bare necessities of life; innumer-

able firms collapsed. What the experts saw was a great industrial plant which had almost ceased functioning. To start the plant, credit and confidence were needed. After ten years of almost uninterrupted suffering, the courage of the German people was exhausted: They had hoped during the war; that hope proved false. They had hoped for a peace of reconciliation; that hope proved false. They had tried first to fulfil and then to break the treaty; both attempts failed. Now, the middle class was ruined, its savings wiped out by inflation. Inflation had consumed all the liquid capital which the Allies had left, so that the buying of raw materials and the payment of wages could not be financed; business could not revive until new capital was found. The apathy of despair hung over Germany: why make new efforts when the demands of the Allies will bring new collapse? Before German economic life could revive, hope must revive.

On one side of the Rhine, Germany sunk in despair; on the other, France angrily insistent on her treaty rights. The experts were economists. The problems before them were so intimately connected with morbid emotional conditions that solutions which were economically possible might prove unworkable. Furthermore, economic conditions ever since the war had been disturbed. The experts must end these disturbances, so far as reparations were the cause of trouble. It was impossible to say what would be economically possible when normal conditions had been established. In these circumstances, the experts decided that it was impossible to devise a definitive reparations plan. A period of experiment was necessary. Therefore, the experts contented themselves with a tentative scheme.

Throughout the Dawes Plan this tentative, experimental purpose was apparent. The first recommendation was that an international loan of 200 millions of dollars be made to Germany. The proceeds of this loan would provide a gold reserve for German currency and would provide funds out of which the initial reparations payment could be made. The machinery thus started, subsequent payments involved two operations which the experts considered separately. The committee thought it possible to determine the amount Germany could collect for reparations. Part of this amount was to be furnished by German industry and railroads, the rest by taxation. A schedule was worked out, calling for small collections at first, rising to over 600 millions of dollars in 1928–1929, and remaining constant thereafter. When the sums were collected, it was necessary to transfer them to the creditor countries. The experts realized that payment could not be made in gold; payment must be made in goods or services. Would Germany develop an export trade large enough to provide the foreign exchange needed for the transfer of reparations payments? Only time could answer that question. Here more than anywhere else the provisional nature of the Dawes Plan was apparent. A collector-general of reparations, Mr. S. Parker Gilbert, was to be stationed in Berlin. He was to receive the funds collected by the German government. If foreign exchange could be bought without endangering the German currency, he was to transfer the marks into francs, pounds, etc. If, for instance, Germany exported in goods and services a million marks more than was imported, Mr. Gilbert would buy up these surplus claims against foreign buyers and reimburse the German exporter out of the funds collected by the German government. If, however, Germany had no surplus of exports in any year, Mr. Gilbert would be unable to buy foreign currencies, except in exchange for gold. The experts prohibited him from transferring collections in gold. Therefore, if Germany did not have an export balance in her favor, funds were not to be transferred to the Allied creditors.

The initial loan to Germany, the ascending schedule of charges, and the safeguards against exporting gold—these were the most important recommendations of the experts. If they were accepted, the experts believed German industry and commerce would revive; prosperity would return; then a final solution of the reparations payments would be possible. The Dawes Plan contained two further important statements. The plan must, the experts warned, be accepted as a whole or not at all. Furthermore, all calculations were based on the assumption that "the fiscal and economic unity of the Reich will be restored." Both these conditions made the French unhappy. They were asked to agree to a scheme which, at best, promised annuities lower than the Allies demanded in 1921, and which might, if German foreign trade did not develop, bring in nothing at all. In order to secure even this reparations settlement, France must promise to get out of the Ruhr. France did accept, after much wrangling. The plan went into effect on October 31, 1924.

From 1920 to 1923 France tried to compel obedience to the reparations clauses of the Treaty of Versailles. Since the Dawes Plan greatly modified the earlier demands of the Allies, the efforts of France might be said to have ended in failure. This was only partly true. The Ruhr invasion demonstrated that the attempt to collect money by armed force was futile and expensive. On the other hand, France had been seeking more than money. France had sought to convince the Germans that, if they defied France, they would be forced to surrender; in that task France had succeeded. In 1918, Germany was defeated by the Grand Alliance; in 1923, Germany was defeated by France. The French now felt reassured. The policy of Poincaré was no longer necessary. He fell in June, 1924, and the moderate parties resumed the task of conciliating the beaten foe. In Germany, the nationalists were discredited by failure. Those who advocated the policy of fulfilment, now led by Stresemann, were once more in power. The Dawes Plan was hailed throughout Europe as a second armistice which would facilitate the making of a lasting peace.

When the French invaded the Ruhr, their motive was as much political as economic: they were convinced that a second defeat of Germany was essential before the *status quo* established by the Peace of Paris could be stabilized. Simultaneously the French were seeking other guarantees for their supremacy. To facilitate the task of repelling a German invasion, France sought to detach the Rhineland from the Reich. To unite the forces of those powers which would suffer from any alteration in the *status quo,* France built up a system of defensive alliances, as Bismarck had done after 1871. To lessen the burden on her strength, France tried to strengthen the guarantees against aggression provided by the League of Nations.

The French have consistently contended that the movement for the separation of the Rhineland from Germany was a purely local affair in which they adopted a neutral attitude. The facts belie the French contention and show conclusively that the separatist movement would never have attained importance without French support. Because of the uncompromising refusal of Britain to countenance the forcible separation of the Rhineland from Germany, the French were obliged to restrict their activities to the encouragement of separatist groups in the districts occupied by French and Belgian troops. At first this encouragement was limited to protection of separatist leaders, like Dr. Dorten, against arrest by the German police. When the Ruhr was occupied, French actions became a travesty of neutrality. In retaliation for German passive resistance, the French expelled many of the regular officials from the Rhineland and confiscated all fire-arms, even those of the police. The separatists, on the other hand, were allowed to bear arms; in fact they were frequently armed with the weapons which had been taken from the police. Separatist bands were transported in official Franco-Belgian trains; French troops, under the pretense of maintaining order, prevented the inhabitants of villages and cities from resisting the separatists. These examples of unneutral French actions might be multiplied many times. With such favoritism shown them, the separatists were able to seize power in the French and Belgian zones. Unfortunately for French hopes, however, the movement was almost completely devoid of local support, while the separatists were incompetent at best and were all too frequently recruited from the criminal class. These circumstances, combined with steady British opposition, ensured the failure of the movement. By February,

1924, the separatists had been forced to surrender their power, and to seek safety in flight. The only result was to intensify the hatred for France which the use of colored troops had already aroused among the Germans of the occupied areas.

French efforts to establish a buffer state along their eastern frontier were prompted by the belief that the Rhine was the only safe protection, not merely for France, but for civilization. Unless the Rhine was held, Foch argued in 1919, Western Europe would be "submerged by the devastating floods of barbarian warfare which find no dyke to arrest them." The French system of alliances also had its origin in the desire to erect a wall against which the waves of barbarism would beat in vain. The Belgians, like the French, were dominated after the war by fear and hatred of Germany. Fear was intensified by two insignificant territorial gains made by Belgium at the expense of Germany —Eupen and Malmédy. Plebiscites were held in these areas, after they had been transferred to Belgium. The Germans claimed with justice that the polling was held under unfair conditions, and they refused to recognize the validity of the result. The Belgians feared that in a new Franco-German war their country would again be the battle-field and that the Germans would seize the districts Belgium had just won. To guard against these dangers, Belgium entered into military discussions with France. In September, 1920, a defensive alliance was signed. Thereafter, joint military preparations were made, and France had the assurance that Belgium would not serve again as the highroad for a German invasion.

Foch and Clemenceau saw only barbarism and confusion east of the Rhine; accordingly, their efforts were concentrated on the acquisition of an impregnable frontier to the east. Clemenceau's successors speedily reverted to the policy pursued by France before the war. The Russian alliance was gone, but the new states of Eastern Europe enabled France once more to expose Germany to the danger of a war on two fronts. In 1920, Poland was saved from a Russian invasion by French munitions and a French military mission under General Weygand. The union thus established was cemented in 1921 by an alliance. Thereafter France bent her efforts to the task of transforming her backward peasant ally into a modern industrial and military state. French efforts secured most of the mining and manufacturing districts of Upper Silesia for Poland, despite the fact that the plebiscite held in March, 1921, showed a substantial majority for union with Germany. The French munitions industry was linked to the Polish; French loans and French experts provided the sinews and the brains for the economic life of the new state. In Poland's thirty millions of people France saw an ally strong enough to be of use and not strong enough to disregard French wishes, as Russia had been able to do.

Czechoslovakia offered similar advantages to France. The long, narrow new state contained substantial, and discontented, German and Magyar minorities. Bohemia was a salient thrust into German-speaking Central Europe. This geographical position was most uncomfortable for the Czechs. If Germany and Austria were united, the enlarged German state would be under strong temptation to seize the Bohemian salient. For France, the situation of Czechoslovakia was an advantage. If war came, the Czechs could, with the assistance of Poland, seize the remnant of Upper Silesia which had been left to Germany. As the Ruhr, the other industrial area of Germany, was placed at the mercy of France by the demilitarization of the Rhineland, Germany would almost at the outbreak of war lose the districts most essential for war. The alliance concluded by France with Czechoslovakia in 1924 was, therefore, the complement to the alliance with Poland.

In turning to the east for allies, France was primarily seeking protection against Germany. The French were anxious, not merely to lessen the chance of a German attack on France by exposing Germany to the certainty of a war on two fronts. France was also guarding against a revival of German strength which would be the prelude to attack on

France. If Germany succeeded in wiping out the Polish Corridor and in reconquering Upper Silesia from Poland, Germany would be greatly strengthened in man-power and industrial resources. If Germany succeeded in her avowed purpose to add the six and a half millions of Austrians to the Reich, Germany would be more populous than before the war and would be in a position to dominate the affairs of southeastern Europe. France had, therefore, a direct and vital interest in seeing that the eastern boundaries of Germany remained unchanged.

The alliances with Poland and Czechoslovakia involved France in other problems as well, problems in which her interest was less direct. Poland feared Soviet Russia no less than Germany. The Treaty of Riga, signed in 1921, settled the Russo-Polish frontier, but there was no certainty that the Bolsheviks might not tear up the treaty if they felt strong enough to do so. For protection, Poland turned to Rumania. The Rumanians had not even a treaty to guarantee their frontier with Russia. The Rumanians had seized Bessarabia; the Bolsheviks refused to surrender their claim to that province. In 1921, Poland and Rumania concluded a defensive alliance by which each promised aid to the other in case of a Russian attack. France had decided that Poland must be made and kept strong; France could not sit with folded hands if Russia defeated Poland in a war caused by the Bessarabian problem. The far-off Russian frontier became the anxious concern of France. French munitions went to Rumania early in the post-war years; in 1926, France concluded a defensive alliance with Rumania. The alliance with Czechoslovakia had similar ramifications. In Slovakia there were large minorities of Magyars living along the Hungarian frontier. Czechoslovakia was, therefore, as much afraid of Hungary as of Germany. Rumania and Jugoslavia were also uneasily conscious of the Magyars within their borders. The natural result was an alliance, the Little Entente, created in 1920–1921 for the purpose of guaranteeing the Treaty of Trianon. The Little Entente involved France in the task of keeping the unruly Magyars from claiming their oppressed fellow-countrymen; and the Little Entente, through Jugoslavia, brought France into contact with Adriatic questions—that is, with Italy. Later, in 1927, France completed the circle of alliances by a defensive treaty with Jugoslavia.

Between 1921 and 1927, France concluded defensive alliances with Poland, Czechoslovakia, Rumania, and Jugoslavia. Like Bismarck's League of Peace, each of these alliances was designed to strengthen some part of the European *status quo*. The French were convinced that, if the *status quo* was violently disturbed at any point, the whole structure created by the peace treaties would be weakened and French security jeopardized. French interests required the alliances, even though the alliances had to be buttressed by loans, and even though they involved France in all the conflicts of a troubled Continent. The French protested that they were serving not merely their interests but the interests of Europe. France sought peace; surely peace would be the greatest boon which providence could confer on Europe. The organization of peace was properly not the task of one power or of one group of powers; it was the task of all nations. Beginning in 1923, the French sought to shift to the League of Nations at least a part of the responsibility for preserving the *status quo*.

During the first years of its existence, the influence of the League on world politics was insignificant. An able Secretariat was organized, composed of experts on all questions of international importance. These enthusiastic believers in international coöperation succeeded in making Geneva a clearing-house for information and in drawing most of the long-established agencies for facilitating intercourse between states under the ægis of the League. In this way, the League quickly demonstrated its usefulness, and its continued existence was assured. The League had, however, been created to ensure peace and thereby to make possible the reduction of armaments. There could be no doubt that the League was not fulfilling the purpose of the Covenant.

Two episodes set the failure in glaring relief. After the war, the frontier between Poland and Lithuania remained in dispute. In October, 1920, a frontier was established by a League commission, and accepted by both governments. No sooner was the arrangement completed than it was upset by the seizure of Vilna, which had been allotted to Lithuania, by an irregular Polish force. All efforts to dislodge the Poles proved fruitless. In 1923, the Allied Conference of Ambassadors acquiesced in the accomplished fact, and awarded the city to Poland. In the same year, the prestige of the League was further impaired by the Corfu episode. In August, 1923, four Italians who were delimiting the frontier between Greece and Albania were murdered. Mussolini, who had seized control over the Italian government, utilized the incident to make a spectacular demonstration of Fascist determination to protect the honor of Italy. An ultimatum, far more severe than that sent by Austria to Serbia in 1914, was despatched to Greece. Greece accepted part of the demands and offered to submit the dispute to the League. In reply, the Italians bombarded and occupied the island of Corfu. The exceptional brutality of the Italian action profoundly shocked European opinion. The League proved impotent. Only when all their demands were satisfied did the Italians quit Corfu.

The French contended that the League was impotent because the Covenant did not provide with sufficient exactitude for the action to be taken against an aggressor. Until the mechanism for repelling acts of aggression was perfected, there could be no guarantee of security except armaments. Therefore, if the League was to serve its function of ensuring peace and of facilitating the reduction of armaments, the Covenant must be strengthened. By 1923, the League committee which was studying the disarmament problem had become lost in a bog of technicalities, and it was alarmed by the swiftly vanishing prestige of the League. The French contention might rescue the League. The disarmament commission laid aside its technical studies and turned to the problem of security. In 1923 the Draft Treaty of Mutual Assistance was submitted to the powers. The treaty met with widespread criticism, especially in the British Empire. In 1924 an effort was made to meet these criticisms in a revised version, the Geneva Protocol.

The Geneva Protocol was, and remains, a perfected scheme of international organization—from the French point of view. Every dispute must be settled by arbitration or by conciliation. There were no loopholes, as under the Covenant. Where existing international law covered the case, both parties must abide by the law. Where no legal precedent could be found, the case must be decided either by the League Council or by a board of conciliation in the way which gave the maximum of justice to the claims of both sides. A solution must be found, and, once found, it must be obeyed. A state which refused to accept the award, or which in any way prejudiced the peaceful solution of a dispute was *ipso facto* the aggressor. Against the aggressor, all signatories of the Protocol bound themselves to act with all the resources, military and economic, at their command. Security would, therefore, be absolute. Reduction of armaments could now commence. The Protocol was to go into effect only after a disarmament conference had been held and brought to a successful conclusion.

Practically, the Protocol would perpetuate the *status quo*. Only where no law existed could changes be made. The Peace of Paris was a conspicuous part of the law of nations. Bound to enforce obedience to law, all boards of arbitration and conciliation must enforce obedience to the Peace of Paris. Defense of the *status quo* as established by the peace treaties would be the duty of all signatories of the Protocol. France would no longer be forced to rely on her own efforts to safeguard her own position and the position of her allies. France must, of course, sacrifice her freedom of action by agreeing to submit all disputes in which she was involved to international adjudication. France was quite willing to make this sacrifice. France wanted only to hold what she had. Under the Protocol the judges must protect what France legally possessed.

France was willing to submit to a rule of law because France was not confident that she could maintain unaided the position she had won in Europe. Britain felt strong enough to protect herself unaided; so Britain was unwilling to place herself under the obligation either to obey or to enforce the decisions of an international tribunal. When the British, and the Americans, spoke of their desire to preserve their isolation, they were actually expressing their determination to tolerate no restraints on their freedom of action. The British did not give impatience at restraint as the reason for their dislike of the Protocol. Instead, they pointed an embarrassed finger at the United States. The Protocol demanded action against any power which refused to submit disputes to an international tribunal. The United States had stated in no uncertain terms its refusal to submit to such restraints. This attitude would make the United States the aggressor in any dispute in which it might be involved. Britain would then have to fight the United States. Britain was not willing to risk an armed encounter with the United States over issues which were not immediate British concerns. So far the British argument was a strong one, and the French would probably have been willing to change the Protocol so that cases where a collision with the United States was to be feared might be excluded from the scope of the Protocol. The British raised another objection. The effect of the Protocol, they pointed out, was to guarantee the territorial *status quo*. England did not feel that her interests were affected by changes in many parts of the world, in Eastern Europe for instance. Conditions in Western Europe did affect vital British interests. Britain would be glad to make an agreement which would apply the principles of the Protocol to Western Europe. Greater responsibilities Britain would not assume.

In modified form, Britain proposed to revive the treaty of guarantee which Clemenceau had sought and which Poincaré had rejected as worthless. In its earlier form, the guarantee had protected France against a German attack. Sir Austen Chamberlain, the British Foreign Secretary, now

wished to protect Germany also against attack. The proposal
was welcomed in Berlin. The Ruhr invasion and the separatist movement had shown that France, in her search for
security, might seize more German territory and that Germany would be powerless to resist. With Germany disarmed
and the Rhineland demilitarized, the Rhine country, including the invaluable resources of the Ruhr, was at the mercy
of France. Even the industrial capitalists of the Ruhr, who
usually supported the nationalists, were frightened by the
realization of this danger. If Germany could get a guarantee against further territorial losses, the German government was prepared to defy the nationalists by formally
abandoning all hope of recovering Alsace-Lorraine. As
either French or German control over the whole Rhine
valley would endanger British defense of the Channel, the
British were willing to extend their guarantee to include
Germany. But further than that they refused to go. By
October, 1924, it was apparent that the Geneva Protocol
would not, for the present at least, go into effect.

The British decision aroused once more in France the
anger which had led to the Ruhr invasion. As in 1922, the
French dismissed as worthless the offer of a guarantee limited to the Franco-German frontier. The *status quo* established by the peace treaty stood or fell as a whole. If
Germany gained territory and power in the east, Germany
would once more be supreme on the Continent. If left to
their fate by France, the states of Eastern Europe must
make terms with Germany. France must aid her eastern
allies or fall to the position of a minor state. Once more
France was filled with a sense of outraged justice: Britain
had helped to establish the Continental *status quo;* Britain
had garnered her share of the fruits of war; now Britain
turned her back on the situation she had helped to create.
France prepared to resist. Under the terms of the Treaty
of Versailles, the Cologne zone of the occupied area was
to be evacuated in January, 1925, if Germany had fulfilled
all her obligations under the treaty up to that date. France
seized on some minor infractions of the disarmament clauses

of the treaty by Germany as an excuse for refusing consent
to evacuation. If France was to be thrown on her own
resources, France would use every legal weapon in her possession to prevent Germany from recapturing Continental
hegemony.

At the beginning of 1925 the favorable effects of the
Dawes Plan threatened to be nullified by a new outburst of
nationalism. France was angered by the defeat of the
Protocol; Germany was angered by the refusal to evacuate
Cologne. Once more, however, the situation was transformed by those swift, incalculable shifts of fortune so
characteristic of the post-war years. The fall of the franc
was halted when the Dawes Plan gave promise of new
reparations payments. The revival of Franco-German antagonism made the future of the reparations plan uncertain.
Faith in French credit began to decline, and the decline was
reflected in a rapid fall in the value of the franc. While
French financial power was ebbing, French military power
was suddenly taxed to the utmost. Revolts in Syria,
Morocco, and Tunis forced the withdrawal of nearly all
available troops from Europe. France saw what such an
opportunity might mean to Germany in the future. The
British guarantee against a German attack, from being
worthless, became essential. The French nationalists once
more were repudiated. Briand, once more in power, took up
the negotiations with Germany and Britain.

Briand made all agreements conditional on German admission to the League. The Covenant was not an absolute
guarantee of the *status quo,* but, if strictly enforced, the
provisions of the Covenant would make it difficult for Germany to revise the Treaty of Versailles. The Germans realized this fact, but they agreed to accept membership if
Germany obtained a permanent seat on the Council. A seat
on the Council would imply the reinstatement of Germany
as a great power and would enable Germany more effectively
to protect German minorities in the states of Eastern
Europe. Briand agreed to the German conditions. He next
sought to obtain part of the guarantees which the Protocol

had given. Germany agreed to arbitration treaties with Belgium, France, Czechoslovakia, and Poland. Under these treaties, the signatories agreed to settle all disputes which might arise by arbitration or by conciliation. Germany had, therefore, given up the right to compel a revision of her frontier by force of arms. Germany retained the right to seek a peaceful modification of her eastern frontiers. In the west, Germany, France, and Belgium agreed to respect their existing frontiers with each other and to refrain from war with each other except in self-defense or in accordance with the provisions of the League Covenant. England and Italy pledged their support of the arrangements regarding Germany, France, and Belgium. In case of aggression or refusal to settle a dispute by peaceful means, Britain and Italy promised armed support to the injured party.

The omissions are as significant as the actual terms of these agreements. The possibility of war between Germany and either France or Belgium was diminished by the recognition of the territorial *status quo,* by the agreement to settle all disputes by peaceful means, and by the Anglo-Italian guarantee. Germany promised to settle all disputes with Poland and Czechoslovakia by peaceful means; but Germany did not recognize the inviolability of existing frontiers, and there was here no Anglo-Italian guarantee. France endeavored to remedy this last shortcoming by separate treaties with Poland and Czechoslovakia, promising aid in case of attack. France had, therefore, not got the security provided by the Geneva Protocol. France was determined to maintain the eastern *status quo.* To effect this purpose, France might be forced to fight Germany. Temporary financial and military difficulties forced the French to accept this partial solution of the problem of security. France continued to believe, however, that nothing except absolute and complete guarantees against any disturbance of the *status quo* would give the security necessary for the real pacification of Europe. The problem of security was still unsolved.

In October, 1925, Briand, Stresemann, and Chamberlain met at Locarno to arrange the final details of the treaties,

which were already substantially completed. Locarno was
a perfect conference, because Briand was a perfect dramatic
artist. By his genius he made unwilling French acquiescence
seem an epochal reconciliation between victors and vanquished. The meetings at Locarno were secret, but Briand
provided an abundance of the picturesque details which the
readers of newspapers relished—birthday parties, boat-rides,
luncheons at tiny hamlets, and above all, gracious courtesies
paid to the ladies present. By his skill Briand accomplished
the most difficult task of the diplomat: he gave labors in the
cause of peace the same news value that strife and warlike
gestures possess. The idyllic scenes staged at Locarno appealed to the popular imagination. The war-weary peoples
of Europe were eager to think that strife was past. Locarno,
millions believed, was the beginning of the era men had
looked for in 1918.

CHAPTER IX

CONCLUSION

CHAPTER IX

CONCLUSION

The years following the Peace of Paris exposed the difficulties confronting the post-war world. To each difficulty palliatives were applied. The worth of these palliatives was incontestable: they gave time for the discovery of real remedies. The opportunity was not used. Instead, men mistook palliatives for cures, and were indignant when the evils recurred, often in more virulent form than before. The Washington Conference temporarily lessened the tension which had marked American relations with Britain and Japan before 1921. Contrary to American belief, the questions of naval armaments and the Far East were not solved. Britain had not conceded parity in all categories. Japan had not abandoned her claims in Manchuria. The Dawes Plan took reparations out of politics for a few years and, by helping to restore confidence, allowed Europe to enjoy four years of economic prosperity. The question of reparations was not solved, as men insisted on thinking. Locarno and the entrance of Germany into the League were followed by four years of comparative tranquillity in Franco-German relations, tranquillity which permitted the evacuation of the Rhineland. The French thought Locarno meant German acceptance of the Treaty of Versailles; Germans thought Locarno would be followed by revision of the Treaty of Versailles. Both the French and the Germans were mistaken.

Economic dislocation and political instability remained, their operation temporarily checked. To trace in detail the recurrence, one by one, of the unsolved difficulties would be merely to repeat the analysis already made. New names, new episodes, but all the old elements, enter the story of the years following 1925. Detailed description is, therefore, superfluous. It is merely necessary to show briefly how the more important problems revived.

The Washington Conference ended, the United States returned to "normalcy." American "observers" appeared at international conferences and claimed the right to influence decisions; but America refused to accept any part of the responsibility for enforcing the decisions made. The League was ignored; the Senate refused to permit American entrance into the World Court established by the League. The European nations which owed war debts to the United States were compelled to make funding agreements. In some cases coercion was necessary. The sum total of the debts was over ten billions of dollars. By the terms of the original contracts the United States was entitled to demand interest at the rate of 4¼ per cent. It soon became obvious that none of the borrowers could pay such high interest. Capacity to pay was accepted as the basis for settlement. As capacity varied, the settlements varied. Comparing what would have been received on principal and interest, under the original terms, with the agreements finally made, Britain received a reduction of 19.7 per cent; France, of 52.8 per cent; and Italy, of 75.4 per cent. Of the total obligations, the United States sacrificed by reduction of interest about 43 per cent. Americans liked to speak of this reduction as evidence of generosity; Europeans saw little generosity in asking for all that they were capable of paying. Europeans also complained that the United States made payment in goods difficult by a high protective tariff. With typically nationalistic lack of logic, many of the governments which made this complaint were impeding the payment of reparations by tariffs no less high.

Before the debt question had been disposed of, the naval question revived. Britain was building a fleet of small cruisers. The Americans placed more reliance on large cruisers. The United States asked for a conference to discover means of balancing small and large cruisers, so that American and British strength would be equal. The conference was held at Geneva in 1927. Japan also participated.

The conference turned into a battle of naval experts over technical points, and broke up after six weeks without achieving agreement. Not one man in a hundred in either Britain or America understood the debates at Geneva, but each government blamed the other for failure. Undoubtedly the British had refused to agree to parity as defined by Americans: equality of fighting strength between the two fleets. The British insisted that a true definition of equality must consider "the whole position of the two countries on the sea and their respective risks and vulnerability." America need not defend a world empire: America was protected by two oceans; a blockade of America would be less disastrous, and more difficult, than a blockade of England. Therefore, Britain could not consent to mathematical parity. Americans saw in the British argument a determination to ensure American defeat in a naval engagement; the British saw in the American argument desire to secure a fleet which, concentrated, could defeat the divided British fleet.

Like all unsuccessful conferences, the Geneva conference led to violent debate in Britain and America. In the United States, the "big navy" party immediately introduced a bill for the construction of cruisers: Britain was to be shown the futility of refusing mathematical parity. The peace party insisted that conciliation be tried. The result of the efforts of the peace party was the Kellogg Pact, signed at Paris in August, 1928. Although it originated in a suggestion made by Briand, the pact perfectly expressed American pacifist sentiment. All the signatory powers bound themselves to renounce the use of war as an instrument of national policy. What did this promise mean? It did not mean, first of all, that defensive wars were outlawed. The obvious difficulty of distinguishing between offensive and defensive war was at once suggested. Briand wished to provide means for determining whether or not a war was aggressive, and for punishing an aggressor. The American government rebuffed these suggestions. The pact must rely for enforcement on the good faith of the signatory powers. How much dependence could be placed on good faith? To what extent had security against attack been furthered by the pact? These questions could not be definitely answered. The extent to which the American government relied on the pact could easily be inferred, however. The United States Senate agreed to ratify the pact for the outlawry of war only after an agreement had been reached for the simultaneous passage of the cruiser bill. The question might pertinently be asked: Who had gained the more substantial advantage, those who relied on international coöperation, or those who relied on arms for the prevention of war?

As far as immediate results are concerned, the cruiser bill was more effective than the Kellogg Pact in forcing Britain to come to time. The peace party in England argued that a naval race was unnecessary, because the interests of Britain and America were not in vital conflict. More effectively, the peace party in England argued that a naval race was dangerous and futile, because Britain could not stand the pace. The British public was convinced by the latter argument. When Ramsay MacDonald became Prime Minister in 1929, he immediately opened negotiations with the new American President, Herbert Hoover, for a truce. In June MacDonald visited the United States and another idyl was arranged: sitting on a log beside the Rapidan, President and Prime Minister decided on another conference for the promotion of peace.

The conference was held in London in 1930. Its purpose was to prolong the truce in the building of capital ships and to extend the Washington Conference ratios to other categories. Substantial agreement had been achieved in advance between Britain and America; the demands of Japan could be compromised. As in 1921, however, France and Italy had been ignored during the preliminary negotiations, and the omission was even more disastrous than in 1921. Since the advent of Mussolini, Italy had been filled with imperialistic fervor. The Fascists frankly avowed their determination to secure colonies where the growing millions of Italy could find homes. North Africa and the Balkans were the "logical" fields for expansion. To Italy, with a population as

large as that of Continental France and with no worth-while
colonies, expansion seemed justified. To France and Jugoslavia, whose possessions were menaced, the Italian claims
seemed aggressive. The conflict of interest was reflected in
the conflict over naval ratios: Italy insisted on a fleet as
large as the French; France, with two coasts to protect,
insisted on a fleet as large as the combined navies of Italy
and Germany. The Franco-Italian feud had been obvious
for many years, yet Britain and America called the London
Conference without regard for this unsettled dispute over
ratios. The oversight prevented not merely reduction, but
limitation, at London. To Britain, naval supremacy in the
Mediterranean seemed vital for the maintenance of communications with the east. Therefore, the British fleet must
be able to muster strength in the Mediterranean equivalent
to the combined forces of France and Italy. If the latter
powers refused to reduce their forces, Britain must continue
building cruisers for some years to attain equality. If France
and Italy refused, not merely to reduce, but to stop building,
Britain could not even limit her building. Anglo-American
agreement would be useless without Franco-Italian agreement.

Italy would consent to nothing less than parity with
France. France would grant parity on one condition, which
was that the great naval powers should agree to a consultative pact similar to the Four-Power Pacific Treaty. If
France had security against Italian aggression, France could
be content with a fleet no larger than the Italian. If the
consultative pact was not forthcoming, France would continue to build, confident that her resources would enable her
to build faster than Italy. The American delegates were
apparently willing to purchase agreement by a consultative
pact. There was an outcry against entangling alliances in
the American Senate. President Hoover denied that a consultative pact was contemplated. His announcement ended
all hope of reduction. An agreement limiting the tonnage of
the three great naval powers was made, but the agreement
was tentative. If French and Italian tonnage increased,

Britain would increase her building; American and Japanese building would then increase proportionately. This was a meager achievement—limitation at such a high figure that extensive new building was necessary, with the probability that even these high figures would soon be raised. A small achievement it was, and purchased at great price. The Franco-Italian quarrel, brought into the open, became more intense. In England and America, some blamed France for the failure, some blamed Italy; few saw that both France and Italy were claiming only the right to determine what strength was needed to protect their interests. Neither Britain nor America could justly condemn others for national egoism. Britain and America might be condemned with more justice for summoning a conference which was bound to end in failure.

If the fruit of three naval conferences was tentative limitation purchased at the price of bad feeling, the fruit of incessant discussion of land armament was angry recrimination without tangible benefits. By the Treaty of Versailles, Germany was forced to disarm as a prelude to general disarmament. The victorious powers were forced to consider reduction of their own armaments or provide Germany with an excuse for demanding freedom from the restriction enforced by the treaty. Furthermore, the burden of armaments aroused popular discontent, even in France. Discussion was necessary, if only to justify existing expenditures for arms. In 1925 the League of Nations created a commission which was to draft a treaty preparatory to the calling of a disarmament conference. The preparatory commission labored five years. The discussions were able and exhaustive. A few questions considered may be given as illustrations. How should air forces be limited? A civil airplane could be transformed into a military plane with little difficulty. It was impossible to limit the number of mail and passenger planes. Therefore, limitation of air forces seemed impossible. How should effectives, trained troops, be limited? The countries with voluntary service wished to limit trained reserves. The countries with compulsory service wished to limit only peace-time strength. Both sides argued effectively; no final agreement was reached. How should *matériel*—guns, rifles, ammunition, and the rest—be limited? Most countries wished to limit the amount which might be spent. The United States opposed budgetary limitation. Again there was no agreement. Finally, how should what the French call "war potential" be regulated? Obviously, if the United States and Mexico went to war with equal forces, the United States would win. Population, resources, geographical location, education, patriotism, and a host of other elements determined the potential war strength of a nation. What relative weight should be attached to each element? The French asked the question, but they did not believe it could be answered. So long as fear and ambition existed, the French contended, each nation would determine its armaments by its fears and ambitions; and the result would be competitive armaments. Disarmament could only be effected when fear and ambition were banished. Security must precede disarmament. The British and Americans, seeing the purpose and cogency of the French argument and unwilling to give the pledges France sought, maintained embarrassed silence through most of the discussions of war potential.

In 1930, the preparatory commission completed its draft treaty, or rather, set of treaties. At the end of the sessions, France pointed out that it was necessary to safeguard earlier disarmament conventions such as the Treaties of Washington, London—and Versailles. The German delegate immediately protested. He would not sign if "this factitious piece of work" was to be regarded as the fulfilment of the disarmament promises made by the Allies at Versailles. Germany would not give new assent to the disarmament imposed at Versailles in order to secure "a Convention which, instead of leading to genuine disarmament, would only serve to draw a veil over the real state of land armaments throughout the world, or—which would be worse—would make it possible to increase these armaments." Thus the fundamental divergence of objective was revealed. France was not prepared to surrender the military preponderance which the Peace of Paris gave her and her allies until her demands for security were met. Neither America nor England was prepared to promise aid should the defeated powers attempt to alter the *status quo* by armed force. Germany was not prepared to sign a new armaments convention unless the artificial military preponderance of France and her allies was ended. What the preparatory commission had assiduously done for five years was to ignore this, the core of the problem. Embarrassed by the lack of tact shown by the French and German delegates, the preparatory commission shuffled off the stage with as much grace as possible. The League solemnly invited the powers to convene at Geneva in February, 1932, for the purpose of converting the recommendations of the commission into a treaty of disarmament.

The Americans and the British succeeded in convincing themselves that the London naval conference had solved the problem of naval armaments, and that at the Geneva disarmament conference the Continental nations could be forced to complete the work so nobly begun. The French were under no such illusion. They knew arms were only a symptom of the "disease called fear." Fear must be banished before the armaments race could be ended.

The French proudly contrasted their logic with Anglo-Saxon muddle-headedness, but the French themselves showed a divided mind in their efforts to banish fear during the years following Locarno. As before, the protagonists were Briand and Poincaré. As before, Briand said that fear could only be banished by a real reconciliation between France and Germany. His views were shared by Chamberlain in England and by Stresemann in Germany. These three statesmen regarded Locarno as merely the first step in a long process. German sovereignty was still limited in ways any nation would resent. The reparation problem was merely in abeyance; it was not solved. German territory was still occupied by Allied troops. The Germans were determined to secure modification of the territorial settlement. The Germans could not be expected to submit forever to unilateral restrictions on their military establishment. As soon as Germany was admitted to the League, Stresemann and Briand tried to advance another step. They met at Thoiry in September, 1926. What they discussed is not definitely known. It seems that Briand proposed to secure the evacuation of the Rhineland and the Saar, and the retrocession of Eupen and Malmédy. In return, Germany would pay for the Saar mines, give Belgium financial compensation, and make a large, apparently a final, reparation payment. Thus reparation, the occupation of the Rhine, and all western frontier problems would be wiped off the slate by a huge capital transaction.

As at Locarno, Briand captivated the imagination of Europe by this secret luncheon with Stresemann at a village inn. This time Briand failed. Poincaré was again premier, brought back to power to save the falling franc. Probably it was Poincaré who balked Briand. In any case, nothing happened. Locarno remained the limit of French concession. Poincaré was willing to let Briand try to convert the League into an instrument for preserving the *status quo,* but Poincaré placed his trust not in conciliation but in French strength. Under his guidance, the franc was stabilized and French finances made impervious to attack. The land frontiers of France were strengthened by a wall of steel and iron. The armies of the eastern allies were improved in strength and efficiency. With French loans, Poland built a great new harbor on her own territory at Gdynia. Danzig could now be confronted with the alternatives of ruin or acquiescence in Polish immigration, which would eventually mean Polish ownership. Poland, strong and prolific, was eyeing the sparsely populated fields of East Prussia. By interfering with transport through the Corridor, Poland could make the economic position of the Germans in East Prussia intolerable. In the future, German conquest of the Corridor would be less probable than Polish conquest of East Prussia and Danzig. Under Poincaré's guidance, Locarno was being used to strengthen the material and military foundation of French hegemony.

Only reparations remained unsettled. In 1928 a new reparations conference was called. Poincaré asked that the temporary Dawes Plan be replaced by a permanent settlement. In return, he was willing to permit the evacuation of the Rhineland. The German delegate treated this concession as negligible. He boldly demanded colonies and a revision of the eastern frontier as the price of German acceptance of a permanent settlement. The demand caused consternation. To bring the Germans to time, the French resorted to an action later used on a larger scale. They suddenly began withdrawing French money deposited in German banks. The sudden withdrawal of such large sums threatened to cause a financial panic. The Germans yielded, and accepted the schedule which had been worked out in large part by the American chairman of the conference, Mr. Owen D. Young. The annuities were somewhat smaller than those called for by the Dawes Plan. The average payment was to be about 500 millions of dollars a year. Of this sum, 165 millions was unconditional. The remainder might be suspended if payment threatened to weaken the gold reserve of German currency. If suspension became necessary, a new commission of experts was to examine the situation and decide what payments were possible in addition to the unconditional annuities. If reduction were made in the inter-allied debts, German payments were also to be reduced. The reparations payments were to continue until 1987.

Then came 1930: the close of an era, the era of reconstruction, men said. Reparations were settled. The war debts were settled. The Allied troops, and the Allied commissions had left Germany. Naval armaments had been limited; land armaments would soon be limited. At Geneva, the League sessions, under Briand's dextrous guidance, became pageants symbolic of the new era of peace. To be sure, the German delegate at the reparation conference had been rude and overbearing, but good taste was not a German virtue. To be sure, the American security markets had taken a spectacular fall, but that was only a temporary setback. The world was entering a new political and economic era. Then, in September, 1930, came the German election. From the

election a man hitherto regarded as a fool, and a party
hitherto regarded as a collection of beer-hall revolutionists
emerged as the most conspicuous forces in German political
life—Hitler and his Nazis, who demanded the repudiation
of the Treaty of Versailles. Confidence was shaken. Within
a few months it vanished. The world plunged into a devastating economic crisis.

The sudden emergence of Hitler forced consideration of
political and economic conditions in Germany. What had
been going on there since 1925? On the surface everything
had seemed well. The Dawes Plan had worked, in the sense
that payments were promptly made. The industrial life of
Germany, stagnant in 1924, had revived and flourished in
the years following. The trouble was, as Mr. Gilbert pointed
out again and again, that Germany was living on borrowed
money. International finance, particularly American, had
disregarded the experimental nature of the Dawes Plan.
Thinking reparations a settled issue, and finding the Germans willing to pay high rates of interest for loans, bankers
floated huge loans to equip industries and to finance governmental works. The Germans set busily to work. There was
little unemployment. Taxes were easily raised for reparations. The transfer problem gave Mr. Gilbert no trouble.
He, and some economists, pointed to disquieting symptoms.
Germany was prospering because the improvements were
being financed by foreign borrowings. The sums raised for
reparations were transferred without difficulty because the
foreign borrowings gave Germany large dollar and sterling
balances upon which Gilbert could draw to effect transfers.
Germany was not, however, paying her way. Theoretically,
the improvements being made in Germany should stimulate
German productive capacity; but by no means all the borrowings were going into the development of German industry. Much of the proceeds was used for public buildings, housing, even parks and swimming pools, which were
at best only indirectly productive. Furthermore, the Germans were not saving. Inflation had wiped out a large section of the capitalist class, the group which traditionally

saved a large part of its earnings. German labor was getting
more than before the war, and labor proverbially spends
most of its earnings. Germany was living on borrowed capital, and was not piling up capital upon which to base its
industrial life when borrowing ceased. Foreign trade told
the same story. Germany continued to have an unfavorable
balance of goods and services. While Germany could bor-
row abroad there was no trouble. The unfavorable balance
of trade and the reparations payments were settled with
foreign gold. Some day Germany would have to stop borrowing. Then Germany must export enough, not merely to
balance her imports, but to pay both reparations and the
interest on the foreign loans. The Dawes Plan was not really
working. Germans were paying their taxes and transferring
payments on borrowed money. What would happen later?
This question was asked, but it was disregarded. While the
world was prosperous no one worried about the future.

The Germans began to worry in 1928, when Americans
began to use their money for stock-market speculation at
home instead of for lending abroad. Prosperity waned in
Germany. As loans fell off, building and employment fell
off. The calling of the reparations conference precipitated
discussion in Germany of the international and internal situation. What had been the result of ten years of Republican
rule? In the field of foreign affairs the record was disappointing. The Germans saw their country unarmed, while
other countries were strongly armed. Germany seemed
powerless, not merely to change, but even to defend, the
precarious eastern frontier. The Germans saw themselves
debarred from union with their fellow-Germans in Austria.
They saw themselves the only great power deprived of colonies. They saw themselves and their children doomed to
pay "tribute" until 1987. And they saw far less justice in
their lot than they had seen in 1919. During the intervening
decade, there had been much study of the origins of the war.
The Germans had convinced themselves, not merely that
Germany had not caused the war, but that the Entente had
been guilty of this crime. Germany was being punished for a

crime committed by the victors. The thought was intoler-able. The "spirit of Locarno" seemed a lying fantasy. France spoke of reconciliation, but France was using the truce to make her hegemony so secure that Germany could never hope to regain equality.

Waning prosperity discredited the record of the Republic at home as well as in foreign affairs. Deprived of work, labor began to move to the left, toward the Communists. The bourgeoisie and the old aristocracy drifted further to the right. Before the war, the middle and upper classes had property, a monopoly on the posts in the army and the civil service, and assured social position. Inflation wiped out the investments of the propertied class. Agriculture, the profes-sion of the aristocracy, was suffering from world overpro-duction. The army was small, too small to enable many young aristocrats to become officers. The civil service was underpaid. The revolution had shaken the old class lines. Sons of the proletariat were crowding into the universities, the civil service, and the professions. The old possessors of power were hard pressed, financially and socially. They blamed their troubles on the Republican government and on the Treaty of Versailles.

On internal questions, the Germans were hopelessly at odds; on questions of foreign affairs they were becoming increasingly united. This confused situation gave Hitler his chance. Hitler's internal program was a strange conglomer-ation of contradictory and unrealizable promises and theo-ries. He caught the ear of the old governing classes by prom-ising to throw out what he called the Marxist Republic. He caught the ear of the proletariat by promising to throw out what he called Jewish capitalism. He fascinated all classes by promising to rid Germany of the incubus of the Treaty of Versailles. Practically, Hitler said Germany had not really been defeated. Germany had been betrayed by the corrupt Republican politicians. The Republic gone, Ger-many could repudiate the treaty. Germany was stronger than France. "France," he declared, "must free herself from the delusion that we are a second-rate power and must learn to treat us as a cultured people. We are not Carthage, nor is France Rome, and it should also be recalled that Rome subdued Carthage single-handed."

The election of 1930 made apparent what the world had refused to see: Germany, made desperate by years of suffering and thwarted hope, was losing faith in democracy and moderation. Both the Communists and the National Socialists made heavy inroads on the Socialists and the moderate bourgeois parties. The Bruening government tried to stem the tide of radicalism by adopting, so far as it dared, the program of the nationalists. Ministers made speeches declaring that a revision of the eastern frontier was necessary. At Geneva, the German representative protested against the oppression of German minorities in Poland. In March, 1931, a customs union between Germany and Austria was announced.

The steadily rising tide of nationalism in Germany and Hitler's wild language aroused misgivings among those who had invested money in Germany. A large proportion of these loans were short term, that is, the investor could demand repayment on a few weeks' notice. Uneasy, more and more foreign investors demanded repayment. The announcement of the Austro-German customs union changed uneasiness into panic. The customs union, every one realized, was the prelude of political union or *Anschluss,* as the Germans called it. France promptly protested with a vigor which showed that Paris was determined on a test of strength with German nationalism. International finance took fright and tried to withdraw almost overnight the sums which had been showered on Germany in the years preceding. All the phenomena of a run on a bank were present, but on a colossal scale. The American and British central banks vainly tried to stem the panic by placing credits at the disposal of Germany. In June, President Hoover tried to avert the crash by the dramatic gesture of proposing a moratorium on all inter-governmental indebtedness. France held back, and insisted that the unconditional payments under the Young Plan be protected. The French demands were accepted, but only after a delay which allowed the panicky withdrawals to have effect. By the time the moratorium was adopted, German economic life was paralyzed. The damage did not stop there. Loss of confidence in German credit undermined confidence in the credit of other governments. The weak financial structures of the small eastern European countries collapsed completely. Britain and Japan found it impossible to maintain the credit of their currencies and were forced to abandon the gold standard. Even the United States, with half the gold in the world, was frightened. Exuberant confidence in the new economic era gave place to the paralysis of despair.

Alone among the great powers, France emerged apparently unscathed, and with relentless precision France proceeded with the task of reducing the rebellious Germans and Austrians to complete submission. To vindicate her legal rights, France compelled Austria to submit the customs union proposal to the World Court on the ground that the union violated the promise of Austria not to take action prejudicial to her independence. To demonstrate her physical power, France, in advance of the court decision, compelled Germany and Austria publicly to renounce the union.

France won, but at heavy cost, not only to the rest of the world but to herself. France had vindicated her right to payments under the Young Plan, but only by helping to plunge the world so deep in economic ruin that there seemed little hope that Germany would ever be able to resume payments. France had shown her power to coerce Germany, but open coercion not merely alienated world opinion from France, it also goaded the Germans to desperation and made the triumph of the German nationalists certain. France secured a favorable decision from the World Court, but in doing so dealt a serious blow to the prestige of that body. The decision proved suspiciously partisan: France, her allies, and the other Latin powers made up a bare majority against the customs union. Italy was with the majority because *Anschluss* would make the persecuted Germans in the Italian Tyrol turn to Germany for aid. The judges of the World

Court, it seemed to many, were not impartial jurists, but national partisans. The agencies of international conciliation which for a few years had seemed to hold much hope for the future were discredited.

As in 1923, so in 1931, Poincaré's policy gave victory, but a Pyrrhic victory. France stood triumphant, but over a ruined and a hostile Europe. Of what value, even to France, was the policy which could destroy, but could not create, European tranquillity? The followers of Poincaré sought desperately to vindicate themselves during the months following the crash of July. They sought to salvage something from the wreck of reparations. That failed. In January, 1932, Bruening announced that Germany could pay no more reparations. The French government blustered, but financial opinion everywhere supported Bruening's contention. France could do nothing. In February, when the disarmament conference convened, the French presented a program for ensuring security. The plan followed in general the lines of the Geneva Protocol, but in addition the League of Nations was to possess a small army and was to control all civil aviation. Unless complete guarantee was given against aggression, declared the French Premier, Tardieu, discussion of disarmament was futile. His plan was received in silence; only the allies of France spoke in its favor. A month later Tardieu made his final drive. The weakness of the French system of alliances lay in the fact that it rested on a political, not an economic, basis. The small countries of eastern Europe, including the allies of France, felt the pinch of economic depression with peculiar force, and while the Balkanization of eastern Europe continued, economic distress must also continue. Tardieu proposed an economic union between the succession states of the Dual Monarchy; he promised that the tremendous gold reserves of France would be used to start anew the economic life of the member states. Again the French failed. Germany, Britain, and Italy refused to sanction a plan which would extend French political domination to include Austria and Hungary. French nationalists had been unable to rebuild the political and economic structure of Europe; in the elections held in the spring of 1932 they were repudiated by the French people. Herriot assumed power, pledged to return to the policy of conciliation.

While the French were losing faith in the cold, legalistic logic of the followers of Poincaré, the Americans were learning, slowly and painfully, that complete lack of logic was no less costly. America is a young nation, but in no country does tradition exercise a stronger hold over men's minds. In the post-war world, America tried to live in accordance with nineteenth, even eighteenth, century traditions. From the days of Washington and Jefferson, Americans inherited the belief that their safety depended on keeping clear of European affairs. From the days of Hamilton, Americans inherited the belief that their prosperity depended on a protective tariff. These traditions worked with moderate success in the nineteenth century. Politically, Europe and Asia were far away. Economically, America was a debtor nation, borrowing money for her industrial development, paying the interest on her debts by exporting large quantities of farm products, and importing as little as possible. The war, however, effected a revolution which was already impending in 1914. From a debtor, America was suddenly transformed into a creditor, country. Every year a large sum was dropped into the lap of America, payments on interest and principal made by foreign borrowers, public and private. Simultaneously, American industrial capacity expanded mightily; markets were sought abroad for the surplus products which the American market could not absorb. Agriculture also expanded and became even more dependent than formerly upon the ability of foreign purchasers to absorb the growing surplus. Americans rejoiced to think of this rain of gold which would still further fructify their land.

America had gained much but she had also lost, lost her political and economic self-sufficiency. The World War had demonstrated that it was impossible to keep clear of the vortex of European politics unless America was prepared to cut all economic ties with Europe. When, after the war, American finance, business, and agriculture pushed out boldly into the markets of the world, American prosperity was irrevocably tied to world prosperity. If the world was torn by strife or economically impoverished, debtors could not pay their debts nor buyers continue to buy. Default on foreign debts meant that Americans could not pay their internal debts; falling sales abroad meant business stagnation at home. Naturally the stake of some Americans in world affairs was, directly, negligible. The manufacturer producing only for the domestic market thought himself safe by comparison with, say, the wheat grower. In fact, both were involved, because if the wheat grower could not sell his crop he could not buy the products of the manufacturer. America had given hostages to world peace, world order, world prosperity. Furthermore, in becoming a creditor nation, America could no longer determine her tariff policy solely on the basis of protecting the domestic market. It was not a rain of gold which fell on America, it was a deluge of claims on foreign borrowers and foreign buyers. Borrowers and buyers could not pay in gold; all the gold mined since the beginning of time would not suffice to quit the world of its debts. The debts must be paid in goods, and if they were to be paid it must be possible for foreigners to give Americans either goods or services.

New economic conditions demanded new national traditions. That, the Americans refused to see; they credited their good fortune to the zeal with which they had adhered to the traditions of their fathers. Flushed with success, they were disposed to think of the outside world as a horde of ragged tricksters seeking to cheat them of the fruit of their toil; at times suspicion verged on morbidity. To preserve their spoils the Americans held firmly to their belief in the danger of entangling alliances, and to their faith in the protective tariff. Republican Presidents found themselves powerless alike to secure senatorial approval of agreements calling for international coöperation, or to prevent Congress from raising still higher the tariff wall. Alike in what it did, and what it refused to do it cannot be denied that Congress faithfully reflected the views of most Americans. Protected against foreign goods by the tariff, protected against foreign malice by the fleet, the American people were confident that they were insulated against the woes and the wiles of an unregenerate world.

For almost a decade America succeeded in enjoying the advantages of both the old and the new economic and political order. Since the causes of political success were transient they may be ignored. The causes of economic success were also transient, but they left a legacy to the future. America was able to be an exporting and creditor nation, and still to preserve a prohibitive barrier against imports because American investors lent billions of dollars to foreign borrowers. Out of the proceeds of these loans the world outside was able to pay interest on old debts and to pay for goods purchased. While America was willing to lend prodigally it was not necessary that goods should enter America. But that could not and did not last forever. In 1928 American investors suddenly turned away from foreign investments; speculation in American securities seemed to offer greater prospects for quick profits.

The sudden cessation of American lending had an immediate effect on German economic life, but the American people saw no connection between the rapidly developing European crisis and their own lives. Even after the collapse of the stock market boom in October, 1929, little heed was paid to Europe. Instead, the familiar panacea of a heightened tariff schedule was applied. The German elections of 1930 alarmed Americans who had funds in Germany, but the public in general remained unperturbed. To the great majority, the proposal of a moratorium on intergovernmental debts by President Hoover in June, 1931, came like a bolt from the blue. In general his action was applauded because he promised that the moratorium would afford a breathing space during which the economic crisis could be ended. When, however, the expected revival did not take place, when instead the fall in prices and in industrial activity persisted, enthusiasm rapidly vanished, to be replaced by heightened suspicion of Europe. The feeling was that Europe, aided by unpatriotic American financiers who were willing to sacrifice the public interest in order to protect their own investments, had tricked the President into an action which imperiled war-debt payments in the future. By the time Congress met in December, 1931, opinion had so hardened that Hoover's action was only ratified with difficulty. His request that the debt commission be reëstablished, in order to ascertain whether or not the capacity of the debtors to pay had been altered by the depression, was met with a blunt refusal. Instead, Congress put on record its opposition, not merely to cancellation, but even to reduction of the war debts.

If, as many students maintain, traditions are most emphatically defended when their hold begins to weaken, the closing months of 1931 may in the future be taken as a turning point in American foreign relations. Certainly the supposed sins of Europe were then more vehemently denounced than earlier. When the French Premier, Laval, visited America seeking aid in the task of world economic reconstruction he received a frigid reception. Americans freely admitted that affairs in Europe influenced American affairs, but only to the detriment of American interests. The woes of the world were laid to the "poisoned springs" of the Versailles Treaty, and Laval was frankly told by prominent Americans that the demands of the German nationalists with regard to the Polish Corridor, Upper Silesia, Austria, and even reparations must be met before Europe could again have peace and prosperity. While eagerly, rudely, offering gratuitous advice, however, Americans showed complete unwillingness to aid the task of reconstruction by assuming responsibilities or making sacrifices; indeed, with strange lack of humor, Americans angrily rebuffed all suggestion or criticism.

The irritability of American opinion in the autumn of 1931 was a symptom of disillusionment. Two years of unparalleled economic misery had badly shaken faith in the old traditions which were supposed to have enabled America to establish an earthly paradise in the midst of a troubled world. The months following gave Americans a rough education in world politics and world economics.

Manchuria was the first lesson, and because the Manchurian question so completely illustrates the complex nature of the task of establishing world order, the problem deserves analysis. The Manchurian crisis resulted from the explosive impact of two expanding nationalisms. On one side was China, politically disorganized but united in nationalistic feeling. To Chinese nationalists the political and economic privileges which foreign powers had been able to wrest from earlier weak and corrupt Chinese governments seemed intolerable. For many years before 1931 the Chinese government and people had been attacking these privileges, openly and covertly, peacefully and violently. The Chinese appealed to the right of self-determination as justification for their course. On the other side, were the foreign powers with treaty rights. Japan was only one of the powers which felt injured by the anti-foreign agitation, but Japan suffered most. The Chinese market was essential to Japanese prosperity. The anti-foreign boycotts, by depressing Japanese industries, threatened the whole structure of Japanese society: impoverished workers were more and more thinking the "dangerous thoughts" assiduously spread by Communist agitators. To Japan, therefore, Chinese nationalism seemed intolerable. The Sino-Japanese conflict was most acute in Manchuria. There Japan possessed treaty rights unparalleled in any other region supposedly part of an independent country.

During the decade following the Washington Conference the merchant class, which was in temporary control of the Japanese government, followed what the western nations would call a liberal policy. Since Manchuria was of vital strategic importance to Japan as a buffer state, separating Communist Russia from China, and since Manchuria possessed great economic importance as a source of raw materials and as a market, the Japanese refused to surrender privileges which were legally theirs under existing treaties. On the other hand, more than three fifths of Japan's foreign trade was with China and the United States; these powers must not be antagonized. Conciliation was tried, but, at least by 1931, the attacks of Chinese nationalism on Japanese trade and vested rights had not been ended. The world economic depression brought the situation to a head. The old aristocratic and military groups in Japan, alarmed by the growth of revolutionary forces at home, and impatient with the failure of conciliation abroad, defied the bourgeois parliamentary leaders and embarked on a policy of strong action.

In September, 1931, on the pretext that the Chinese had tried to destroy a Japanese railroad in Manchuria, Japanese troops began an advance which proceeded, slowly at first, then with increasing rapidity. By February, 1932, all Manchuria was in Japanese possession. In retaliation, the Chinese sought to boycott trade with Japan. Undaunted, the Japanese sent troops to Shanghai. The troops met with unexpected resistance, and before this "diversion" ended thousands of civilians had been killed, and property to the value of many hundred millions of dollars had been destroyed. The next stage was to separate Manchuria from China. A puppet state, backed by Japanese troops was created—Manchukuo. In September, 1932, Japan officially recognized Manchukuo as an independent state and announced that the existence of this state would be protected by Japanese arms. Further, the Japanese proclaimed that throughout they had been acting in self-defense. They pointed out that the United States Senate, in ratifying the Kellogg Pact, had voted that self-defense might compel a nation to take armed action outside its own frontiers; on many occasions, notably in quarrels with Mexico, the United States had despatched troops to the territory of other countries, justifying this action by the plea of self-defense. As for the Nine Power Treaty signed at the Washington Conference, Japan had not impaired the territorial integrity or independence of

China: the people of Manchuria had exercised the right of self-determination, and Japan was determined that the Manchurians should not be deprived of this right.

The advance of Japan in Manchuria gave America, and the world, much to think about. Since the end of the World War, the nations had been trying to devise some method of settling international disputes other than that of force. Those efforts had centered to an unusual degree on Chinese affairs, because every one realized that the absence of a stable government in China, combined with the rich spoils which Chinese territory offered to the acquisitive instincts of other powers, made the Chinese question a standing menace to world peace. Three agreements were pertinent to the problem: The League Covenant, the Kellogg Pact, and the Nine Power Treaty of Washington.

The League Covenant provided that conciliation must be applied to all problems, and that if any nation, refusing conciliation, resorted to war, the other member states must give full economic and military support to the party attacked. When the Japanese advance began, the League Council was in session and China promptly appealed for aid. The Council was inclined to force Japan to accept neutral aid in solving the question. The American government was sounded out. Washington held back. Apparently the Washington government hesitated to associate with the League which American opinion had rejected in the name of national independence. Apparently also, Washington hesitated to concur in a precedent for coercing a great power. Whatever the motive, the aloofness of America gave the other great powers an excuse to avoid the unwelcome necessity for applying the League machinery to a great power. The League Council lamely adjourned the problem to a subsequent meeting. Almost immediately the truth of the theory behind the League mechanism of conciliation became apparent, the theory that a dispute is easiest settled in its initial stages. In September, 1931, the civil government in Japan was still struggling against the demands of the military. Strong action by the powers might have halted the advance. The moment escaped unused. Subsequent meetings of the Council made obvious the weakness of the League. None of the great powers represented relished the thought of crossing swords with Japan. Furthermore, England, the power with the naval force which must bear the brunt of any action against Japan, had herself felt the force of the Chinese boycott in earlier years, and half sympathized with Japan's actions. If the United States had been willing to take the lead, offering a policy which it was prepared to back by force of arms, indecision might have been overcome. The United States was not prepared to go so far. Although alarmed and angered by Japan's rapidly developing campaign, the United States would only promise to "endeavor to reinforce" League action. What was needed was a leader, not a possible follower, and the Council gladly shirked its duty by accepting the Japanese proposal that a neutral commission undertake a comprehensive examination of Sino-Japanese relations. In the League Assembly, which met early in 1932, the smaller powers tried to compel action, but the larger powers, notably England, forced delay until the neutral commission had reported. In the autumn of 1932 the commission reported its findings. It found that the lack of stable government in China had invited, and would continue to invite such incidents as had led to the Japanese advance. To end this dangerous condition international coöperation was essential. In other words, the problem, still unsolved, was to find means of grappling with unstable conditions before they reached dangerous proportions. As for Manchuria, the Lytton Commission found that the Japanese plea of self-defense was untenable; conciliation should have been tried before force. Manchukuo, it decided, was a puppet state. It had not grown out of, and it did not rest upon, the desire of the Manchurians for independence; Manchuria must remain a part, though an autonomous part, of China. Japan flatly rejected these findings, and clearly intimated that the refusal could be overcome by force alone.

Clearly the machinery of the League had broken down on

a decisive test. What of the Nine Power Treaty by which the powers, headed by America, had promised to respect and defend the territorial integrity of China? Japan denied that she had violated that treaty, and insisted on her sovereign right to interpret her international obligations. The United States flatly asserted that Japan had violated the treaty. How was this divergence of view to be reconciled? Secretary Stimson gave one answer in February, 1932. The treaties signed at the Washington Conference, he said, stood or fell together. If America became convinced that the Nine Power Treaty had become void through the violation of its provisions, the United States would hold that the treaty limiting naval armaments was also void. In other words, the United States was prepared to begin the naval race anew, with the objective of enforcing its demands by the usual weapon, the threat of armed force. This was nothing more and nothing less than a confession that the United States was prepared to surrender the thesis of the Kellogg Pact that war must be abandoned as a means of enforcing the national will.

Stimson's threat of February, 1932, logically meant that the United States was prepared, unless its interpretation of international agreements was accepted, to rescind its promise to abandon war as an instrument of national policy. Logic, however, was not a characteristic of American thought. Stimson simultaneously was seeking means of enforcing obedience to the Kellogg Pact. That Japan had violated the promise made when she signed the Pact at Paris, Stimson did not doubt. Slowly, tentatively, he felt his way toward methods by which violation of the Pact might be punished or, better still, prevented. In January, 1932, he had already put forward a program to accomplish the first of these objectives. In a note to China and Japan he gave notice that it was the policy of the United States not to recognize any new settlements or arrangements which were brought about in violation of the Kellogg Pact. Force might win territory or privileges; but these acquisitions, illegally gained, remained illegal. There were two flaws in this position. First of all, it was negative; it could not prevent the use of force. Further, who was to determine when the Pact had been violated? Was each signatory to decide for itself? These questions were asked, but the American government was embarrassed by the American tradition that any obligation which prejudiced the free decision of the American people in any crisis was an intolerable restriction on American sovereignty. For several months, Stimson was silent.

The Manchurian crisis revealed the weaknesses of the treaties by which the post-war world had sought to "outlaw" war, to make arms useless as a means of national policy. The revelation came at an embarrassing moment. In February, 1932, the long awaited disarmament conference opened at Geneva. The French were quick to see that the breakdown of existing means of ensuring safety, other than arms, reinforced their thesis that solid guarantees of assistance to repel aggression must be given before France could abandon her arms, her one effective defense. The argument was double edged, however. Germany could use the same argument, to prove that, deprived of arms, she was also deprived of security. The old dilemma found the old solution; the conference tried to evade the central problem by debating technicalities. This time the old device failed to work. The world was sick to death of expensive conferences which dodged issues. The clamor for action became irresistible. President Hoover, faced with an unbalanced budget and an outcry against the burden of armaments, sought to break the deadlock by a dramatic gesture. In June, 1932, the American delegate presented a comprehensive scheme for the reduction of all existing forces—land, sea, and air— beyond the number necessary for police purposes, by one-third. The armaments race, he argued, must be halted. At Paris in 1919, the victorious powers had decided what forces and what arms were necessary for police purposes. Everybody was entitled to that quota. Many nations, however, possessed arms in excess of the police quota. To reduce this excess by one-third would save at least a billion dollars and leave the relative positions of the powers unchanged. President Hoover's proposal was hailed as an ideal solution in America, and justly. The plan was ideal, from the American point of view. The concentrated forces of America would be lowered, to be sure, but so would the forces of all the powers. America after the reduction, would have a fleet second to none. Actually, the American position would be improved; for America had not built up to the limits of the London treaty and much of the tonnage to be scrapped existed only on paper.

To the surprise and indignation of the Americans, Mr. Hoover's plan met with a reception almost as cool as that which had been accorded M. Tardieu's plan to achieve security. The British pointed out that their fleet must be kept dispersed over the globe and every new reduction made it increasingly difficult for Britain to possess effective strength throughout the vast area of her empire. The British cleverly suggested that reduction be by size, not number, of vessels. This idea was repellent to America; America relied on massed force concentrated in a small number of units. Other powers, notably Japan, held back. They were reluctant to state their motives because their motives were illogically called immoral by the standards of the age. Japan was a growing power, desirous of expansion. To expand, as the world was now organized, she felt she must rely on force. America and Britain had once done the same; but now they were agreed in believing that expansion by force was evil. They did not, however, suggest any other method by which expansion could be effected. France and her allies, on the other hand, opposed the Hoover plan because it provided no security against the states which desired to alter the *status quo,* states whose power would, under the Hoover plan, be increased relatively to that of France and her allies.

The conference adjourned to a later date. Everywhere there was a cry of disappointment. Everywhere popular opinion, ignorant of the complex problems involved, naturally accepted the proposal of the home government as the only correct method of lessening the burden of armament, and accused the other powers of evil designs because they opposed the true method of disarmament. The governments, however, did realize the nature of the problem, and in some capitals, notably in London, Paris, and Washington, there was a feeling that the time for evasion was past.

While the first session of the disarmament conference was ending in failure at Geneva, in June, 1932, another and more fruitful conference met at Lausanne for the purpose of settling the cancerous reparations problem. The year which had elapsed since the Hoover moratorium came into effect had disillusioned those who had hoped that a rapid economic revival would again make it possible to put the Young Plan into effect. The year had been marked by continuous financial panic. In the first wave of panic, English currency had been driven from the gold standard, carrying the currencies of many smaller countries with it. In most other European countries the gold standard existed only in theory, while in fact the free movement of exchanges, upon which financial and economic life depended, had disappeared. When the conference met the most spectacular panic in currency history was just ebbing: the frightened effort of Europeans and Americans to convert their dollars into gold or foreign currency. While credit was in this hysterical condition the relentless fall of prices and trade must continue. As MacDonald said in his opening address to the conference, capitalist society was "crumbling under our feet." Every one realized that the seizure of power by the military party in Japan and the Manchurian adventure were in large part efforts by the old possessing classes to check the growth of Communism in Japan. In Germany there had been a similar development. If, to silence nationalist attacks Bruening had himself become more violently nationalistic, in his internal policy Bruening had yielded step by step to the demands of the parties of the left. To halt this process, President von Hindenburg in May, 1932, executed what was in effect a *coup d'état* with the aid of the army. Bruening was dismissed and a new cabinet recruited from the leaders of capitalism and agriculture was entrusted with the task of making a final stand against Marxist doctrines.

The leaders at the Lausanne conference, MacDonald, Herriot, and von Papen, the new German Chancellor, were united in believing that a final settlement of the reparations problem was the indispensable prelude to the economic recovery upon which capitalism depended for salvation. They also realized that it was futile to hope for large reparations payments in the future. MacDonald and Herriot had been able to convince their constituents that reparations were a thing of the past only by promising that war debts would also be abolished. If both debts and reparations were wiped out, the countries entitled to reparations payments would lose little. In making this promise MacDonald and Herriot were gambling. There was no guarantee that the United States would cancel the debts. The gamble seemed justified by the fact that there was no other way to secure popular consent to an essential step. Even then, agreement was difficult. The French people were reconciled to the loss of reparations payments; they insisted that their right to collect reparations be recognized. This was no mere quibble over words; the French suspected that the attack on the reparations clauses of the Treaty of Versailles was merely the first of a series of German attacks on the treaty. The justice of the French suspicion was shown when von Papen presented the German terms. He was no blind chauvinist. This he showed when he freely admitted that France was entitled to "compensation" for surrendering her claim to reparations. Immediately there was a cry of indignation from the German nationalists who declared that Germany owed France nothing. Further, declared the nationalists, von Papen must bring home the abrogation of the "war guilt" clause of the Treaty of Versailles and the recognition by France that Germany was entitled to equality of armament. The outcry in Germany provoked fiery words in France; Herriot was warned that he must insist on reparations, and must do none of the things German nationalists demanded. Under this cross-fire the negotiators at Lausanne did what they could. The questions of war guilt and of equality of armaments were eliminated as impossible of compromise.

Germany, in return for the cancellation of reparations payments, was to make—not "compensation"—but a "voluntary contribution." The contribution was to be in the form of bonds to the sum of 300 million marks, about seventy-five million dollars. These bonds were to be payable after a three-year moratorium, if German credit would stand the strain. Thus in ten years reparations claims had dwindled more than 99 per cent., and whether the remaining fraction would ever be paid was dubious. Here, if anywhere, the suicidal folly of post-war nationalism finds illustration. As MacDonald said, reparations had proved, not a punishment to one nation, but an affliction to all. Theoretically, of course, Lausanne was not a final settlement. The agreement was not to be ratified by the creditor states until they had made a "satisfactory settlement" with the United States. Practically, reparations were dead. No matter what the United States might do, sensible men realized that the reparations issue could not be revived.

From misery Europe had learned at least the beginning of wisdom. America also was proving not completely impervious to instruction. Americans could and did attribute the failure of the Hoover disarmament plan to the incorrigible lust of Europe for war. This was poor solace. The important fact was that arms had not been reduced, and that the American military budget could consequently not be reduced. That fact brought the United States a small step closer to the French position. In the campaign of 1932 the platforms of both major parties vaguely endorsed the principle of consultation between the powers in case of a threat of war. Stimson was even more precise. The Kellogg Pact, he said, had made war "an illegal thing." When there was war one party or the other must be a law-breaker. If there was a threat of force, consultation between the signatories of the Pact "becomes inevitable." These principles he enunciated as self-evident, but previous American practice was at variance with his words. Was America awakening to the need of international coöperation?

On a questioning note any study of diplomatic history

written in 1932 must end. To what extent have the experiments of the two generations just past taught the peoples of the world to regulate their relations so that peace and concord may ensue? It would be easy to say that nothing has been learned. It would be easy to demonstrate that international rivalries have increased, not diminished, in complexity and in number. It would be easy to demonstrate that the experiments in international coöperation have uniformly ended in failure, while statesmen have become increasingly timorous in opposing the demands of chauvinists. To abandon as insoluble the problem of peaceable adjustment of the forces of growth and decay in the world seems all too easy. But in reality the problem cannot be abandoned, because it is a problem which must be answered if civilization, as the Western nations have known civilization for centuries, is to survive. Almost a century ago Karl Marx flung his defiant challenge to the Western nations: "A spectre is haunting Europe—the spectre of Communism." The years since 1848 have not exorcised that spectre. Rather, the shadow has become a reality. To say that the disruptive forces of capitalistic nationalism cannot be restrained is to say that our culture is doomed.

SUGGESTED READINGS

The purpose of these suggestions is to facilitate the task of students who wish to obtain a more complete picture of diplomatic history than is afforded by this volume. Only works in English are given, and only works which treat of a fairly large segment of the field. Such a selection must be arbitrary, but it is hoped that the books suggested may prove of sufficient interest and value to lead the student to seek further reading from the more detailed bibliographies contained in many of the works mentioned. G. P. Gooch's *Recent Revelations of European Diplomacy,* 3d revised edition (London, 1930) is a good introduction to the sources. Fay's first chapter and his foot-notes form the best bibliography in English. Langer contributes an excellent list of current publications to *Foreign Affairs.*

GENERAL

Gooch, G. P., *History of Modern Europe, 1878–1919* (New York, n.d.).
    Remains, despite the appearance of much new material, the best detailed survey.

Hayes, C. J. H., *Essays on Nationalism* (New York, 1926).
    An excellent introduction to a subject which is just beginning to receive critical study. Bibliography.

Moon, P. T., *Imperialism and World Politics* (New York, 1927).
    Bibliography.

Feis, H., *Europe, the World's Banker* (New Haven, Connecticut, 1930).
    An account of European foreign investment and the connection of world finance with diplomacy.

1871–1890

LANGER, W. L., *European Alliances and Alignments* (New York, 1931).

Langer attempts, with great success, "to take due account of economic developments, of changing military considerations, and of strong tides of national sentiment, as well as of individual leadership."

1890–1914

FAY, S. B., *Origins of the World War*, 2d ed., 2 vols. in 1 (New York, 1930).

The best account, particularly of Balkan problems and the evolution of the alliance systems. The second volume is entirely devoted to the outbreak of war in 1914.

DICKINSON, G. L., *The International Anarchy, 1904–1914* (New York, 1926).

A thoughtful, well-written defense of the thesis that "whenever and wherever the anarchy of armed states exists, war does become inevitable."

BARNES, H. E., *The Genesis of the World War*, 2d ed. (New York, 1927).

The most important American contribution to the "revisionist" cause.

1914

Fay's second volume, mentioned above, is the best treatment of this vexed subject.

RENOUVIN, P., *The Immediate Origins of the War* (New Haven, Connecticut, 1928).

The best defense of Entente views of the origins of the war.

SCHMITT, B. E., *The Coming of the War, 1914*, 2 vols. (New York, 1930).

The most detailed study. Hostile to Germany.

1914–1932

There is no satisfactory treatment of the latest years. The biographies listed below furnish the best introduction.

BUELL, R. L., *Europe, a History of Ten Years* (New York, 1929).

Useful.

SIMONDS, F. H., *Can Europe Keep the Peace?* (New York, 1931).

An excellent, and pessimistic, analysis of the troubled conditions in Europe by a well-informed journalist.

GIBBS, PHILIP, *Since Then, the Disturbing Story of the World at Peace* (New York, 1930).

Impressionistic pictures by another famous journalist. Less substantial than Simonds's work and more obviously prejudiced.

MADARIAGA, S. DE, *Disarmament.* (New York, 1929).

Excellent.

KEYNES, J. M., *Economic Consequences of the Peace* (New York, 1920).

Already discussed.

McFADYEAN, SIR ANDREW, *Reparation Reviewed* (London, 1930).

A vigorous and authoritative introduction.

PATTERSON, E. M., *The World's Economic Dilemma* (New York, 1930).

An able analysis of the effects of nationalism on an economically interdependent world.

Foreign Affairs.

A quarterly published by the Council on Foreign Relations. Prints many valuable articles. Langer's bibliography is very useful.

Survey of American Foreign Relations.

An annual volume published by the Council; contains analyses of European problems.

Survey of International Relations.

A volume published annually by the British Royal Institute of International Affairs. Very ably edited.

SPECIAL TOPICS

JASZI, OSCAR, *The Dissolution of the Habsburg Monarchy* (Chicago, 1929).

Badly written, but filled with invaluable material which is not accessible elsewhere. Repays careful study.

PRIBRAM, A. F., *Austrian Foreign Policy, 1908–1918* (London, 1923).

A good introductory account.

——, *The Secret Treaties of Austria-Hungary, 1879–1914*, 2 vols. (Cambridge, Massachusetts, 1920).

The second volume contains the best history of the Triple Alliance.

CARROLL, E. M., *French Public Opinion and Foreign Affairs, 1870–1914* (New York, 1931).

An able attempt to analyze the main currents of opinion and to determine the effects of these currents on official policy.

BRANDENBURG, E., *From Bismarck to the World War* (London, 1927).

The best history of German foreign policy in English.

GOOCH, G. P., *Franco-German Relations, 1871–1914* (London, 1923).

Brief but excellent.

PRIBRAM, A. F., *England and the International Policy of the European Great Powers* (Oxford, 1931).

A brief, thoughtful commentary on the facts.

KANTOROWICZ, H., *The Spirit of British Policy* (London, 1931).

A ponderous but valuable defense of British policy and indictment of German policy. The view of British policy is too charitable, and that of German policy too harsh, but the reader who is on his guard against bias will find the book provocative of thought.

COOKE, W. H., and STICKNEY, E. P., *Readings in European International Relations since 1879* (New York, 1931).

A discriminating selection from a wide variety of sources. Over two-thirds of the material treats of the period after June 28, 1914.

BIOGRAPHY AND AUTOBIOGRAPHY

CECIL, LADY GWENDOLEN, *Life of Robert, Marquis of Salisbury*, 4 vols. (London, 1921–1931).

By Salisbury's daughter. Gives an excellent picture of international politics as seen by the great Conservative statesman during the early years of the age of imperialism.

GREY, VISCOUNT (SIR EDWARD GREY), *Twenty-Five Years*, 2 vols. (New York, 1925).

The most charming and convincing of the innumerable defenses written by pre-war statesmen. For an equally convincing criticism, see Hermann Lutz's *Lord Grey and the World War* (New York, 1928).

NICOLSON, HAROLD, *Portrait of a Diplomatist* (Boston, 1930).

At once a life of Sir Arthur Nicolson, and a study of the origins of the war. Brilliantly written, replete with cogent argument.

BÜLOW, B. VON, *The Memoirs of Prince von Bülow*, 4 vols. (Boston, 1931–1932).

Thoroughly unreliable, but unconsciously self-revealing. Full of stories about the great and the near great.

POINCARÉ, RAYMOND, *The Memoirs of Raymond Poincaré*, condensed English translation in 3 vols. (London, 1926–1929).

Also unreliable. A very astute defense; vulnerable points are protected by an almost impenetrable barrage of words.

HENDRICK, BURTON J., *The Life and Letters of Walter H. Page*, 3 vols. (New York, 1922–1925).

A most valuable introduction to Allied war psychology.

SEYMOUR, C., editor, *The Intimate Papers of Colonel House*, 4 vols. (Boston, 1926–1928).

Contains much valuable material on the war and the peace conference.

BAKER, R. S., *Woodrow Wilson and the World Settlement*, 2 vols. (New York, 1922).

A very valuable source of information about the peace conference. Marred by bias, but the very emotional fervor of the style is a valuable aid to understanding the atmosphere of the peace conference.

CHURCHILL, WINSTON, *The World Crisis*, 5 vols. (New York, 1923–1929).

The war and the peace as seen through the eyes of a British imperialist; an admirable work to set in contrast to Baker.

INDEX

Abdul Hamid, and Germany, 75
Aehrenthal, Alois, policy of, 116 ff.
Afghanistan, 29, 33, 34, 35, 114, 326, 327
Agadir crisis, 154 ff.
Agreements, political, *see* Alliances
Albania, 161, 176 ff., 184, 185
Alexander, King, of Serbia, 116
Alexander, Prince, of Bulgaria, 37, 38
Alexander II, Tsar, 14 ff., 18, 21
Alexander III, Tsar: and Bulgarian crisis, 37 ff.; and France, 53
Alexandria, bombardment of, 32
Algeciras Conference, 108–111
Algeciras, Treaty of, 110, 111, 155
Alliances, ententes, and political agreements: growth of, after *1871*, 5, 25, 26; and balance of power, 146 ff.; in crisis of *1914*, 202
Anglo-French Entente: Fashoda crisis and, 64; formation of, 81, 90 ff.; *see* Triple Entente
Anglo-German alliance: proposed by Bismarck, 46; William II and, 51–53; British Unionists and, 60; Germany and, *1893–1895*, 71–73; proposed by Chamberlain, 76, 78, 79; negotiations in *1901*, 79, 80
Anglo-Japanese alliance: formation of, 79–81; failure to check Russia, 88–90; renewed and extended, *1905*, 106; ending of, 335–337
Anglo-Russian Entente: sought by Salisbury, 60, 61, 64 ff.; by Lansdowne, 90; formation of, 107, 111 ff.; British Liberals and, 127; *see* Triple Entente
Austro-German alliance: formation of, 18 ff.; and Bulgarian crisis, 39; and reinsurance agreement, 43, 44; *see* Triple Alliance

Alliances—*Continued*
Austro-Serbian alliance: formation of, 22; collapse of, 116
Continental coalition against England: proposed, 60; Germany and, 72–74; rumors of, *1899–1904*, 77, 78, 89, 90; proposed by Germany, *1904–1905*, 101, 102, 105, 106, 147, 148
Dreikaiserbund: *1872–1878*, 7, 8, 11, 14, 18; *1881–1887*, 21, 22, 38 ff., 45
Dual Alliance, 29, 30, 45; formation of, *1890–1894*, 52 ff.; French disappointment with, 62; and Far East, 81; in *1912*, 174, 175; *see* Triple Entente
France, post-war alliances of: Anglo-American treaty of guarantee, 279, 326, 331, 345, 346, 354, 355; with Belgium, Poland, Czechoslovakia, Rumania, and Jugoslavia, 363–366, 385, 391, 392
Franco-Russian Alliance, *see* Dual Alliance
Little Entente, of Czechoslovakia, Rumania, and Jugoslavia, 365, 366
Mediterranean Agreements, of *1887*, 41, 42; of *1907*, 133
Reinsurance agreement, Russo-German, 42 ff., 51
Russo-Japanese agreement, *1907*, 107, 112, 114
Triple Alliance: formation of, *1882*, 23–26; renewal of, *1887*, 41, 42; *1891*, 51, 52; *1902*, 95; *1907*, 134; *1912*, 178; William II and, 50; growing weakness of, 95, 103, 124, 125, 134, 167, 176
Triple Entente: effect of, on French policy, 99; and Bosnian crisis, 99; and Agadir crisis, 155; British interpretation of, 126, 127, 129 ff.; Poin-